The age of the crowd

# The age of the crowd

*A historical treatise on mass psychology*

Serge Moscovici

*Ecole des Hautes Etudes en Sciences Sociales*

Translated by J. C. Whitehouse

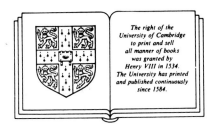

The right of the
University of Cambridge
to print and sell
all manner of books
was granted by
Henry VIII in 1534.
The University has printed
and published continuously
since 1584.

## Cambridge University Press

*Cambridge*
*London   New York   New Rochelle   Melbourne   Sydney*

## Editions de la Maison des Sciences de l'Homme

*Paris*

Published by the Press Syndicate of the University of Cambridge
The Pitt Building, Trumpington Street, Cambridge CB2 1RP
32 East 57th Street, New York, NY 10022, USA
10 Stamford Road, Oakleigh, Melbourne 3166, Australia
and Editions de la Maison des Sciences de l'Homme
54 Boulevard Raspail, 75270 Paris Cedex 06

Originally published in French as *L'âge des foules* by Fayard 1981 and ©
Librairie Arthème Fayard
First published in English by Editions de la Maison des Sciences de l'Homme
and Cambridge University Press 1985 as *The age of the crowd*
English translation © Maison des Sciences de l'Homme and Cambridge
University Press 1985

Printed in Great Britain at
the University Press, Cambridge

Library of Congress catalogue card number: 84-29370

*British Library Cataloguing in Publication Data*
Moscovici, Serge
The age of the crowd: a historical treatise
on mass psychology.
1. Collective behavior – History
I. Title
302.3'3   HM283
ISBN 0 521 25774 3 hard covers
ISBN 0 521 27705 1 paperback
ISBN 2 7351 0110 x hard covers (France only)

WV

# Contents

---

Author's note      *page* vii
Introduction      1

## PART I: THE STUDY OF THE MASSES

1   The individual and the masses      13
2   The revolt of the masses      20
3   What do we do when faced with the masses?      29
4   Eastern and western varieties of despotism      40

## PART II: LE BON AND THE FEAR OF CROWDS

1   Who was Gustave Le Bon?      49
2   The Machiavelli of mass societies      55
3   Four reasons for saying nothing      67
4   The discovery of the masses      71
5   Mass hypnosis      81
6   The mental life of crowds      92

## PART III: THE CROWD, WOMEN AND MADNESS

1   Collective matter: the impulsive and conservative crowd      107
2   Collective form: the dogmatic and utopian crowd      115
3   The leaders of the crowd      122
4   Charisma      129
5   The strategies of propaganda and mass suggestion      138
6   Conclusion      150

## PART IV: THE LEADER PRINCIPLE

1   The paradox of mass psychology      155
2   Natural crowds and artificial crowds      160
3   The leader principle      170

## Contents

**PART V: OPINION AND THE CROWD**

1   Communication is the Valium of the people          183
2   Opinion, the public and the crowd                  193
3   The law of the polarisation of prestige            201
4   The Republic in France: from a democracy of the masses
    to a democracy of publics                          207

**PART VI: THE BEST DISCIPLE OF LE BON
AND TARDE: SIGMUND FREUD**

1   The black books of Doctor Freud                    219
2   From classical to revolutionary mass psychology    230
3   The three questions of mass psychology             237
4   Crowds and the libido                              244
5   The origin of affective attachments in society     255
6   Eros and mimesis                                   270
7   The end of hypnosis                                283

**PART VII: THE PSYCHOLOGY OF THE
CHARISMATIC LEADER**

1   Prestige and charisma                              289
2   The postulate of mass psychology                   296
3   The primal secret                                  303

**PART VIII: HYPOTHESES ABOUT GREAT MEN**

1   'The Man Moses'                                    313
2   The family romances of great men                   319
3   Creating a people                                  330
4   Mosaic and totemic leaders                         342

**PART IX: SECULAR RELIGIONS**

1   The secret of a religion                           353
2   The prohibition of thought                         361
3   The cult of the father                             368

Conclusion: The planetary age of the crowd            381
Notes                                                 386
References                                            395
Index of names                                        400
Subject index                                         405
vi

# Author's note

This book takes up, in a considerably extended form, the theme of a series of lectures that I had the privilege of giving in the University of Louvain under the aegis of the Franqui Chair. I am deeply appreciative of the welcome extended to me there by my colleague Jean-Philippe Leyens and of the interest shown by those researchers and students who attended the lectures and gave me the benefit of their criticism.

I have since been able to fill a number of gaps in my documentation, more particularly during a period of residence at Churchill College, Cambridge, where I became acquainted with the many English-language works in the field.

I should also like to express my sincere thanks to Nelly Stéphane for kindly reading my manuscript and making valuable suggestions.

# Introduction

## I

THE IDEA of writing about mass psychology first came to me when I resigned myself to accepting a fact which, for good or evil, is more blindingly obvious than any other. By this I mean that at the beginning of the century we were certain that the masses would triumph, whereas towards the end of it we are all the prisoners of leaders. One after another, the social upheavals that have shaken most countries in the world have brought to power a regime headed by a charismatic leader. Mao, Stalin, Mussolini, Tito, Nehru, Castro and a number of those emulating them have exercised total control over their subjects and continue to do so. In return, the latter worship them fervently. If we move down a step from the level of the nation to that of parties, churches, sects or schools of thought, we can see that imitative behaviour irresistibly produces the same situation throughout the social body.

Revolutions are successful, one regime follows another and old institutions crumble away, but there is no stopping the rise of leaders. They have, of course, always had a part to play in history, but never such a decisive one, and never have we wanted them so much. The problem that is beginning to take shape can be formulated as follows: is such a rise compatible with the principle of equality (on which all governments in civilised countries are based), an increase in power and culture for the masses and the dissemination of knowledge? Is it an inevitable consequence of those characteristics of modern society with which one would deem it to be incompatible? When the majority seizes power, it passes temporarily into the hands of a minority until one exceptional man, who alone embodies the law, takes it from everyone else. He can lead the multitudes into heroic struggles and make them perform massive works of construction. For him, they sacrifice their clear interests, their manifest needs, their very lives. The leader orders his horde of followers to wreak immense destruction, to carry out unimaginable crimes, and they obey him without demur. Authority of that kind is not exercised without depriving individuals of their responsibility and freedom. It also demands their wholehearted support. We may well be so accustomed to these paradoxical effects that we are no longer affected by the cumulative

1

weight of them, but they still surprise us and sometimes even shock us, depending on how we see their causes.

We thought it axiomatic that the notion of the law as being the will of a single man was a thing of the past, known to us merely by hearsay, no more than a historical curiosity, like the cult of heroes or witch-hunts, things to be read about in old books. But here, where we are dealing with one of the oldest questions in the world, it is difficult to do anything new. Far from innovating, all we have done is to push to its limits what other ages, with their Caesars and their tyrants, had only had an inkling of. We have made the exception into the rule and systematised their rule-of-thumb first attempts. Let us be clear from the start that over the whole diverse range of cultures, societies and groups an identical power has arisen, encouraged on all sides and endowed with increasing strength of personality. I mean the power of the leader. He may be called the *lider massimo*, the *presidente*, or the *caudillo* in Spanish, the *duce* in Italian, or the *Führer* in German, but the name does not matter much. It always describes an identical reality, and the word corresponds faithfully to the phenomenon. Of course, it is not one and the same thing to live under the authority of a Mussolini or a Hitler, a Tito or a Stalin, a Castro or a Pinochet, or to follow a Gandhi or a Mao. By definition, each situation is unique and in its concrete form differs from the others as much as siblings do. But with leaders there emerges a new quality in politics and hence a new cultural characteristic, and this characteristic is so unprecedentedly widespread and powerful that it would be pointless to try to find analogies in the past.

This relative novelty is the first point. There is a second. Historians and sociologists have taught us to find the hidden and impersonal causes behind events and human actions. They show us how we are dominated by the objective laws of economics and technology. Behind the apparatus of so-called great men, they reveal to us the work of the people and the creations of those who control industry and finance. They put us on our guard against the myth of the hero, that man sent by Providence whose appearance is thought to be enough to change the course of history. But what happens? If we look up from their books to the stage of history, we see that the myth is still enjoying great success. It is arising from its own ashes as a result of a carefully-orchestrated ritual of ceremonies, parades and speeches. In stadiums or at mausoleums crowds take part in enormous productions going far beyond the festivities organised by the emperors of Rome or China. My reason tells me that such spectacles are illusions, even if the whole world is present when it watches them on the cinema or television screen. But like the whole world, I believe in what I see. These compelling rituals and grandiose productions have become an integral part of our civilisation, like the circuses of ancient Rome, and meet a need. They are important for its psychology and its survival. On the stage of history, of course, everything that happens has a personal cause and is attributed to the exceptional prowess and qualities of the great man, whether it be a case of a successful revolution, scientific progress, unequalled production records, or of rainfall and the curing of the sick, the heroism of the soldiery or artistic inspiration. Social phenomena and historical tendencies are explained by the subjective laws of genius – as happened with Stalin and Mao – and the poverty of words and the insufficiency of superlatives to indicate the immensity of that genius are bemoaned.

In most cases – and those I have just mentioned are in no way unusual – leaders are invested with an extraordinary mission. They are seen as long-awaited messiahs who will lead their people to the promised land. Despite the warnings of one or two enlightened minds, the masses see themselves in such men and recognise themselves and their essence in them. They venerate and worship them as if they were omnipotent and omniscient supermen able to use men by dominating them. Fascinated and awe-struck, they change these latter-day Zarathustras into demigods whose every judgement is infallible, whose every action is just, and whose every word is true. Their power, which first came into being under the pressure of circumstances and then grew as a result of expediency, henceforth takes on the form of a system which is automatically and universally applied. Thus, within society as a whole, a society of prestigious commanders (or charismatic leaders, if you prefer the term) creates itself. It is smaller than the wider society, but more energetic and endowed with greater will-power. It has no difficulty in directing the world without the world knowing anything about it.

## II

By its sheer size, the phenomenon took most social sciences and theories by surprise. Thinkers could not accept the evidence of their own eyes when it occurred in Europe, more precisely in Italy and Russia, for the first time. Some saw it as a pathological aberration of the human mind, others as a passing disturbance in the march of events. Chiefly it was seen as a necessary expedient to maintain social order in the capitalist world or to bring to birth a new order in the socialist one. It was a catalyst, it seemed, since dictatorship is reputed, as Plato said, to be the form of government which makes it easier to produce rapid change. There is, of course, no dictatorship, even that of the majority, without a dictator, and no dictator, whether his name be Mao Tse-tung or Pol Pot, without abuses and crimes. It was quickly pointed out that such things were slip-ups or accidents on the way to achieving a goal. In the long run, they served the cause of progress and the liberation of nations and would continue to do so.

There is only one branch of science which right from the start tackled the burning subject of the power of leaders, which indeed was created to make it its sole object of investigation. This was crowd or mass psychology. This discipline foresaw its rise when no-one was thinking of such things. Sometimes involuntarily, it provided the practical and intellectual instruments for the increase in the power of leaders and, when that power triumphed, it fought against it. In it and in its manifestations, it saw one of the characteristics of modern society, the sign of a new life for humanity. I find it astonishing that even today we believe that we can ignore its concepts and dispense with them. They must be of value, since they have made it possible to describe and show what the other sciences never even saw, a reality which they still ignore because in their view it is inconceivable. And yet, as we shall see throughout this book, the effect they have is still considerable. I have no hesitation in saying that, along with economics, mass psychology is one of the two human sciences which have provided ideas that have made history. By that I mean that in a concrete way they have left a mark on the events of our time. In comparison, sociology, anthropology and linguistics are sciences that have been made *by* history.

That branch of psychology sees that economic or technical factors clearly increase the power of leaders. But there is a magic word which alone indicates the real cause of that power, and the word is *crowd* or, more exactly, *mass*. It has often occurred in popular speech since the French Revolution, but not until the twentieth century has it been possible to say exactly what it means or to give it a recognised scientific sense. A mass is a transitory collection of equal, anonymous and similar individuals within which the ideas and emotions of each individual member tend to express themselves spontaneously.

A crowd or mass is the social animal which has broken its leash. Moral prohibitions loosen their hold. The differences between human types melt away. Men express, in action which is often violent, their dreams and their passions and all the heroism, brutality, delirium and self-sacrifice they contain. A human group in fermentation, a constant seething, these are the real characteristics of the crowd. It is also a blind and uncontrollable force which can overcome any obstacle and move mountains or destroy the achievements of centuries.

Collectivities are constantly being made and unmade by the break-down of social ties, the speed of communications, the continual mixing and fusion of populations and the accelerated and exhausting pace of urban life. Once they have been reduced to their component atoms, they are reconstituted in the form of unstable and ever-greater crowds. The phenomenon is taking place on a scale hitherto unknown, and this explains its absolute historical novelty. It also explains why, in a civilisation in which crowds play a major part, the individual is losing both his reason for existing and his sense of himself. He is an outsider, forced to function as an anonymous cog in a machine composed of other individuals with whom his relationships are exclusively mechanical and impersonal. Hence the uncertainty and unfocussed anxiety within each individual, who sees himself as the plaything of hostile and unknown forces. Hence too his search for an ideal or a belief, his need for a model which will enable him to restore his longed-for wholeness. The psychological wretchedness of the masses of which Freud speaks is assuming world-wide dimensions. It is the background against which prestigious or charismatic leaders, whose vocation is to rally men to them, recreate powerful ties amongst them. They propose an example and an ideal and an answer to the question of what makes life worth living. In an age when we no longer have a unitary view of nature, and no model in society or any of our vanishing religions can provide a valid reason for the mere fact of our existence, that question is pre-eminently a political one.

In short, the birth of a form of collective life has always coincided with the appearance of a new type of human being. Conversely, the decline of such a form always sees the disappearance of a human type. We live in an age of mass societies and mass men. To those qualities shared by every person who has to direct and manage his fellow-men, leaders have to be able to join those other, more magical, qualities of the prophet and to arouse admiration and enthusiasm. The masses are like a heap of bricks without course or mortar, liable to collapse at the first hint of bad weather, since there is nothing to hold them together. By giving each individual the impression of a personal relationship, by enabling him to share in the same identical idea and view of the world, the leader offers him an ersatz togetherness and the illusion of a direct man-to-man tie. All that is needed is one or two striking images, a few high-sounding and emotionally-appealing formulas, or a reminder of a great collective belief. Such is the cement that binds individuals and holds the edifice of the masses together. Spectacular ceremonies, frequent assemblies, shows of strength and faith, projects to which all assent and the like all form the apparatus which ensures that energies are combined and that the collective will is paramount and creates an atmosphere of drama and exaltation.

The leader stands out from this sea of humanity, receiving its adulation and homage. His image fascinates, his words charm, the awe he inspires embraces everyone. For the multitudes of atomised, isolated individuals reconstituted as a mass, he is the mass made into an individual. He gives the mass his name, his visage and his active will.

Napoleon did this magnificently for the soldiers of the French revolutionary armies. Stalin succeeded in producing amongst the Communists of the entire world what Michelet called 'the agreement of the people in one man'. Both ensured the limitless devotion of the masses for whom they had undertaken to provide a model. Transforming a large crowd into a single entity gives the leader an attraction which is both visible and inexplicable. From that unwanted combination there emerges a whole, a captivating character who holds and binds as soon as the leader speaks or acts. But the skills used to achieve such ends involve first the heart, then faith, and finally hope. Reason plays a very secondary part. If we look closely, in our mass societies, the art of motivating crowds, *politics, is a religion revived.*

## III

With crowd psychology then, we have to see what unites the leader to his people like a man to his shadow. Clearly, it is power. The people have wrested it from those who held it and now hold it themselves. The leader is as avid for it as the believer is for eternal life. Indeed, his struggle for it begins in a spirit of loyalty. He wants to wipe out all the injustice of the past, acquire the means of curing a wasteful and inefficient economy, give the under-privileged the well-being without which life is wretched and re-establish the authority of his nation. At the end of a period of crisis, war or revolution, a programme of that kind demands a sense of efficiency and a more skilful administration of public affairs.

It is a commonplace to think that chaos reigns wherever there is anarchy, in the correct sense of the word, a lack of authority, whether that of a man or of a party. That is a mistaken view of things. But the leader, of whatever kind, can use it to strengthen his internal power at the expense of his rivals by putting institutions and production on a sound footing again. Success in this enables him to rally the masses, make them see his struggles as their own and to ask the necessary sacrifices of them.

The first of these sacrifices is renouncing the control of power and the satisfactions freedom brings in order to help him, those close to him and his followers to command and to make themselves better obeyed, and to do so using the shortest and fastest means. Thus, by using expedient but illicit methods, he speeds up the seizure of power. The people, too trusting, authorise and approve abnormal procedures of surveillance, suspicion and oppression. The same thing happens in any number of spheres. Principles are first respected and then fudged. What at first seems merely a temporary expedient finishes up as a permanent abdication of responsibility, as happened with the legislative assemblies in the case of Napoleon and the soviets in that of Stalin, as history bears witness.

All these machinations go hand in hand with a reorchestration, around the leader, of all the ideas that have brought him to the top. Without them, of course, all tigers are made of paper and all power is a flash in the pan. Every election, all the actions of everyday life, work, love, the search for truth, reading a newspaper and so on all become so many votes of confidence in him. Thus his authority, whether obtained with the consent of the masses or seized after a coup, rests on universal suffrage or, in other words, has a democratic form. We should remember that even Hitler and Stalin became heads of government as a result of proper elections which they subsequently transformed into *coups d'état*. In short, in all such cases, social anarchy is abolished to make way for violence and subordination.

What is called in the East the cult of personality and in the West the personalisation of power are only, in spite of the enormous differences, extreme variants of one and the same kind of exchange. The people daily renounce the responsibilities of sovereignty and ratify their action in each opinion poll and at each election. This is bartered for an equally day-to-day right on the part of the leader to exercise the power he has assumed and which is never given to him definitively. What Le Bon called 'the leaders of crowds' operate this kind of barter skilfully and ensure that its terms are accepted wholeheartedly. In doing so, they follow to the letter the principle of political society, which is that *the mass reigns but does not rule*.

**IV**

There is a mystery about the masses. The timidity of current social thought acts as a brake on our curiosity, whereas a reading of classical authors keeps it alive. We can tacitly ignore the mystery, emasculate it and even push it from our minds, but we cannot be rid of it for ever or destroy it. The Soviet philosopher Zinoviev wrote not long ago in his book *Without Illusions* that generally such phenomena of mass psychology escape the attention of historians, who see them merely as secondary elements leaving no trace, whereas in fact they play a very important part indeed. It could not be better or more succinctly expressed. Mass psychology was born when the pioneers of the discipline asked the questions on everybody's lips: how do leaders exercise such a power over crowds? Is mass man made of a different stuff from individual man? Does he want a leader? Why is our own time the age of the crowd? The success of the answers to these questions was striking to a degree that is hard to imagine today. This branch of psychology was very influential in politics, philosophy and even literature, and it has continued to make progress. Of course, it took up facts which were already known and ideas which had been popularised by poets, political thinkers and philosophers. But it showed them in a new light and laid bare surprising aspects of human nature. The analyses it provided gradually built up a profile of mass society as we know it in its final form today, when it is perhaps just beginning to decline.

I cannot over-emphasise the scope of the analyses which Le Bon, Tarde and Freud, the three founding fathers in this field, used in attempting to solve the mystery. Nevertheless, when I started writing this book I was, like everyone else, ignorant of them. At first, I studied them as if I were a learned antiquarian, seeking to establish them, to reconstitute their origins and to put a date to the circumstances in which they were made. I shook off a great deal of the dust that has settled on much of the work of Le Bon and Tarde in particular and tried, so to speak, to make up for an omission in our knowledge or fill in a gap in it. As I got further on in my work, however, I realised that in following received opinions I was taking the wrong path. It became clear to me that I was not dealing with books that were no more than the vestiges of work that had succumbed to the ravages of time or relics to which one might justifiably prefer more recent writings which make a significant contribution to knowledge, as they say.

In fact for almost a century we have often done little more than repeat and paraphrase them in less raw and more refined, and hence relatively more hypocritical, language. Of course, in the intervening time, we have made some advances and opened up other perspectives, but within a framework for which they had provided the bare outline. I have become very much aware of the obvious common ground of questions and answers in mass psychology and the profound relationships between the work of all three. This means that they must all be dealt with together and that each one must be a starting-point for an understanding of the others. Once I had realised this, I approached them, I suppose, like a traveller entering an unknown town who visits house after house and street after street and suddenly realises that he has gone through a whole community built to a plan which he then sees in a flash.

What I am proposing, then, is to map out the whole area of mass psychology. I must make it clear that it is not a question of explaining the ideas of each writer, but rather of seeking a link between them and casting light on what lies at their root. I first reflected on what the classical architecture of the general area might be and what value the scientific material with which it had been planned might have. I then went on to what is known as a logical reconstruction of each theory with the aim of showing the progress its proponent had made in providing solutions to problems which his predecessors had left unanswered. I am bound to say that this progress is the sign of a coherent system which it is possible to accept or reject but whose existence simply cannot be denied. As a final step towards establishing such a system, I took into account the effects of this branch of knowledge in order to give it the current reality which, despite appearances, it has never really lost.

I had to proceed in this way as the work of Le Bon, Tarde and Freud on mass psychology is in each case diverse, fragmentary, repetitive and incomplete. None of them ever reached the end of his projects, either because of the difficulties involved or because he died before he had completed his work. We are often faced with first fine careless raptures rather than with rigorous concepts. Hence, in order to achieve the logical reconstruction, which is always an invention, I simplified basic principles. This means that I took each writer's line of reasoning to its logical extreme and made the links between them more coherent than they really were. In one or two cases, I was obliged to create concepts which could be deduced from them. If I had not done so, the theory would have remained incomplete. I have tried throughout to make mass psychology an analytical science (which no-one had previously attempted and which the data make difficult) just as there has been an attempt to do with mechanics or economics. Thus the reader will find here not so much the ideas of Le Bon, Tarde and Freud as the intellectual framework of the science that they jointly established.

## V

This brings me to the last point that had to be made, that of my own position. Establishing the system of mass psychology is not, despite the abundance of material, an easy task. It is also a painful one. At every turn, one discovers a rather unflattering picture, to put it mildly, of public life, leaders and masses. It describes as necessary all those attributes which make power insupportable: its scorn for reason, its violence, cunning and despotism. Nor is the image of the crowd contained within it any less disheartening. Crowds are eager to submit, a prey to their impulses and, by definition, unconscious. In addition, mass psychology takes no account in its hypotheses of those familiar economic, historical and technical factors which determine the content of power and explain how societies develop. Whatever their political position, mass psychologists insist on the primacy of the psychic element in collective life. They criticise dominant theories, from those of Durkheim to those of Marx, for leaving out affective and unconscious forces. That is their Achilles' heel when they want to leave the world of ideas and enter the world of realities. Their reply to the ancient question of whether mankind is good or evil is also that man as part of a crowd is pretty evil, as if this was something they knew for certain. It would seem that if one wants to avoid the pitfall of lofty sentiments and the danger of appearing woolly-minded, the safest thing is to follow Bradley's maxim that when something is bad, it must be good to know the worst. So one eschews all illusions and remembers that a pleasant surprise is better than certain disappointment.

As you might suppose, we are a long way from the pieties normal in a branch of knowledge drawing its inspiration from a lucidly rational philosophy and the certainty that all our present dramas are merely preludes to some future happy ending. And yet even now, when I have reflected assiduously on the bases of mass psychology, I still find it very hard to understand them. This is precisely because I recoil from the vision of man and society that it proposes, which is so radically different from the convictions I have examined in several of my books.

Of course, I am quite convinced that we must avoid an idealistic view of man and society and that in view of our recent history dismantling our dream-factories is a wholesome thing. Nevertheless, I find it difficult to insist that certain ideals of democracy and freedom have no necessity or social strength. That is why there have always been men willing to struggle to make them prevail and to change a state of affairs which, by maintaining itself, seems to have become the very destiny of our own species, with the leaders at the top and the led at the bottom.

That is where the real difficulty lies. The more one studies the psychology of crowds, the clearer it becomes that it draws its power from its very refusal to view men through the spectacles of customary morality and its insistent repetition of the belief that because we are what we are it will be a long time before we achieve our ideals. We can criticise its founding fathers for seeing things in this way and reject their vision for being so avowedly conservative. But that would mean viewing those first exponents as mediocrities incapable of seeing anything outside their own social class and the age they lived in. What we must not forget, however, is that their theories sprang from a reflection on the liberal democracy they supported and on the course of the revolutions which they witnessed in our century. That reflection draws on the age-old common sense that both the masters of this world and its peoples understand very well. The attraction of mass psychology lies in that complicity with common sense, to such an extent that it gives the sense of dealing with permanent tendencies in human societies.

The most disturbing aspect of it, however, is still its practice, that is, the success with which its ideas have been applied. They may perhaps sometimes be rather simple and sometimes verge on the ridiculous, but they have nevertheless been almost too successfully justified in the events of the recent past and even of the present, and several perspicacious commentators have stressed this fact.

This success means that it has been at the source of too many things in our civilisation for us to be able to ignore it. Mass psychology holds at least one of the keys to the power enjoyed by leaders in our age. Counting one's democratic chickens before they are hatched is a rather frivolous undertaking if one does not seek to ascertain in what ways and for what reasons that power might reduce their number or indeed take their place. This is what this book sets out to do. It aims to penetrate as deeply as possible a branch of knowledge which has taken a long, hard look at our age, examined the domination of man by man without indulgence and shown the ways of using this power in mass societies. I refuse its view of history, I doubt its truth, but I accept the phenomenon.

My method then is as follows. The first part of the book is devoted to the reasons why a science of the masses came into being and the themes it deals with. The second and third parts are concerned with the invention of that science by Le Bon, firstly with the description of crowds and of the leader, and then with the methods he prescribed for governing them, which have been popularised by modern propaganda and publicity. In the fourth and fifth parts I show how Tarde generalised that description to cover the whole range of the forms of social life and analysed the power of leaders over the masses. His decisive contribution, which is still strikingly contemporary, was his theory of mass communications. A hidden face of the human sciences in France emerges as this section progresses. Finally, in the last four parts I reconstitute, on the basis of several sketches, Freud's explanation of mass phenomena. This was both a synthesis and the final development of his predecessors' work, but by using a new perspective it changed their hypotheses into deductions from a system. It is, in fact, the only explanation of that branch of psychology that we have, and can thus be seen as classical.

## PART I

# The study of the masses

## 1. *The individual and the masses*

I

IF ASKED to name the most important invention of modern times, I should have no hesitation in saying that it was the individual. From the first appearance of *homo sapiens* to the Renaissance, man's horizon was always 'we' or 'us', his group or family, to which he was bound by powerful obligations. But once major voyages, trade and science had separated the independent atoms of humanity, those monads with their own thoughts and feelings, man operated within the perspective of 'I' or 'me'. There was and is nothing easy about this position. An individual worthy of the name, we believe, has to behave in accordance with his reason, judge people and things dispassionately and act in full knowledge of what he is about. He should only accept the opinions of others advisedly, after considering them and weighing up the arguments for and against them with scientific impartiality and should not bow to the judgement of authority or the greatest number. We expect each person to act after due thought and guided by his intelligence and his interest both as an individual and when he is in the company of his fellows.

But observation shows us that it is not at all like that. At some time or another, every individual passively submits to the decisions of his chiefs and his superiors. He unreflectingly accepts the opinions of his friends, his neighbours or his party. He adopts the attitude, language and tastes of those around him. What is worse, as soon as a human being joins a group and is caught up into a mass, he becomes capable of excessive violence, panic, enthusiasm or cruelty. He performs actions repugnant to his conscience and contrary to his interests. In situations like these, it is as if he had completely changed and become someone else. That is the enigma that constantly baffles and amazes us. In a classic work, the English psychologist Bartlett quotes an observation by a statesman that sets it out clearly. 'The great mystery of all conduct is social conduct. I have had to study it all my life, but I cannot pretend to understand it. I may seem to know a man through and through, and I still would not dare to say the first thing about what he will do in a group' (Bartlett 1932: 24).

What is the cause of this lack of certainty? Why is it impossible to say how a friend or someone close to us will behave at a professional meeting, a political gathering, as a member of a jury or in a crowd? That question has always been answered by saying that in a social situation individuals do not act totally in accordance with their conscience or show their best side and that what usually happens is the opposite. Far from coming together and improving, their good qualities tend to diminish and deteriorate. In fact, the level of a human group falls towards that of its lowest members, which means that all can take part in collective action and feel they are all equal. One cannot therefore say that in such cases actions and thoughts tend towards the 'average'. They are those of the lowest common denominator. The law of numbers is seen as the law of mediocrity, and what is common to all is measured by the standards of those who have least. In short, in a group the first shall be last.

It would not be at all difficult to compile a huge anthology showing that this is a universally-held idea. Solon, for example, maintained that an individual Athenian was as cunning as a fox, but that when they were all assembled in the Pnyx they were as witless as a flock of sheep. Frederick the Great had the highest esteem for his generals when he spoke to each of them individually, but said that when they were together in a council of war they were simply a collection of imbeciles. The poet Grillparzer maintained that each separate human being was bearable, but that in the mass they came far too close to the animal kingdom, and Schiller fully agreed with him, remarking that each particular person is fairly intelligent and understanding, whereas men in a body become so many fools.

It is not only the German poets who have expressed opinions of this kind. Long before them, the Romans invented a proverb which has enjoyed amazing fortune: *Senatores omnes boni viri, senatus romanus mala bestia* (The senators are all good men, the Roman Senate is an evil beast), defining thus the contrast between the likely qualities of each individual senator and the lack of wisdom, consideration and moral rigour which blemished the joint deliberations of the august assembly on which the peace of the whole of the ancient world depended at the time. Referring to this proverb, Albert Einstein exclaimed, 'How much misery does this fact cause mankind! It is the source of wars and every kind of oppression, which fill the earth with pain, sighs and bitterness' (Einstein, 1954: 54).

And the Italian philosopher Gramsci, who had abundant experience of men and had long meditated on the nature of the masses, interpreted it very precisely. In his view, it meant that a crowd of individuals dominated by their own immediate interests or a prey to passions aroused by events of the moment and passed on uncritically by word of mouth would come to a wrong collective decision made in accordance with the lowest instincts. The observation, he thought, was true of fortuitous crowds that had come together 'like people sheltering from a shower under an arcade' and made up of men with no ties of responsibility towards other men or groups of men or any concrete economic reality, which in his view was a degradation and diminishment of individuals (Gramsci, 1953: 149).

This interpretation highlights the two sides of a single haunting fact. Taken individually, each of us is ultimately reasonable. Taken as a whole, as part of a crowd, at a political meeting or even with a group of friends, we are all willing to commit the worst acts of madness.

## II

Whenever individuals come together, a crowd is soon born. They mix, fuse, radically change, acquire a shared nature which stifles their own, are subject to a collective will which silences their own. Pressure of this kind is a real threat, and many people feel engulfed.

When they see this social animal embodied, moving and milling about, some individuals hang back for a moment before throwing themselves headlong into it, others are truly repelled. These reactions all bear witness to the power of the crowd and the psychic echoes it evokes and through the latter to the presumed effects we attribute to it. These have been admirably described by Maupassant with a precision equalled by few specialists in the field:

Moreover, for another reason, I have a horror of crowds. I cannot go into a theatre or watch a public festival. They fill me with a strange and unbearable unease, a frightful distress, as if I were struggling might and main against an irresistible and mysterious power. And indeed I am struggling against the soul of the crowd, which is trying to enter into me. How many times have I noted that when one lives alone the intelligence increases and rises, whereas once one mixes with other men once more it diminishes and falls. Contacts, widespread ideas, all that is said and all that one is forced to listen to, to hear and to reply to, all this has an effect on one's thought. Ideas ebb and flow from head to head, from house to house, from people to people, and a level is established, an average intelligence for every large group of individuals. The qualities that every individual person has – intellectual initiative, free will, wise reflection and even perspicacity – in general disappear when that individual becomes part of a mass of his fellows.

(Maupassant, 1979: 102)

All that, no doubt, is a catalogue of Maupassant's preconceived ideas, his prejudice against the herd and his high but not always justified estimation of the individual. Perhaps I should even have said a catalogue of those of his time and his class. Nevertheless, his description of the contact between the individual and the collective (or between the artist and the masses) with its three phases of instinctive fear, shock and anxiety followed by irresistible deprivation, and finally a vast movement to and fro of almost palpable if not visible influences, has the inescapable ring of truth.

It also shows the supposed effects of immersion in the crowd: the levelling of intelligence, the paralysis of initiative and the annexation of the individual soul by that of the crowd. These are not the only ones, but they are the ones most frequently mentioned. The horror Maupassant felt helped him define the two causes of his unease, namely a belief that he was losing the use of reason and a sense that his emotional reactions were excessive and extreme. This makes him ask the very same questions as those later posed by scientists reflecting on the phenomenon he described:

A popular saying tells us that crowds 'do not reason'. But why not, if each individual member of them does? Why should a crowd unreflectingly do what none of its component units would? Why is a crowd subject to irresistible impulses, fierce desires and stupid, uncontainable impulses and carried away by the latter, to the extent that it commits acts that none of its members would commit? A stranger cries out, and suddenly everyone is seized by a kind of frenzy, and all are caught up in the same unreflecting movement which none tries to resist. Carried along by the same thought which immediately becomes common to all, despite differences of social class, opinions, beliefs, customs and morality, they will hurl themselves upon him, massacre him, drown him, without any real reason, whereas each of them, if he were alone, would dash forward to risk his life saving the very man he is now killing.                    (Maupassant, 1979: 103)

The thought and tone of these lines are so accurate and precise that they need no commentary. It is not possible to improve on what the novelist has expressed so well. Maupassant is wrong about one thing, however. The popular saying is not alone in denying reason to collectivities and human groups. As the two following samples show, the notion is echoed in what the philosophers, following a widespread view, have to say. Zinoviev writes in *The Yawning Heights* that correct and profound ideas are individual ones, and that false and stupid ones come from the mass, which seeks blindness and sensation. Simone Weil, a French philosopher universally known for her moral fervour, corroborates his opinion:

With regard to thought, the relationship is reversed. In this connection, the individual is greater than the mass as much as something is greater than nothing, for thought only forms in a single mind face-to-face with itself. Collectivities do not think.                    (Weil, 1955: 108)

Remarks of this kind show clearly that there is a wide consensus about a basic idea: groups and masses live in the grip of strong emotions and extreme affective movements, all the more so since they do not have sufficient intelligence to control their elementary affective states. A single individual who becomes part of a crowd finds his personality profoundly modified along these lines. Although he is not always conscious of it, he becomes someone else. The collective 'we' speaks through his individual 'I'.

I have spent a lot of my time, and hence the reader's, in stressing the importance of these ideas, since in general we tend to ignore them because they are common. We often pay no attention to them, but they are in fact the basis of so many social relationships and actions.

## III

And so the problem is posed. There are only individuals. How, starting from these social atoms, does one obtain a collective totality? How can each one of them adopt and express an opinion coming to him from outside? The fact is that the individual unknowingly interiorises the attitudes and feelings that come his way. He abandons himself to brutal or orgiastic demonstrations whose causes or aims elude him, although he believes he knows them. He even believes that he sees things which do not exist and believes any rumour whispered into his ear without thinking to check it. It is in such ways that innumerable men come to wallow in social conformity, taking what is in reality the general consensus for a truth established by each individual reason.

It is *suggestion* or *influence* that produces such an extraordinary metamorphosis. What we are really witnessing is a kind of hold on people's consciousness. An order or a message causes an idea, an emotion or an action to be accepted as if they were convictions by someone who has no logical reason to do so. Individuals have the illusion that they are making their own decisions and do not realise that they have been subjected to influence or suggestion.

Freud described the specific nature of the phenomenon very well:

I should like to put forward the view that what distinguishes a suggestion from other kinds of psychical influence, such as a command or the giving of a piece of information or instruction, is that in the case of a suggestion an idea is aroused in another person's brain which is not examined in regard to its origin but is accepted just as though it had arisen spontaneously in that brain.                (Freud: I, 82)

The consequent reversal is also part of the puzzle. Each person thinks that he is the cause of something instead of only the effect, the voice instead of the mere echo, and has the illusion of possessing himself what in reality he simply shares with everyone else. In addition, he splits and changes. When he is with others, he is not what he is when he is alone. His public and his private behaviour are two different things.

I should like to conclude this overview with an analogy. At the collective level, suggestion or influence is what neurosis is at the individual one. Both presuppose on the one hand a turning-away from, or even an avoidance of, logical thought and a preference for illogical thought, and on the other a split in the individual between the rational and irrational sides of his nature, between his internal and his external life. In both cases there is a loss of the connection with reality and of self-confidence. Consequently, the individual eagerly submits to the authority of the group or the leader (who might well be the therapist) and docilely accepts the orders of the person suggesting how he should think and behave. He is the victim of an inner struggle in which his individual personality is at war with his social one. What he does as part of the group is in total contradiction to what he knows to be reasonable and moral when he is alone with himself and obeys his need to respect truth. We can take the analogy further. Just as external influence can invade and devour the individual and make him part of an undifferentiated mass in which he is simply a bundle of imitative patterns, so neurosis eats away the conscious layer of his mind until his words and actions are no more than living repetitions of his traumatic childhood memories.

But their effects are obviously quite different. The former enables the individual to exist in a group and ultimately makes him unfit to live alone. The latter prevents him from living with other people, removes him from the mass and imprisons him in himself. In short, influence makes human beings social and neurosis makes them asocial. The list of the tensions arising between these two mutually-opposed tendencies would be endless. Modern society has exacerbated them and pushed them to extremes. One thing is clear and must be borne in mind: what we call 'collective madness' is not of the same nature as what we call 'individual madness', and it is not legitimate to come to the facile conclusion that one follows from the other. From what I have just said, it can be seen that the former arises from an over-emphasis on the social and the total incorporation of the individual into the group and that the latter is the result of an inability to live with others and to make the compromises necessary in community life.

These comparisons are not, of course, fortuitous. Right from the start, it has been the same men who have studied both suggestion or influence and neurosis. The former was associated with collective hysteria, the latter with individual hysteria. Once again, we must recognise the admirable courage of Le Bon and Freud in giving a scientific sense to these phenomena. The former was bold enough to put suggestion at the centre of mass psychology and the latter to place neurosis at the heart of individual psychology.

No-one has seriously attempted to verify these hypotheses about influence or suggestion. And yet we are pretty certain that in social life the lower layers of the psyche take over from the higher ones and that the heat of the instincts takes over from the coldness of reason, just as in nature the highest forms of energy, like gravity and electricity, are broken down into its lowest form, namely heat. This conviction goes hand in hand with the widespread belief that in the struggle between reason and passion the latter always wins. Precisely because we are social beings.

For thousands of years the peoples of the world have had similar ideas and have sought to explain why men as individuals are logical and consistent in their behaviour, but once they become part of a mass they lose these qualities. However, if we want to create a science, we have to make a close analysis of causes and effects. Only by doing so can we go forward in an area in which the wisdom of the world and of its poets and its philosophers has made so little progress. As for the object of our curiosity, it remains the same, intriguing us as it intrigued those who have gone before us.

## 2. *The revolt of the masses*

FOR A SCIENCE TO COME INTO BEING, the mere existence of a phenomenon is not enough. We have been aware for thousands of years of the one we are dealing with. Nor is it sufficient that it is strange enough to whet the intellectual appetite of one or two novelty-seeking scholars. The phenomenon has to lose its episodic and harmless nature and increase and multiply to such an extent that it gives us all sleepless nights and becomes a problem that we simply have to solve. Who bothered about the exchange of goods for money before society became a series of markets or about hysteria before the mentally ill were locked away and mental illnesses spread? Virtually no-one. Similarly, suggestion or influence has the power of transforming individuals into masses. But it was not drawn out of the darkness of common sense, highlighted and made into the central theme of crowd psychology until crowds increased in number and size. We all think that we see it all over the place as we note the changes individuals undergo when they are plunged into the crowds in streets, offices, factories, political meetings and so on. Suggestion did indeed become a widespread phenomenon towards the end of the nineteenth century as a result of a series of crises which produced a radical upheaval in society. The symptoms were as follows.

The first was the collapse of the pre-capitalist *ancien régime* under the repeated onslaught of capital and revolutions. With it collapsed too the traditional religious and political framework and spiritual institutions. The stable world of families, neighbourhood groups and the countryside was breached and split. Men were uprooted from their land and their church spires and siphoned off in huge numbers to the unstable world of growing and developing towns. The move from tradition to modernism threw onto the market a multitude of anonymous individuals, social atoms with no links between them. This change has been described by the German sociologist Tönnies in the well-known image of the movement from community to society. More precisely, the movement is from a warm, natural and spontaneous collectivity based on kinship, neighbourhood life and shared beliefs to a cold, artificial and constrained one based on the profit motive, mutual advantage and scientific logic. This image, since it illustrates one of the major aspects of the break between past and present society, has had a very wide general appeal.

The rapid mechanisation of industry epitomised by the steam engine, and the concentration of men, women and children, crushed into shape by the factories, subject to the discipline of the machine and exploited by the entrepreneurial class, turned the towns into battlefields where the new poor confronted the new rich. In every country, all these effects were expressed in the massive and angry rise of the working class, a class which took as its weapon new means of action such as strikes and acquired hitherto unheard-of forms of organisation in the shape of trades unions and political parties. These channelled the human tide, gave it form and direction and changed the way political cards were dealt. In those days, when the 'mob' took to the streets it was no longer to celebrate a patron saint, to take part in a carnival or stage a peasants' revolt. The people fought their masters, shouted down their not over-saintly employers and claimed what was justly theirs. Eric Hobsbawm has pointed out the permanent nature of their claim:

The classical mob did not merely riot as a protest, but because it expected to achieve something by its riot. It assumed that the authorities would be sensitive to its movements, and probably also that they would make some sort of immediate concession; for the 'mob' was not simply a casual collection of people united for some *ad hoc* purpose, but in a recognised sense, a permanent entity, even though rarely permanently organized as such. (Hobsbawm, 1971: 111)

This passage stresses the existence of the crowd or mob, its place of assembly (the street) and its action in support of its claims. In particular, it brings out the threatening character of the whole phenomenon, the mere presence of which is enough to make the authorities yield.

Increasingly, the working class was inflamed with the ideals of the coming revolution, for which its leaders were conducting a dress rehearsal. Socialism was perhaps a very new idea grafted onto the undying myth of justice, but in many people it nevertheless aroused memories of terror and subversion. This was particularly so in France, where ever since the Revolution of 1789 revolutions and counter-revolutions had followed each other in a seemingly unending sequence. Did not Auguste Comte declare that the major problem of social reform was that of achieving a consensus and re-establishing moral unity? At the speed with which things were moving, however, the real problem was barricades and regularly-recurring and bloody street fights. They were a foretaste of what was to come in the future and the tangible sign that new masses of humanity had been launched into the arena of history.

Another characteristic of the times was the creation of a new kind of man in the overcrowded towns. Baudelaire spoke of a 'swarming city, a city full of dreams', but for the workers it was full of disappointments. Its immense market led to the mass production of culture and consumer habits. One after another the collective bureaucrat, the collective intellectual and the collective consumer made their appearance on the social stage, and thoughts and feelings were standardised. All these social cyclotrons simply reduced individuals to ever-tinier particles and condemned them to an anonymous and ephemeral existence. The popular press was already acting as a communications factory, pouring minds into a uniform mould and ensuring that each human unit conformed to the pre-ordained model. Gramsci was aware of these developments and noted that in the contemporary world the trend towards conformity was wider and deeper than in the past and that the standardisation of modes of thinking and acting had reached national and even continental proportions (Gramsci, 1953: 150).

He also pointed out the emergence of a new mass man, completely dependent on others, shaped by this unusually widespread current of conformity and subject in reality to two kinds of conformity, that of the minority, from above, and that of the majority, from below. He saw a constant struggle between the two, a battle between two kinds of conformity, a fight for hegemony and a crisis in civil society (Gramsci, 1953: 130).

If we pursue Gramsci's idea as far as we can, we are forced to the conclusion that in the age of mass man what is at stake in the conflicts that torment society is not exclusively or predominantly *power*, which is taken or abandoned according to relative strength or weakness, but *influence*, as the latter is gained or lost depending on whether one of the two conformities is enjoying an ascendancy over the other.

## II

The image of the nineteenth century that remains with us is clear. It is that of an age in which the *mobile vulgus*, the violent and malleable crowd, was uncontainable. The external observer saw in it a concentration of amorphous human matter incorporating and dissolving every individual and a prey to a kind of social delirium. Flaubert had already described his hero, Frédéric, struck by the collective intoxication of the 1848 revolution as 'caught up by the magnetism of the enthusiastic crowds' (Flaubert, 1952: 323).

It is precisely the exaltation produced by a moving crowd taking on the appearance of a collective Frankenstein that fascinates and disquiets. Flaubert describes the crowd forcing its way into the Palais-Royal as 'a swarming mass going ever upwards like a river pushed back by an equinoctial tide, with a drawn-out roar, acting on an unforeseeable impulse' (Flaubert, 1952: 319–20).

These strong impressions give the common image a solidity: men come together in social herds and, intoxicated by the mysterious force that emanates from any over-excited group, lapse into a state of suggestibility like that produced by drugs or hypnosis. As long as they remain in that state, they will believe all they are told and do all that is required of them. They will obey even the most senseless exhortation. Individual reactions are always heightened, as happens with pilgrimages, patriotic parades, music festivals and political rallies. Flaubert reveals in his hero the symptoms proper to the state of mass man, depicting him as 'shivering as an immense love, a supreme and universal tenderness washed over him, as if the heart of the whole of humanity were beating in his breast' (Flaubert, 1952: 323).

Until modern times, however, such crowds appeared only sporadically and played a quite secondary part. They were thus not really a problem and did not call for any particular science. As soon, however, as they became current and common, the situation changed. If we are to believe Le Bon, the power of the crowd to influence the course of events either by the vote or by revolt is something new in history and is a sign that society is changing. Increasingly, in fact, the latter seems to be breaking down group solidarity, loosening traditional ties and destroying religious belief. Like isolated atoms, individuals are left to their own solitude, a prey to their own needs in the jungle of our towns, the desert of our factories and the greyness of our offices. These various atoms, these grains of the multitude, come together in violent and unstable mixtures. They form a kind of gas tending to explode in the vacuum of a society stripped of its authority and its values, a gas with an explosive power that increases in proportion to its volume and is predominant everywhere. As Le Bon, an interested witness, wrote:

While all our ancient beliefs are tottering and disappearing, while the old pillars of society are giving way one by one, the power of the crowd is the only force that nothing menaces, and of which the prestige is continually on the increase. The age we are about to enter will in truth be the ERA OF CROWDS.

(Le Bon, 1952: 14)

## III

We can always add a few touches to this image and perhaps even need to do so to bring it closer to reality. But it is universally accepted that crowds of this kind are a symptom of a new state of humanity, a revolt from below threatening the way society is organised. Agreement about the state of affairs, however, does not inevitably mean agreement as to why it has come about. And so it is scarcely surprising that the upheavals of history are used in support of two diametrically opposed concepts, that of mass society and that of class society.

Class society was given a theoretical form by Marx and Weber, who both drew on political economy to do so. In that science, crowds are seen as the striking signs of a new form which is specifically revealed by the dislocated and pauperised masses mobilised against oppression by bureaucracy and capital. Capital brings men and machines together in large concentrations, socialises the forces of production and transforms society into a huge market in which everything, including labour, is bought and sold. In doing so, it creates an entirely new class, the proletariat. We may accept or reject that idea, but it certainly sees classes as the actors in history with one particular class, the proletariat, emerging as the herald of the modern age and the symbol of the coming revolution. The crowds swarming into the towns, engaging in civil war and taking part in every uprising, are thus seen as the raw material and the forms of the working masses. The level of consciousness varies amongst them, ranging from that of the passive sub-proletarian to that of the active true proletarian proposed as a hero.

Consequently, the more enormous they are, the clearer a vision such crowds have of their strength and their aims and the greater their effect on the way society changes. They turn away from the past, break the myriad slender links which bind them to religion, the nation and the superstitions of the dominant classes and go forward towards a new world of science and technology, leaving the old one to go into decline. Illuminated by the sunlight of history, this model of society gives a meaning to collective movements. It also offers an explanation of how they have come into being since the first tentative struggles. Everything else is merely the froth and dross of an alienated ideology.

There have been several successive versions of the second concept, based on the original one and born in and with crowd psychology. We can leave aside precursors such as Taine and de Tocqueville, but not writers like Le Bon and Tarde, who first began to shape the discipline. As one sociologist said in connection with the hypothesis of the mass society, 'It is probably the most influential social theory in the Western world today' (Bell, 1960: 21).

For such a society, the froth and dross are everything. In it, the agglomeration of individuals stripped of all their ties, of all the privileges of birth and station, disorientated by incessant change, gives an unwonted impetus to the emergence of those human nebulæ we call crowds. Of course, there have always been unheard and unseen crowds, but now, as history so to speak accelerates, they have burst their bonds and made their revolt visible and audible. They even, by their tendency to mix and standardise everything, threaten the existence of individuals and classes. Once their masks are off we see them in their simplest form. As Canetti writes:

Since the French Revolution these eruptions have taken on a form which we feel to be modern. To an impressive degree the crowd has freed itself from the substance of traditional religion and this has perhaps made it easier for us to see it in its nakedness, in what one might call its biological state, without the transcendental theories and goals which used to be inculcated in it.     (Canetti, 1973: 23)

We need only look around us: in the street, the factory, in parliamentary assemblies or barracks, even in holiday areas, we see nothing but stationary or moving crowds. Some individuals emerge from contact with them like a soul from purgatory. Others are permanently swallowed up by them. Nothing better expresses the fact that our contemporary society is primarily and preponderantly a *mass* society. We can see this in the number and the instability of the links between parents and children, friends and neighbours. We are aware of it in the metamorphosis each newly anonymous individual undergoes, for the desires, passions and interests that subsist in him depend on a great number of people for their fulfilment, and he is subject to moods of social anguish and pressure to accept and conform to a collective model.

In this concept, change is seen neither as the result of the proletarianisation of man nor of the socialisation of the economy. What we are really seeing is *massification*, the mixing and blending of the social classes. Where they come from, whether they are proletarians or capitalists, educated or ignorant is of little importance, for identical causes produce identical effects. From diverse and different fragments a homogeneous human composite, the mass made up of mass men, is formed. They are the actors of history and the heroes of our time. The reasons for this state of affairs lie hidden not in the concentration of the means of production and exchange, as the notion of the class society would maintain, but in the means of communication, the media, the press, the radio and so on, and in the phenomenon of *influence*. All these find their way into every household, are present even at work and on summer beaches, directing and standardising opinions and changing individual minds into mass minds. By means of a kind of social telepathy, the same thoughts and images are conjured up for millions of individuals and spread from one to the other like radio waves. The result of this is that such individuals are always ready to be part of a mass. When that actually happens, what we see is the troubling and unforgettable spectacle of a

25

multitude of strangers who, without ever having seen each other, are spontaneously swayed by the same emotion and respond like a single being to a band or a slogan and spontaneously fuse into one collective entity.

Marcel Mauss has described this metamorphosis at length. This is what he has to say:

The whole social body is animated by the same movement. There are no longer any individuals, for they have all become, as it were, the parts of a machine or, to use an even better image, the spokes of a wheel, turning in enchantment, singing and dancing. This has become the ideal symbol. It has its roots in very early societies, but is still reproduced in our own age, both in the case we have mentioned and elsewhere. This rhythmical, uniform and continuous movement is the direct expression of a mental state in which each individual consciousness is possessed by a single feeling, a single idea, the hallucinating idea of the common aim. Each body has the same swing, each face the same mask, each voice utters the same cry. In addition, there is the same depth of impression resulting from rhythm, music and song. Everyone sees on everyone else's face the image of his own desire, hears the proof of his own certainty in everyone else's mouth and is irresistibly carried along by the universal conviction. All are at one, caught up in the dance and enraptured by their agitation, and become a single body and a single soul. It is only at that point that the social body truly becomes real, for it is then that its cells, the individuals composing it, are as close to each other as the cells in an individual organism. In such conditions (which are never achieved in our societies, even when crowds are in their highest state of excitement, but which are still to be seen elsewhere) consent can create reality.

(Mauss, 1973: 126)

The passage is certainly striking.

It is time to look at consequences. The intellectual operation undertaken by those originating this concept is a simple and a bold one. For all of them, the mass was the unshackled crowd, without conscience, leader or discipline and the slave of instinct, as it appeared on the barricades to the sage, a frightening, enormous, howling and hysterical monster. In Freud's words:

It is just as though when it becomes a question of a large number of people, not to say millions, all individual moral acquisitions are obliterated and only the most primitive, the oldest, the crudest mental attitudes are left.    (Freud: XIV, 288)

We might add that sometimes the opposite happens and millions of men make unheard-of sacrifices and give their lives for the highest ethical values of justice and freedom.

But once we begin to see in them the emblem of our civilisation the masses are no longer the result of the breakdown of the former system, social classes incarnate or spectacular forms of the by-play of the life of society, something to be colourfully and poetically described by fascinated onlookers. They become an omnipresent aspect of our society and provide a key to politics and modern culture and an explanation of the discontents our society is a prey to. This radical shift of intellectual perspective has thus meant that crowd psychology has put the masses at the very centre of an overall view of twentieth-century history. It has also provided a rival theory to that of the class society, and so far no-one has been able to reconcile the two or to eliminate this alternative.

## IV

I have tried to show above that starting from the same still-recurring phenomena we have simultaneously imagined two opposing and mutually exclusive explanations, a duality which is commonplace in the sciences. I admit that in comparison there is something extremely simple and perhaps even simplistic about this concept of mass society. It postulates the individual as an impregnable fortress into which others steal by suggestion, which they then destroy and wash away with the silt of the collective, impulsive and unconscious tide. Such an idea seems to us both old-fashioned and insufficiently aware of the complexities of contemporary history. But it is not the first time that simple and apparently old-fashioned ideas have shown us unexpected truths.

Let us also look at the consequences of the twin explanations. What for one of them is a class revolt and a hope for the future is for the other the revolt of the masses – Ortega y Gasset's phrase has acquired universal currency – and the disturbing herald of an age of critical chain reactions. Crowd psychologists believe that revolt to be a decisive one, since it puts political power into the hands of masses who cannot exercise it and who show their fear of it. This fear has been enough to awaken a desire to know the masses in order both to exorcise their power and to rule them and also to study them scientifically. It is easier to see the mote in one's neighbour's eye than the beam in one's own. Their avowed enemies have also taken them seriously and struggled to discover the sources of their strength in order to do battle with them more successfully. Those who support them mostly do no more than sing their praises and talk of them in abstract and idealised terms. They too have not properly understood them.

The crowd psychologist makes no bones about denying that the masses have any claim or any ability to change the world or run the state, even if his words may shock some readers. By definition, they have neither the ability to reason nor the gift of self-discipline necessary for survival and culture, for they are to a high degree the slaves of momentary impulse and susceptible to the influence of anyone who cares to exercise it. In our times we are experiencing the decline of the individual and the high point of the rise of the mass, which is thus dominated by irrational and unconscious forces emerging from their subliminal lair and spontaneously showing themselves. In Le Bon's lapidary phrase, 'The substitution of the unconscious action of crowds for the conscious activity of individuals is one of the principal characteristics of the present age' (Le Bon, 1952: 6).

Who nowadays could still make such an abrupt and summary declaration? Experience has taught us to be more circumspect. Nevertheless, that declaration has had and still has historical consequences that no-one can now erase. In addition, its meaning has been universally understood. What it signifies is that the solution to the revolt of the masses depends on their psychology which, as Nietzsche says, becomes 'once more the way that leads to fundamental problems'. Sociological and economic explanations are only valid fortuitously and in particular situations.

What Nietzsche was the first to glimpse is becoming something of a general conviction. This is explicable by the creation of the new science of crowd psychology. Deciding how valid that science is is another matter. But what is certain is that it becomes more important in relation to the growth in importance of the masses. The great German writer Hermann Broch sees in the dramatic upheavals in Europe between the two wars the change in direction that encouraged it and defends the need for such a psychology in the following terms: 'The new political truths will be based on psychological truths. The human race is about to leave behind the economic stage of its development and enter the psychological one' (Broch, 1979: 42).

It is therefore not surprising that in the enormous flow of knowledge, which changes more than the sea or the seasons, this branch of science should be seen by all as having a universal application. The use by Le Bon, Freud or Reich of 'crowd' or 'mass' rather than 'social' or 'collective' psychology should not be seen as fortuitous. Each of them shows that he is portraying a view of our civilisation which is characterised by a specific form of group, the mass. Thus, the first writers in the field did not consider their subject to be a supporting science for other, more considerable, fields of investigation such as sociology or history. In fact, they saw it as a rival discipline, and set themselves a single goal, that of solving the enigma of how masses are formed, as Freud put it. Only a major science could claim to reach that goal.

## 3. *What do we do when faced with the masses?*

I believe that recent political innovation means nothing less than political domination by the masses.

J. Ortega y Gasset

## I

T HE INDIVIDUAL IS DEAD, long live the masses. That is the brute fact that the observer of the contemporary world discovers. The masses, it seems, have everywhere conducted a stubborn and violent campaign and their surprising and definitive victory has been equally universal. It is the masses that have raised new questions and necessitated new replies, since their strength is a new reality to be reckoned with. As Ernst Cassirer has noted:

In the last thirty years, in the period between the first and the second World Wars, we have not only passed through a severe crisis of our political and social life but have also been confronted with quite new theoretical problems. We experienced a radical change in the forms of political thought. (Cassirer, 1961: 1)

It is undeniable that in the period starting with the First World War and still in progress we have seen radical changes. Its major characteristic has been the irruption of the masses, their particular way of thinking and their irresistible beliefs. Crowd psychology perceived the basic nature of these changes, but that was not all it did. Of course, like any science, it attempted to describe phenomena, to seek their causes and to foresee their effects. But clearly too it had to create its own methods and rationale if it was to influence events. What is the point of knowledge without the power to act? Why discover ills for which one cannot prescribe a cure? When we demonstrate causes, we are answering the question 'why?', but when we formulate a practical solution we are answering the question 'what do we do?' The latter is of greater consequence than the former, since our curiosity is only exercised during moments of respite, whereas action is a permanent necessity.

Crowd psychology was created to answer both these questions at once. At the very start, it made much of its aim of explaining the 'why' of mass societies, but this was done in order to teach the governing classes what to do when faced with the masses who were upsetting the whole play of political life, an arena which will not see the last of them in the foreseeable future. In short, its aim was to solve the puzzle of how masses come into being, in order to deal with the even more difficult one of governing them. It addressed itself as much, and perhaps even more, to leaders as to men of science. In the manifesto of the new science, Le Bon wrote that

A knowledge of the psychology of crowds is today the last resource of the statesman who wishes not to govern them – that is becoming a very difficult matter – but at any rate not to be too much governed by them.

(Le Bon, 1952: 19)

## II

Crowd psychology was thus the science of a new kind of politics. Those pioneering it were all convinced that it provided the Ariadne's thread to the labyrinth of power relationships, in the absence of which so many rulers and ruled were left lost and bewildered. Right from the beginning they rejected the old political view based on the individual, for which a mass was simply a collection of a thousand or ten thousand such people. This old view was therefore one in which men were moved by their particular interests as workmen, industrialists or fathers and, after due reflection, acted solely in terms of those interests, thus suppressing their beliefs and feelings.

Crowd psychology rejects politics based on interest and reason and refuses to believe that men join a party, vote for a candidate and generally behave in order to obtain the greatest personal advantage. It does not see them as being aware of possible gains or losses, like buyers or sellers on the market. All that, crowd psychology maintains, is an illusion. What creates it is the fact that conventional politics sees the masses as an epiphenomenon of alienation which will pass away as education, technology, science and the fair distribution of the fruits of the earth progress.

Traditional politics thus believes that it is possible to fill in the gap between social action and acting on things as they are. To do this, it proposes the same methods and practices in both cases. It is quite true that science and technology are continually making new conquests. This shows the power inherent in the ways of thinking they represent. Consequently, we use them as models in every area of life. We imagine that if we adopt scientific methods which are based on rational principles we can make similar progress in the political field to that achieved in the industrial sphere, and think that we can rule and possess society as we rule and possess nature. Sooner or later, we think, this will enable us to create individual relationships between rulers and ruled which are free of passions, hatred and love and resemble our relationships with objects. In short, in Saint-Simon's famous phrase, we would move from ruling men to ruling things.

This familiar traditional view hinges on the idea of the rational nature of politics and a perception of it as progressing hand in hand with knowledge and the society we live in. Seen in this way, mass manifestations look less important and take on a similarity to other lingering traces of human immaturity apparent in less developed and advanced societies. The result of this is a certain political practice. It operates in a quite objectively scientific way, distinguishing between logic and belief and factual judgements and feelings in an attempt to decide which means are most suited to its ends. It addresses itself to reason and relies on figures and rational arguments, indicates what the realities of the matter in hand are and attempts to convince individuals that they should choose the solution which conforms most closely to their interests. It believes that the support of human beings is most easily obtainable when they are made aware of what is at stake in their work, class or party situation and so on (Oberschall, 1973), and, since unity creates strength, of the aims they can achieve together.

Crowd psychology accuses the traditional view of not seeing the real importance of crowds, which are a fact, and of misunderstanding their nature. When individuals are lost in the mass, they forget their own interests and accept common desires, or those desires which their leaders tell them are common to all. Whether they are in or out of work, they are the playthings of the waves of irritation and excitement produced by urban existence and possess nothing, not even the time to think. They are always dependent on others for their housing, their food, their jobs, their ideas and their dreams. All this means that their own interests are too weak and insubstantial to inhibit impulses that are exacerbated from every side.

Human kind, as T. S. Eliot wrote, cannot bear very much reality. Crowds can bear even less. Once men have been drawn together and fused into a crowd, they lose most of their critical sense. This is a result of both fear and a desire to conform. Their consciousness gives way to the thrust of illusions like a dam swept away by a river in spate. Thus, individuals forming a crowd are borne along by limitless waves of imagination and tossed about by emotions which are strong but have no specific object. The only language they understand is one which by-passes reason, speaks directly to the heart and makes reality seem either better or worse than it in fact is.

We may, of course, want them to be different from what they are and hope that they will be as minimally important as they were in the past.

That would mean that the masses would be in the position of consciously and deliberately choosing and supporting authority. Nothing of the kind will happen in the immediate future. It would be stupid to try to reform them, to say that they are anything other than what they are or to claim that we can change their mentality or reduce it to that of the constituent individuals. We can no more do that than change the laws of nature, which are not the same for an isolated atom at an ordinary level of energy as for a bundle of atoms at a higher one.

These basic facts mean that those in power are obliged to choose between two equally-justifiable but mutually incompatible ways of envisaging their action, one of which is concerned with individuals, the other with masses. Those choosing the former and banking on human interests and human reason must be aware that a policy of such a kind, which is scientific in both the way in which it is conceived and carried out, is suitable for a handful of statesmen, savants or philosophers and was useful when the masses played no part in political society, that is, before the age of the crowd. But choosing this path means rejecting the burning ambitions of those who found nations or religions and losing the ability to carry out even their most urgent responsibilities. For those who choose it are the products of the traditional system of parliaments and offices and are ignorant of the strength of passions and beliefs. They rely solely on intelligence when trying to persuade and on calculation when trying to show the rightness of a decision. They are disconcerted by the violence of collective emotions of individuals in the mass. Outrageous words or actions are as repugnant to them as a lack of taste. They can only conceive of guile or compromise between the right sort of people. They leave character out of account or laugh at it. But when they run out of courage, statesmen are vacillating and embarrassed, irresolute and wordy, and unable to measure up to their task. They argue without conviction or principles, deliberate without coming to any conclusion and act half-heartedly, letting things work themselves out. They are democrats, but they often prepare the way for a tyrant, call for a Cæsar, a strong man, and facilitate oppression as if it were liberation. When that happens, the paradox of liberty appealing to despotism takes form. Reason condemns politics and politics condemns reason.

In short, what such men lack as leaders is the instinct that allows of an understanding of the masses and a passionate sharing of their hopes. Instead of listening to the mighty voice of the multitude, they pay attention to the whispers of counsellors and flatterers. They can never say the right word or do the right thing at the appropriate time. They are undermined by the lack of certainty in their shifting and relative world and overwhelmed by events which they do not expect. They are first nonplussed and then turned out of office. The conclusion seems obvious: no-one can be a great political leader without a feeling for the masses.

Crowd psychology maintains that in the civilised world the masses keep alive an irrationality which, like the chaos of a primitive era of gods and madness, had been thought to be disappearing. But rather than becoming less important as civilisation advances, the part it plays is continually becoming greater and more attractive. Irrationality has been removed from the economy by science and technology only to become concentrated in the area of political power, where it is now of pivotal importance. This importance is becoming continually greater as men have less and less time to devote to the *res publica* and less chance of resisting collective pressure. Individual reason yields to mass passions, which it cannot control. We cannot stop an epidemic merely by wanting to.

This is why anyone who wants to devote himself to affairs of state and to govern men must appeal more to their feelings of love or hate, revenge or guilt, than to their understanding. It is better to awaken their memories than their minds, for in the present the masses can more easily see the traces of the past than the shape of things to come. What they see is not what is changing, but what is happening again. In short, the would-be ruler must thoroughly absorb the idea that mass psychology is not interested in individual psychology. Individuals succeed in their aims by using analysis or by a higher experience of reality. The means the masses use are no less effective, for they are passionately enamoured of an ideal and a man who is its incarnation. As Proust wrote about nations,

The logic which drives them is a completely interior one which is constantly being re-shaped by passion, like that driving people on opposite sides in some amorous or domestic quarrel, such as that between father and son, cook and mistress or husband and wife.                                    (Proust, 1978: III, 773)

I have to say and say again that traditional politics is based on reason and interest. It cannot but fail, as it follows scientific logic and treats the mass as a collection of individuals. It is not that the latter are without intelligence or will or are so dominated that they can no longer see what is in their interest or use their reason. Quite the contrary, for each of them is capable and even desirous of introducing democracy in the lofty sense of that term. Otherwise, there would be no concept of democracy or any attempt to achieve it. If individuals do not always succeed in this and their efforts are often counter-productive, it is because they are caught up in the crowd. They are subject to the law of human masses, and so everything turns out in an unexpected way and the psychic conditions are always different. The difference can be summed up very simply. Individuals have to be convinced, masses have to be swayed.

The basis of my argument can be summed up equally briefly. The masses overthrow the bases of democracy set up by bourgeois liberals and accepted in their turn by social democrats. The wish of the latter is to govern by means of an elite chosen by universal suffrage. Their policies take account of technological and economic realities alone, and refuse to recognise psychological ones. Policies of this kind may well be inspired by lofty ideas and have absolute merits, but they are based on a kind of blindness which invariably stops them forming a stable political regime. We can say that those who practise politics of this kind are working with the wrong society or the wrong nation (mass psychologists mostly make an exception in the case of Great Britain and the United States, which they admire, and where they claim that democracy has found its true form) and invariably in the wrong age. This wrong age can be recognised by one particular characteristic, that of revolutionary and anti-revolutionary movements involving the masses. That is why it demands a new kind of politics.[1]

## III

When faced with the masses, the task of politics is to organise them. Since they are swayed by two things, passion and belief, both have to be taken into account. Whenever men come together, they are all filled with similar emotions. They share in a higher faith, identify with someone who draws them from their solitude and admire him without reservation. That is a brief description of the synthesis that turns a collection of individuals into a collective individual. Their interests are only the velvet gloves on the hands of their passions. Take off the gloves and the hands are still there; cut off the hands and the gloves serve no purpose. Their reason is simply the froth on the surfaces of deep and abiding convictions.

This explains the character of political practice, which Gramsci explained better than I could, describing politics as a permanent action producing permanent organisations and hence identical to economics. The latter, however, he saw as also different from it, which was why it was possible to speak of politics and economics separately and to talk of 'political passion' as an immediate impulse to action coming into existence in the 'permanent and organic' sphere of economics, but going beyond it and involving feelings and aspirations providing an incandescent atmosphere in which the same way of assessing an individual human life obeyed laws other than those of individual accountancy (Gramsci, 1953: 13).

As a result, there is in fact in political life a profound lack of symmetry, which means that it is impossible ever to reach a point of equilibrium and stability. When men act on the material world in order to produce and survive, their technical and economic actions obey a rational law, and time brings an increasing rationality in the methods and the knowledge they use for this purpose. The main thing, if one is to succeed, is to subordinate means to the desired end and always to follow the results of experience. Logic-based machines show that this can be done, and this is why their use is becoming progressively more widespread.

Human relationships, on the contrary, are characterised by a degree of irrationality. This cannot be avoided, particularly if the aim is to mobilise the masses in terms of an ideal, whether it be positive or negative. Reich – and he was not the only one to do so – has shown the disastrous effects of ignoring this fact and how much it helped the rise of the Nazis in Germany:

Thanks to Marx, Engels and Lenin, the economic conditions of forward development were appreciably better understood than those forces that acted as a brake. No-one thought to raise the question of *the irrationalism of the masses*. Hence, the development towards freedom, which was so promising at the beginning, came to a standstill and then regressed to an authoritarian form.

(Reich, 1975: 254–55)

Indeed, those social processes which turn men into masses always make them more irrational and mean that they cannot be governed by the use of reason, even with the most worthy of intentions on the part of those controlling the processes. There are three aspects to this lack of symmetry in politics.

In the first place, there is a yawning gap between the two areas of human life. Rational thought and practice belong squarely to the field of the administration of things and wealth. They create increasingly important, efficient and automatic tools and instruments. On the other hand, managing human beings and hence political power involves less and less of this kind of thought and practice. In this area, society creates only beliefs and motive ideas. The former are admirable and urge justice and emancipation. The latter are cruel and preach revenge and oppression. They help to mobilise and unite men, and to this end they are poured into the mould of a dogmatic religion which has been prepared beforehand. This is the inevitable price that has to be paid if an idea is to be one of the factors moving the masses, and even Marxism has not escaped it.

Secondly, there is purely and simply the move towards unreason always present in the masses. This is evident in the release of those underground emotional forces which are ready to erupt like a volcano when the time comes. They are always powerfully present and when the time is right they assume the domination which is their due. That moment is when men are spurred on by some crisis and come together,

35

when individual awareness dims to some degreee and can no longer control the impulses such forces set up. The unconscious emotions, those burrowing moles of history, are free to take over. What comes to the surface is not something new, but something which already exists in an agglutinated but non-explicit form, latent forces which have been more or less concentrated and repressed and are now coherent and ready to advance. The masses are carried along in their mighty flow, driven on by panic or enthusiasm and controlled by the magic wand of a leader who has taken his place at their head. And with Shakespeare, the fascinated observer may cry out, ''tis the times' plague, when madmen lead the blind'. The total aptness of the quotation is striking. When we think of Hitler, Pol Pot and so many others, those maniacs who ruled the masses whose eyes were sealed with fear and hope, the economy of Gloucester's words strikes home. The extreme example such leaders provide shows us, rather as illness instructs us about health, what happens in less extreme situations: power is exercised by means of the irrational.

There is a third and final aspect. In many fields – technology, economics and demography, for example – there has been positive progress. Methods of work are improving, there is increased trade, the population is increasing, and so on. In politics there is no progress, any more than there is in art or morality. History teaches that power is exercised and is repeated from one generation to another in the same ways and the same conditions. The many never cease to be dominated by the few. As Freud writes:

One instance of the innate and ineradicable inequality of men is their tendency to fall into the two classes of leaders and followers. The latter constitute the vast majority; they stand in need of an authority which will make decisions for them and to which they for the most part offer an unqualified submission.

(Freud XXII, 212)

So it would be futile to talk of a movement towards a society without gods or masters, as new leaders are constantly appearing amongst us. What explains the autonomy of the area of politics and emphasises its difference from other fields is therefore this lack of progress. Relatively speaking, historical developments are irrelevant to it. In all societies, even the most advanced ones, where authority is concerned the past dominates the present and the dead hand of tradition casts its spell on living modernity. Moreover, if we are to act, the most archaic levels of the human psyche have to be influenced. The whole contrast can be summed up in a single sentence: economics and technology obey the laws of history, politics obeys those of human nature.

Contemporary society, in which there are so many material and spiritual imbalances, accentuates each of these three aspects. All that can be done is to adapt available instruments and knowledge to the permanent data of the exterior and interior life of men. Essentially, *politics is the rational form of exploiting the irrational substance of the masses*, and always has been. This is confirmed by mass psychology. Every propaganda method it proposes and every technique that leaders use to influence the thoughts and behaviour of crowds is based on that perception. Such methods and techniques play on the emotions of individuals with the aim of transforming them into a collective and uniform material. We know of course that they will be eminently successful.

## IV

The freeing of irrational forces means that the leader is the solution to the problem of the existence of the masses. Some would propose a very different solution. They suggest creating political parties, ideological movements or institutions capable of controlling the masses. But sooner or later any political party, movement or institution acquires a leader, who may be living or dead, and so the second solution is no different from the first. They have in common a Cæsarian element which is to authority what hydrogen is to matter, namely its universal component. Finding out its origin and composition is one of the most difficult scientific undertakings. Every science puts forward an explanation based on the facts within its field of enquiry. Since the days of Tarde, mass psychology has been developing its own. The father is the source and prototype of authority of all kinds. His ascendancy began with the family in the mists of time and continues and grows in our own days amongst masses composed of individuals torn from their families. This means that the history of political regimes merely illustrates the slow changes which have taken place in paternal government. Once we try to expose the bare bones of that branch of history, all we see beneath the species of bureaucracy, party, state and so on are the ramifications of the original power of the head of the family, who is both a model and an ideal.

When the appearance of the masses was a sporadic phenomenon, this explanation seemed a rather shocking one. People were unwilling to admit that the leader was just as much the necessary solution to the problem of the masses as the father to that of the family. But what do we see on our television screens every day? Muslim crowds acclaiming the Ayatollah Khomeini on his return from exile, Christian crowds rushing to welcome John Paul II, who has flown in as a pilgrim to bring them the Good News, or else secular masses enthusiastically thronging around one of their leaders and singing his praises.

The media have made us contemporaries of and participants in all the great gatherings in the world and their adulation and ecstatic genuflections. There is no longer anything exotic about idolatry or surprising about the succession of events. A whole people shoots at supersonic speed from enthusiastic liberation to rigid submission, losing its natural diffuseness and solidifying and crystallising around one man. Very few people indeed resist this or even realise what is going on. It would seem that the masses delight in satisfying a kind of unconscious impulse to bow down. Tarde for his part states this openly:

It has often been said – and it is an attractive theme which lends itself to oratorical development – that there is nothing more intoxicating than the sense of freedom, of the non-necessity of any submission to others and of any obligation towards them. Naturally enough, I certainly do not deny this lofty feeling. I do, however, feel that it is far less general than the fact of its frequent expression might suggest. The truth is that for most men there is an irresistible sweetness inherent in obedience, credulity and almost lover-like servility towards the admired master. What the *defenders* of the Gallo-Roman cities were after the fall of the Empire, the *saviours* of our democratic and revolutionary societies are now. That is, the objects of enthusiastic idolatry and passionate submission. (Tarde, 1895b: 25)

Why does the leader attract such a following? Because he offers, in simple terms full of imagery, an answer to their questions and gives a name to their anonymity. Not as a result of reasoning or calculation, but from the very depths of their intuition, the masses grasp it as if it were an absolute truth, the offering of a new world or the promise of a new life. When the mass accepts the leader, it is exalted, converted and transfigured in the real sense of the term. Its affective energy draws it on and also gives it the courage to endure the martyrdom and the brutality necessary for violence. This is proved by the revolutionary armies Napoleon bewitched and who followed his eagles across the breadth of Europe.

The energy drawn by the masses from their dreams and illusions is used by leaders to turn the wheels of state and to lead the multitudes towards an aim dictated by reason and sometimes by science. General de Gaulle who, as we shall see, had understood better than most the teachings of mass psychology, recognised its practice, pointing out that however much reality there might be, he would perhaps be able to surmount it, since he had the gift of achieving what Chateaubriand had called 'leading the French by dreams' (De Gaulle, 1955: I, 120).

The experience of peoples confirms the conviction that the shortest way from an all-embracing idea to specific action and from the intelligence of an individual to a mass movement is through dreams. When illusions lose their power or fade away, groups and their beliefs lose their form and substance and have no more life or solidity than a body drained of blood.

Men no longer know whom to follow, what to obey or what they should devote themselves to. There is nothing or nobody to impose on them the discipline necessary if civilisation is to be maintained and extended or to feed their enthusiasm or their passion. The world of admiration and loyalty is left empty. There are no longer any friends or enemies. The boundaries marking off groups or communities have all but disappeared, and 'the people' is simply an amorphous collection of individuals. In a mass society such as ours, the cure for the 'psychological wretchedness of the masses' is the leader, if only he can avert the danger of panic. Thus Napoleon, at the end of the revolutionary period in France, gave back to the crowds the object of worship that they had lacked and the ideal for which they were ready to sacrifice everything, including life and liberty. As Broch observes,

The *Führer* is the symbol of a system of values and the vehicle for its dynamics. As we have said, he appears primarily as the sign of the system. His rational characteristics and his deeds are of purely secondary importance.

(Broch, 1979: 81)

## V

What then do we do when we are faced with the masses? Two things, crowd psychology tells us. Find a leader from their own milieu and rule them by appealing to their passions, beliefs and imagination. The first might not appeal to us if we think that individuals play only a minor role in history, or even none at all. In fact, however, a knowledge of that branch of psychology means that we cannot cross it off our list of possible solutions, primarily and particularly because everyone believes in it, even those who should not. Tito, the leader of the Yugoslav Communist Party, retorted to someone who was stressing the decisive role of the masses that he was talking rubbish and that historical processes often depended on a single person (Djilas, 6 May 1980).

In conclusion, mass psychology replies to the question posed by our age of what we should do by suggesting a different policy. It raises it above the empirical level and tries to provide a precise answer to an equally precise question. Hence the part played by suggestion in creating the mass and by the leader who sets it in motion. At present we are dealing with a solution that has been put forward without much in the way of explanation. In the following chapters I shall set out the reasons for choosing it. First of all, however, I want to set out one of them immediately to give a better idea of the particular importance mass psychology attaches to it. The reason is that the masses do not spontaneously tend towards democracy, but towards despotism.

## 4. *Eastern and western varieties of despotism*

I

IN THE CENTURY that saw the birth of the masses, we consider domination by a single person to be a barbarous survival. We talk of such a situation in terms of intense disapproval, speaking of absolute dictatorship, the blighting effect of a lack of culture or material resources or a deplorable return to an outdated morality. On the whole, it is seen as a product of ignorance or base instincts. For us, our destiny lies in moving forward hand in hand with a developing humanity advancing towards complete democracy. Each victory marked up by civilisation also means a victory of the people over their hereditary enemies, the despots. Anyone refusing such a view of the march of events is of course moving against the flow of history. Yet this was the stance that Le Bon took, and most of the mass psychologists were associated with it. For him and for them, the appearance of the masses, given their psychological make-up, meant in the long run an appeal to leaders and the installation of a despotic regime. As Le Bon himself said, 'A series of such typical facts shows very clearly that in Europe there is a widespread turning towards despotic forms of government' (Le Bon, 1924: 231).

Mass society is after all defined by the democratisation of this kind of authority, in the sense in which one might say that cars, leisure activities, newspapers and the mass media have become democratised. In the past they were the preserve of elites and then the bourgeoisie but are now available to everyone. Why has despotism managed to become accepted and practised by the masses? (Le Bon, 1910: 117). Both because governments are no longer able to govern or impose their authority or, in Thomas Mann's phrase, to act as masters whom it is possible to serve with a good aristocratic conscience and also because of the rise of those same masses, who have their own hierarchy and organisations and take parliamentary social debates into the street and rob democratic institutions of their prestige. To quote Le Bon once more:

Nowadays leaders tend gradually to replace public authorities as the latter are contested and weakened. As a result of their tyranny, these new masters receive from the masses a more complete docility than any government commands.

(Le Bon, 1910: 117)

Without making it explicit, Le Bon is talking about trades union leaders, seeing in them the real masters of the world of work.

But that is not all there is to it. If we take a wider look over a long period of history, we can see signs of a recrudescence of despotism more or less everywhere. In every ideology and all political life it reappears with remarkable constancy, introduced by civilisations which have nothing in common with each other. As soon as a nation learns to use writing and produces its first texts, the theme is hauntingly present. So we cannot simply limit ourselves to the causes I have just mentioned to describe how it develops or to understand the meaning this ancient form of authority has in our own days. I should like to show this development by means of a contrast. Like all comparisons, it is not totally coercive, but in this case it is justified. Here it is.

History would seem to show that before our era there was an eastern despotism with imperial China and the Egypt of the pharaohs as its high points (Wittfogel, 1964). It was based on the principle of inequality, which was common in the societies of those times, and met the need to make a system of production based on the creation of towns and the maintenance of an effective system of irrigation work. The hierarch – king, emperor or pharaoh – exercised his absolute power by controlling the water supply of peasant communities, whether by building dikes or digging canals. The human multitudes were brought together and co-ordinated by his officers to carry out massive works, of which the pyramids still give us some idea. The despot was the apex of a rigorously hierarchical society, a sacred god in its religion, at once the infallible master of the state and the universe, and demanded absolute obedience. Those are the characteristics which we ascribe to despotism. On looking back into history, we see that they were widespread and occurred independently – that is, without being transmitted – over several continents. This identical solution to the same problem, found by so many scattered peoples, is a disturbing enigma of human history.

We shall now jump quite unjustifiably several thousand years forward to modern societies and look at the reasons for talking about *western despotism*, an idea that was very clearly to the forefront at the time of the French Revolution. Before Le Bon and Tarde had asserted its general significance, Chateaubriand had already seen its chief characteristics, pointing out that daily experience showed that the French undeniably directed their attention towards power, that they had no love of liberty and that equality was their god, and stressing the hidden links between equality and despotism.

This is not merely metaphorical language or rhetorical flourish. It shows the hidden nature of the link in question, which needs expressing in plain words. Political systems which are dominated by parties govern by means of discussion and argument and solve difficulties by frequent voting. In theory, however, they are unstable and uncertain. As Napoleon said to Molé, 'balanced' governments, as they are so inappropriately called, are the quickest way to anarchy. It is precisely to avoid chaos that in practice there is recourse to a despot. This has been known since the earliest times and is axiomatic in crowd psychology, which deduces from it that in an age in which crowds are bigger and more fluctuating than in the past there will be increasing appeals to despots.

## II

Thus, wherever a mass society exists, it will use one means or another to achieve stability, but will only be able to reach its goal by modifying one of the two basic elements of equality and freedom. One of the two possible solutions to the equation, re-introducing civic inequality, would seem to be ruled out. No party or politician would advocate it, no scholar or orator would argue its merits or put it forward as a necessary change or the lesser of two evils. To do so would be to go against the nature of the mass, which is characterised by the equality of the individuals of which it is composed:

It is of fundamental importance and one might even define a crowd as a state of absolute equality. A head is a head, an arm is an arm, and differences between individual heads and arms are irrelevant. It is for the sake of this equality that people become a crowd. (Canetti, 1973: 32)

For this reason, all political action and all political plans leave equality as it is and infringe freedom, by either persuading or forcing individuals to relinquish it. The process is rather like urging people to take the plane rather than the train to reduce travelling time from one town to another if the distance between them cannot be reduced.

It seems as if the instability of mass society is a result of the inevitable demand for equality and a misuse of freedom. There are two possible solutions to this problem. Either power is given to a single individual or to no-one, in the sense that it is put into the hands of a kind of anonymous directorate, as if it were simply a matter of some economic or technical business. In such a case, the effect produced by a shortage of resources or poverty is exactly the same as that obtained by a leader by persuasion or coercion: freedom disappears. There is no third possible solution.

Where there is a leader, the end result is the *democratic despot*, a familiar figure in Europe since Napoleon invented him. An English writer has said of Bonaparte that he achieved absolute government supported by popular feeling. In him, democratic means and imperial aims went hand in hand. The features of the brother, the symbol of popular equality, overlay those of the father, the image of unlimited authority. Each Roman emperor, as we know, was the successor of Cæsar, and a statue was erected to him bearing the inscription 'to the father of the fatherland'. He nevertheless kept the title of tribune, which meant that he was the spokesman for the citizens and their defender against the omnipotent state he symbolised.

In very recent times, Stalin too held every political and military command, like a true emperor. At the same time, he kept all the responsibilities of the people's commissar, which meant that his task was simply to carry out collective decisions. One of the overweening privileges of such men is to have at once the power to control and the power of stopping power, to be the only recourse against their own repression, with the result that the only limit to their authority is their own will.

Prestigious or charismatic leaders of this kind preserve the externals of democracy. By means of regular plebiscites they reaffirm the equality of the masses, who are summoned. Questions are put to them, which they answer by a simple yes or no. They have no real chance to meet and deliberate, and have no authority to discuss the leader's decisions or to offer him advice. All they are called upon to do, and all they can do, is to approve a policy, or in extreme cases to reject it. Plebiscites are the sign of a freedom which is relinquished at the very moment it is exercised.

When power has not been mandated to any one person, we can talk of the *despotic democracy* of a bureaucratic and anonymous party which acts in the manner of an administrative body or a management committee and deals with the state or society as if they were nationalised industries. The question of power itself seems quite secondary. It will not even be raised if the majority of the population shows no interest and remains passively silent. There are governments like this in several one-party states or in ones that have had a major party in control for fifty years or so, as has been the case with the liberal democrats in Japan, the Christian Democrats in Italy, the revolutionary party in Mexico, the liberal–Gaullist alliance in France and so on. Governments of this kind are a state within a state, and the end result is inevitably pallid uniformity and the kind of conformity which favours a balance of the forces supporting it. Freedom is kept within strictly defined limits by the monopoly control of the police and the media.

In order to maintain their own continuity, majority parties recruit their officials and leaders from a restricted circle which is constantly renewed by controlling the class origin of recruits in the case of Communist parties and their religious one in the case of Christian parties. No-one else is entrusted with keeping up the stock of future statesmen by keeping an eye on their careers to date. Such men are part of a system of internal promotion that leads them towards power. By appointing them to various functions – deputy, mayor and the like – the system gives them the opportunity of claiming to represent the people. They have to be recruited by some system of co-opting, since hereditary selection is contrary to the principle of equality and must be ruled out (even though the secretary of the French Socialist Party chooses his own successor). Real elections would re-introduce free competition amongst candidates, and so they are all selected by some top-level body such as a management committee, a politburo or a secretariat according to how close they come to the desired model and how great their loyalty to the party is. They are then subject to a process of popular ratification which is often purely formal and automatic, as in Mexico or Poland. This is a kind of plebiscite on the anonymous leader in the form of a group of people, a plebiscite disguised as an election based on universal suffrage.

In both cases, the margin of freedom left to persons and communities is reduced and their desire to conduct public affairs is suppressed either by overt force or hidden manipulation. All the real features of democracy – majority agreement, the authority of parliament and respect for the law – have a *de jure* existence but perish *de facto*. Like all general statements, this observation must be modified to fit the concrete facts of each individual country and age. We are, however, quite justified in observing that mass societies oscillate between democratic despots and despotic democracy. They sometimes use one formula rather than the other in the hope of regaining in time an equilibrium that they cannot achieve in space. Here, the history of France is an excellent example and has, since the Revolution, been a *locus classicus*. Since then, as we have seen over the intervening years, both formulas have become part of the political air we breathe. What was once an exception has become a pattern and a body of knowledge. Just as the French Revolution raised the armed masses to fight and conquer and introduced the classical age of war, so the chain of revolutions and counter-revolutions in our own age has brought about the classical age of despotism. That is why the network of institutions and administrative bodies in which men receive advancement for their skill in depriving their fellows of freedom covers larger areas of our lives.

## III

Because it is more outspoken, I prefer the term 'western despotism' to that of the totalitarian system, the cult of personality or authoritarian regimes. But even superficial reflection shows the limits of the analogy with the notion of eastern despotism and the differences between the two.[1] On the one hand, rather than being concerned with the means of production, this type of power needs and has as its nervous system the means of communication, whose ramifications extend to every place in which individuals meet, associate and work, penetrate the furthest recesses of every district and every home, imprison men in a cage of dominant images and impose on them a common picture of reality.

Eastern despotism met an economic need, that of irrigation and the control of labour. Its western counterpart, however, corresponds rather to a political need. It presupposes the control of the means of influence or suggestion, that is the education system, the press, the radio and so on. The former controlled the masses by controlling the things they needed, such as water and food. The latter achieves the same end by controlling the belief of the majority in a man, an ideal or even a party. It would appear that there has been a development between the two types, with external submission giving way to an internal one, and very visible control to a spiritual and invisible one which is all the harder to resist.

On the other hand, in the older form, the leader was the guardian of a permanent order of society and nature. He was the pinnacle of the human hierarchy by virtue of an accepted inequality. No-one disputed the position he held, even if some people rebelled against him as a person. His fall or his death, like those of a god, were seen as signs of fundamental disorder, provoking fear and anguish which were cunningly exploited by his appointed successors. In modern despotism, however, the appeal to the leader is of an exceptional and extremely tense nature. What makes the social framework totter and leads to large-scale mass movements is economic crises and the processions of the unemployed, the inflation and the poverty they bring with them, political crises and their concomitant risk of civil war, and failures of the system involving the alternation of revolution and counter-revolution.

At such times new forces make themselves felt. Power changes hands, prisoners are released and promptly jail their former captors, exiles return in triumph and others are banished. Exceptional times demand exceptional men. To these the masses delegate sovereignty, just as the Romans delegated it to their dictators. They choose them for the years they have spent in prison, for their resistance to the enemy, for their open revolt in difficult times and for heroically breaking with their own caste (hence General de Gaulle's appeal on 18 June 1940). All forms of heresy, disobedience and usurpation – the usurper was the title given to Napoleon, the prototype imitated by all the great statesmen who have left their mark on our century – are both the source of new power and the sign of the chosen one. They are what lie behind what we call prestige or charisma, the mysterious quality that changes someone unknown into a personality commanding total adoration. Prestige suppresses all moral scruples, sweeps away all the legal obstacles in the leader's path and changes the usurper into a hero. Everyone sees him with the same starry-eyed admiration that Hegel felt when he saw Napoleon at Jena on 13 October 1806:

I saw the Emperor, that soul of the world, riding his mount through the streets of the town. . . . It is an incredible sensation to see such an individual at the same time on horseback in one place and bestriding and dominating the whole world.

The illustrious philosopher felt what all the men of the Old Guard who gave their lives for that 'soul of the world' must have felt. He did not see them or the trail of millions of dead on the battlefields, without whom Napoleon would have had no world to bestride and dominate.

What has just been said leads to an obvious conclusion, namely that *he who leads the masses is always a usurper and is recognised as such by them*. This is not only because what he does is done in opposition to the norms of legitimacy and because his power comes into being in extraordinary times. It is also due to the necessary respect for equality, which rules out the possibility that any individual can remain indefinitely above the collectivity. This means that any true leader must *ipso facto* be illegitimate. However, as long as he maintains his position, the masses are his to do with as he will.

It might be objected that neither the means of communication nor the power of leaders is as important as I make them out to be and that there are other factors at work which explain this historical development. I would not dream of denying this, for the latter is very complex. However, I have set myself the task of explaining as fully as I can one of the hypotheses of crowd psychology, that of the trend towards despotism in contemporary society. That discipline saw in it a symptom of the decline of our civilisation: the impotence of the individual in the face of the collective and the abandoning by political and intellectual elites of their responsibilities towards democracy. There are many things in the subject which might turn us wholeheartedly against it, but whenever it is clear that the masses reign but do not rule we see the unambiguous sign of western despotism, just as in times gone by a king who reigned but did not rule meant a victory for democracy. As Paul Valéry said, 'It is remarkable that nowadays dictatorship is as contagious as freedom was in the past.'

## IV

Long before mass psychology came into being Burckhardt, the historian of the Renaissance, had glimpsed the same conclusion. The future, he said, belonged to the masses and to those who could explain things to them simply. Mass psychology did not invent despotism or the authoritarian type in Europe any more than economics invented, rather than simply studied, profit or entrepreneurial capitalism, but it is sometimes accused of having done so. Hence the way in which it is criticised and marginalised. We perhaps imagine that that is how to encourage democracy and change its tragic failures into triumphs.

Psychologists have tried to combat this illusion, and despotism has been a major theme in their writings on the masses. From Le Bon, who saw in it a major characteristic of human nature, via Fromm and Reich who explored the roots in the family of voluntary submission to totalitarian power, to the German sociologist Adorno studying the personality of the despot, they have sought to go beyond soft words and softer feelings and reach the bedrock, that part of man which makes him ready to relinquish freedom and what we call human rights as soon as a leader emerges at a decisive moment in history. And since in the final analysis this is their concrete aim, they expect their subject to give a realistic account of things in the light of what things might turn out to be like if we decided to change them.

This, as can be seen, is the very opposite of detached and neutral observation. They are the only people to take western despotism seriously. Whether it be a matter of the influence of the media or the authoritarian structure of the masses, it is not something chosen fortuitously or out of mere intellectual curiosity. What they write about is related to reality, and it is with that reality that their theories have to struggle. They are proportionate and related to the conflicts of the age – and the dramas gestating within it. Crowd psychology has done what it had to do when confronted with the conditions of the age – of which the rise of Nazism has been one of the most revealing features – and has exerted and still exerts considerable influence on, and on more than, political thought and action. At one time or another, every one of us has had to have recourse to it.

The German writer Broch, a late-comer to a subject that had already begun to establish itself, wrote thus:

Along the whole way of the earlier problem, that led us through the fields of theories of the state and politics and economics, there has scarcely been any stage that has not raised problems of mass psychology. That a central place of this kind had to be accorded to mass psychology has been clear to me for a long time now, even if only as a supposition. (Broch, 1979: 274)

It sees mass democracy as the stance to be adopted in the struggle against those forces in human nature which are opposed to it and demands a generation of men capable of resisting the pressures around them. As well as being able to defend reason doggedly, such men must also have the strength to exercise a certain amount of restraint in the enjoyment of goods and freedoms. There are severe penalties for any breaches of vigilance when one is on that kind of active service. Flexibility and survival at any price have the worst effect on morale. Giving way on what appear to be very minor points can mean letting go of things that are really fundamental and opening the floodgates to the waters of lukewarm submission.

## V

In the first part of this book I have tried to sketch in a map of the mental landscape of mass psychology and give some idea of its origins, the phenomena it examines and the quite practical problems it attempts to solve. I have also stressed the fact that it is first and foremost a political science, and always has been. This is why its two major concerns have always indefatigably been the individual and the masses and the masses and leaders. The first of these has meant that it has raised the basic problems of mass society, the second that it has sought practical solutions. All this is very right and proper.

I must now add more detail to the map and colour in the landscape with an account of the theories themselves. This will provide an opportunity for establishing a coherent system and establishing whether it can introduce any sort of order into a mass of largely unrelated facts.

## PART II

# Le Bon and the fear of crowds

***

## 1. *Who was Gustave Le Bon?*

***

I

EVERYONE KNOWS that Le Bon was the founder of crowd psychology. There is, however, a kind of Le Bon mystery. For the last fifty years, works in French have made no mention of his extraordinary influence on the social sciences, preferring to devote inordinate space to minor scholars and amorphously general schools of thought. Why should he receive such unfavourable treatment? How has it been possible to ignore one of the dozen or so most decisively influential thinkers in the field of the social sciences in the twentieth century? To be quite honest, no French thinker apart from Sorel and probably de Tocqueville has had an influence as great as Le Bon's. None of their books has caused anything like the same stir. For those reasons, we should first of all look at the man himself and his place in his time. This will help us to understand the circumstances in which the discipline came into being and why it did so specifically in France.

Le Bon was born in 1841 at Nogent-le-Rotrou in Normandy and died in Paris in 1931, and his life was remarkable from many points of view. He happened to be born in a period of incipient social progress, and his adult life spanned the Second Empire, a time of industrial revolution, military defeat and civil war. He also lived long enough to see the triumph of science, the crises of democracy and the spread of socialism and the popular forces whose rise he had anxiously observed and whose increasing power he had condemned.

He seems in his person to have continued the long line of amateur scholars and pamphleteers previously represented so illustriously by men like Mirabeau, Mesmer and Saint-Simon. He continued a tradition, but did so within an environment marked by rapid changes. This provincial physician, short in stature and fond of good food, had abandoned the practice of medicine to become a populariser of science. He was successful enough to be able to live from his writing, to mix freely

49

with men of letters and to rub shoulders with the greatest of them. Why was he so eminently successful? Was it perhaps a case of an outstanding talent imposing itself on a milieu which had initially been unfavourable and even hostile? Should his writings be seen as incorporating both new and progressive scientific ideas and an older literary tradition? Or had he an outstanding flair for discovering and expressing currents of thought and a hidden sensibility in his age? No doubt there was something of all that in Le Bon, but his own particularly highly-developed gift was for synthesising and expressing in a direct and telling way ideas which were in the air but which others had either not had the courage to articulate or had only put forward unsystematically. An unusual combination of circumstances turned the studious doctor into the founder of a new branch of science and the originator of a new kind of politics.

## II

After the humiliating defeat of her army in 1870, France (and the French bourgeoisie in particular) discovered within the space of a few months just how fragile the latter was and how ill-prepared to govern the country and control the social forces operating in it. Under Napoleon III, it had applauded Offenbach's operettas and been charmed by their music without understanding their words. The country had unconsciously played the most spineless of roles and had not recognised the signs of the impending catastrophe or the lack of seriousness that was paving the way for it. Armand Lanoux made this point forcefully when he said that when nowadays we look at Offenbach in a historical perspective, we cannot help seeing his work as a kind of *danse macabre* leading to Sedan. And from Sedan to its logical consequence, the Commune. As always, the bourgeoisie saw the cause of the disaster in urban disorder, disobedient workers and undisciplined soldiers and the welter of social movements swarming towards Paris as the Huns had once swarmed over Europe. Sluggish governments and divided political factions were powerless to contain the insurrection.

Logically, the only answer was a strong government capable of re-establishing authority. 'The only reasonable thing,' Flaubert wrote to George Sand on 29 April 1871, 'is a government of mandarins, as the people will remain minors all their lives.' And all this at a time when the Paris Commune, with its insolent claim to be changing the world, was proclaiming a glorious future at the very moment when France was on her knees, the territory of France reduced in size and the army defeated. The Commune was in fact a fairly good manifestation of the link between defeat and popular uprising, between the collapse of state power and the rebellion of the citizens. The intellectuals shuddered with their mother, the bourgeoisie, at the spectacle of the humiliation of the nation, at the same time raising their voices against the hereditary enemy, Germany, the chief external danger, and the French Revolution, which had never been completed in the years since 1789, was seen as the chief internal one despite its perpetual defeats. As François Furet writes, 'The whole of French nineteenth-century history was that of a struggle between Revolution and Restoration, passing through 1815, 1830, 1848, 1851, 1870 and 16 May 1877' (Furet, 1978: 16).

We only need to read Taine or Renan to appreciate the strength of the disquiet brought into the open again by the last two of those dates and the response it evoked in the thought of the time, and its effect on society can be seen in the new interest in social movements and the popular classes. Zola's novels are as striking an indication of this as more purely historical studies. The whole of society saw the masses at work and judged their importance or the threat they posed in terms of individual political convictions. Rather than concern, it was fear that 'illicit and shifting populations' and 'the anti-social scum', as they were described in expressions used at the time, caused in the hearts of the French citizenry.

If the threat was to be overcome, there had to be some explanation for what was happening. What was perhaps even more necessary was how to find the key to the modern world. The eyes of the whole of France were on the social order, and everyone was aware of the shaky foundations on which power was based. The attempts at returning to an earlier order and restoring the old regime with its monarchy and its Church had not had the hoped-for results. Views which condemned the modern world, the claims of science, universal suffrage and the overriding principle of equality and the like were very much in vogue. Those who supported progressive ideas were held up to public obloquy. None of this, however, stopped political parties from proliferating, the bourgeoisie from hanging on to its control of society, or revolutionary ideas from taking root. Some drastic remedy was needed, some bold, clear and simple idea that would purge minds, bring men to their senses and channel their energies. There had to be a convincing counter-blast to socialism, some proof that France could regain her strength and become mistress of her fate. It was clearly no easy undertaking, but everyone knew what was at stake and was aware of the need for a fresh solution.

## III

At last, one is tempted to write, Le Bon's time had come. The scientist *manqué*, the man of the people without a platform, had understood what was involved. He was completely obsessed with curing the ills of society, and once his medical studies were completed he associated with men concerned with the same problems, politicians, philosophers and many learned writers. He was anxious to make a career for himself, to become a member of the Academy or obtain a University post, and embarked on a whole range of research which included physics and anthropology, biology and psychology. This last was still in its infancy, and he was one of the first to see its future importance. Despite his many contacts and his enormous scientific industry, however, his deepest ambitions were never fulfilled. The doors of the University and even of the Academy of Sciences remained firmly closed to him.

It was thus as an outsider, excluded from official circles, that he worked so indefatigably, handling knowledge as a financier handles money, setting up intellectual project after intellectual project without ever achieving any remarkable discoveries. His dilettante research and his scientific popularisation did, however, give him considerable skill as a synthesiser and perfected his gift for presenting broad outlines and telling phrases. He acquired the journalist's sixth sense for the facts and ideas that will grip the mass of readers at a particular time. The academic resistance he encountered meant that increasingly he sought success in the political and social field. In dozens of works published over many years he perfected the same brew of biological, anthropological and psychological theories, suggesting the main lines of a psychology of peoples and races inspired by both Taine and Gobineau. Historians say that his contribution in that field was decisive enough to ensure him a place amongst the not very glorious list of the forerunners of racialism in Europe.

In his psychological studies, Le Bon was naturally struck by the phenomenon of crowds, and particularly that of popular movements and terrorism, which his contemporaries found so disturbing. Indeed, a number of books on this topic had recently been published, particularly in Italy, which stressed the fear caused by what some saw as a return to barbarism. Le Bon skilfully took up the theme, which had been discussed in general and purely legal terms, and erected around it a plausible if not entirely coherent body of doctrine.

He first gave his diagnosis of parliamentary democracy, its sickness and lack of resoluteness. The strength to govern, he maintained, led to social order, the lack of it to social disorder, the will to govern to political security and the lack of it to public danger and incitement to revolution. The ruling classes in such democracies, he maintained, had remained intelligent, which caused irresoluteness, but lost the will which is the source of all strength. They no longer had the necessary confidence in their mission, and this meant that political functions and institutions were foundering in a morass of indecision and irresponsibility. Such classes did not even have the virtue of honesty, for although in a democracy the majority vote, it is the minority who govern.

It is important to be clear here. Le Bon was not accusing the governing classes of dishonesty or a lack of principles, but of being unable to turn their backs on the past and of being ineffectual. In troubled and demoralised times, decisions lay with them. By choosing a democracy which combined Jacobin ideas and oligarchical practices and wrapped everything up in general and vague speeches, they had condemned themselves to impotence and the risk of being manipulated and out-flanked, crushed by ambitious, intelligent and unscrupulous men supported by popular forces under their own control. If they were not to fail in their task of bringing civilisation and progress, they would have to recognise the facts of the situation and the real nature of the conflict which was tearing society apart. And Le Bon, of course, gave them the long-awaited answer: in that conflict, the masses played the major part, and they alone held the key to the situation in France and the modern world.

As a recent writer on the subject notes, 'Writing in a prophetic mood, Le Bon began by putting the masses right at the centre of any possible interpretation of the modern world' (Giner, 1976: 58). Towards the masses, Le Bon certainly felt the traditional bourgeois contempt for the lower classes and the scorn of the socialist for the sub-proletariat. But the masses are a fact, and the scientist does not scorn facts but respects and tries to understand them. Le Bon, faced with this situation, did not hanker after the restoration of the monarchy or of an aristocratic regime. What he dreamed of was rather a patrician and individualist democracy in the English style.

From the Second to the Fifth Republic, and including both of them, English liberalism continued to have a considerable impact on French social thought, but never made a decisive intellectual breakthrough. Neither did the French financial and industrial upper middle classes have any definitive political impact on the French state, which was conceived by and for the middle reaches of a mercantile, administrative, peasant and even working-class bourgeoisie. France's distinctly uneasy and rather abstruse relationship with modernity, the fact that she was torn between the English model which was close in time and German power to which she was close in space, her loyalty to a kind of crusading national-ism based on an inner picture of a world distinctly French-looking, for which the eighteenth century provided the model and the sense of nostalgia, all went to explain these part-failures.

Le Bon was anxious about what was happening in France, and sought a cure for the disorders brought about by the masses. This he found not in history or economics, but in psychology, which showed him that there was a 'crowd soul' consisting of basic impulses and shaped by strong beliefs and taking little account of experience or reason. Just as an 'individual soul' responds to the suggestions of the hypnotist who has put someone to sleep, the 'crowd soul' responds to those of the leader who has imposed his will on it. In such states of trance, everyone does what under normal circumstances individuals neither would nor could do. The leader, by conjuring up images which replace reality, takes possession of the group soul. The crowd, like the patient hypnotised by a doctor, is at his mercy.

So the basic idea was a simple one. All the catastrophes of the past and the difficulties of the present had been caused by the masses breaking in. The weakness of parliamentary democracy was accounted for by the fact that it went against the findings of psychology. The dominant classes had made mistakes and failed to recognise the cause of crowds and the laws that govern them. To cure the evil and return to a status quo that had long been compromised, all that was needed was a recognition of past errors and an awareness of those laws.

The expression of this idea in lively and straightforward language and supported by a quasi-scientific content explains why his books were so successful that he 'finished by gaining a reading public no other social thinker could rival' (Nye, 1975: 3). Overnight, the scientific populariser became an intellectual mentor, a role which he was to play for the rest of his life. In the words of his only biographer (English, of course) 'For the rest of his life . . . Le Bon bent his efforts towards educating the elites to their growing military-political responsibilities' (Nye, 1975: 78).

For thirty years, this work brought to his home, which he rarely left, a stream of major politicians, men of letters and scientists, amongst whom were the psychologists Ribot and Tarde, the philosopher Bergson, the mathematician Henri Poincaré, that unclassifiable genius Paul Valéry, and the princesses Marthe Bibesco and Marie Bonaparte, who both played a large part in spreading his ideas. Nor should one forget the politicians who knew and, as far as one can see, respected him, such as Raymond Poincaré, Briand, Barthou and Theodore Roosevelt. It should also be mentioned that all these admirers were convinced of the import-ance of his view of human nature, although it was a difficult one to accept. In social and political matters, they took his imperative advice seriously. Indeed, his ideas were at the height of their influence in the nineteen-twenties, when 'the appeal of the new discipline was strongest for the democratic elites who saw it as a conceptual device that confirmed their deepest fears about the masses, but also gave them a body of rules for the manipulation and control of their violent potential' (Nye, 1975: 169).

# 2. *The Machiavelli of mass societies*

## I

IT IS GENERALLY AGREED that Le Bon's *La Psychologie des foules* was what nowadays we call a best-seller and that the total number of copies printed makes it one of the greatest scholarly successes of all times. I should now like to assess his achievement in terms of the quality of his readership and the influence he exerted. To take the most obvious thing first, *La Psychologie des foules* was the manifesto of a branch of knowledge which still exists under various names (social psychology, collective psychology and so on) in our own day. This is worth noting, for it is not given to everyone or to every book to be as innovative. As two American scholars write of the work of Tarde and Le Bon in France, it was very influential in shaping the immediate background from which modern social psychology emerged (Sherif and Sherif, 1956). The two names are often linked, but it is clear that, as Allport states, *La Psychologie des foules* is still the most influential book on social psychology. It was read and re-read, discussed, criticised and, obviously, plagiarised. The book formed much of the inspiration and matter of the first two textbooks of social psychology, McDougall's in England (McDougall, 1908 and 1920) and Ross's in America, and is still influential. I am one of the few writers to have rejected its basic arguments (Moscovici, 1976a) but I nevertheless believe that the judgement of two seasoned American scholars is on the whole relevant:

> Le Bon's work also hit the mark in social psychology. There is scarcely a discussion in his book that is not reflected in the experimental social psychology of this century. . . . And it is not merely a highly general discussion that Le Bon provides, but a rich storehouse of imaginative, testable hypotheses.
>
> (Milgram and Toch in Lindzey and Aronson, 1969: IV, 545)

It has played a no less important part in sociology, although this tends to be forgotten. Even the most cursory examination is enough to show the influence, the vogue almost, that the ideas and propositions put forward by Le Bon and Tarde enjoyed in Germany, for example. Thinkers of the rank of Simmel (Simmel, 1908), Von Wiese (Von Wiese, 1924) and Vierkandt (Vierkandt, 1928) developed them, refined them and incorporated them into their systems of thought.

Mass psychology thus entered the university field and became part of academic impedimenta, and the ground was consequently prepared for its spread in political circles. It also provoked a response in a very different area of German sociology, the Frankfurt School. In the writings of Adorno and Horkheimer the name of the French psychologist is mentioned several times. There is nothing surprising in that, as mass society is a central theme in their thought. The recent 'textbook' of that school contains a chapter on him, containing these words:

After the experience of the last decades one will have to admit that the assertions of Le Bon have been confirmed to an astonishing degree, at least superficially, even under the conditions of modern technological civilization, in which one would have expected to be dealing with more enlightened masses.

(Horkheimer and Adorno, 1973: 75)

At several points in this study I shall have occasion to return to the links between the Frankfurt School and mass psychology and the attention paid to Le Bon and his 'famous work' (Horkheimer and Adorno, 1973: 73). For the moment, I am simply giving a general idea of his influence. The general shape of it is clear until the time when Hitler came to power, that is, until German sociology collapsed. As one of its best-known representatives wrote, it is undeniable that up to that time *The Crowd* had remained a classic and its half-truths were repeated in the overwhelming mass of sociological works (Geiger, 1926). This includes the work of American sociologists, who are too numerous for even a satisfactory sample to be mentioned. But there is nothing unique about the case of Robert Park, one of the founders of the famous Chicago School. From his doctoral thesis, which was submitted in Germany and dealt in fact with the crowd or the public, and right down to his most recent writings, the mark of Le Bon and his 'epoch-making volume on *The Crowd*' (Park, 1975: 24) can be easily seen.

The Chicago School has produced important work on the masses and collective behaviour. In that field, Le Bon and Tarde are still seen as the pioneers. Even if many of those writing about the former seem to have read his work superficially or at second hand and criticise him rather off-handedly, they have to admit that he has had an influence (Oberschall, 1973: 8). What is true of Germany and the United States holds good for the rest of the world too. The merest glance at Becker's and Barnes's encyclopaedic work (Becker and Barnes, 1961) is enough to convince the reader of this, and shows just how much of a classic, as the cliché has it, Le Bon had become. Consulting a certain number of histories of sociology (published outside France, of course) has convinced me that until the Second World War, Le Bon's name, with that of Tarde, was at least as frequently mentioned as that of Durkheim and that his ideas had a greater influence (House, 1936: 113).

But crowd psychology also influenced related areas of investigation and inspired a whole series of works on political science and history. The models it proposes can be found even in psychoanalysis. Robert Michels has written a book which is universally considered to be a classic study of political parties[1] (Michels, 1971). On examination, his ideas can be seen as a synthesis of the German sociologist Max Weber's ideas on the forms of domination and Le Bon's psychological explanations. It is even more obvious that Michels makes no mystery of this. The very idea of treating political parties exactly as if they were masses comes straight from Le Bon.

History was also inevitably affected by the passion for his ideas. Considerations of space preclude any lengthy treatment of this subject, and I shall content myself with a quotation and a brief comment. In 1932, a year after Le Bon's death, a session on 'the crowd' was organised during the *Semaine de synthèse*. For Academe, it was a left-handed way of burying and commemorating the man it had wanted to ignore but whose thought had included it. The great historian Georges Lefebvre, adopting an occasionally rather forced critical approach, and clothing in the currently fashionable Durkheimian language ideas that had nothing at all Durkheimian about them, paid him a rare compliment:

The specific notion of the crowd was introduced into the history of the French Revolution by Dr Le Bon. It implied the existence of a problem to which previously no attention had been paid. But although, from that point of view, his merit is incontestable, that is its limit.                    (Lefèbvre, 1954: 271)

The judgement is a fair one and in no way petty. Introducing a new idea and discovering a hitherto-unsuspected problem in a field as unadventurous as history is no minor achievement. Lefebvre himself paid Le Bon an even greater compliment by going beyond the limit he mentioned and applying the notion of the crowd to the basis of his own research and of extant documents. The result of this was *La Grande Peur de 1789*, a work unique among its own kind in that it bridges the gap between crowd psychology and history.

Logically, I should pay greater attention to what psychoanalysis took over from crowd psychology and developed, something of major importance. Since, however, a considerable part of this book is devoted to Freud, I shall merely remind the reader of a view expressed by Adorno which makes the basic point here and makes it very well. Writing of *Group Psychology and the analysis of the Ego*, he has this to say: 'The method of Freud's book is that of a dynamic interpretation of Le Bon's description of the mass mind' (Adorno, 1972: VIII, 411).

In this context, there can be no question of ignoring Jung. His idea of the collective unconscious was one of the main ones that Le Bon had an inkling of and used and abused. Once more, a historian has something apposite to say:

In no area does there seem to be greater agreement between Freud and Jung than that of mass psychology. Both accept Le Bon's classic definition of the mass and agree that the individual in the mass operates at a lower, more primitive and emotional level.               (Odajnyk, 1975: 128)

Of course, listing these links and rapid comparisons gives no more than a very incomplete picture of an influence that went beyond the boundaries of scientific knowledge and had its effect on culture in general. This was so to such an extent that one writer has felt able to describe the tendencies of our century as 'deeply coloured by Darwinian biology and Wagnerian aesthetics, by Gobineau's racialism and Le Bon's psychology, by Baudelaire's anathemas, by the black prophecies of Nietzsche and Dostoyevsky and, at a later stage, by Bergsonian philosophy and Freudian psychoanalysis' (Sternhell, 1972: 11).

A sombre company, no doubt, but an inclusive one, and whether we like it or not Le Bon's name is there. That simple fact is more eloquent than all the acknowledgements of the exceptional importance of his work and his major influence that I could add. All this makes it harder to explain why he is something of a poor relation in the extended family of psychologists and sociologists. Everyone has read him, but no-one boasts of having done so. Everyone makes unacknowledged and shameful use of his writings, like the heirs of Balzac's cousin Pons destroying and scattering his collections for monetary gain. A whole book would not be enough to contain all the relevant documents that have come to my attention.

## II

There are many oddities that form a stumbling-block for the modern reader of Le Bon's work. Nevertheless, his prescience is amazing. All the psychological and political developments of the twentieth century were anticipated in his writings. His analyses and prophecies are so passionate because he saw himself as the Machiavelli of mass societies, called to take up the work of his illustrious predecessor on a new basis. 'Most of the rules of the art of governing men that Machiavelli taught us,' he wrote in 1910, 'have long been impossible to use, and yet although the great man has been in his grave for four hundred years no-one has tried to rewrite his work' (Le Bon, 1910: 5).

He did try to do so, successfully he thought, and turned to statesmen and party leaders, the princes of the modern world, seeing them as the audience to whom he was directly or indirectly addressing himself. Nor was he short of disciples. By giving a psychological framework to the precepts of political common sense (and in particular to those of a Robespierre or a Napoleon) Le Bon opened a new intellectual door and destroyed the taboos of liberal and individualistic thought. He made it possible for statesmen to approach the reality of the masses in a new way and lawful for them to behave as leaders. In fact, it was mainly new men and parties who espoused his ideas and paraphrased his books with the zeal of converts. Or at least they were obliged to take them into account and to adopt a stance. This was the case over the whole of the political spectrum, from the left to the right and including all ideological nuances and political positions.

Let us first look at socialist movements. One might have expected that for them crowd psychology would be something alien, even something that they could not absorb. The workers' parties, however, were those chiefly concerned with the problem of the masses. Their policies were based on the assumption of rationality and class interest, just as were those of the liberal and bourgeois parties. Both groups shared the philosophy that what men do depends on an awareness of their aims and education in that direction.

Le Bon's ideas impressed socialist thinkers because they were the opposite of their own, and in particular his insistence on unconscious factors and the crucial role of the amorphous and unorganised masses. They were also striking because they pinpointed a reality that they had observed but not reacted to. They were used to the phenomena of class, namely of a relatively restricted and more or less organised working class, but the phenomena of the masses took them unawares.

The liveliest reaction to these ideas came from Georges Sorel, the author of the famous *Reflections on violence*. His review of the work on crowd psychology contains a series of reservations about their conservative nature and the lack of a sociological basis in the new psychology (Sorel, 1895: 121). On the whole, however, his attitude was positive and even enthusiastic, and as the years passed he was to move closer to Le Bon and echo his ideas. He also found inspiration in his work, and the idea that the working class must embrace a powerful and hence irrational myth in order to become revolutionary is a proof of this. He also declared his admiration for Le Bon on many occasions. All this meant that Sorel, whose writings and ideas had a great impact on the political thought of the time, was instrumental in helping crowd psychology become part of the thinking of socialists. There are echoes of this in the work of Gramsci, the Communist, who had read and critically meditated on the writings of Sorel and Michels, the two men who, each in his own individual way, had best assimilated Le Bon's ideas.

These ideas, by some path as yet unknown to us, appeared at the centre of a debate that shook the German Social-Democratic Party, which before the Russian Revolution was the model for all workers' parties. The matter under earnest discussion was the nature of the relationship between a class party, conscious and organised, and the non-organised mass, the sub-proletarian populace, the 'mob'. Le Bon had very clearly brought the increasing importance of the latter out into the open. Karl Kautsky, the great German theorist, saw how important this development was and wrote that it was abundantly evident that the political and economic struggles of the time were increasingly becoming mass actions (Kautsky, 1970: 233).

At the same time, he thoroughly rejected any explanation of crowd phenomena caused by suggestion and psychological factors in general. This did not stop him reluctantly accepting Le Bon's theory. In whatever social class they appear, crowds have the same characteristics. They are destructive, unpredictable and, to some extent at least, conservative. Thus, quoting as examples anti-Jewish pogroms and the lynching of blacks, he came to the conclusion that mass action did not always help the cause of progress and did not destroy only what was most harmful to development. It had been ruled by reactionary elements just as often as by revolutionary ones in those cases when it had emerged victorious (Kautsky, 1970: 245).

Pannekoek, one of his adversaries, therefore vehemently accused him of seeing the crowd as imbued with a dynamic of its own, unrelated to the historical period and independent of class content, of being unaware, in short, that a crowd is always made up of either proletarians or bourgeois. For him, a crowd was merely an epiphenomenon to which workers' parties should pay no attention. He maintained that, given the diversity of basic (class) character, the contrast between organised and non-organised masses was not totally unmeaningful, since training and experience brought about a considerable difference, other things being equal, in working class people, but was nevertheless secondary (Kautsky, 1970: 282).

To the best of my knowledge, this debate was never brought to a conclusion. Neither of the two protagonists put forward a new point of view or any new tactics aimed at the non-organised urban masses.

I have perhaps spent too little time on this crucial episode. It does, however, give some idea of the effects of crowd psychology over such a short period. There has just not been enough research done for anyone to have a fine enough scale to determine just how great these effects were on the socialist and revolutionary camp. My own suspicion is that they were not great enough to open the eyes of democrats of all shades of opinion when unashamedly despotic regimes, with Fascism in the lead, took the centre of the stage of contemporary history with the enthusiastic support of the masses. They were so convinced that a victory achieved in such a 'primitive' way was impossible that they could not see them under their noses.

The Italian writer Ignazio Silone has described the process:

> On the other hand, it must be pointed out that the socialists, with their eyes fixed on the class struggle and traditional politics, were astonished by the sudden irruption of Fascism. They did not understand the reasons for and the consequences of its slogans and symbols, which were so outlandish and unusual, nor did they imagine that such a primitive movement could take over and keep the power of such a complicated machine as the modern state. The socialists were not prepared to accept the efficiency of Fascist propaganda, as their doctrine had been formulated by Marx and Engels in the previous century and had not progressed since. Marx could not have foreseen the discoveries of modern psychology or anticipated the forms and political consequences of present-day mass civilisation.
>
> (Silone, 1962: 66)

Everyone thinks that certain things cannot happen until just before they do, for instance wars and scientific discoveries. The short-sightedness of the socialists (and the Communists) cut them off and still cuts them off from the working-class masses. Even if they vote for them. Shallow water cannot carry a big ship. When the passions of the mass of men are shallow, they cannot live out a great idea. That is what has happened.

## III

Le Bon's works have been translated into every language, and indeed into Arabic by a Minister of Justice and Japanese by a Foreign Minister. The President of the United States, Theodore Roosevelt, insisted on meeting Le Bon, whom he read assiduously, in 1914 (Hanotaux, 1925: 45). Another Head of State, Arturo Alessandri, wrote in 1924, 'If you ever meet Gustave Le Bon, tell him that the President of the Republic of Chile is a fervent admirer. I have drawn sustenance from his work' (Suares, 1939: II, 437–9). There is illumination and food for thought there. From a distance, we can see that crowd psychology and Le Bon's ideas were one of the dominant intellectual forces of the Third Republic. They provide us with a key to it. We need only note how those who understood their message fully and followed Le Bon's precepts helped them permeate the world of politics. Aristide Briand was one of the major figures amongst those who knew and listened to Le Bon. Louis Barthou also knew him and said that he considered Dr Le Bon to be one of the most original minds of the age (Barthou, 1931). Raymond Poincaré was quite willing to mention his name in public debate, as was the case with Clemenceau later. In the latter's *La France devant l'Allemagne*, published while the war was raging, Le Bon was the only living author mentioned (Clemenceau, 1916: x-xi). To that necessarily incomplete list the name of Herriot too can be added, who wrote in 1931 that he felt, as he had done for a long time, the liveliest, the most considered and the most loyal admiration for Dr Gustave Le Bon and considered him to be one of the widest-ranging and most penetrating thinkers alive. No doubt such remarks contain an element of courtesy and polite exaggeration. Those five men, however, held power and shaped the Republic. Their words, along with other indications, bear witness to the very real nature of the permeation I have spoken of.

Crowd psychology also found a place in other circles, starting with military ones. It was studied by the various armies of the world and gradually became an integral part of their practices and beliefs. At the beginning of the century, Le Bon's theories were taught at the Ecole de Guerre by, amongst others, generals Bonnal and Maud'huy. Some of them – General Mangin, for example – were self-declared disciples, and he is thought to have deeply influenced several military leaders, notably Foch (Nye, 1975: 149). What they probably found attractive was his view of the leader's power as being supported by the direct will of the nation. They no doubt also approved of his criticism of a democracy governing without conviction, not matching its actions to its words and resigning itself to defeat so as not to have to give battle. After the catastrophe of 1870, language of that kind would not fall on deaf ears. As it had the backing of a scientific approach, people were ready to believe it. During the 1914–1918 war, it was thought capable of galvanising the necessary energy. Appeals were made to Le Bon on several occasions, and he drew up papers for the military and political leaders.

His psychology was all the more credible in that it provided ways of motivating men and strengthening military discipline, that precious and fragile thing that every wise soldier must needs preserve and foster. De Gaulle's genius lay in bringing this cluster of ideas out of the military academies and into the political arena in a systematic form. There is no doubt that he gave them a particular style and majesty. At a time of danger he used them to recreate the myth of France and to imbue the French with patriotism. With all due academic caution, it seems to me that Le Bon provides us with a key to the Fifth Republic, just as he did to the Third. He foresaw what was to become the formula for it, a president whose task it was to summon the assemblies and a parliament whose role was to give its consent. He had urged this from as early as 1925:

The most likely form (of government) will no doubt be that of virtually omnipotent Prime Ministers, like Lloyd George in England and Poincaré in France. The problem is to find a way of making Prime Ministers independent of parliamentary votes, as is the case in the United States. (Le Bon, 1925)[2]

We know that de Gaulle solved the problem and found the way. Indeed, he did more than that. He very consciously personified the leader as Le Bon had seen him and adapted this view to a democratic situation and the French masses. This can be seen in his book, *Le Fil de l'épée* (1944), which contains a great number of aphorisms from Le Bon, particularly those concerned with the nature of the masses and the prestige of the leader. This borrowing has been noted by Mannoni: 'General de Gaulle has taken over the idea [of the leader] lock, stock and barrel. We decry Le Bon, but ransack his work' (Mannoni, 1952: 62).

Two politicians in particular engaged in this ransacking, putting his principles into practice and codifying their use with extreme precision. I mean, of course, Mussolini and Hitler. One interesting detail is worth noting. Le Bon's ideas reached Italy through revolutionary socialist publications and achieved rapid popularity. A glance at the origins of Fascism is enough to convince one of the important part such ideas played:

In [Mussolini] the ideas of Pareto, Mosca, Sorel, Michels, Le Bon, and Corradini were to find expression. These were the ideas critical to his youthful social and political thought. They were the ideas that were to constitute the first doctrinal statements of Fascism and were to ultimately provide the doctrinal rationale for the first frank totalitarian nationalism of our time. (Gregor, 1969: 92)

If Sorel and Michels owed a great deal to Le Bon and Pareto borrowed widely from him, each of his works must have been doubly effective in the Italian counter-revolution. In any case, Mussolini recognised this and spoke of the fact warmly, declaring in 1932 (with perhaps just a touch of exaggeration):

Nevertheless, I can tell you that philosophically speaking I am one of the most fervent admirers of your illustrious Le Bon, whose death has meant an irreplaceable loss. I have read all his massive and profound works, and his *Psychologie des foules* and *Psychologie des temps nouveaux*, are the two works, along with his *Traité de psychologie politique*, that I often turn to. I also used some of the principles in them when setting up the present regime in Italy. (Chanlaine, 1932: 61)

Words like those would have delighted the old man. He had already replied with compromising gratitude to other praise coming from Machiavelli's native land. It is true that the curtain had not yet gone up on two of history's darkest decades and that at that time no-one knew that concentrating the masses was to lead to masses in the concentration camps.

The person who followed Le Bon most methodically, however, and who did so with true Teutonic thoroughness, Adolf Hitler, did not come to power until after his death. One characteristic of *Mein Kampf* is the way in which Le Bon's reasoning is closely followed and his sentences paraphrased without style or any of the loftiness of the original. The book and Hitler's other writings aimed at influencing the masses have been aptly described as reading like a cheap copy of Le Bon (Horkheimer and Adorno, 1973: 75).

This long-standing following of Le Bon's ideas has given rise to the view that he played a much more decisive role than is at first apparent. A recent German historical study in fact suggests that 'Le Bon's theory, constantly assessed and tested against the real world, had given him [Hitler] the conviction that he was in possession of the true categories of revolutionary thought. . . . Le Bon was the only writer to give him a knowledge of the qualities necessary for a revolutionary counter-movement and the basic principles of the way of influencing the masses' (Stein, 1955: 366).

Such bald declarations should of course be examined very critically, as there were other intellectual and political traditions at work in the shaping of the future dictator. Nevertheless, it would seem that there is a certain amount of truth in them. Hitler may have changed Le Bon's ideas into clichés, but he certainly also gave them scientific validation. As a skilful manipulator of men's minds, he put them into practice. The result of this was that

There is far less difficulty in establishing the more important sources of Hitler's ideas on propaganda as set out in *Mein Kampf*; they are Le Bon's *The Crowd – A study of the Popular Mind* and McDougall's *The Group Mind*. A number of expert and knowledgeable witnesses have confirmed that he knew both these books well. Many of the *Mein Kampf* statements, moreover, prove that Hitler had not only read Le Bon and McDougall but had stored away their teaching in his memory and adapted it logically to the circumstances of his time.                    (Maser, 1970: 70)

Further confirmation is supplied by Goebbels, Hitler's terrible Propaganda Minister. This 'easy tool, deferential, glad to be of use' drew his theories and practices from the same sources as his master, and had thus read *The Crowd* and absorbed its half-truths. These he summarised, paraphrased and dinned into his subordinates until the end of his life. One of his assistants wrote in his secret diary that 'Goebbels thinks that since the Frenchman Le Bon nobody has understood the masses as well as he does.'

In a totalitarian state, what the great mind thinks becomes gospel truth for a hundred thousand lesser ones. An American writer has shown that practically the whole of Nazi propaganda – one of the most effective that the world has known – and its underlying political theory consist of the practical application of Le Bon's ideas, and it is easy to believe it (Herzstein, 1979).

That is neither an isolated nor an extreme point of view. Most historians who have studied the development of totalitarian movements mention Le Bon's name at some point and describe his influence (Biddis, 1980; Masser, 1972). The American historian Mosse sums up this judgement very well:

> The Fascists and the National Socialists are merely the most recent of the movements to have brought the theories of men like Le Bon to life. It would have been more pleasant to describe modern politics as a failure, but tracing its history over a fairly long period of time, this proves impossible.　　(Mosse, 1975: 16)

In my view, the nearest idea to Le Bon's is still that of de Gaulle. The author of *The Crowd* was bound by every fibre of his being to the democratic tradition and deeply attached to republican freedoms. He was disappointed that France was not another – right-wing – England and like many people both within his class and outside it dreamed of a political power that was stable without being authoritarian (Nye, 1975). History has decreed otherwise. But it was the modern Cæsars, the dictators, who took his propositions literally and made inflexible rules of action of them. It might be argued that what they really did was to draw on the accumulated wisdom of the ages in their search for a way of dominating men and that they had no need of Le Bon.[3] That may be, but it was he who during their lifetimes had the gift of systematising that wisdom and clothing it in characteristic formulations. In that sense, I have no hesitation in seeing him as the inventor of it. Like many of his kind, he did not guess the scope of his invention or its explosive power.

## IV

The reader will perhaps feel that I am over-concerned with certain details, exaggerate others and ignore much. This does not claim to be a definitive book. If we glance back, we will see that on the one hand Le Bon's postulates about the masses were taken up, shuffled around, tailored and spread about until they became part of the common stock in psychology and sociology, and that this went on for a century. Few researchers have had that privilege, even if those who have benefited from his work make little or no mention of the rich veins from which they have mined their wealth.

On the other hand, in spite of the contrasting political uses to which it has been put, the method he urged and worked on like the good intellectual producer and entrepreneur that he was has become an integral part of our practices. In this field more than anywhere else what he predicted has become a very visible reality. Anyone who examines mass society sees at once that every government, whether democratic or autocratic, has been brought to power by a propaganda machine operating on a hitherto-unknown scale. In the past only the Church, and that at specific times, had equalled that kind of performance. Linking the means of suggestion and influence to politics and all forms of communication and learning the secret of reducing individuals and classes to a single mass is the really novel feature of our age, and it was Le Bon's concepts that made this possible. We knew the rudimentary elements of the matter, but Le Bon systematised them and presented them as scientific rules. In his study of mass psychology, Reinwald writes that 'the description Le Bon gives of the means of action the leader uses has influenced modern mass-orientated propaganda and greatly helped its success' (Reinwald, 1949).

There can be no doubt at all that everything that has been used and discovered in the field of influencing public opinion and communications (including, of course, advertising) has a basis in it which has changed little over the years (Tchakhotine, 1939). We simply see a gradual coming together of methods that have become uniform and standard, as common everywhere in the world as Coca-Cola or television. The social sciences have often been accused of having no practical value and of being unable to change the course of collective life. These are not, as we have seen, the failings of crowd psychology. Right from the start, that discipline has had an effect on historical events and a utility which is no more likeable than that of the atomic bomb and which far exceeds that of most known theories. This is incontrovertibly shown by the one or two facts I have brought forward in connection with Le Bon's work.

# 3. *Four reasons for saying nothing*

IT IS THE SCHOLAR'S DUTY to face up to unpleasant facts and to describe things as they really are. It is not hard to guess what you are going to ask. If Le Bon was such an important figure, how is it that no-one has ever mentioned him or mass psychology in general? Why has his work been looked upon as unworthy of attention and perhaps even as being of somewhat ill repute? I am not trying to rehabilitate him or his ideas, which certainly do not need it. I do, however, want to explain why, in my view, the silence has existed.

In the first place, Le Bon's books were very mediocre in quality, written as and when the occasion arose, and their function was to please the reader, strike his imagination and tell him what he wanted to hear. To hold a large readership, an author has to have the knack of informing, explaining and drawing conclusions in short and simple terms. That means taking every risk, including that of being shallow. It must be admitted that Le Bon had the gift of making discoveries but not that of following them up and developing them. His reasoning was too partial and his observation impoverished and there was very little depth in his work. It is difficult to read his sharp judgements on the masses, the revolution and the working classes without being swept along by the flood of prejudice and aggression directed at something which, in my opinion, fascinated him.[1]

The second reason is a rather more sophisticated one. As a result of his social origins, Le Bon belonged to a liberal, middle-class tradition, on behalf of which he argued against revolution, socialism and the weaknesses of the parliamentary system in a crude and rough-and-ready language. Things have changed since then. What was a dim possibility at the beginning of the century is now a sharply-defined reality. The same tradition, however, still has to face up to the same problems – revolution, socialism and so on – but in a much more ecumenical and muted way. Consequently, it sweeps aside its Le Bons and its Tardes and replaces them with subtler masters, its Webers, Durkheims, Parsons and Skinners, to speak only of the dead and leave the living in peace. Their arguments are couched in more refined terms and their science is more cosmetic and frankly more ideological.

It is also more acceptable to an academic and intellectual milieu which is orientated towards the left in a country in which power has always been held by the right and the centre. This milieu has also determined the form of a development in ideas and the social sciences which does not question such a compromise. Le Bon was of course excluded from it right from the start, and therefore does not exist. 'Primarily, he was a violent enemy of the French university system, which had never accepted any of his ambitious scientific work (save *Psychologie des foules*) as authoritative; it chose to destroy him through silence' (Nye, 1975: 3).

Thirdly, every party, the media and advertising and propaganda specialists apply his principles or, as I was about to say, his recipes and tricks. No-one, however, is ready to acknowledge him, for if they did every party propaganda machine, the parade of leaders on the television screens and the public opinion polls would be seen for what they are, the elements of a strategy of the masses based on their unreasoning nature. We are quite willing to treat the masses as if they had no capacity for reason, but we have to keep it quiet, as we have told them the opposite.

We also make a basic, clear-cut distinction between psychology and politics and are loud in our claims that the former has little influence on the latter. Let us be clear about the situation. There is a kind of politics for which psychology does not exist, just as there is a kind of psychology for which politics does not exist. That means that a kind of politics which has a psychological basis and a kind of psychology which has a political basis are upsetting both to those who advocate a classical concept of revolution and democracy and those who advocate pure knowledge. Le Bon, who linked what everyone wanted to be kept separate, is thus a disruptive figure, presenting us with certain unbearable facts. Schumpeter, the great German economist, supports this view:

Of the many sources of the evidence that accumulated against the hypothesis of rationality, I shall mention only two. The one – in spite of much more careful later work – may still be associated with the name of Gustave Le Bon, the founder or, at any rate, the first effective exponent of the psychology of crowds (*Psychologie des foules*). By showing up, though overstressing, the realities of human behavior when under the influence of agglomeration – in particular the sudden disap-pearance, in a state of excitement, of moral restraints and civilised modes of thinking and feeling, the sudden eruption of primitive impulses, infantilisms and criminal propensities – he made us face gruesome facts that everybody knew but nobody wished to see and he thereby dealt a serious blow to the picture of man's nature which underlines the classical doctrine of democracy and democratic folklore about revolutions. (Schumpeter, 1976: 256)

The fourth reason is to be found in his political influence. His ideas came into being in France and passed into Fascist ideology and practice. It is true that they were put into practice more or less everywhere as a systematic means to the conquest of power, but only in Germany and Italy were they openly acknowledged. And that explains everything. If you ask why Le Bon should be ignored, you will be told that it is because he was a Fascist. A pathetic reason, of course. If we wanted to purge the world (but not, of course, using the methods of *Fahrenheit 451*) of every book that expresses ideas similar to his, we should have to include those of, for example, Freud and Max Weber.[2] All that is true of the latter is true of Le Bon too, except that he had the depressing honour of being read by Mussolini and Hitler. Flaubert was right when he said that honours dishonour. They also diminish the recipient.

In the circumstances, it is perfectly understandable that the founder of crowd psychology should be severely criticised, even if we know from his writings that he preferred the anguish of democracy to the serenity of dictatorship. He urged the former and saw the latter as no more than a stop-gap. His view was that every dictatorship was a response to a crisis situation and could last no longer than the crisis itself. 'Its usefulness is transitory and its power must be ephemeral' (Le Bon, 1924: 232). If they were extended for longer than necessary, society would be faced with two deadly dangers, the erosion of values and the slow collapse of character. At the end, he warned France, which in one century had already experienced the rule of both Napoleons, against the temptations and risks of a new dictatorship. In short, he wanted to safeguard freedom in a country for which the real revolution would be to have no more revolutions. He totally condemned all dictatorships including the one he was accused of supporting, Fascist dictatorship (Le Bon, 1924: 232). So at the very least he has been wrongly labelled. I would not, however, have taken the not inconsiderable risk of breaking this silence if I had not discovered that it is a uniquely *French* phenomenon. Some of the very foremost German thinkers, who were staunchly anti-Nazi – Broch, Schumpeter and Adorno – refer to him freely in their attempts to understand the phenomenon of totalitarianism. Adorno even denounces the exclusive way in which crowd psychology is linked with Fascism, seeing it as far too facile. He wonders why applied group psychology is more specific to Fascism than to other movements seeking mass support, and goes on to say that neither Freud nor Le Bon had envisaged this distinction, since they had simply discussed crowds as such without differentiating between the political aims of the groups in question (Adorno, 1972: VIII, 428).

A generation cannot understand and judge ideas in any other way than by referring them to its own ideas and experience, any more than a man can separate himself from his own shadow.[3] Those ideas and that experience have led us to ostracise Le Bon and mass psychology in general. I had to explain the reasons for this and to get rid of what was most unfounded in them. There is no need for further discussion of either them or the reservations I share. My task as a biographer is finished.

# 4. *The discovery of the masses*

## I

WHEN THE MASSES APPEARED more or less everywhere in Europe, posing a threat to the social structure, the question of the nature of the crowd was raised. Three answers, all equally ubiquitous and equally superficial, were proposed.

1. Crowds are collections of individuals who temporarily come together outside and in opposition to institutions. In other words, crowds were antisocial and composed of antisocial individuals, the result of a temporary or permanent dissolution of groups or classes. A worker or wage-earner leaving his workshop or office to go home to his family might escape from the normal social framework for an hour or two and become an atom in a swarming and multiple crowd in the street or the *métro*. While strolling around or watching what was going on, he might be drawn to some group that was assembling and melt into it with intense pleasure. Baudelaire, in *Le Spleen de Paris*, describes this as an art.

The lonely and pensive stroller derives an intense and pleasurable intoxication from that kind of universal communion. The man who finds no difficulty in losing himself in the crowd experiences heady pleasures forever denied to the egoist in his iron self-sufficiency or the slothful man as limited in his contacts with the external world as a mollusc.

The crowd was still equated with the 'populace', the 'mob', the *Lumpenproletariat*, in short with what had always been thought of as the plebs, men and women with no specific identity, on the fringes of society, pushed into ghettoes or industrial suburbs, with no jobs and no aims and living outside laws and customs. Or at least thought to be living in that way. It was therefore an accumulation of disintegrated social elements, human waste swept out of society and hence hostile to it. Consequently, for sociologists the crowd was neither a separate nor an important nor a new phenomenon, but simply an epiphenomenon. It was not an object of investigation, and was seen merely as a perturbation following upon a breakdown in the normal functioning of things. Society was order, the crowd its related disorder and ultimately a collective rather than a social phenomenon.

2.  Crowds are *mad*. This second answer, seen and proposed as a truth, was as clinging and tenacious as ivy and part of the stock wisdom handed down from generation to generation. We still have the madness of crowds of fans worshipping a pop star or of thousands of fans rising to their feet as one man and waving flags and banners when their team scores, or of tumultuous masses coming to see a great man or lynch some unfortunate out of hand, or of the faithful rushing to places like Lourdes or Fatima where a miracle is supposed to have occurred (De Felice, 1947: 372).

Numberless lurid fables or books (see for example Mackay 1847 and 1932) tell of the unlimited enthusiasm or the unbridled panic of popular masses travelling over whole continents singing or flagellating themselves. Full of fervour for a religion or a man, they followed it or him like the Jews their false Messiah or the Christians their fanatical monks until the final catastrophe. As their whim changed, they burnt today what they had adored yesterday, changing ideas like shirts and, depending on the situation, changing serious history into a grotesque carnival or a bloodbath.

Colourful and extravagant crowds have always stimulated the eloquence and aroused the interest of witnesses who have remained miraculously sober. Their exploits have sometimes been described as mad voyages in a ship of fools, sometimes as the criminal misdeeds of a band of brigands. When those writing such accounts adopt the 'eye-witness' formula, their work achieves Dantesque dimensions, its columns fleshed out with tens and hundreds of thousands of men, medieval crusaders or heretics, leaving their families, possessions and homes under the spell of a shared illusion and, despite their faith, perpetrating terrible destruction and frightful slaughter without the slightest hesitation or the least remorse. If their faith evaporates, they adopt a new illusion and follow it just as stubbornly, making the same sacrifice for it and committing equally great crimes in its service.

In the minds of both the writers and the readers of such tales these mass phenomena are fits of madness which feed obscure dreams, unveil the darker side of human nature and exorcise it by presenting it as a spectacle. Their extraordinary, crazy and pathological nature is captivating because, in Claudel's words, order is the delight of our reason, disorder the frenzy of our imagination. Beyond this spectacular aspect, however, it would seem that crowds offer no interest. They have the inconsistency of dreams and exert no real effect on real history.

3.  The third reason takes the first two a stage further. Crowds are *criminal*. They are mobs, scum, made up of angry men attacking, injuring and destroying anything. They are the incarnation of violence unleashed without any apparent motive, the uncontrolled sweep of unlawful as-

semblies. Bodily harm and offences against property are ascribed to them. They resist the authorities and act with a total disrespect for the law. At the end of the nineteenth century, there was an enormous increase in the number of crowds, and their unexpected actions began to alarm the authorities. It was at that point in particular that the expression 'criminal mobs' began to be heard, designating criminal assemblies threatening the security of the state and the peace of its citizens. The fact that it was not possible to apprehend them, impose a penalty on them or attribute responsibility for what they had done to any particular individual was disturbing for jurists and meant that any law applied to them would be purely arbitrary. The most that could be done was to arrest one or two people at random, mere small fry or perhaps innocent onlookers, as unlike the maddened monster as the millpond the stormy ocean.

It is not by chance that amongst the first to try to explain crowd behaviour was Lombroso, whose theory of the born criminal had become notorious. In his view, crowds were either composed of or led by individuals with criminal tendencies. He also claimed that mass psychology could be treated simply as part of 'criminal anthropology, criminality being the internal characteristic of any crowd'. This was an aspect of a general trend quite new at the time. There was an attempt to produce a body of law aimed at penalising illegal collective acts. As one scholar wrote, 'What is characteristic of our time is the attempt to introduce into criminal law the principle that the crowd can have its own guilt and hence its own responsibility' (Fauconnet, 1920: 341).

The Italian Sighele extended the theory put forward by his compatriot, Lombroso, and was the first to give a technical meaning to the term 'criminal crowds'. For him, the expression included every social movement and political group from the anarchists to the socialists and, of course, striking workers, street assemblies and so on. His analysis prepared the ground for the introduction of repressive measures by preparing public opinion and providing arguments and a justification for the politicians, if not for the lawyers.

Crowds thus became an object of study as a result of their legally suspect nature. This 'criminality' needs to be described and understood, for it explains their violence, their terrorist acts and their destructive instincts. The general agreement was that it was a question of groups operating like bands of thieves or highwaymen, mafia killers or any other criminal association without a moral conscience or any legal responsibility.

A society which is convinced of its own *de facto* and *de jure* stability is relatively tolerant of deviant and nonconformist movements. It is always indulgent towards those who have lost their reason and perhaps even gone beyond what the law allows, and although it may occasionally punish them it does not agonise about them. Their asocial and anomalous nature does not threaten the established order, and they are seen as harmless or even as complete fabrications. But if a society is internally unstable or attacked from outside, the danger to its internal and external security means that such movements are a more serious threat. It is at that stage that they are judged to be harmful and abnormal. That is why crowds, a product of urban and working-class surroundings, were seen right from the start as psychologically and legally suspect, as showing pathological symptoms or symptoms of deviation from normal collective life. This meant that they were diseased growths in a healthy body trying as best it could to expel them. In short, because of their criminal, mad and plebeian nature, crowds seemed to be the waste products or maladies of the existing social order. In themselves, they had no reality and were of no interest.

## II

Le Bon's bold idea, his stroke of genius, was to ignore this way of looking at things. None of the three answers to the problem of the nature of the crowd was acceptable to him. His reasoning was simple and direct. The basic characteristic of crowds is the fusion of individuals into a common spirit and feeling which blurs personality differences and lowers intellectual capacities. Everyone tries to follow his neighbour. By its very weight, the aggregate draws him in its direction, as the tide carries pebbles along with it. That is what happens whatever the level of education and culture or the social class of those involved: 'To combat what precedes, the mental quality of the individuals composing a crowd must not be brought into consideration. This quality is without importance. From the moment that they form part of a crowd, the learned man and the ignoramus are equally incapable of observation' (Le Bon, 1952: 42).

In other words, whatever the wealth or culture of the individual members of a crowd, their own characters will disappear and their personalities fuse in the group in just the same way. It would be wrong to suppose that the educated or upper classes of a society are better able to resist this collective influence than the uneducated or inferior ones or that forty members of the French Academy would behave differently from forty housewives. One commentator stresses this particularly: 'Both the examples and the systematic explanations in Le Bon show that he had not only street riots and popular assemblies in mind but also all bodies – parliaments, castes, clans within a people, the broad masses of the more developed races and the originators of national intellectual movements and trends, and hence the whole people as a cultural community. The mass for him was almost the exclusive opposite of the individual' (Vierkandt, 1928: 432).

Masses made up of aristocrats or philosophers, of readers of *Le Monde* or the *Nouvel Observateur*, that is, non-conformists very aware of their own individuality, would react just the same as any other. The author of *L'Education sentimentale* was expressing the same idea when, within the space of a few pages, he spoke of 'le peuple sublime' and then of 'universal madness' and described the repression in the following terms:

Fear overflowed everywhere. . . . Equality, as if to chastise its defenders and deride its opponents, was triumphally evident. It was an equality of brute beasts, a universal level of base and bloody acts, for fanatical partisan interests balanced out the delirium of need, the aristocrats were as full of furious outbursts as the scum, and the cotton bonnet was no less hideous than the revolutionary one.

(Flaubert, 1952: 432)

The universal nature of these effects, the identical transformation to which all individuals assembled in groups are subject means that the mass is not synonymous with the plebs, the populace, the poor, the ignorant, the proletariat, the *hoi polloi* as opposed to the elite or the aristocracy. The crowd is everyone, you, me, all of us. All men, when they come together, become a mass, and there are no distinctions in this matter.

And what was seen as the criminal nature of crowds is an illusion. Of course they are violent and anarchical and are often easily carried away by a destructive fury. As a group, they pillage, demolish, lynch and engage in acts that no individual member would dare to perpetrate. And Le Bon is quite happy to see their historical role as an eminently negative one. For him, civilisations had always been created and led by a tiny aristocracy and never by crowds, whose only power was to destroy. If they were dominant, it was always at a period of disorder (Le Bon, 1952: 18).

Crowds can also be more heroic and just than individuals, and have the enthusiasms and generosity of simple beings, and when they are offered an ideal or a strong faith, they are capable of almost limitless unselfishness. For Le Bon, their inability to reason meant that they could develop great altruism, something that reason inevitably suppresses, but which is a very useful social virtue (Le Bon, 1910: 129).

He criticised in stubborn detail all those who held criminality to be the distinctive feature of crowds. To that end, he pointed out that even at the worst moments of the French Revolution they took care to set up tribunals and judge their future victims with equity. Their honesty was just as marked, because they brought back to the tables of the revolutionary committees all the money and jewels taken from the condemned men and women. Their crimes were therefore just one particular aspect of their psychological make-up, and were for the most part committed at the instigation of a leader.

In short, crowds were neither preponderantly criminal nor preponderantly virtuous, and violence was no more a characteristic of them than heroism. They could be violent and heroic at the same time. For Le Bon, that was where those writers who had only studied crowds as criminal phenomena went wrong. Crowds were, of course, often criminal, but they were also often heroic. They could easily be led to sacrifice their lives for a belief or an idea, be filled with enthusiasm for glory and honour or be led, as in the crusades, without bread or weapons to free the tomb of a God or, as in 1793, to defend the soil of their native land. Such heroism, Le Bon maintained, was perhaps unconscious, but history is made up of it. If all that could be attributed to the peoples of the world was coldly calculated major acts, the annals of the world would be distinctly empty (Le Bon, 1952: 33–4). It is also worth adding that the best way of motivating a crowd is by appealing to its collective idealism.

In the last analysis there is nothing mad or pathological in the so-called madness, crazes or illusions of the crowd. If, that is, we accept the hypothesis that they are composed of normal individuals like you or me. Quite simply, when such individuals become part of a crowd, they feel, reason and react on a different mental plane. Of course, the way they think and react is far from being the way in which an isolated individual would think and react, but the contrast does not imply any anomaly. And we have no grounds for passing a severe judgement here, except in extreme cases of overt mental illness. Even then, we cannot be sure whether we are dealing with a real kind of madness or a stereotype that allows us to escape from what we do not understand and which consequently frightens us. It is too easy to label the bizarre behaviour or excesses of a crowd (the brawls after a football match, panic after a disaster, the surging of a mass of people cramped into insufficient space and so on) as hysteria or collective madness. The label may be wrong, the behaviour wrongly understood. What Georges Lefebvre wrote about the revolutionary assemblies is universally valid:

Attributing excesses of this kind to 'collective madness' or 'criminal folly' is very superficial. The revolutionary assembly was not unconscious and did not consider itself guilty. Indeed, it was convinced that it was punishing justly and advisedly. (Lefèbvre, 1954: 282)

It would be just as superficial as attributing the abuse of power of a despotic leader such as Hitler to an 'individual madness' or a 'criminal individual'. A despot of that kind acts to maintain his authority and enforce his law. And indeed, when we examine a crowd at close quarters and over a long period, the impression of hysteria vanishes. We merely observe that crowd and individual psychology are quite dissimilar. What seems abnormal in one case seems perfectly normal in the other.

These various responses to the problem of the nature of crowds are still widespread and we still think and talk in terms of them. For the reasons I have given, however, we cannot accept them. Crowds or masses (from the psychological point of view, the two words are synonymous) constitute an autonomous reality. The question of whether they are plebeian or bourgeois, criminal or heroic, mad or sensible, no longer arises. They are a collective form, the outstanding form of collective life, and that is enough.

In what way, you might ask, is that a discovery? Current notions hide the fact that the mass is the basis of society, as the animal is in man or wood in a carving. It is, after all, the raw material of all political institutions, the potential energy of all social movements and the original state of all civilisations. Until modern times, so Le Bon and Tarde believed, it was not even noticed. It took social collapse and social upheavals for them to strike men's minds. The masses existed in the past, in Rome, Alexandria and Carthage. They re-appeared in the Middle Ages with the crusades and in the Renaissance in the towns. They were at work in the revolutionary period, particularly during the French Revolution, which saw their rebirth. From then on they spread like an epidemic as a result of contagion and imitation, toppling states and overthrowing societies.

As long as their role was a peripheral one, governments showed little interest in them. They were a source of amusement for moralists and historians. The theorists pointed them out on their way to more important things. They were merely the supporting players in a play, carrying out the lowlier jobs and having virtually only walking-on parts. But their role in the drama of states has increased impressively. They claim the centre stage and the chief part, that of the ruling class. Le Bon declares that:

The progressive growth of the power of the masses took place at first by the propagation of certain ideas, which have slowly implanted themselves in men's minds, and afterwards by the gradual association of individuals bent on bringing about the realisation of theoretical conceptions. It is by association that crowds have come to procure ideas with respect to their interests which are very clearly defined if not particularly just, and have arrived at a consciousness of their strength. The masses are founding syndicates before which the authorities capitulate one after the other; they are also founding labour unions, which in spite of all economic laws tend to regulate the conditions of labour and wages. They return to assemblies in which the Government is vested, representatives utterly lacking initiative and independence, and reduced most often to nothing else than the spokesmen of the committees that have chosen them.

(Le Bon, 1952: 15–16)

So that is what the workers were for Le Bon: crowds. But why should their power be opposed? What reasons does he give for condemning them in this way? For him, these waves of men raised and carried along by waves of ideas were tolling the death-knell of civilisation, destroying it as water penetrating into the hull of a ship will sink it. Left to their own devices, the masses were the evil genius of history, the force that would destroy everything created by an elite. Only a new elite, or more precisely a leader, could change them into a constructive force to create a new social structure. The working-class masses were no exception. This was not because of their jobs, their poverty, their hostility towards the other social classes or any intellectual inferiority, but simply because they were masses. The reasons given were therefore psychological and not social.

If they sometimes gave the opposite impression and seemed to have opinions, be guided by ideas and respect the law, such things never came from within the masses, but were always inculcated from outside. To quote Le Bon once more:

It is only by obtaining some sort of insight into the psychology of crowds that it can be understood how slight is the action upon them of laws and institutions, how powerless they are to hold any opinions other than those which are imposed upon them, and that it is not with rules based on theories of pure equity that they are to be led, but by seeking what produces an impression on them, and what seduces them.                                  (Le Bon, 1952: 20)

Those are very hard words. Le Bon made no bones about saying that the masses were irrational or reducing them to the level of children or savages. And indeed the idea that the consciousness of the masses comes to them from outside sources and cannot be acquired spontaneously has always been a very widespread one and even persists in the Bolshevik concept of the working-class party. As Porchnev, a Soviet psychologist, writes, 'In Lenin's works, the question of the relationship between psychology and ideology is often presented as that existing between spontaneity and consciousness. . . . Here, the contrasting concepts are blind unconsciousness in human behaviour and scientific awareness.'

And, as is well known, the function of the party and the revolutionary elites is precisely to inculcate such consciousness into all the masses and to impose on them a discipline of thought and action.

**III**

Thus it was that a set of phenomena, crowds, which had previously received very little attention, came out into the foreground. For established scholarly thought, such human aggregates had been anomalous, exceptional states without any unity and of no interest. Only classes, social movements and their institutions, which were seen as real associations, regular social states, were worthy of study. But things changed radically, and the 'abnormality' of the crowd was now a reflection of the hidden forces of history and a vehicle for the explosive force of real life breaking through the shell of a congealed and repetitive civilisation. Crowds were no longer simply oddities, a string of feverish outbursts and historical accidents and an excuse for breathtaking and colourful tales. They had become an intellectual category, a subject of study and a basic aspect of society.

Historical parallels are always a little clumsy and unconvincing. There is, however, an element of truth in the following one. With Freud, dreams and unconscious actions, which had hitherto been brushed aside as accidents or non-events, assumed the status of symptoms of mental life and scientific fact. There was a similar development in Le Bon's case. The masses and their strange behaviour and ways of thinking became scientific phenomena which could be described and needed explaining. Misunderstanding or ignoring them meant running the risk of understanding nothing of the contemporary world, which is chiefly characterised by the creation of mass societies and in which the chief actors are the masses.

The importance of the establishment of a previously ignored field of research cannot be emphasised enough. Irrational behaviour, emotional explosions and the so-called disturbances of crowds and the human mind were no longer merely aberrations or errors or distortions of human nature. They were periscopes showing movements beneath the waters, the hidden patterns of our lives working themselves out as we go about our daily tasks and society follows its grey and meaningless routine. But if crowds were not 'criminal' or 'hysterical' (and hence pathological) products of individual psychology, a new science, a different kind of psychology, had to be created in order to study them. Le Bon wrote that crowds, about which so much was beginning to be said, were a phenomenon about which virtually nothing was known, that professional psychologists had had little direct contact with them and had ignored them, considering them only from the point of view of the crimes they might commit (Le Bon, 1952: 18–19). The new psychology that was needed was of course crowd psychology, and Le Bon predicted a great future for it.

But there is a further point. Science could seek neither a psychiatric nor a legal solution to the problem raised by crowds, which were neither essentially mad nor essentially criminal. This meant that the only solution was a political one, and the only task that could be allotted to that discipline was that of finding a method of government consonant with mass psychology. This could be done by amassing scientifically verified data. The results of such investigations would make it possible to teach politicians how to lead crowds. This would mean that, in politics, intuitive psychology would be replaced by scientific psychology, just as in medicine old wives' cures had been replaced by scientific knowledge and techniques. Le Bon's burning ambition for his new science was that it would provide a method and a solution for the problem of governing mass societies.

# 5. *Mass hypnosis*

O NCE A NEW CLASS OF PHENOMENA has been discovered, those phenomena need to be explained. Why did the individual change when he became part of a crowd? Since the earliest times the state of a man plunged into the collective tide has been seen as a twilight one. His consciousness is dimmed and allows him to drift off into dreams or mystical ecstasies, or else completely extinguished, in which case he abandons himself to panic or nightmare.

Crowds seem to be carried along by the flow of a dream. This well-known and striking truth has attracted the attention of the sages and politicians of all peoples and all ages again and again. It would seem that certain twilight states between sleeping and waking are the real cause of both the fear that crowds arouse and the fascination they exert. Those watching them are struck by the strength of their ability to affect the way in which men, who seem to have lost all contact with it, see reality. And there is a further and equally outrageous fact: it is in that state that the individual can most easily become part of the mass. A sense of total solitude makes him seek a form of unconscious life like that produced in him by the feeling of belonging to the mass.

Psychologists no less than politicians and philosophers have reflected on these basic characteristics of crowds. In doing so, Le Bon arrived at a second discovery (or intuitive conclusion) which was to have a considerable effect on psychology and politics. He thought that the psychic modifications produced in an individual incorporated into a group were in all respects analogous to those brought about by hypnosis. Collective states were similar to hypnotic ones. This similarity had already been noted by others, Freud in particular. Le Bon investigated it thoroughly and explored all its consequences, including its least convenient ones.

At the very time when Le Bon was following up his interest in crowds, Liébeault, Bernheim and Charcot were presiding over the noisy entry of hypnosis into the world of medicine and psychology. This was not quite pure coincidence. Liébeault in particular had done very valuable pioneering work in the methodical large-scale use of verbal suggestion. It was not known at that time, and nor do we know now, why a kind of 'magnetic' trance was produced in the patient when the doctor looked at him or got him to look at a shiny object, but both the therapeutic and the psychic effects were indubitable. The educated and indeed the general public still had the fascinating 'animal magnetism' fresh in their minds and saw hypnotism as a new version of it. It could alleviate suffering and satisfied the desire for a magic cure that lies in all our hearts. This new form of direct action by one human being on another was universally fascinating, both intellectually and emotionally. It was not known whether it was effected over a distance by means of the spoken word or at close quarters by a kind of electromagnetic medium circulating inside and outside all of us.

Whatever the case may be, it is difficult for us nowadays to imagine the excitement caused by hypnosis or its fascination for both the learned and the popular imagination. It was as enthralling as the discovery of electricity in its own time. Everyone wanted to attend a session of hypnosis, just as a hundred or a hundred and fifty years earlier everyone had wanted to give or receive an electric shock and see things and people jump as it hit them.

## II

If crowd psychology was born in France rather than in Italy or Germany, it was because of the effect of the simultaneous existence of waves of revolutions and the appearance of schools of hypnosis, the aftermath, so to speak, of the Paris Commune and the Nancy hospitals or the Salpêtrière. The former created problems, the latter seemed to offer solutions. One might think that in linking the collective and hypnotic states Le Bon was illicitly turning individual relationships into social ones. This was far from being the case. The fact is that hypnosis was a group practice. That is how Freud described it in his account of what he had seen in the sessions run by Bernheim and Liébeault:

Every patient who is making his first acquaintance with hypnosis watches for a while how older patients fall asleep, how they are obedient during hypnosis and how, after waking up, they admit that their symptoms have disappeared. This brings him into a condition of psychical preparedness, which causes him, for his part, to fall into deep hypnosis as soon as his turn comes. The objection to this procedure lies in the fact that the ailments of each individual are discussed before a large crowd, which would not be suitable for patients of a higher social class.

(Freud: I, 107)

Freud's criticism of the practice was precisely that it was collective and took place in public, thus preventing any private and individual relationship. Bernheim, on the other hand, saw this as the only way in which hypnosis could be carried out successfully, or indeed carried out at all. In his classic book on the subject, he boasts of having created in his sessions 'a real suggestive atmosphere' which meant that 'the proportion of somnambulists is much higher' than elsewhere (Bernheim, 1888: 11).

The 'hypnotic crowd' could thus be seen as a small-scale, indoor model of the larger crowd acting freely outdoors. The phenomena observed in the microcosm of the hospital acting as a laboratory would represent those occurring in the macrocosm of society. Analogies of that kind are common in science, and their value depends on how fertile they are.

But we must examine these phenomena more closely and see how they were produced. We shall understand both their spectacular nature, which struck the general imagination, and the way in which they were explained. We still know very little about hypnosis and the way in which suggestion acts on the nervous system (Chertok, 1979). We do at least know that it is very easy to put some people to sleep. When they are in the sleeping state, some part of their mind makes their body obey the suggestions of the hypnotist, who is usually a medical practitioner. He gives his instructions in a very firm voice. So that the patient may not detect the slightest trace of hesitation in it, which would prevent the desired result, he must take great care not to contradict himself. The hypnotist vigorously denies the existence of the symptoms the patient describes, assures him that he can do a certain thing, and orders him to do so.

There are thus two aspects to every session, one involving an affective relationship, the other a physical manipulation. The former consists of a relationship of absolute trust and the submission of the subject to the therapist. The essence of the latter is the limitation of the field of vision and sensation to a very small number of stimuli. This sensory deprivation restricts contact with the outside world and the effect is to put the patient into a state of hypnotised waking dream. The subject is emotionally dependent on the hypnotist, who limits his range of sensations and ideas and plunges him into a trance. He does exactly as he is told, carries out the actions he is instructed to perform and says what he is told to say without being in the least aware of what he is doing or saying. In the hands of the hypnotist he becomes a kind of puppet, raising his arms, walking and shouting without knowing why he is doing it or even that he is doing it.

And it is quite extraordinary to read what hypnotists claim to have been able to make their patients do. Some say that they have made their patients feel a sensation of freezing or burning, others have made them drink a glass of vinegar and think it was champagne, others have thought a broomstick was an attractive woman, and so on. During public demonstrations, the patient has been told that he is a baby, a young woman dressing to go to a dance, or a soap-box orator, and has been induced to behave accordingly. We read in one scientific work that 'One can almost say that *suggestion can bring anything into being*' (Binet and Féré, 1887: 198).

The range of hallucinations affecting every sense and the variety of illusions of all kinds cannot but impress. From the point of view of crowd psychology, two are of particular significance. One consists of focussing the patient exclusively on the hypnotist and isolating him from all the other individuals in the group. Once in a trance, the subject is blind and deaf to everyone except the hypnotist and, if such is the case, the one or two individuals the latter may specifically indicate to him. However hard the others try to attract his attention, he pays no heed to them, but continues to obey the slightest sign from the hypnotist. If the latter touches someone or even points him out almost imperceptibly, the subject answers that person at once. There is a very close analogy there with the direct relationship established between the leader and each member of a crowd, and the control which is exerted is very comparable.

The second illusion is that created when the hypnotist suggests that a certain action should be performed at a given time after the trance is over and the patient back in his normal waking state. The hypnotist has gone, and the subject has no memory of the instructions he has received. Nevertheless, he is forced to do as he has been told. He believes that he performs the action of his own volition and often, when he is obeying his instructions, he invents some excuse to make it plausible to those around him.[1] He thus acts feeling that he is his normal self and not as if he were obeying instructions planted in his mind:

One can order the thoughts and resolutions of the hypnotized person in advance for a certain time when the hypnotist is no longer present. One can further give the suggestion of resolutions of a freewill. More than this, one can give the suggestion that the hypnotized person will have no suspicion that the impulse originated from the hypnotist. (Forel, 1906: 132)

Delayed effects of this kind are like all the forms of influence observed in a society. We commonly see someone unconsciously and unintentionally take up again the gestures or words that he has seen or heard long ago or adopt ideas that he unconsciously realised would brook no denial. They indicate that many of the thoughts and much of the behaviour that seem to us deliberate and conscious and to come from a decision within ourselves are in fact the automatic carrying-out of an order received from outside.

It would be superfluous to expatiate any further on the results obtained by hypnotists, but we must briefly examine the psychic modifications revealed by the state of hypnosis and what the inventors of the technique believed to be their cause. It is thought to be an idea which has been introduced into, and fostered and reinforced in, the mind of the subject, who may have been told, for example, that he is Napoleon, that he is healthy, that he must feel cold, and so on. 'It is an *idea* that creates hypnosis, a *psychic* and not a physical or fluid influence' (Bernheim, 1888: iv).

The idea takes root in the person who has been more or less put to sleep and provides him with a new way of seeing the world and himself and a rapid and direct judgement which is accompanied by a deep conviction. What then works the miracle, gives the idea the strength to bring it about? Ordinary ideas could never achieve this state, but the hypnotic idea draws its strength from the images which it carries and suggests, that is from its concrete and not its abstract content. By means of a series of transformations it releases a cluster of images into the subject's mind, which re-awaken and arouse a whole series of elementary sensations. There is thus produced the orderly transformation of an abstract idea into an immediate perception and a movement from conceptual to eidetic thought.

This hypothesis is supported by the fact that hypnotised subjects describe themselves as invaded by visible illusions, as if in a dream, and experience a keen sense of rapport with the ideas suggested. In addition, and this offers an explanation of the foregoing, the subject's memory is very rich and extensive, much more so than when he is in a normal waking state. To the great astonishment of all, and to his own in particular, he can remember, in the state of of trance, places, phrases and songs which he cannot normally recall. Hypnosis liberates memories and heightens the ability to recall to such an extent that 'One is sometimes led to believe that the subjects have a mysterious lucidity' (Binet and Féré, 1887: 100). Being put deeply or lightly to sleep, however, never abolishes conscious life. It simply gives way to another and separates it into two. Thoughts subsist in the background and are still able to comment on the suggestions even though they cannot prevent their fulfilment or their mental or physical effects.

## III

Binet and Féré see what is happening in the subject's mind in the following way:

Thus in each image in the mind there is a potentially hallucinatory element simply waiting to develop and grow. It does this during hypnosis, when it is enough to name any object to the subject, to say for example, 'There is a bird', for the image suggested by the experimenter to produce an immediate illusion. We can see that between the object and the illusion of the object there is only a difference of degree.                                                         (Binet and Féré, 1887: 163)

This is too cool and clear an explanation for such a mysterious and increasingly puzzling phenomenon. It had to be put forward, however, because, as we shall see, hypnosis was very influential in crowd psychology. It gave it all the authority of both experimental and clinical science, and put forward nothing that had not been properly established. It was particularly influential because, in the mind of the crowd as in that of the individual hypnotised subject, 'every idea becomes an action and every idea which has been called up a reality and they cease to make any distinction between the real world and the imaginary one which has been suggested to them' (Bernheim, 1888: 579).

In this connection, it would perhaps be useful to note the three almost invariable elements of crowd psychology: the strength of the idea on which everything depends, the immediate movement from image to action, and the non-distinction between experienced and suggested reality. What conclusions can be drawn? In hypnosis, doctors go beyond personal consciousness and the area of reason and clear feelings to an area of unconscious psychic life where, like radiation from a source, the influence of the deep memory is strongly felt. It is as if the individual, once he is put to sleep, is removed from his normal world by another one and then wakes up in this new region.

An analogy between a group of hypnotised subjects and another of non-hypnotised ones would not, however, enable us to transpose the phenomenon from one to the other. This is perhaps helpful without being decisive, for doubts spring readily to mind. Perhaps the hypnotist influences the subject with his eyes and not his voice, or perhaps hypnosis is due to a particular pathological state such as the suggestibility of the hysterical patients psychiatrists deal with and hence cannot be achieved with normal subjects. If, as has been said, hypnosis is an artificial madness or an artificial hysteria, we should be deluding ourselves if we expected to find it in crowds if, as we have just established, they are neither 'mad' nor 'hysterical'. What way would there be of moving from one field to the other if they belong respectively to the medical and political spheres? It would be all the more difficult as there is only a minority of 'abnormal' people in crowds as, in principle, the groups we belong to contain a majority of normal individuals.

It was doubts of precisely this kind that Liébeault and Bernheim raised. Basing their views on their clinical practice, they maintained that hypnosis was brought about by the verbal suggestion of an idea by wholly psychical means and that it was this and this alone that determined its success or failure. But was every individual susceptible to this kind of suggestion or only those of a neurotic or hysterical disposition? The reply was a categorical negative. All the phenomena observed with hypnotised subjects are the result of a mental predisposition to 'suggestibility' common to all of us to some degree. We are suggestible in the waking state but do not realise it, as the tendency is neutralised by our critical faculties and our reason. When we are put to sleep, it is freely observable: 'The imagination reigns supreme and the impressions which reach our senses uncritically are transformed by the brain into sensations, movements and images' (Bernheim, 1888: vi).

This removes the final obstacles and means that we can move from the field of individual to that of mass hypnotism. Man is then seen as a psychic automaton acting in response to external impulses, carrying out with ease what he has been instructed to do and unconsciously reproducing a *habitus* impressed on his memory. Psychiatrists in their clinics seem to be imitating the automata Vaucanson produced in his workshops. They are as enthralling as such creations and fascinated not only Le Bon and Tarde but also the poet André Breton. The comparison seems unavoidable: surrealism transposed the discoveries provided by hypnosis to the artistic level and crowd psychology made use of them at the political one. The surrealists' automatic writing and psychic dreaming owed a great deal more to the masters of Nancy than to the master of Vienna. Freud was well aware of this when he refused them the patronage they had asked for.

Here too Le Bon proceeded in the same way, introducing into the social sciences what seemed to be a curiosity and a non-fact. As MacDougall writes:

Suggestion is a process which can be wholly ignored by psychologists so long as they are not concerned with social life; and, as a matter of history, for a very long time it was so ignored; and especially the very striking and immensely instructive phenomena of suggestion working on the hypnotic subject were thrust on one side as curiosities, monstrosities, or fraudulent displays; and even to this day there are many professors of psychology who ignore them, shun them, or even deny them. (McDougall, 1936: 2)

Yet since it was seen as a widespread and ever-recurring phenomenon, it was felt to be at the heart of crowd psychology. Suggestion, it was declared, perfectly described and explained why man in a group is different from a man alone, exactly as a man under hypnosis is different from one in his normal waking state. It was believed that in observing a crowd, one was seeing individuals affected by a kind of intoxication. Like any other kind of verbal or chemical intoxication, it was characterised by a movement from a state of lucidity to one of dreaming, and was a sort of twilight state in which many physical and mental reactions were modified.

All this helps us to understand why the ordinary view of human nature as being rational and conscious refuses to accept the phenomena associated with this state and denies their influence on political and social action. Le Bon, however, did accept them and rejected the 'normal' view when he saw that it was suggestion that determined the fusion of the individual into the mass. In his view, it was a scientific fact that the individual, once in such a state, obeys

all the suggestions of the operator who has deprived him of it [i.e. his conscious personality], and commits acts in utter contradiction with his character and habits. The most careful observations seem to prove that an individual immerged for some length of time in a crowd in action soon finds himself – either in consequence of the magnetic influence given out by the crowd, or from some other cause of which we are ignorant – in a special state, which much resembles the state of fascination in which the hypnotised individual finds himself in the hands of the hypnotiser. (Le Bon, 1952: 31)

Thus, under the influence of that magnetism, individuals lost their consciousness and their will. They became sleep-walkers or automata – robots, as we should say today – bending their wills to the suggestions of the leader, who commanded them to think, see and act in unison. Unless, by a process of natural imitation, they simply copied each other. This produced a kind of social automaton incapable of reasoning or creating but capable of committing all sorts of reprehensible acts repugnant to a waking individual. If crowds seemed so threatening to us, it was because they seemed to live in another world and be a prey to a dream which was devouring them.

# IV

For crowd psychology, hypnosis is the main model of social actions and reactions. The leader is the epicentre from which a first wave originates, to be followed by other concentric waves which take over from it and, like an earthquake, spread the same idea further and further. It is clear that these two forms of propagation, the direct and the indirect, will gradually widen the concentric circles and make them carry still further the kind of hypnotic wave that the leader has set in motion. Thus the work of collective suggestion, taken up by lesser leaders and speeded on its way by the mass media, like a malicious rumour that no proofs or denials can stop, is carried along by its own momentum.

But large-scale hypnosis demands a setting. The crowd's attention has to be attracted in some way, and once things are happening outside the confines of the consulting-room, it has to be turned away from reality and its imagination must be fired. Inspired no doubt by the Jesuits – and by the French Revolution – Le Bon urged that the methods of the theatre should be taken up in the world of politics, with the stage as a model of social relationships in dramatic form and a place where those relationships were observed.

For mass psychology, this theatre had to be a hypnotic one. Suggestion had to be its mainspring, and its rules had to be enforced if the anticipated results were to be obtained. This was so because:

Nothing has a greater effect on the imagination of crowds of every category than theatrical representations. The entire audience experiences at the same time the same emotions, and if these emotions are not at once transformed into acts, it is because the most unconscious spectator cannot ignore that he is the victim of illusions, and that he has laughed or wept over imaginary adventures. Sometimes, however, the sentiments suggested by the images are so strong that they tend, like habitual suggestions, to transform themselves into acts.

(Le Bon, 1952: 68)

Le Bon's assiduous reader, Mussolini, to mention him alone, must have kept this and similar passages in mind. He organised stirring parades and assemblies in majestic squares, soliciting rhythmically chanted responses from huge crowds, and since his time such proceedings have become an integral part of the art of assuming power. One has of course only to watch documentary films and read specialised works to see this. There has been a gradual standardisation of the processes of propaganda. A parade in Peking in Mao's honour looks just like a larger-scale version of Mussolini presiding over a mass parade in Rome or a ceremony in Red Square under Stalin's eye.

It is difficult to judge the consequences of this model of hypnosis at the intellectual and practical level, so universal have they become. It is also a fact that no-one mentions the model much any more, although we continue to think in terms of it and to act within the framework it provides. One thing is certain: by indicating it, Le Bon gave the world of politics an archetype and a method. Fromm, who saw it spread, describes it as being quite precisely a parallel to the hypnotic situation in the relationship of authority, helping social psychology to provide a new and original analysis of the urgent historical problem of the new authoritarianism (Fromm, quoted in Sollner, 1979: 52).

The effect of this analysis was to replace the orator by the hypnotist, to replace eloquence by suggestion and the art of parliamentary discourse by propaganda. The masses are no longer to be convinced, but to be galvanised into action by the methods of the theatre, disciplined by organisation and subjugated by the press or the radio. Indeed propaganda, the epitome of this change of perspective, ceased to be a means of communication or a developed form of rhetoric and became a technique

89

which made it possible to subject individuals to the power of suggestion and hypnotise them in large numbers. In other words, just as industry mass-produced cars or guns, propaganda became a way of mass-producing the masses. That, of course, is why it is so effective and why we cannot do without it.


## V

It is clear that the domain of crowd psychology was shaped (and it is here that its novelty lies) by three major perceptions: (a) the masses are a social phenomenon; (b) the total incorporation of individuals into a mass is explained by suggestion; (c) hypnosis is the model of the action of the leader on the mass. These perceptions transformed a collection of odd phenomena, exceptions and minor facts into major data of reality and objects of science. They enabled Le Bon to provide a sketch for the first version of a system of crowd psychology. This system included a number of key ideas, the following half-dozen in particular:

1. In psychological terms, a crowd is a collection of individuals endowed with mental unity and not a group of individuals coming together in the same place.

2. Both the individual and the mass act, the former consciously and the latter unconsciously, since consciousness is individual and unconsciousness collective.

3. Despite their outwardly revolutionary aspect, crowds are conservative. In the end they always re-establish the order they have overthrown, since for them as for any hypnotised subject, the past is infinitely more powerful than the present.

4. Whatever their cultural background, their beliefs or their social status, masses need to submit to a leader. He neither sways them by reason nor dominates them by force but, like a hypnotist, wins them over by his glamour and prestige.

5. Propaganda (or 'communication') has an irrational basis, collective beliefs, and an instrument, immediate or long-distance suggestion. Most of our actions are the result of our beliefs. Critical intelligence and a lack of conviction and passion are the two obstacles to action. These can be overcome by suggestion, which is why mass propaganda necessarily makes use of language which is allegorical, active and full of images and of straightforward and imperative formulas.

6. All politics aimed at governing the masses, whether they be a party, a class or a nation, is of necessity a politics of the imagination.[2] It must be based on a sovereign idea (revolution, the fatherland) or indeed an

obsession implanted and cultivated in the mind of each mass-man until he is susceptible to its suggestive power. This is subsequently transformed into collective acts and images.

These key ideas reflect a certain picture of human nature which is hidden in individuals but obvious in masses. Crowd psychology sees itself above all as a science dealing with those masses and not with society or history.

# 6. *The mental life of crowds*

I

CROWDS COULD BE SEEN as comparable to hypnosis, that strange drug which arouses in all of us the obscure need to be at one with everything, releases the individual from his solitude and carries him off to a world of collective intoxication and triumphant instincts in which he is euphorically aware of his own omnipotence. Baudelaire called this immersion in the crowd 'an ineffable orgy, a holy prostitution'.

What happens when someone suppresses his individuality and exalts the collective part of his nature to its highest point? In order to explain that, we need to know how crowd psychology sees the psychic system as working. The latter consists of two parts, one conscious and the other unconscious. The conscious part is proper to each individual, acquired over a lifetime and diverse, hence unequally present in society. The conscious life of some people is richer than that of others. The unconscious part, on the other hand, is inherited, common to all and present to the same extent throughout society. Conscious life is tenuous and perishable, a mere fraction of unconscious life, which is massive and permanent. Unconscious life influences us greatly and dominates us without our knowing it, because it comes to us from our ancestors with an inherited accretion of instincts, desires and beliefs.

Let us now look at what happens in a group when each individual is in a state of mutual suggestibility. The universal tendency is to stress those things that bring them together, namely all that they had in common before coming together as a group. These elements minimise personal differences which might lead to mutual antagonism and, over a whole process of contacts and exchanges, increasingly suppress and eradicate the individual consciousness that separates individuals and makes them dissimilar. The part of themselves which brings them together becomes stronger, as it is common to all of them. Similarly, people who live together for a long time stress those things that unite them and eliminate those that separate them.

The mental unity of crowds resulting from this process is no more and has no other intellectual and emotional content than the unconscious itself, which is engraved on the mind and body of each individual: beliefs, inherited traditions, shared desires, the 'tribal words' beloved of Mallarmé, and so on. But it would perhaps be better to let Le Bon himself tell us what happens when consciousness and personality dissolve:

We see, then, that the disappearance of the conscious personality, the predominance of the unconscious personality, the turning by means of suggestion and contagion of feelings and ideas in an identical direction, the tendency immediately to transform the suggested ideas into acts; these we see, are the principal characteristics of the individual forming part of a crowd. He is no longer himself, but has become an automaton who has ceased to be guided by his will.

(Le Bon, 1952: 32)

Thus there is only one way out of individuality, and that is through the unconscious. The mass draws us as the magnet polarises iron filings and holds us by its affective and irrational energy. This also includes rational forces, which it mixes according to the situation. The successful dissolving of the individual into the mass, however, presupposes that everything is ready for the irrational tendencies to be liberated. This idea caused an immediate stir and imposed on a whole generation a new way of mobilising and governing human beings. Scientifically speaking, however, it took the form of the postulate that *everything collective is unconscious and everything unconscious is collective*. As we have just seen, the first half of the statement is the result of Le Bon's work, and from it he drew out all its consequences in practice.[1] The second comes from Freud, who formulated it as a self-evident truth: 'The content of the unconscious, indeed, is in any case a collective, universal property of mankind' (Freud: XXIII, 132).

We must keep the postulate in mind and let it fertilise our thinking, for it is the key to the mental life of crowds in the same way that that of the conservation of energy is the key to nature. Every fact of that life is of course of interest, but knowing how crowds and mass-man think is particularly fascinating. If we are to be able to describe these processes, we must once again assume, as has been the case throughout this book, that crowds and single individuals think differently, just as the hypnotised subject and the conscious person do. We have all come across that difference so often that there is no need to insist on it.

## II

So how does a crowd think? To answer that question, we have to assume the existence of other laws than those of reason, for reason, of which only the individual is capable, has no power to sustain action or inculcate a belief. There is a limit, and Pascal has pointed it out for us: 'For make no mistake, we are automata as much as we are minds, and that is why the

93

instrument of persuasion is not demonstration. How few things are demonstrated! Proofs convince only the mind. Custom creates our strongest and crudest proofs, inducing submission in the unthinking part of our nature which draws the mind all unwitting with it.'

Crowd psychology inevitably perceived the contrast between totally conscious individual thought and a largely unconscious crowd thought drawing the mind 'all unwitting with it'. In everyday life it is the first kind that is manifest; in the case of the hypnotised subject, it is the second. Using that analogy, Le Bon applied to crowds conclusions drawn from observing people under hypnosis. I should now like to look at the various aspects of the two kinds of thought in turn. It is easy to recognise them and illustrate them by means of contrasts.

Individual thought would seem to be critical, that is, logical and making use of conceptual ideas which are mostly abstract in nature. It describes objects and explains events with the help of theories linking a chain of reasoning that can be discussed and corrected in the light of observations of known facts. We know that contradictions can be involved and are aware of the gap between our reasoning and reality. If we eliminate the contradictions, we can achieve a coherent view of the facts we are examining and the techniques we are using. Individual thought is also independent of time, and the laws of logic alone determine the way in which ideas are linked together, which depends neither on our memories of the past nor the conclusions we wish to obtain. It is also orientated towards reality, which in the final analysis is all that matters, and that is why we question it and discuss it in detail, often polemically. We subject proofs to tests of their validity. Experience settles the argument and pronounces its verdict. Nothing, in the long run, is accepted if it cannot be shown to be true, and individual thought is therefore *objective*.

Crowd thinking, on the other hand, would seem to be *automatic*, being determined by stereotyped associations and remembered clichés. It makes use of concrete images. Le Bon indefatigably went on saying in every possible way that the masses were unable to use abstract reasoning and that it was consequently pointless to address them with an appeal to a faculty that they simply did not possess. In one of those tirades which are for authors what histrionic gestures are for barristers, he writes:

A chain of logical argumentation is totally incomprehensible to crowds, and for this reason it is permissible to say that they do not reason or that they reason falsely, and are not to be influenced by reasoning. Astonishment is felt at times on reading certain speeches at their weakness, and yet they had an enormous influence on the crowds which listened to them; but it is forgotten that they were intended to persuade collectivities and not to be read by philosophers.

(Le Bon, 1952: 66)

That perhaps does not sound too unlike a barrister arguing that the defendant was not responsible for his actions and at the same time smiling in complicity with the jury of 'thinking men' and 'philosophers'.

If speeches of this kind have been so influential, the reason is to be found in their power to evoke images, to change sounds into visible signs, words into memories and names into characters. In short, crowds do not think of the world as it is, but as they are led to see and imagine it. They have no grasp of reality and are content with appearances. It is not that they flee from reality, but simply that they cannot distinguish between what things are and what they seem. Truth irremediably escapes them. They replace a hardly-bearable reality with an image and a scarcely tolerable present with the past. In Le Bon's view, 'Appearances have always played a much more important part than reality in history, where the unreal is always of greater moment than the real' (Le Bon, 1952: 68). The thought of the crowd is always composed of the already seen and the already experienced, and that is why, when we are caught like fish in the net of the crowd and have become waking dreamers, ideas enter our minds in the concrete form of diagrams, snapshots and other images.

No-one has bothered to check these biting assertions. They cannot of course be totally false, since mass communications or mass propaganda use them successfully every day. They are based on a solid tradition. St Thomas Aquinas had already said that *nihil potest homo intellegere sine phantasmata*, that no-one can understand anything without images (and hence illusions), and Giordano's dictum that thinking is speculating with images repeats the same idea. Studies of hypnosis seemed to support this long-held view and to show that the ideas suggested under hypnosis are associated with lively images before being expressed in action. But a handful of suppositions is not a proof, a view which I accept without difficulty.

## III

These reservations must not stop us going on. Let us then try to see how an automatic manner of thinking is created and how one can 'reason' using images. There have so far been very few studies of this question, and the description I am going to give will unavoidably be an incomplete one. But we do know enough about the matter to be able to talk about it. At first glance, it seems we can distinguish two processes, which we can call *superimposing* and *projecting*.

*Superimposing* means linking the ideational images that come together for the slenderest of reasons and which, once they have been juxtaposed, make it look as if the reasoning process has moved from premiss to conclusion without going through the intermediate stages. Le Bon's example is worth studying *in extenso*, as it is very revealing about both the man himself and the kind of thinking he was decrying:

The mode of reasoning of crowds resembles that of the Esquimaux who, knowing from experience that ice, a transparent body, melts in the mouth, conclude that glass, also a transparent body, should also melt in the mouth; or that of the savage who imagines that by eating the heart of a courageous foe he acquires his bravery; or of the workman who, having been exploited by one employer of labour, immediately concludes that all employers exploit their men. (Le Bon, 1952: 66)

One might well wonder about the stereotypes behind Le Bon's reasoning and his conclusion that workers are savages. His own logic is a perfect example of automatic thinking. He selects and amasses a series of clichés and from them creates the image of a primitive mass of workers. A good illustration of what is meant by 'superimposing' is the artistic technique known as collage, in which the artist juxtaposes and overlaps bits of photographs, scraps of newspaper, drawings and the like and makes a picture of them.

*Projecting* reflects the inability of the crowd to distinguish between reality and a representation of it and to recognise the difference between things as they are and as they would like them to be. Since it cannot discriminate in this way, the crowd unconsciously exteriorises its internal ideational images and sees as a datum of the world, an event, something that is merely the product of its wishes and its fantasy. It quite simply takes its desires for reality and acts accordingly. We can consider an example from a situation involving crisis or panic. Let us suppose that, with very little justification, a crowd believes it has discovered that some group or other, perhaps the Jews or the blacks, is threatening it. It ascribes imaginary crimes to them – ritual murders or rape, for example – and eventually organises pogroms or lynchings. The same process helps create legends around some particularly admired person. These are embroidered with striking episodes – for the French, Napoleon's martyr-like exile on St Helena, for the Christians, Christ's crucifixion, and so on – in which he figures as the crowd wants him to be rather than as he actually was. In present-day France, the legend of the 'people's de Gaulle' is beginning to grow up, which some future Balzac will chronicle, just as the real Balzac drew the 'people's Napoleon' from life.

Le Bon believed that:

The images evoked in their mind by a personage, an event, an accident, are almost as lifelike as the reality. Crowds are to some extent in the position of the sleeper whose reason, suspended for the time being, allows the arousing in his mind of images of extreme intensity which would quickly be dissipated could they be submitted to the action of reflection. (Le Bon, 1952: 67)

This might well happen when the crowd disperses, in which case individual reason would be dominant. Until that time, it would accept everything uncritically, seeking to test its judgements not against experience but against majority opinion. The latter would always be seen as more convincing than reality. Its persuasive force is extraordinarily strong and irresistible to the individual in a crowd.

It is a particular characteristic of automatic thinking to confuse the interior and exterior worlds. The process may not help reflection, but it is advantageous to practice, since it makes it possible *to move directly from the idea to the act*, to move effortlessly from the imaginary to the real. Incidents like the following lend support to this view:

> The story has often been told of the manager of a popular theatre who, in consequence of his only playing sombre dramas, was obliged to have the actor who took the part of the traitor protected on his leaving the theatre, to defend him against the violence of the spectators, indignant at the crimes, imaginary though they were, which the traitor had committed. We have here, in my opinion, one of the most remarkable indications of the mental state of crowds, and especially of the facility with which they are influenced. The unreal has almost as much influence on them as the real. They have an evident tendency not to distinguish between the two. (Le Bon, 1952: 68–9)

## IV

Automatic thinking, whether it superimposes or projects ideational images, has no concern at all for their rigour or coherence. This is taken care of at a more primordial level by the beliefs and feelings which regulate its flow, as locks control that of a river. Its main concern is to stay as close as possible to life as it is concretely lived. When someone says something or provides an image, there is an immediate reaction. This is different from critical thought in three ways, being *indifferent to its own contradictions, lively* and *repetitive*.

The *indifference to its own contradictions* can be seen in the fact that a crowd makes no bones about accepting and putting together ideas that are mutually exclusive, such as narrowly patriotic concepts and socialist ones, or fraternal ideas and those involving hatred, and finds nothing disturbing in their illogicality or the clash of words. Indeed, it appears that this twisting of logic gives ideas an air of mystery and confers some sort of extra authority on them, as happens in the thoughts of Mao: 'Within the people, democracy is correlative to centralism and freedom to discipline.' The principles of elementary logic are abolished, and a thing can be correlative to its opposite. Such an indifference to the principle of contradiction explains why a crowd can change its mind overnight, believing one day the exact opposite of what it believed the day before without either noticing that it has done so or trying to correct it if it does notice. All the twisting and turning that takes place in a party or a movement and all its inconsistencies are above the heads of those caught up in it. Hence the ease and casualness with which they contradict themselves and suddenly change tack.

Le Bon states that:

These image-like ideas are not connected by any logical bond of analogy or succession, and may take each other's place like the slides of a magic-lantern which the operator withdraws from the groove in which they were placed one above the other. This explains how it is that the most contradictory ideas may be seen to be simultaneously current in crowds. According to the chances of the moment, a crowd will come under the influence of one of the various ideas stored up in its understanding, and is capable, in consequence, of committing the most dissimilar acts. Its complete lack of the critical spirit does not allow of its perceiving these contradictions. (Le Bon, 1952: 62)

This does not explain why, from the social point of view, the members of a party and those who vote for it remain faithful to it in spite of its frequent changes in course, despite the fact that it says one thing on Mondays and another on Tuesdays and that those who were its friends yesterday are its enemies today. (The last fifty years of Socialist/Communist relations in France offer a good example of this.) But the fact that the masses are not aware of such contradictions and, intellectually speaking, do not notice such chopping and changing, is still an important historical factor.

Shakespeare has described this kind of inconsistency vividly. His vision is admittedly a dramatic one, but it certainly keeps to historical truth as reported by Plutarch. In *Julius Cæsar*, the crowd acclaims Brutus, who explains, with a beautifully impeccable logic, why he has killed Cæsar. One of the crowd even calls out 'Let him be Cæsar', and yet shortly afterwards that same crowd, swayed by Mark Antony, is howling for his and his companions' deaths as traitors to Rome. A few images have been enough to arouse the desired emotions: Cæsar's mantle, rent by daggers and bloodstained, a veritable relic, the 'dumb mouths' of 'sweet Cæsar's wounds', the will leaving his goods to the people of Rome and even the biting irony with which the word 'honourable' is repeated, making a mockery of that desired epithet. On the one hand, the rule of reason and an ignorance of men as political animals. On the other, a welter of magical images and unleashed passions, the art of the orator playing the crowd like an instrument, coaxing from it at will sounds of love, violence and hatred.

*Vividness* is an intuitive quality which makes it possible to select the decisive idea from amongst a mass of possible ones. When this is expressed extremely brilliantly and interestingly it calls up familiar memories. It makes an absent person or thing immediately present in the mind's eye. The words 'de Gaulle' at once conjure up the man's tall silhouette, his measured tread and his distant gaze. 'Nazi' means a whole crowd of goose-stepping automata, arms raised in the 'Heil Hitler' salute, howling slogans against a background of swastika banners, burning books or human beings.

It is its power to *show*, not to demonstrate, that makes the difference between a 'lively' idea and one which is less so. It does not inform; it creates enthusiasm. For the person receiving it, it 'rings a bell' because it is directly and intensely related to a person or a familiar object. These qualities fix it firmly in his mind and make sure that it is used often and devastatingly consistently. A certain kind of highly-informative knowledge has no impact, because it has no such emotional colouring. A speech full of figures and statistics is boring and not much of it is retained. A few colourful images, a striking analogy or two, a film or a comic strip will have a stronger effect on the imagination and produce emotional echoes.

To catch the imagination of crowds, who are 'rather like sleepers', half-measures are useless. What is needed is exaggerated arguments, spectacular examples and gripping short-cuts. Proverbially, what is excessive is false. For the crowd, the exact opposite is the case. Everything excessive is true, or at least can be.

The writers of antiquity taught that the mind and the memory could be impressed if emotional shocks were produced by means of unusual and striking images of a superb, hideous, comic or tragic nature. If a character was to make an impact, he had to have outstanding features and unusual characteristics, come close to an extreme prototype such as the hero or the traitor and experience unusual adventures and situations. When those conditions are met, ideas or individuals become *active images* for the crowd. And, as with drugs, the dose and frequency has constantly to be stepped up:

Whatever strikes the imagination of crowds presents itself under the shape of a startling and very clear image, freed from all accessory explanation, or merely having as accompaniment a few marvellous or mysterious facts; examples in point are a great victory, a great miracle, a great crime, or a great hope. Things must be laid before the crowd as a whole, and their genesis must never be indicated. A hundred petty crimes or petty accidents will not strike the imagination of crowds in the least, whereas a single great crime or a single great accident will profoundly impress them, even though the results be infinitely less disastrous than those of the hundred small accidents put together. (Le Bon, 1952: 70)

This suggests that an ideational image contains an evocative charge in much the same way as a bomb contains an explosive one, tearing apart the filters of memory and bringing to the surface what is normally compressed and hidden in the concept.

The repetitive quality has the particular virtue of changing a conceptual idea into an ideational image and turning an abstract content into a concrete one. If doctrines and theories are to be popularly accepted, all that makes them specific and individual – their intricate arguments and precision of language – has to be abandoned. There is no other way. Crowds have neither the time nor the appropriate circumstances to discuss all the arguments, weigh up all the pros and cons and ponder all the facts. In addition, being always composite, as we have seen, they bring little intelligence to bear on such matters. Paradoxically – and this is well worth noting – the very places where they are brought together and demonstrate (such as meetings, assemblies, processions, markets, stadiums and streets) and where their leaders claim to be instructing and informing them, are the worst possible ones for such things. In such places there is a great deal of room for suggestion and very little for reason. Crowds listen to their spokesmen, see them and see themselves, work themselves up into enthusiasm or indignation and do everything in fact except reflect, since they have been brought down to an elementary level of thought and feeling. If ideas are to have a place at that level, they must of course be greatly simplified and the information or content be condensed and presented in the form of images. In Le Bon's words, 'Whatever be the ideas suggested to crowds they can only exercise effective influence on condition that they assume a very absolute, uncompromising and simple shape. They present themselves then in the guise of images, and are only accessible to the masses under this form' (Le Bon, 1952: 61–2).

Ideas become universally accessible if they are constantly mass-produced and repeated, like machines or cars. And anyone can use them, whereas at first a driver or a skilled mechanic was needed. Once they are reduced to a simplistic formula, they capture the imagination. Natural selection becomes 'the survival of the fittest' and socialism 'the class struggle' and 'workers of the world unite'. Anyone knowing the formula seems to have a key, a rather straightforward way of understanding and solving the most complex problems. When they are reduced to one or two simple propositions and repeated often and at length, ideas act on the deep motives for our actions and automatically trigger them off. That is of course what terse slogans and catchwords are for, and the same is true of extraordinary or exemplary events, such as a revolution or the launching of the first moon rockets, which both strike the observer and produce a haunting and riveting image.

It is clear that there is more than a mere analogy between automatic thinking, with its indifference to its own contradictions, its liveliness and its repetitive nature, and symbolic thinking. The latter belongs to the dreams we have when asleep in bed, the former to the waking dreams the mass experiences when it is in a highly-suggestible state. In both cases, sleep dissolves consciousness and reason. Put bluntly, that means that crowds are automata. They are sensitive to whatever strikes a chord in their memory and react to the visible aspect of an abstract idea. They like a simple, frequently repeated answer that will cut through a complicated question like a sword through the Gordian knot. In short, they should ideally be given the answer before they have bothered to listen to the problem. To sum up, the logic of the crowd begins where the individual's finishes.

## V

In the foregoing, we have defined the conditions of automatic thinking, stating that it expresses a susceptibility to lively, stereotyped and repeated images. But in the last analysis, that susceptibility is impressed by the suggestive power of words. Hence the importance of choosing them carefully. It is not a question of precise expression or the clarity of the information furnished by this or that word, but of the number and strength of the images it calls up, irrespective of their real meaning, in the mind of the crowd. Le Bon insists that:

Words whose sense is the most ill-defined are sometimes those that possess the most influence. Such, for example, are the terms democracy, socialism, equality, liberty, etc., whose meaning is so vague that bulky volumes do not suffice to fix it precisely. Yet it is certain that a truly magical power is attached to those short syllables as if they contained the solution of all problems. They synthesise the most diverse unconscious aspirations and the hope of their realisation.

(Le Bon, 1952: 102–3)

When a leader sets out to rouse a crowd, he has to use such words. If he uses current ones, he must know exactly what they mean at the time. Some of them (the gods, honour) are worn out and have lost their evocative power. Others are too new and fresh to set up echoes in the mind. The leader and the statesman have to try to find 'telling' words, to baptise the things that the masses love or hate by encapsulating them in pithy expressions. Thus they induce their imagination to concentrate on the points at issue, since 'certain transitory images are attached to certain words: the word is merely as it were the button of an electric bell that calls them up' (Le Bon, 1952: 103).

Once the image has appeared, action follows. Le Bon had total faith in language. Not of course as a means of reflection or communication, but as a vehicle for verbal suggestion. In his eyes language, the appropriate use of words and phrases, had a magical power. When it has that power, where does it come from? From its ability to evoke strong feelings and lasting beliefs in the masses. In other words, language is powerful when it links past and present, fleshes out today's ideas with feelings inherited from past times and transfers old-established relationships to new situations. A declaration made by Maurice Thorez in 1954 illustrates this admirably. He gathered around the Communist Party all France's strictly national images and emotions and changed her revolutionaries into the heirs of her traditions, drawing all their representative figures into a corona of metaphors pregnant with the history of French feelings:

To Joan of Arc, the shepherd-girl of Domrémy betrayed by the king, condemned by the Church and distorted by subsequent reaction, we have restored her true face, just as we have restored the true meaning of the *Marseillaise*, the revolutionary song of the barefoot army of Valmy and the volunteers of Year II. We have united the red flag of our hopes and the tricolour of our ancestors.

(Birnbaum, 1979: 132)

The suggestive power of such language comes from the fact that in each member of the crowd it arouses the memory of events and age-old beliefs and feelings, all of which are part of the common inheritance of the mass of the people. Even if one is not aware of it or perhaps rejects it, it is nevertheless still the substratum created by history – in this specific case, by French national history – and secretly influences our opinions and our actions. In Durkheim's view, there is present in each of us, to varying degrees, the man of yesterday, and this man is necessarily predominant, since the present is insignificant in comparison with the long past in the course of which we have taken shape and of which we are the result (Durkheim, 1938: 16).

Le Bon, Tarde and Freud wrote in a similar vein, for one of the most constant hypotheses of mass psychology is that nothing in the life of a people, a religion or a group is lost, and so everything, or almost everything, changes. That is why it is essential, when addressing a crowd, to choose words that reach far back into the collective memory and bring back ideas and images drawn from a deep-rooted common past. That is why Georges Marchais says that the socialist society that the French Communist Party will create 'will be blue, white and red' (*Le Monde*, 23 January 1980).

Only words and pregnant phrases such as 'France for the French' and 'the have-nots and the haves' suggest that around the visible crowds there are others that are invisible, shameful, sometimes unknown, and these phantoms, once they have been summoned up at the touch of a button, exert enormous and irresistible pressure. Le Bon declares that:

The dead are infinitely more numerous and powerful than the living. They govern the immense area of the unconscious, that invisible field that controls the manifestations of intelligence and character. . . . The dead generations impose not only their physical make-up but also their thoughts. They are the only undisputed masters of the living.                                    (Le Bon, 1895: 15)

They are also the cement that holds their language together, and those who are summoned up by words and images (Joan of Arc the shepherd-girl of Domrémy, the barefoot army of Year II etc) surface spontaneously and make their presence inescapably felt. The leader has therefore to address the 'old' man in us and invent a language he can use to arouse crowds and draw them fascinated and incapable of reflection towards the predetermined end. If he wants to keep his mental hold over them, he will constantly have to widen the linguistic register, and hence its unconscious basis, by aiming at new beliefs and new sectors of the collective imagination and going to the furthest limits of legend. This is what Napoleon, Stalin and others did, uniting the ancestral heritage of revolutions and the masses with that of the fatherland, empires and tsars and so on and, in the case of Napoleon, with that of religion. Once these ways of speaking no longer have a master, an artist capable of renewing them, they lose their hold. We saw it happen in France immediately after de Gaulle's death, when the crowds weakened and evaporated almost without trace overnight.

## VI

In conclusion we can say that there are two, and only two, modes of thought aimed at expressing reality, and these are the conceptual idea and the ideational image. The former depends on the laws of reason and proof, the latter appeals to memory and suggestion. One is proper to the individual, the other to the mass. Trying to convince and sway the mass by means more suited to individuals would be a serious mistake, rather as if a man were trying to apply to the state budget the rules he followed for his own family finances. Le Bon states critically that 'logical minds, accustomed to be convinced by a chain of somewhat close reasoning, cannot avoid having recourse to this mode of persuasion when address-ing crowds, and the inability of their arguments always surprises them' (Le Bon, 1952: 114).

They could avoid such surprises if they used striking images and used them often, like Maurice Barrès attacking 'the Jewish upper middle class' for 'reducing thousands of workers to a state of starvation', or Maurice Thorez declaiming that 'the fourteenth of July is the occasion when the nation is reconciled and united against the two hundred families' (Birnbaum, 1979: 23 and 31 respectively). The two hundred families and Jewish bankers are a bit more colourful than capitalists and bourgeois.

It would be very wrong to assume that Le Bon suggested that crowds should be manipulated coldly and calculatingly. That would go against both his intention and the data of his science, since no-one can persuade the crowd to accept an idea by which he himself is not fascinated or indeed hypnotised. In the light of what he saw as his own rigorous observation, he argued that there was no other way of addressing a crowd. Embarking on a collective action in the same way as one would embark on an individual one would be pointless and even dangerous, and would mean ignoring the shape of his thought and the nature of his psychology and treating the masses just as if they were not the masses. All that would happen is that they would be made apathetic rather than encouraged to action. There was no way of infringing the laws of mass psychology, which were as strict as those of economics or physics and meant that the art of governing the masses was that of directing their imagination.

The power of those who ruled the world was based on that imagination. By acting on it they had brought about great religions and major historical events – Christianity, Buddhism, the French Revolution, the Reformation and, in our own times, Socialism. No-one, not even the 'most absolute despots', had been able to rule in opposition to it, even those who had always tried to appeal to it in their speeches, their dazzling battles or their fabulous legends. One thinks not only of Napoleon, but also of Churchill or Mao. The last word on this chapter is Le Bon's 'To know the art of impressing the imagination of crowds is to know at the same time the art of governing them' (Le Bon, 1952: 71).

Hitler followed Le Bon's thought and paraphrased it as follows: 'The art of propaganda lies in the fact that it applies itself to those areas in which the imagination is exerted, those of the masses dominated by instincts, and finds an appropriate psychological way to reach their emotions'. He also urged 'the use of all forms of images', since in that way 'human beings are still less obliged to use their reason. The most they need do is look at and read the shortest texts.' We learn from his biographers that his seizure of power and hold over the German people were the result of applying that principle.

Thus for Le Bon the age of the crowd was the age of the imagination, and he who rules there rules by imagination. Writing at a time when the cinema and television were still unknown, he explained how the skilful use of language could bring about that reign, since repeated words and phrases produce and fertilise in us a whole world of images that we see in our mind's eye. But however wonderful it might be, their power was nevertheless limited. After all, words and phrases are only substitutes for images. The latter, if they were directly presented, would have a greater power: 'Words evoke mental images, but images in the form of pictures are even more powerful' (Le Bon, 1911: 146).

He was obviously thinking of the images of his time, such as posters, photographs and theatrical spectacles. It would be a considerable and worthwhile undertaking to investigate how such illustrated illusions were produced and distributed and how they impressed and captured the crowds. Le Bon's intuition has been proved right time and time again. Since his day we have vastly increased the number of material devices for which he had very presciently provided a theoretical justification. No doubt, since it has often been said to be the case, the advent of the mass media had economic and technical causes. But their prime and major purpose has been to influence and sway the masses and hence to produce them on a large scale. The way they have developed can be seen to fall into two stages. First the evocative power of words was greatly increased by the radio, then the images that they call up were brought into being by the cinema and television.

There has been a constant move from one to the other. Fifty years of cinema, television, comic strips, political posters and advertising placards have brought to full growth, and hence confirmed, all that was embryonic in the analyses that crowd psychology proposed. Over a single generation we have moved from a culture of the word to one of images, which are more powerful. This means that in a short space of time radio and television have provided automatic thinking with a technical basis and a strength beyond anything that could have been foreseen, just as printing provided the basis for critical thought. The means of communication have turned it into a factor of history, a factor that will remain with us as long as we have a mass society.

## PART III

# The crowd, women and madness

## 1. *Collective matter: the impulsive and conservative crowd*

I

C ROWD PSYCHOLOGY is interested in only two elementary phenomena, how individuals are fused into a crowd and how the leader controls the masses. So far we have looked at the first of the two. I have tried to show how the power of suggestion leads from the dissolution of individual consciousness to a collective mental unity. Like hypnotised subjects, men change into automata governed by their unconscious. When they are asked, as in the play by the German dramatist Toller, who they are, their reply is that the mass is anonymous.

We must now look at the second phenomenon, that of the control exercised by the leader. We can question the need for him, condemn what he does and play down his role, but we cannot talk of human groups without taking into account the fact that they are divided up into leaders and followers, who are rival powers and persons. Anyone who wants to understand how they are organised always asks the same questions: who is in command and why is he obeyed?

The most disturbing enigma on earth is still the fact that the few always manage to rule the many, and with their consent. The few themselves always finally become one single person, the leader, like firelight concentrating in a fireplace.

All the work undertaken in mass psychology arose from one particular problem. In mass society, the masses were no longer obedient and were showing their power, whilst the leaders were no longer in command, but hid their power and hesitated. Power which is uncertain and called into question is dangerous, a sign that a civilisation is growing old, that the people are losing their energy. Leaders therefore had to be taught to recognise a goal and lead the crowd towards it. In its attempt to solve the problem, crowd psychology devoted itself exclusively to the enigma I have mentioned, seeing the study of the crowd as a way of understanding the human drama as events occurring on stage and the study of the leader as a way of understanding what is going on in the wings. It also saw crowds and leaders as primary and irreducible forces to be confronted directly. The laws governing them had nothing to do with technology or economics. The new science did not deny that other factors were involved, but in each and every case the factors of control and obedience were seen as the chief ones and as having a greater effect on a culture than those of wealth and production.

What was at stake was no less than the survival of a civilisation and a fight between two ways of seeing human beings. As Rimbaud wrote, a spiritual battle is as brutal as a physical one, and this was a war of beliefs and ideas. Whoever won it would gain power and all that went with it. This point of view can be summed up by saying that for crowd psychology, the link between the leader and the crowd was the outstanding human tie, for it was through it that prehistory became history. There are good reasons for not accepting its axiom that in the beginning were the leader and the mass (Moscovici, 1976b). Since, however, it is one of the major themes of this branch of psychology, let us accept it without prejudice, as the legal phrase has it.

## II

Let us first look at the mass seen as a whole. To help us detect some kind of logic behind the range of varied symptoms, we shall make use of Aristotle's old schema. He maintained that everything in the universe consists of both a passive and malleable matter and a stable and active form. Just as there is a matter (wood or bronze) and a form (round or pointed) in a table or an arrow, so there is a matter and a form in crowds. Their unity is achieved in a specific object, a human group such as a parliament, a political party, a state and so on.

We have seen how collective matter is produced: individuals are transformed into crowds. What are the characteristics of the latter? On the one hand they are impulsive, open to suggestion, on the other, extremist in nature. Their openness to suggestion means that they are swayed by every inner impulse and instinct and react, without any self-control, to every external stimulus. Their permanently receptive state means that they are exposed to every event in the outside world and that their reactions will be excessive.

If we ignore the exaggerations in his picture, we can see that Le Bon is offering a serious hypothesis on the social origin of the emotions. Indeed, it has been verified experimentally. The American psychologist Stanley Schachter has shown, in a series of classic experiments, that someone in an uncontrollable state of excitement is sad or happy when in the presence of another sad or happy person. In other words, sadness or happiness do not exist in their own right. All that does exist is a state of uncertainty and instability which becomes sadness or happiness according to the surrounding emotions.

Le Bon saw individuals incorporated into crowds as being permanently in such a state, which would take on a gloomy or a rosy tinge according to the stimuli received from the outside world. Their constant changes were explained in the following terms:

The exciting causes that may act on crowds being so varied, and crowds always obeying them, crowds are in consequence extremely mobile. This explains how it is that we see them pass in a moment from the most bloodthirsty ferocity to the most extreme generosity and heroism. A crowd may easily enact the part of an executioner, but not less easily that of a martyr. (Le Bon, 1952: 37)

Indeed, their most distinctive characteristic was perhaps disinterest or altruism, and they were more capable of sacrifices and unselfish acts than individuals.

Such sudden collective changes of mood occur all the more rapidly in very critical situations. A Parisian bourgeois, Guitard de Floriban, saw Robespierre and his comrades being led away to execution, noting in his diary that 'They were led there along the rue Saint-Honoré, and were everywhere insulted by the people, who were incensed at the way they had been duped. Their heads were cut off at five in the afternoon.'

Such total and apparently inexplicable changes of attitude meet with no resistance when leaders take the initiative with regard to them. The German socialists had declared that they would oppose war, but in 1914 they voted for it. Rosa Luxemburg wrote that 'The powerful organisation and famous discipline of the Social Democrats has produced a splendid result. It took a mere handful of parliamentarians to give the order and in twenty-four hours that mass of four million men did an about-turn and let themselves be harnessed to the imperialist cart, although the day before their raison d'être had been to destroy it.'

As well as being fickle, crowds were credulous. How could they be otherwise? They could not learn from experience. They lived in an imaginary world, were obsessed by the images and illusions stored in their unconscious and were ready to swallow all they were told and act accordingly. 'Reality and experience have no effect on them. They can be made to accept anything and see nothing as impossible' (Le Bon, 1910: 117).

They could not distinguish between dreams and reality or Utopia and scientific fact and could not see the obstacles between them and their desires. Nor did they understand the words which were to arouse them to make them give up what they were shouting for. Lost in their hypnotic dream, they could be made to accept anything, and had to be told that they could have anything, for to talk thus was to speak the only language that reached them and impressed them. The recipe for success was obvious. If they asked for the moon, they had to be promised it (Le Bon, 1910: 130).

Rarely had demagogy been proposed and advocated with such conviction as a truth originating in the most basic tendencies of the human psyche. Le Bon wrote page after page containing a flood of aphorisms addressed to the politicians of his time, telling them that to take a good aim they had to aim low, always at the most elementary and primitive level of humanity. The tip was put to good use. If Hitler had not used it, he would probably have remained a house-painter.

We are coming to one of the central ideas of crowd psychology. What do fickleness, credulity, shifting moods and the like suggest if not women? In one of his idiosyncratic passages (which could perhaps be set to the tune of 'La Donna è mobile'?) Le Bon writes thus:

Crowds are everywhere distinguished by feminine characteristics, but Latin crowds are the most feminine of all. Whoever trusts in them may rapidly attain a lofty destiny, but to do so is to be perpetually skirting the brink of a Tarpeian rock, with the certainty of one day being precipitated from it. (Le Bon, 1952: 39)

On the basis of these characteristics, which have so often been said to be feminine, an obdurate conclusion has been reached. A crowd is a woman. A woman's supposedly emotional, capricious, temperamental and flighty nature means that she is susceptible to suggestion, and her passivity, traditional submissiveness and capacity for endurance fit her equally well for devotion. She is the harlot and the housewife, a mistress to be conquered and a betrothed to marry. There was no need for Le Bon to invent the idea that there are strong links between the eternally feminine and the eternally collective. The crowds of the French Revolution were largely made up of women, and the women who harangued them haunted the nightmares of the leaders of the mobs for years to come. Napoleon spoke of them as an emperor and a lover: 'I have only one passion, one mistress – France. I have slept with her.' Many of his successors would have liked to be able to say as much, but none dared.

Seeing women, crowds and disorder as similar phenomena is another constant element in political and literary confidences and rumour. One contemporary writer has described the crowd in the following terms: 'Yes, anyone who reads the listeners' letters has probed all the wounds of that plaintive female monster, the crowd, and has a pretty good idea of what God and the saints hear day in and day out in the prayers sent up to them' (Tournier, 1977).

As a part of mass psychology, this prejudice, which was no more than a half-truth away from it, became a political principle. The quickest to understand and apply it was Mussolini, who repeated to Emil Ludwig what he had read in Le Bon, that crowds, like women, loved strong men. His great ally Hitler went on at greater length, declaring that the mass of the people were mostly so feminine in nature that most of their actions and opinions were the product of sense impressions rather than pure reflection and that those impressions had nothing subtle about them. They were, he maintained, very simple and straightforward, containing no nuances, but only positive or negative feelings of hatred or love, right or injustice, truth or falsehood, and there were no half-feelings.

Such statements undeniably constitute a concrete and striking summary of one of Le Bon's major ideas, and one on which he expatiated at great length and with evident gusto. Hitler, however, was not content merely to think that the crowd should be treated like a woman. He also invented a means of dealing with women as if they were a crowd. What Ernst Bloch, the great German philosopher, had to say about female support for the Nazis is of interest:

It began with the charmers. Emotions erupted and hearts were won. There is nothing surprising in the fact that a number of them belonged to women. Feelings, after all, are their speciality. But it is not as simple as that. Women are not made up of instincts alone, and Hitler's toothbrush moustache was not enough to draw them. One of the early Nazis, when they were looking for the best gimmick, had said that he would have to be a bachelor, as that would bring in the women. (Bloch, 1979)

What he certainly meant was that they would see in him their lover and husband, in short the man they were lacking in the years just after the war. And the 'gimmick' worked. This is confirmed by Tchakhotine, who worked on the socialist side in the nineteen-thirties, fighting Nazi propaganda. In his view, propaganda based on suggestion naturally worked well with women, who fell for it despite the anti-feminist ideas of the Nazi movement (Tchakhotine, 1939: 46).

Turning a piece of prejudice into a technique does not make it true. A number of such techniques have in fact been based on incorrect theories. It does raise a serious problem, however. How did the swing from crowd suggestibility to female suggestibility come about? The Nazis were not the only ones to make use of what I take to be a complete about-turn. In mass society women, who had previously been disregarded and seen as a negligible factor, became the prime target for advertising, propaganda and other means of persuasion. This was the case to such an extent that men, who are the ones in control of these means, now talk of a *feminisation* of the media which is parallel to their democratisation. But the tendency I referred to goes back much further in our culture, and can be traced to Aristotle. For us as for the Greeks, the image of matter has always been woman, like her a receptive creature to which man aspires to unite himself and which he desires to dominate, as does the demiurge the stone he is carving or the wood he is shaping.

The extremism of crowds can be seen in the speed with which they adopt one-sided opinions and push them to their positive or negative conclusion. This reflects an ever-present tendency towards action which, if it is to come to fruition, needs a pole of attraction. The latter can be a person – the leader, foreigners, the Jews, the rich, the Americans – or an idea: peace or war. It can be some place towards which everyone is to march together: the Bastille in the French Revolution or the Winter Palace in St Petersburg in the Russian Revolution. By choosing a pole, an idol or a scapegoat, we eliminate all the wavering, doubts and differences of opinion that might create friction and divide the crowd, in whose warm and exalted atmosphere doubters begin to find faith, the Hamlets become resolute and the moderates extremists. This is all the more so if exaggerated emotions have been induced. If orators have dinned far-fetched notions into it, or urged it to cheer or boo a particular person or idea, contagion does the rest. Once the mood of the crowd is swinging towards an extreme, the general approval a particular opinion receives increases its capacity to exclude any other. Subtlety disappears as the crowd continues to focus on a particular feeling, view or course of action. In Le Bon's words:

The simplicity and exaggeration of the sentiments of crowds have for result that a throng knows neither doubt nor uncertainty. Like women, it goes at once to extremes. A suspicion transforms itself as soon as announced into incontrovertible evidence. A commencement of antipathy or disapprobation, which in the case of an isolated individual would not gain strength, becomes at once furious hatred in the case of an individual in a crowd. (Le Bon, 1952: 50)

Odd as it may seem, this suggestion has also been verified, in a rather more sober form, in laboratory conditions. Le Bon's description lacks foundation and coherence and is no more than a web of prejudices, but it does contain a grain of truth. The focussing process in the crowd corresponds to a need to avoid doubts and uncertainties and makes it possible to achieve unity round a fixed point by accepting an unswerving view of things. A fixed and unshakeable purpose is the best way of inducing extreme forms of action.

# III

Under hypnosis persons subjected to suggestion recall forgotten memories which are clearer and more numerous than when they are in the waking state. They also have an imperative and irresistible quality not present in conscious thoughts. Le Bon transposed this observation and maintained that through the irritations and exaggerations of crowds memories and habits always return. Even after great upheavals the broken thread of continuity is knotted together again. Contrary to revolutionary slogans, there are no fresh starts and new beginnings, for we cannot control the past. We may escape from it for a time, but it is our master.

That proposition might upset some people, for after all, when it was put forward, the masses appeared to be bent on a revolutionary transformation of society for reasons of tradition and self-interest. Habits of thought put masses and revolution together as they did childhood and innocence. To do so, said Le Bon, was an error. Thought was not reality. The masses were not drawn into revolution by their own instinct, but by parties or leaders:[1]

It is merely their tendency to violence that deceives us on this point. Their rebellious and destructive outbursts are always very transitory. Crowds are too much governed by unconscious considerations, and too much subject in consequence to secular hereditary influences not to be extremely conservative. Abandoned to themselves, they soon weary of disorder, and instinctively turn to servitude. It was the proudest and most intractable of the Jacobins who acclaimed Bonaparte with greatest energy when he suppressed all liberty and made his hand of iron severely felt. (Le Bon, 1952: 55)

Le Bon saw this conservatism as an opportunity rather than as an obstacle, as it could prevent the apparently imminent revolution. He therefore argued that the crowds on the barricades waving red flags and shouting revolutionary slogans were deceptive and should not be taken at face value. In reality they were tortured by a desire to return to things as they had been in the distant past. If society responded to that desire and fostered it with the appropriate phrases, it would be possible to bring them back to that past from which they had temporarily freed themselves, and hence to order. Here, he was echoing Nietzsche's dictum that the herd instinct meant immobility and conservatism and had nothing creative about it.

There were immediate reactions to this apparently rather anodyne argument. Sorel was the first to take it up, suggesting that there was a great deal of truth in such judgements, which were based on a wide knowledge of civilisations, but that they were not valid for class societies.

Kautsky was next. We have seen, in an earlier chapter, that he adopted more or less the same point of view.[2]

But it was left to someone like Mussolini and those who followed and imitated him to adopt this position wholeheartedly. This meant that they did something which the bourgeoisie had never dared to do, to treat the working classes as a conservative mass and blend Marxism or socialism with chauvinistic beliefs and the worn-out ideas of tradition and thus revive the myth of the nation. This bold move produced the desired results, since the Fascist parties and the Nazi storm-troopers captured a considerable section of the working classes from the Socialist and Communist parties, thus converting revolutionary into anti-revolutionary militants fighting for one of the most reactionary forces the world has ever seen.

To sum up, we can say that crowds are open to suggestion and given to extreme attitudes. Superficially, they change easily and often. They can be carried from one extreme to the other with no resistance. From this, it was concluded that the crowd was like a woman. In a deeper sense too it is like a woman, who is a prisoner to traditions, customs and the ancient unconscious and yet is opposed to overthrowing them. If they are overthrown, she immediately sets about painfully rebuilding all that she has happily demolished. A revolution can be prevented or stopped by an appeal to sentimental nostalgia, past glories and the desire of the masses to respect the memory of the dead.[3] The recipe was simple and crowd psychology provided a rough-and-ready explanation of it. But using it has produced and still produces the desired results.

## 2. *Collective form: the dogmatic and utopian crowd*

### I

**B**ELIEFS ACT AS FORMS. Once they are combined with the prime matter composed of individuals joined together, they make up what, in psychological terms, are organised crowds, cementing together the parts of the collective group and shaping them in pursuit of a common aim. If they are ill-founded or sloppy, the beliefs crumble away and the structure collapses. There are no crowds without beliefs any more than there are houses without architecture or mortar. Contrary to what both Marxist and non-Marxist history and sociology tell us (that is, that crowds are flimsy superstructures built upon a solid economic base) crowd psychology sees them as the permanent bases of social life. If human groups have no beliefs or driving ideas they are, crowd psychology insists, inert and empty. Like a man who can no longer see any meaning in life, they decompose and collapse into apathy.

Thus it is that, thanks to general beliefs, the men of every age are enveloped in a network of traditions, opinions, and customs which render them all alike, and from whose yoke they cannot extricate themselves. Men are guided in their conduct above all by their beliefs and by the customs that are the consequences of those beliefs. These beliefs and customs regulate the smallest acts of our existence, and the most independent spirit cannot escape their influence. The tyranny exercised unconsciously on men's minds is the only real tyranny because it cannot be fought against. Tiberius, Genghis Khan, and Napoleon were assuredly redoubtable tyrants, but from the depth of their graves Moses, Buddha, Jesus, and Mohamet have exerted on the human soul a far profounder despotism. A conspiracy may overthrow a tyrant, but what can it avail against a firmly established belief? (Le Bon, 1952: 145–6)

It is not sciences or philosophies that provide the mental unity of the mass, but beliefs, from which there is no escape. No society, including our own, can do without them.[1]

Faithful to its ideas of progress, sociology has striven to see an end to ideologies and looked forward to the arrival of a post-industrial society wholly founded on science and reason. A desirable aim, in the eyes of crowd psychology, but a completely impossible one. The masses of humanity, in its view, can neither live according to the rules of reason nor act in a scientific manner. They need the mortar of beliefs, which will

115

certainly not disappear but will remain a crucial factor. In the age of the crowd, their importance is on the increase.

## II

It is not therefore because they are true and strong that ideas conquer and become beliefs, but because they take on a traditional dimension. They have to move from the individual consciousness to the collective unconscious of the crowd and gain the backing of the folk memory of the peoples of the world. Thus the notion of liberty and equality preached by the philosophers of the Enlightenment became part of the traditional memory of bourgeois freedoms and Roman virtues in the French Revolution.

If it is to reach the 'soul' of the crowd, a belief must acquire the inflexible nature of customs. It cannot be a matter for discussion. It imposes itself by its self-evidentness and the strength of the irresistible feelings it arouses and also by its power to reshape reality by invoking either a world which has gone, the golden age or paradise lost, or one which has yet to be born, the just society or the last judgement. In short, a belief of the kind we have in mind has to be dogmatic and utopian. Why is this so?

Crowds have a constant need of mental coherence and emotional certainty to enable them to understand events and make sense of an unstable and complex universe whose plaything they seem to be. The dogmatic aspects of belief meet this need, which is similar to that experienced by children. If a changing reality can be explained by a single, visible cause – the workers, the Jews, capitalists, imperialism – by giving simple and compelling answers to questions and categorical definitions of what is true or false, good or evil, then the desired coherence and certainty can be provided.

It also removes any possibility of argument. Every conclusion is logical, every judgement infallible. This is the way of ideologues and parties when they show that they have never been wrong, prove that they foresaw everything and that their policies have never varied, when, in short, they declare that they have always been right about everything. The following declaration by Georges Marchais, the secretary-general of the French Communist Party, will serve as an example:

The French Communist Party was right in 1934.
The French Communist Party was right in 1939.
The French Communist Party was right in opposing the Algerian war. The French Communist Party was right in opposing the war in Indo-China, and in all the major events of national and international life it stood alone as a party.

(Marchais 23 January 1980)

By repeatedly stressing its permanence and infallible rightness, it turns the events of history into unquestionable doctrinal tenets.[2]

When they are imposed under the guise of absolute truths and repeated as a form of constant suggestion, beliefs are no longer subject to reasoned argument, doubt or the pressure of facts that go clean against them. This is all the more so as, generally speaking, crowds will have nothing to do with argument or criticism. They have neither the necessary objectivity nor the capacity for self-examination for reflection. In Le Bon's view, the proof of this lay in the howls and invective that greet the slightest objection made by an opponent at a public meeting.

The effect of this dogmatic aspect of their make-up is to make them more intolerant: 'One of the most constant general characteristics of beliefs is their intolerance. This is particularly intransigent when beliefs are strong. Men who are in thrall to certainty cannot tolerate those who do not accept it' (Le Bon, 1911: 235).

All collective beliefs are uncompromising, radical and puristic. They free the believer from ambiguity at the level of the intelligence and from half-heartedness at that of the feelings, and endow him with a sense of exaltation and omnipotence, which is nourished by the conviction that he belongs to a group that is *right*. They justify his zeal and save him from apathy, the deadly sin of sloth, that lifeless disgust with existence, and ensure that passion will conquer. The hold that fanaticism has on crowds comes from the conviction that they are following their own authentic ideal, which creates a world of fixed values which is free of inner doubts and protected from all outside dangers. The world of the crowd is a partisan world, every crowd engaged in action is a partisan crowd and can only be made to act if it is made partisan.

Le Bon thus saw logical coherence and certainty, qualities to which we give priority in education, as leading directly to fanaticism, authoritarianism and intolerance, not perhaps in individuals, but certainly in crowds (Le Bon, 1952: 53).

If that is so, what should we think of governments, parties and social movements which nowadays more than ever have the urge to provide the masses with totally scientific coherence and certainty? In contradiction to what they believe and state, their efforts do not bring about greater tolerance. They have and always will have the opposite effects to the ones aimed at. Once they have the comfortable feeling that there is intellectual or scientific support for what they believe, crowds become even more pitiless towards those who do not share it or who question it. It was that state of mind, according to Le Bon, that had produced the Inquisition and the Terror and would feed their modern counterparts. The dilemma was that knowledge enlightened the individual but made crowds fanatical.

Some solution other than a simple hymn of faith in human reason was hoped for, but history had already announced that this was not to be.

Atomised and anonymous crowds live in a world that is not always an agreeable one. They seek happiness and more often than not find unhappiness. Such failure is a hard school. But individuals, impervious to experience and torn between unsatisfied desires, never cease to believe that their situation can be changed and must be changed radically. That hope provides the energy that makes them do the best or the worst things and makes the crowd heroic or criminal. As Le Bon saw things, 'People of all races all worship the same god, Hope, although they give it many names. In this sense, they are all monotheistic' (Le Bon, 1911: 150).

Since their worship is so constant, crowds are receptive to beliefs that refer to it and depict the earthly achievement of their longed-for happiness.

That may be an illusion, but if so it is an illusion that has shown itself able to move the human mountain. They may be dreaming of Utopia, but it is a Utopia based on desires which creates a full, authentic society without injustice or corruption, the opposite, in short, of the one they live in. These warm-hearted illusions are not necessarily fallacious. The worker dreams of a world where he can work freely without enduring want or the oppression of his boss and co-operate consciously with other workers in a common task. And does not that dream sometimes come true?

Belief tries to create a more satisfying reality than the everyday one, offering in its place a more glorious future. Behind the appearance of a total break with the past, however, it is always a paradise lost that emerges again – primitive Communism, the Greek city, the Roman empire – a golden age that the crowd wants to believe in.

'We carry out', wrote Proust crudely, 'that brainwashing on ourselves through hope, which is a figure of a nations's instinct for self-preservation if one is really a living member of it' (Proust, 1978: III, 773). Utopian belief is that tendency carried to its extreme limits. It is not faulty logic, but logic taken as far as it can go, and it gives the tiniest details of the working drawings of the world as it should be. Its internal perfection is fascinating.

Le Bon's quick-fire language takes him to extremes. In the creation of that picture, quickened by hope, he saw a profound and inescapable necessity. The potential state of the living masses was a messianic one. They saw themselves as having a mission to carry out and as able to save themselves and the world. That mission would always justify their actions, whether they were lofty or base. It is reason that leads the individual to reject morality; the crowd does so out of faith. One of the leaders of the Hungarian Communist Party, an expert on the matter, has requested for that very reason that those with messianic tendencies should be declared guilty of 'crimes against humanity' (A. Hegedus, *Le Monde*, 3 August 1980), perceiving that in the atomic age such people, whatever their ideology, can embark on catastrophic policies. Leaders are well aware of the temptation. It is an easy move from the first reasonable proposals to a stage when the crowd is told to entrust its hope to someone in return for happiness, just as in past times they were told by the priests to give them their souls to be taken to heaven.

If men's faith, their capacity for illusion, was taken away from them, they would never undertake anything. Beliefs renew and refresh it. They reproduce in their structure the need for certainty and hope that crowds experience in the same way that knowledge and science embody the aspiration felt by individuals towards proven truth and objective reality.

# III

There is an infinite variety of beliefs. Some are universal, others local, some presuppose a god, others exclude the idea. They govern our daily social life or establish our proper relationship with God. Making a catalogue of their origins, listing the kinds of language they use or drawing up a map of their geographical distribution in one single country, such as France, would be a labour of Hercules. It is an essential undertaking, however, and it is regrettable that there is no overall comparative science of beliefs.

If we keep to their essential features – dogmatism and utopianism – it is striking to see how closely they resemble the system of beliefs that has best held civilisation together for millennia and weathered the storms of history, namely religion. If they are to reach the 'soul' of a crowd, all beliefs must be like it and come to be like it, wherever they come from. This is a generally valid law, and Le Bon declared that:

> The convictions of crowds assume those characteristics of blind submission, fierce intolerance, and the need of violent propaganda which are inherent in the religious sentiment, and it is for this reason that it may be said that all their beliefs have a religious form.
> (Le Bon, 1952: 73–4)

It can be seen in the intensity of faith, the exaltation of feelings and the propensity to see as enemies those who will not accept them and as friends those who will; in the sacrifice of human lives that all the great founders of great faiths have demanded and obtained; and in the quasi-divine nature that the human heart has invested them with. Such leaders, by inspiring a worship that knows no bounds and imposing unquestionable dogma, command blind obedience, and one after another they join the gallery of legendary heroes who people and illuminate history. We no longer raise altars to them, although the great have their Panthéon in Paris and Mao has his mausoleum in Peking. We no longer pray to them,

but they have statues, or their portraits are in the hands of their admirers, and the cult of which they are the object is not notably different from that accorded to their predecessors. An understanding of the philosophy of history is only to be got by a thorough appreciation of this fundamental point of the psychology of crowds. The crowd demands a god before everything else. (Le Bon, 1952: 75)

From Alexander to Cæsar and from Hitler to Stalin, the list of those who understood that is a long one. To support that view, I will simply mention the contagious growth, in our own time, of what is specifically called the cult of personality.


**IV**

Crowd psychology takes religion seriously.[3] This it does of course because of its psychic value for the masses, and not because of its content, with which it is not concerned. As Le Bon said:

A person is not religious solely when he worships a divinity, but when he puts all the resources of his mind, the complete submission of his will, and the whole-souled ardour of fanaticism at the service of a cause or an individual who becomes the goal and guide of his thoughts and actions. (Le Bon, 1952: 73)

Every large-scale action depends on it.

Every prestigious leader has the art of using it, and to this the greatest add the gift of prophecy. But only a civilisation which respects customs, can pray to the gods and imagine a supernatural world, can have a sacred religion. This is not the case with our own, which professes atheism, cultivates disbelief and extols the secular virtues. After such massive doses of humanism and irreligion, no return to the faith of the past or restoration of bygone forms of worship is possible. It is not even worth being tempted by it, for in the westernised world religion, in comparison with a nationalist or socialist faith, has lost the power to move hearts and souls, exalt fidelity and move the disbelieving masses. This is confirmed by a *reductio ad absurdum*: it is not religion, but the charisma of the leader that brings the masses to the feet of the Pope or Khomeini.

And yet our civilisation can also have a religion, with its dogmas, its orthodoxy and its infallible texts that are not to be criticised, a religion woven from contemporary ideas, based on scientific knowledge and without any spiritual god. In short, a secular religion. That is how

Auguste Comte's positivism saw itself, but was not, and that is what Marx's socialism is without wanting to be. Since there is clearly a need for them and since the ones we once had are now obsolete, we can create new religions just as efficacious as the old ones. These religions of an irreligious civilisation, which are certainly secular and man-made, must in any case proliferate to meet all those longings for certainty and hope that were once met by 'God-made' faiths.

Crowd psychology almost provides a formula for the process. It does indeed provide a pattern for tailoring and mass-producing collective beliefs, and without such a pattern it is impossible to act on the masses or to make them act. It looks as if it has been successful, for there is now scarcely a party or country that does not want its own bespoke religion as soon as it feels the need for it. In Ernst Cassirer's words:

> The new political myths do not grow up freely; they are not wild fruits of an exuberant imagination. They are artificial things fabricated by very skilful and cunning artisans. It has been reserved for the twentieth century, our own great technical age, to develop a new technique of myth. Henceforth myths can be manufactured in the same sense and according to the same methods as any other modern weapon – as machine guns or airplanes. That is a new thing – and a thing of crucial importance.                                    (Cassirer, 1961: 282)

What he says is clearly exaggerated, and the comparison he makes is a bad one. Contemporary religions (the word 'myth' is inaccurate in this context and pointlessly pejorative) are in the first place grafted onto others and then expertly cultivated according to the laws of psychology, rather as if they were plants in a greenhouse. However, the statement is not without some foundation. The mass-production of beliefs to the same pattern is incontestably an invention of our own industrial age in which anything that exists in nature can be artificially reproduced, including the impression of naturalness. From being a human art, and one of the oldest, religion has become, since man cannot do without it, an applied science.

# 3. *The leaders of the crowd*

---

*Everyone could be like that, but almost no-one is.*                    Hofmannsthal

## I

T O  C O N T I N U E.  Crowds have a *matter* and a *form*. They are composed of suggestible, polarised, malleable and changing individuals who are subject to the vicissitudes of the external world. Their
form is one of strong, essentially dogmatic and necessarily utopian beliefs
which are similar to religious ones. Crowds therefore combine what is
most primitive in man with what is most permanent in society. The
problem lies precisely in knowing how the form impresses the matter and
becomes its matrix. If we follow Aristotle's scheme, we know that we
need a third term, a *demiurge*, an artisan capable of combining the two and
making them into a work of art, like the joiner shaping wood into a table,
the sculptor casting bronze into a statue or the musician capturing sound
in a melody.

This demiurge is the leader, who transforms the suggestible crowd into
a collective movement welded together by a faith and acting with a goal in
view. His artistic field is social life and his art that of government, just as
carpentry is the art of the joiner and sculpture that of the sculptor. It is he
who, working in that region where life is at its most concrete and intense,
prepares the mass to receive an idea that will make it incarnate and
purposive. The secret of the leader is that he embodies the idea for the
mass and the mass for the idea, the twin sparks of his power.

He exercises his power not by organising violence, which is always
secondary, but by organising beliefs, which are primary, just as the
sculptor exercises his gift not by hammering and splitting stone but by
creating a statue.

The arousing of faith – whether religious, political or social, whether faith in a
work, in a person, or an idea – has always been the function of the great leaders of
crowds. . . . To endow a man with faith is to multiply his strength tenfold.
(Le Bon, 1952: 119)

In other words, faith for a crowd is what atomic energy is in matter, the greatest and almost the most terrifying power a man can have at his disposal. Belief acts, and whoever controls it has the power to change a collection of sceptical individuals into a mass of convinced believers, easy to mobilise and even easier to lead. Let us therefore look at the leader, the master of that art.

## II

Ideas rule the masses, but the masses are not ruled by means of ideas. To bring that essential task to fruition, to work that alchemy, a particular kind of man is necessary. Such men translate the visions which have been produced by the reason of the few into the acts of passion of all. Through them, the idea becomes matter.

They are, of course, men who have emerged from the crowd, who are possessed by a belief and hypnotised by a common idea before the rest of their fellows. They become one with their idea and change it into a passion. Le Bon writes that:

The leader has most often started as one of the led. He has himself been hypnotised by the idea, whose apostle he has since become. It has taken possession of him to such a degree that everything outside it vanishes, and that every contrary opinion appears to him an error or a superstition. An example in point is Robespierre, hypnotised by the philosophical ideas of Rousseau, and employing the methods of the Inquisition to propagate them.

(Le Bon, 1952: 118)

Men of that kind, driven by their passion and obsessed with their mission, are necessarily beings apart. They are abnormal and deviant and have lost touch with the real world and broken with those close to them. A large number of such leaders come chiefly from amongst what Le Bon calls 'the neurotics, the over-stimulated and half-crazy who live on the edge of madness. However absurd may be the idea they defend or the aim they pursue, all reasoning falls on deaf ears. Scorn and persecution merely make them more determined. All is sacrificed, personal interest and family. Even their own instinct for self-preservation disappears to such an extent that often the only reward they seek is martyrdom' (Le Bon, 1910: 242). He writes elsewhere that men like Peter the Hermit and Luther, who were half-mad, radically changed the world (Le Bon, 1911: 132).

The picture of these madmen of faith is complete. Nothing is missing. Alienation, the hunger for martyrdom, dogmatic conviction and unbreakable will are all there. They are the epitome of the crowd, but differ from it fundamentally in their matchless energy and tenacity, in short by their constancy. Their extraordinary obstinacy and their propensity for going on to the very end could well be the sign of their 'madness', for a sane, normal man prefers to accept those compromises necessary to ensure that he and his own will not perish. But those who draw back from such an impossible mission nevertheless respect things they personally cannot do and admit that they are powerless before the superior strength of the reality they are faced with. Le Bon himself never missed an opportunity to insult the working class, but he showed his respect for leaders by describing them as 'extremely tenacious men who always repeat the same things in the same way and are often ready to sacrifice their personal advantage and their life for the success of an ideal that has taken possession of them' (Le Bon, 1910: 361).

The major quality of the leader, then, must be that of a man of faith, whatever excesses and trickery it may involve. Most individuals are uncertain of their beliefs and have doubts about their ideals. They are anxious not to over-commit themselves and keep a certain distance from them. In the character of the leader, there is no room for any uncertainty or reservation. Half-heartedness, that great virtue of ordinary life, is deadly weakness and fatal self-indulgence for him. His idea is not merely a means, the instrument of his ambition, which he uses as he sees fit. It is a *conviction*, imposed absolutely by historical necessity or the will of God. Everything he does is done to ensure that his doctrine or religion or nation will triumph at whatever cost. From the highest to the lowest, all other men are subject to him and in obeying him are merely doing their duty.

The leader overflows with sectarian fanaticism, and every great leader is a fanatic. He communicates to the masses by contagion, so to speak, and with disconcerting ease. His own unshakeable self-confidence kindles a limitless confidence in others, who see him as knowing where he is going and taking others with him. The sharp brilliance of his unwavering discourse casts its irresistible spell over them, and when he speaks the language of power bathed in the translucent light of faith all those who hear him are conquered. Nietzsche said that the religious man speaks only of himself. That 'himself' includes his idea.

The contrast between the totally committed leader and other men has recently been described perfectly by Furet, the historian of the French Revolution. Speaking of Robespierre, an archetypal leader as far as crowd psychology is concerned, this is what he writes:

Whereas Mirabeau or even Danton, another virtuoso of revolutionary rhetoric, were artists with split personalities, moving on two levels of action, Robespierre was a prophet. He believed all he said, and expressed all he said in the language of the revolution. None of his contemporaries had interiorised as thoroughly as he had all the ideological system of codes associated with the revolutionary phenomenon. This meant that for him there was no gap between the struggle for

power and the struggle for the interests of the people, which by definition must be
one and the same thing.                                                    (Furet, 1978: 85)

Thus there is a fusion of individual destiny and the destiny of the
crowd, of the idea and society and of power and faith. If one is to believe
one of those who observed him most intelligently, Charles de Gaulle had
some of the same characteristics. Jean Daniel maintains that 'No prophet
was ever as certain that he was predestined. No passion was ever as
narcissistic. No lover ever loved himself so much in the object of his love'
(Daniel, 1979: 188). That object of his love, as we all know, was France.

The leader's ever-present ambition and his irresistible need to go
forward show the meaning of a vocation, a mission that will brook no
denial. He carries it out as the subject carries out the orders given by
the voice of the hypnotist and repeats the words that have been put into
his mind. No internal or external hindrance stops him, and it is as if he
was pushed along by some indomitable will, the will of the collectivity
itself.

Here is an instructive comparison. Machiavelli's prince was a lucid and
unprincipled individual who could cunningly calculate respective
strengths and manipulate men. He acted off-stage, in a confined space,
and all his thoughts were secret thoughts full of hidden motives. The
leader hypnotised by an idea or a belief is quite different. He is in
physical, outdoor contact with crowds, and knows nothing of plotting in
the wings, the compromises of the corridors of power or the chicanery
that ruling men entails. But his greatest trick is to do what he says he will
do, to have no hidden thoughts and to follow his own road to the end
when no-one expects him to do so, judging him to be less unreasonable
than he actually is. Once that mistake has been perceived, it is generally
too late to do anything about it. That of course is what happened in
Germany. Everyone thought that Hitler would be the prisoner of the
alliances he had made, would put his fulminations against the Jews, the
socialists and so on away in the attic with all the other props necessary for
taking power and would then be denounced as an impostor before the
assembled masses. However, his obstinacy and his total belief in his
terrible ideas ruined such calculations and nonplussed everyone. The
men behind all the clever machinations were crushed by the simple
machine they had helped to set up. The case of Hitler is not unique in
recent history.

The second characteristic of the leader is shown in the superiority of
courage over intelligence. But how can we define such closely-linked
concepts which, like sanity and madness and strength and weakness, can
after all only be defined in terms of each other? Perhaps we should stick to
commonsense ways of looking at things, to the comfortable vagueness of

'generally accepted' meanings that everyone seems to understand. Let us put forward the following idea. In politics as elsewhere, there are many people capable of analysing a situation, reflecting on a problem and proposing a solution. They can examine all aspects of a question, foresee all the terms of a decision and explain how things will develop. They are first-rate advisers, thorough-going experts and excellent at putting things into operation.

But excellent theory and exact reasoning are nothing without the will to act and draw others along in one's wake, and it is precisely courage that turns what is possible into what is real and reasoning into action. In important matters and at decisive moments courage (and hence charac-ter) is more useful than intelligence and has the last word. It turns the adviser into a leader, as with Pompidou, the general into an emperor, as with Napoleon, and the first among peers into the master of his peers, as with Stalin. Goethe stresses that this quality indicates control of one's will: 'The man who possesses self-control and affirms it is capable of the most difficult and greatest tasks.'

It enables him to brave ridicule by doing what considered reflection would never dare do: to kneel and kiss the soil of a concentration camp, like Willy Brandt, to declare, like John F. Kennedy, 'I am a Berliner.' The question of courage is always a central one in government, where friendly forces are unreliable and hostile ones vicious. In comparison, intelligence seems a handicap rather than an advantage.

On occasion, the leader may be intelligent and highly educated, but the posses-sion of these qualities does him, as a rule, more harm than good. By showing how complex things are, by allowing of explanation and promoting comprehension, intelligence always renders its owner indulgent, and blunts, in a large measure, that intensity and violence of conviction needful for apostles. The great leaders of crowds of all ages, and those of the Revolution in particular, have been of lamentably narrow intellect; while it is precisely those whose intelligence has been the most restricted who have exercised the greatest influence.

(Le Bon, 1952: 194)

That is a constant theme. One never has too much character, which is strength, but one can have too much intelligence, which is weakness, drains courage and dispels the blindness necessary for action. The popular saying 'to understand everything is to forgive everything' lends support to the view, and the idea occurs in Goethe's *Poetry and Truth*, where the leaders of crowds are seen as not always being men of superior intelligence or talent and as rarely recommending themselves by the purity of their hearts. Nevertheless, says Goethe, an extraordinary strength emanates from them, and they exert an incredible power over human beings and even over natural forces, a power whose limits cannot be known. The combined forces of morality are powerless against them, and it is in vain that men of more lucid minds seek to make them suspect by accusing them of deception or self-deception, for the mass of men are drawn towards them.

One can criticise crowd psychology, and Le Bon in particular, for hasty and prejudiced, and indeed for superficial, remarks, but it is striking to find that they are compensated for by more recent accounts of the two most exemplary leaders of our times, Hitler and Stalin. Compared with other leaders of the Russian Communist Party, the great orators such as Zinoviev and Trotsky and great theoreticians such as Bukharin, Stalin seems to have been lacking in character and of mediocre intelligence. His knowledge of history, literature and Marxism was very elementary. His writings were unoriginal and indigestible, revealing a limited mind, and he had no polemical skills. 'In a movement accustomed to the most intense discussion of ideas and steeped in romanticism in which only great revolutionary actions and brilliant excursions into the field of Marxist theory conferred an aura, that was indeed *a priori* a crippling handicap' (Robrieux, *Le Monde*, 22 December 1979).

Not only did Stalin suffer from that particular handicap; his doctors had even declared him to be mentally ill. 'Doctors Pletner and Levine had diagnosed madness and even used the word paranoia' (Robrieux, *Le Monde*, 22 December 1979). Khrushchev made great play with that diagnosis in his well-known report on the cult of personality, confirming it for the very good reason that he had helped produce it. In fact, a brilliant mind and great knowledge were a handicap not for Stalin, who had neither, but for Trotsky, who had both to a marked degree. They made him hesitant at crucial moments and likely to come to compromise agreements and to weigh up things wrongly. Yoffe, one of his supporters, wrote to him before committing suicide, 'But I have always thought that you did not have enough of Lenin in you. He was inflexible and would not give in and could go his own way when he was convinced it was the right one, whereas you have often given way, even when you were right, in order to reach an agreement or a compromise that was not as valuable as you thought.'

We know what the verdict of history was and which of the two was for a long time the sole leader of one of the greatest countries in the world and the Communist movement as a whole. The intellectual and educational poverty of the Nazi dictator, despite his habit of devouring books, has been described by all those who knew, heard or read him. It is difficult to understand how *Mein Kampf*, that mass of preconceived ideas and arid prose, could ever have tempted a publisher and found any readers. Yet many people did read it, or at least bought it and talked about it, and to say that they did so simply out of fear is perhaps rather a superficial answer. But the book does give a picture of the limited intellectual horizon of its author, a man whom Thomas Mann described as an extraordinarily lazy failure, a lifelong inhabitant of an idler's hostel and a rejected little artist and whom others described more soberly as a madman obsessed with a single idea. But it was this madman who was to make an extremely powerful nation out of a country which had produced the greatest minds and the scientific, artistic and technological leaders of the twentieth century and a people which had given the world the most important socialist thinkers. By people I mean also the working-class masses, although they did not provide the bulk of its troops or its voters. These examples provide a good illustration of what Le Bon said of leaders: 'They are not gifted with keen foresight, nor could they be, as this quality is generally conducive to doubt and inactivity' (Le Bon, 1952: 118).

There is no need to exaggerate the characteristics, for a portrait is always more than a model. For crowd psychology, the ideal leader has been recruited from a special group, is the prey of a fixed idea and goes to the furthest limits of his 'madness'. He pulls himself up to the top by sacrificing what a more balanced man in full possession of his faculties would cherish. What good is a major ambition without faith? But it is precisely the leader's strong point that he is the man in whom faith and ambition come closely together. His prerogative is also to have more of the courage that mobilises men than of the intelligence that weakens the will. Where courage is absent, nothing great has ever come about, no thought has become reality, no man has aroused admiration. In reality, the picture is less strongly and simply drawn and there are only individual cases, but the ingredients are always and everywhere the same.

# 4. Charisma

LEADERS HAVE A MISSION, for without them the masses, and indeed the whole human race, can achieve nothing, not even their own survival. Le Bon made this idea his special study and the source of his fame. Not for a moment should we forget that he was no impartial, disinterested scholar and observer. He sought to persuade the elites to accept the need for a clear-cut and visible authority before a strong man was thrust upon them by popular power. He used striking arguments to persuade the bourgeoisie, at more or less the same time that Lenin was trying to persuade the socialists, to create an organisation led by a small monolithic group, for, as the latter said, without a handful of able leaders (and able minds are far from plentiful) experienced, professionally trained and perfected by a long apprenticeship and in perfect mutual agreement, no class in modern society could resolutely lead the struggle (Lenin, 1971: 62).

But Le Bon – and this is the crucial difference – saw the existence of a party or a social movement as the work of a leader. For him, the crowd accepted a single individual and submitted to the magnetic force of his personality, as had been the case with Robespierre, Napoleon and Mahomet. What draws the crowd to such men? What particular characteristic marks the leader off from other men? Certainly not a gift of words, physical strength, intelligence, good looks or youth, for many leaders are entirely without such qualities. They dominate and fascinate despite their unattractive physique, their halting speech and their mediocre intelligence. There must therefore be some sign of election, some peculiar stigmata, that make a man the master of crowds.

The indefinable but effective characteristic of the leader, the quality clearly visible beyond faith and courage, is *charisma*. It is difficult to describe, and Le Bon referred to it as a mysterious power, a kind of spell based on admiration and respect that paralysed the critical faculties. The man who possesses it has an irresistible ascendancy and a natural hold over others. A single word or action is enough to impose obedience and obtain what others could only achieve with a large army on war footing or a fully-staffed bureaucracy. Gandhi needed only to say a few words to an armed and over-excited crowd of millions to calm and disarm it.

This gift is the essential advantage of the leader, and the power it gives him over men can seem demoniac in nature. Goethe saw it as 'efficacious in recent times in Napoleon, perhaps, but in no-one else'. It explains his hold over those around him and his control over shifting opinions. It gives him a kind of radiance and makes his each and every gesture delight his supporters and his each and every word cast a spell over his audience. The crowd is mesmerised, at once terrorised and charmed by his presence and magnetised by his gaze, and swoons and obeys. Like the hypnotist, the leader is a master of the art of using his gaze, and his eyes are the instruments of suggestion. Goethe's eyes, said Heine, were 'as calm as a god's, and it is indeed a sign of a god that his gaze is firm and his eyes do not blink uncertainly'. It was not by chance, he also remarked, that in that respect Napoleon and Goethe were equals. 'Napoleon's eyes also had the same quality, and that is why I am convinced that he was a god.'

In the hypnotist, charisma would be the power of inducing hypnosis, the ability to make the crowd receive his suggestions and to dictate to it his will and his fixed ideas. He can make it do what it had no desire to do and did not contemplate doing. He can make it stop or go, destroy or fight, and he can do all this, remember, empty-handed and with no visible external help. He relies on no physical repression, either from himself or from an ally, like de Gaulle faced with the rebellion of the bewildered soldiers in Algeria.

Le Bon himself did not hide the attraction he felt for Robespierre who, despite his sorry gifts as an orator, dominated the assemblies and set them a-tremble with his charm, passion and energy. 'I would willingly suppose in him the existence of a species of personal fascination which escapes us today. His success with women might be quoted in support of this theory' (Le Bon, 1980: 240). (Once more, comparison is used rather than reasoning: Robespierre charmed women and therefore charmed crowds, which are like women!)

But what aroused Le Bon's unalloyed admiration was Napoleon's return from Elba. Alone and defeated, with no allies and no means at his disposal, a man lands with a handful of faithful supporters in a country in which peace has been restored and the king has gained the support of a good part of the middle classes, the police and the army. All he needs to do to make everyone yield to him is to show himself, let himself be seen and heard. 'In the face of his imposing presence, the king's cannons were silent and his armies vanished' (Le Bon, 1910: 199).

There is a recognisable echo there of Chateaubriand's admirable description of that return, with the population stupefied, the police nowhere to be seen and a vacuum around that gigantic shadow:

His fascinated enemies sought but did not find him. He was hidden in his glory like the lion of the Sahara who cannot be seen in the sunlight by his dazzled pursuers. Enveloped in a burning whirlwind, the bloody ghosts of Arcole, Marengo, Austerlitz, Jena, Friedland, Eylau, Muscovy, Lutzen and Bauten formed a procession of millions of dead. From the heart of that column of cloud and fire there issued, as he approached each town, a few trumpet blasts and tricolour standards, and the gates of those towns fell open. When Napoleon crossed the Niemen at the head of four hundred thousand foot and two hundred thousand horse to destroy the palace of the tsars in Moscow, he was a less amazing figure than when, breaking his exile and throwing his chains in the face of kings, he came alone from Cannes to Paris and spent a peaceful night at the Tuileries.

Certain men, then, are surrounded by a charismatic aura. They have no need of a show of force to make men accept them or to make crowds bow down and follow them. The power to arouse admiration is widespread at all levels of society, but we only dare to recognise it in exceptional cases.

## II

Two qualities of the leader, his compelling conviction and his tenacious courage, blend inextricably together to create his charisma, or 'prestige' as it was originally called in French, before German and American thought began to use the Greek term. In the political sense, the two words are more or less synonymous. In the field of crowd psychology, prestige is the precondition for any power, whereas charisma, seen in a historical perspective, indicates a particular form of it.

We can distinguish between 'prestige' and 'charisma' on the basis of the origin of the two qualities. The former can be seen as deriving from a function or an office, the latter as coming from the person. Belonging to a particular class or holding certain titles (professor, doctor, baron and so on) confers on a person a share of the prestige that is traditionally attached to them, even if the person has no personal value or any talent of his own. The company director at his desk, the air hostess in an attractive uniform, the judge in his brocaded robes and the officer with a chestful of medals are immediately marked out from the common run of people and command respect. This is prestige.

Charisma, on the other hand, has nothing to do with any external sign of authority or rank. It emanates wholly from the person who, as soon as he talks or acts, or perhaps simply by the way he looks, charms, captivates and suggests. As de Gaulle wrote, prestige, which is an affective fact, suggestion and an impression produced, depends primarily on an imponderable elementary gift and natural aptitude. The fact is that from birth some men as it were exude a kind of mysterious authority that surprises those around them as they succumb to its effects. Like love, it can only be explained in terms of inexplicable charm (De Gaulle, 1944: 66).

The respective importance of both qualities changes. In the stable and highly hierarchical societies of the past in which rank, title and so on were important, the prestige of function or office was dominant. Everyone literally bowed down before an aristocratic surname, a military or ecclesiastical rank, a decoration and a uniform. In our permanently changing and unbalanced societies all that has changed. It is only personal charisma that can effectively influence the masses. Following the crowd psychologists, de Gaulle also noted the new phenomenon, pointing out that it originated from individual worth and the ascendancy enjoyed by certain men. Everything the masses once attributed to function or birth they now attribute exclusively to those who have managed to impose their will. No legitimate prince was ever obeyed, he maintained, like the dictators we have seen whose only origin is their boldness (De Gaulle, 1944: 65).

In a mass society, one can conclude, the charisma of the leader is almost the only trump card in the game of holding power, the only way he has of influencing the crowd. It is charisma that gives him the power to raise them, shake them, inspire them with fanaticism or to impose a discipline on them. Take that away, and all that is left is government by the police or the administration, by arms or by the computer. When it goes, there is nothing but blood or deadly greyness. And indeed impotence as a principle of government is typical of many of the 'strong' regimes that now cover the face of the earth.

## III

Charisma is essentially a gift. It might be seen as a talent received as part of an inheritance, with other people inheriting a talent for painting, singing or gardening. But a gift is not an inheritance to be shared out as the testator sees fit. It has to be worked on, disciplined and made use of until it becomes a true, useful and useable social ability. As de Gaulle goes on to say, some elements of prestige vary from one individual to another, are absolutely innate and cannot be acquired. But there are certain constant and necessary elements which can be acquired, or at least developed. The leader, like the artist, needs both the gift and the cunning of his craft (De Gaulle, 1944: 67).

The job involves one or two simple rules. The main elements of the discipline a leader must impose on himself are physical fitness, a precise and commanding way of speaking, simplicity of judgement and quickness in making decisions. Where crowds are concerned, there is also the ability to capture and command feelings, a glamorous manner, a gift for the telling phrase and a taste for theatrical settings, all of which set out to inflame the imagination. If they are applied with discernment, such rules arouse the desire to imitate and heighten that admiration without which there is no commanding and – above all – no obeying.

In addition, charisma thus understood only operates if the leader, like the magician and the hypnotist, can keep a certain distance and surround himself with a cloak of mystery and turns his very attitude into one of the factors leading to his success. The distance between him and the crowd arouses a kind of respect and a submissive demeanour. He is put on a pedestal and so cannot be examined or judged. Even when he represents socialist power he takes care to avoid any familiarity. A former companion of the leader of the Yugoslav Communist Party writes that Tito 'carefully protected his reputation. He kept a distance between himself and his closest comrades, even at those moments of high emotion in wartime, when either death or victory was close' (M. Djilas, *Le Monde*, 6 May 1980).

This desire for distance can be seen as a determination on the part of a leader who himself comes from the crowd to break with his past. By separating himself from his former companions, he changes a relationship involving reciprocity and equality into one involving domination and inequality. Once he has become master, a Napoleon or a Stalin no longer has friends. There are only subordinates or rivals, and the change is marked by the unbridgeable gap he has created. Without it, he would not be free to make the decisions he has to make or to command as he sees fit. One day, Napoleon told his biographer Las Cases that he had been obliged to create an aura of fear. Otherwise, coming as he did from the masses, a lot of people would either have taken no notice of him or been over-familiar.

The loneliness of power no doubt stems from such breaks and the consequent rejection of reciprocity in a world in which there are no longer any equals. There is room at the top for one person only. The loneliness also serves to enhance his position and create around him an atmosphere of mystery that sustains all kinds of illusions and means that the masses can ascribe every desired quality to him. The leader is obliged to play up to this love of mystery and this curiosity about his intentions, especially at times of crisis. De Gaulle made this a rule, insisting that there can be no prestige without mystery, for familiarity breeds contempt (De Gaulle, 1944: 67). No man, as we know, is a hero to his valet.

The curtain of mystery hiding the leader always has a few symbolic pictures on it, like the curtain in a theatre with its pattern of masks and dramatic scenes. These present him in a flattering light. His physique, his person and his life are all shielded from the public gaze by a skilfully contrived ignorance of his preferences, his real decisions, his feelings and his illnesses – Wilson on the brink of madness and Pompidou on the brink of death still continued to govern the United States and France respectively – ignorance of, indeed, the man as he really is. Because they are so coherent and deceptive, the images which are spread in this way encourage fear and stifle any discussion at birth. That is the *sine qua non* of any charisma, for in Le Bon's view any charisma that was questioned was no longer charisma. Those gods and men who had managed to retain it for any length of time had never tolerated any discussion (Le Bon, 1952: 140).

It is of course in that sense that the symbolic images I have mentioned are useful. For leaders, they serve to turn the attention of the crowd away from reality and make them feel that they themselves are what is lacking. The mystery shrouding their actions and their decisions raises them above ordinary mortals, and this enables them to work out and stage-manage the illusions they will produce, even the setting for their own end. The faith of the crowd broods on the mystery and embellishes the desired image. Reality can make no impact on a mass of people mesmerised by an illusion, and both masses and leaders work in permanent and perfect unison to produce a world of appearances, the holy of holies of their shared belief. The need for hope does the rest. Le Bon maintained that a characteristic feature of charisma was to hide reality and paralyse judgement. Crowds always and individuals very frequently needed ready-made opinions (Le Bon, 1963: 82).

This amounts to saying that charisma essentially depends on a shared illusion. We are caught up in it as in one created by a magician. We know that it is all a trick, but believe in the magic and allow ourselves to be captivated by it.

It is also true that the only leaders who keep their charisma intact and go on attracting the unlimited admiration of the crowd are dead ones. When they are alive, they are venerated and execrated, loved and hated: venerated because they have the courage to lead the crowd, execrated because the crowd allows itself to be led by them. But there is no restriction on the cult of the dead, who are simply at one with collective ideas and illusions. They are gods, in short, and that is why a dead leader is more dangerous than a living one. It is impossible either to rule in his shadow indefinitely or to demolish his legend and assume divinity without seriously disturbing the crowd itself.[1] I hope to be able to discuss these complex matters more fully later, however, and for the moment I shall conclude by quoting an observation which is still as valid as it was a hundred years ago. Perhaps it is crude, but it is hard to refute:

To-day the majority of the great men who have swayed men's minds no longer have altars, but they have statues, or their portraits are in the hands of their admirers, and the cult of which they are the object is not notably different from that accorded to their predecessors. An understanding of the philosophy of history is only to be got by a thorough appreciation of this fundamental point of the psychology of crowds. The crowd demands a god before everything else.[2]

(Le Bon, 1952: 75)

## IV

But personal charisma, which is an entirely individual phenomenon, is at a distinct disadvantage in comparison with the prestige conferred by office or function, for it lacks legitimacy, a quality which comes with heredity, fortune or election and does not depend on the individual. Charisma is acquired the hard way, and a gift is needed. It lasts as long as the gift is effective, depends on the favour of the masses and can be rescinded at any time. The President of France, a king, a general or a professor have tenure, so to speak. Moses or Napoleon, a military leader like Trotsky or the leader of a movement like Freud are leaders for just as long as their genius allows them to inspire their troops or their followers. The only thing that maintains a leader's charisma and strengthens the devotion of the faithful is success, the proof that his power is active and just as effective as it originally was. Moses needed his tablets of stone, Christ his miracles and Napoleon his victorious campaigns to keep the ascendancy they had achieved with such difficulty and swell the confidence of the crowds.

The latter explained this in his memoirs. 'Situated thus, without the hereditary authority of ancient tradition, deprived of the standing conferred by what men call legitimacy, I could not brook a summons to a tourney. I had to be peremptory, imperious and decisive.' Unlike the legitimate heir, the man brought to power by the favour of the masses is, from the point of view of authority, a *usurper* and is felt to be such. He therefore tries to wipe out that inconvenient image, either by eliminating all the representatives of legitimate power – and history is full of 'wars of succession' – or by assuming all the external trappings of legitimacy: a royal court or followers, flags or insignia. It was probably to legitimise his authority that the de Gaulle of 18 June 1940 kept the title of General throughout his life, wishing to show that France had called upon him in the hour of danger. And it was no doubt for the same reasons that Tito, who had come to the top in similar circumstances, kept up the appearances and rituals that recalled the former traditions of the Austro-Hungarian emperors and the Serbian kings and maintained so scrupulously everything that had appertained to the crown, at the same time increasing its stock.

Leaders of this kind achieve power with no dynastic obligations or debts to anyone, and no-one can say of them that they are what they are by virtue of their ancestors and their wealth. They are self-made men and not links in a chain, and de Gaulle made the definitive statement when he said that he had neither predecessor nor successor. This gives them an extraordinary and almost unlimited power. But one usurper can easily depose another, and from this stems their supreme weakness, the need to fascinate the crowd the whole time, to prove by means of miracles or victories that their charisma is not affected, like an athlete constantly struggling to break his own record. Napoleon frequently admitted this: 'If there was a fault in my person or position, it was that I had suddenly emerged from the crowd. I was aware of my isolation, and so cast out anchors into the sea on all sides.' They were only effective, however, when he achieved victories.

Thus, since the charisma of the leaders of the masses cannot be based on the laws of succession, it is based on those of success. Their authority will only last for as long as they are successful. If their forecasts go wrong or their actions fail, their authority declines at once, since it has no other support or justification. The leader, like the matador in the sunlit arenas of Spain, must win or die.

It is as if his mysterious gift is exhausted and has lost its magic power. In Le Bon's words:

The proof that success is one of the principal stepping-stones to prestige is that the disappearance of the one is almost always followed by the disappearance of the other. The hero whom the crowd acclaimed yesterday is insulted to-day should he have been overtaken by failure. The reaction, indeed, will be the stronger in proportion as the prestige has been great. The crowd in this case considers the fallen hero as an equal, and takes its revenge for having bowed to a superiority whose existence it no longer admits. While Robespierre was causing the execution of his colleagues and of a great number of his contemporaries, he possessed an immense prestige. When the transposition of a few votes deprived him of power, he immediately lost his prestige, and the crowd followed him to the guillotine with the self-same imprecations with which shortly before it had pursued his victims. Believers always break the statues of their former gods with every symptom of fury. (Le Bon, 1952: 139–40)

The exception has become the rule. In the age of the crowd a leader, even one elected by an overwhelming majority, is by definition a usurper. This fact determines the nature of his charisma and his power, the qualities of his composite type with which we are now so familiar. Let us recapitulate the essential ingredients of the mix that creates the all-important admiring crowd on which everything depends – the gifts of the hypnotist, the model of the prophet and the emperor, Napoleon from the front and Robespierre from the back. But there is one reassuring thing:

the fact that a type exists does not mean that all leaders are identical or all political regimes similar. It is not a matter of indifference whether one lives in a country governed by a Mussolini or a de Gaulle, a Salazar or a Roosevelt, a Pol Pot or a Castro. Individual differences, however, do not stop them belonging to the same species.

# 5. *The strategies of propaganda and mass suggestion*

WHAT WE ARE TRYING TO ESTABLISH HERE is a theory of leaders and masses, and hence of politics as a whole, in terms of crowd psychology. The analyses we have conducted so far have already brought out the major part played by mass suggestion, or propaganda, as a way in which the former act on the latter. It is much more than merely a form of communication or persuasion directed from the minority at the top towards the majority at the bottom. The programmes or ideas of a man or a party are determined by external economic and historical factors and by class and national interests, but the method of expressing them in action and transforming them into universal beliefs indicates the kind of relationship existing between leaders and masses, and it alone is decisive.

Charisma, which creates and determines these relationships, presupposes a *policy* of charisma. How can the leader set about bringing it into operation and making sure of his ascendancy over the masses? Force and reason are ruled out from the start.

Force ensures physical control and makes it possible to suppress opposition forces. It also guarantees an external submission based on fear. It does not, however, affect hearts and minds and can only command exterior assent. The masses do not give the leader the close attachment and veneration that he needs if he is to draw them with him, and without these he is merely a hated tyrant.

Can he, then, try to persuade them by plausible arguments, discussion or irrefutable proof? The masses are impervious to reason and any discussion will be the end of confidence in the leader's authority. They do not want to know the truth, which is fortunate for him, since his charisma is based on secrets and illusion. Only theoreticians ignorant of crowd psychology can, in Le Bon's view, believe that reason changes men and rules the world. It certainly produces the ideas which will one day transform it, but on a day-to-day basis in the near future its effect will remain minimal.

Force cannot be used and reason is useless, but there is a third way open to the real leader, that of charm. 'The popular orator and the timorous politician can do no more than slavishly flatter the crowd and blindly accept its will. The real leader first charms it, and the charmed being, whether crowd or woman, then has only a single opinion and will, those of the seducer' (Le Bon, 1910: 137).

Charisma seduces, and the leader is a seducer. Those few words sum up the policy he is obliged to adopt towards the crowd. It is the very basis of what the mesmerist or hypnotist does when he arranges the setting in which he sees his patients, sets the ritual of the session in motion, takes charge of physical contact, looks at the subject in certain ways and pronounces certain set phrases, all in order to encourage attachment to himself and a corresponding relaxation of the will and consciousness. As soon as the spell begins to take effect, the patient falls into a somnambulistic state. The cure, if cure there be, is effected by means of that attachment and relaxation and the illusion of love which they often produce.

The leader too uses the method of arranging appearances and replaces truth with likelihood. He holds the crowd at a distance, removing its gaze from reality and showing it a better and more beautiful reality more in line with its hopes. His talent lies in transforming events and collective aims into striking and exalting images. In his presence, the everyday becomes exceptional, and he always has this in mind. A Napoleon or a Caesar, in the midst of the din of battle, always thinks of the spectacle he is offering and the phrase that can fix it in everyone's mind forever. The former's famous phrase, 'Soldiers, from the summit of these pyramids forty centuries of history are contemplating you', gave an eternal dimension to the presence of the French armies in Egypt.

The Greek philosopher Gorgias taught that by the logic of charm (it has still not been studied in politics!) language became 'a powerful sovereign which, with a tiny and completely invisible body, completes profoundly divine works'. Historic words, incisive phrases and exemplary acts certainly have their own reality, but they were carefully thought out and their effects calculated and pronounced in the appropriate setting, being deceptively frank in order to inflame belief (like de Gaulle's closing words in his speech in French Canada, 'Vive le Québec libre!') and bind the loyalty of the masses.

The leader's charm, like any other kind of charm, does not set out to remain hidden. It shows itself openly and uses all its tricks in the full view of all. The illusion is then so complete that it acquires the strength of reality. Like an artist's work, it is admired when it succeeds, but if it falls short of success, by however little, people feel that they have been made a laughing-stock. Woe to him who rends the well-woven veil of mass illusions, for the crowd may well turn on him and spare the man who has charmed them. More than one politician, from Brutus to Mendès-France, has had that bitter experience and paid for it by his disgrace.

The leader who charms transports the crowd from a world of reason to one of imagination, where all-powerful ideas and words release a spate of memories and inspire strong feelings. You may be disappointed or worried to learn that leaders inflame masses simply by using snares and delusions that turn every genuine social relationship into a bogus one. But Le Bon was not prone to bewailing human nature. The physician of power laid bare its anatomy and described its physiology. Once he had discovered its laws, they were as binding for him as those of physical matter for the engineer. This feeling dominated the laws of the crowd. They called for illusion, and the leader acted through illusion, which was more necessary than reason. This is how Le Bon puts it:

Rational logic governs the area of the conscious, in which the interpretations of our actions are formed. It is emotional logic that creates our beliefs, which are what shapes the conduct of individuals and peoples.          (Le Bon, 1910: 21)

It should not be assumed from this that leaders are deceivers, hypocrites or pretenders; they are not, any more than hypnotists are. But they are the victims of a fixed idea and are ready to give it and themselves all the appearances that will ensure success. Hence that strange air of being sincere and false at one and the same time, which made Talleyrand say of Napoleon that he was a devil who laughed at everybody, simultaneously miming his passions for us and experiencing them.

A leader has to be as spontaneous as an actor. He comes out of his own mind and enters that of the public. He is moved with the crowd in order to persuade it better. He throbs with the masses, brings back their memories, illuminates their ideals and feels what they feel before he turns them round and tries to make them accept his views. Le Bon admitted that 'I will go further than positive science allows and say that souls that know nothing of the charmer and the charmed, of the leader and the led, are penetrated by a mysterious mechanism' (Le Bon, 1910: 139). The mechanism he meant was identification. Crowd psychology was to discover it later, based on the same phenomenon.

## II

We now come to the strategies of propaganda, which are aimed at turning individuals into a crowd and drawing them towards some specific action. The method leaders (or indeed parties) adopt will be different in each individual case, since the desired results are concrete and specific, but they all make use of three main strategies, which are representation, ceremonial and persuasion. The first operates spatially, the second temporally and the third linguistically. Let us consider them in turn.

If they are to assemble and act, crowds need space, which is given a shape and contours by the representational use it is put to. Places are created to receive the masses – cathedrals and stadiums, for example – and to have the desired effect on them. A haven is created where individuals can escape from everyday life together and be united by their common stock of hopes and beliefs. Each individual is closely linked to all the others and feels stronger and more sure of himself since he is reinforced by the mass. The representational use of space in stadiums, avenues and esplanades suits open masses, spread out in a procession like a human carpet or arranged like flowerbeds. Palaces, cathedrals or theatres are better for closed masses that are more inward-looking. As we know, squares have been adapted and buildings constructed specially to take large numbers of people and to be suitable for magnificent ceremonies, that is, to enable the crowd to celebrate itself by assembling around its leader. Monuments, and Fascist ones in particular, are ostensibly built to commemorate a glorious victory or a triumph of the people, but are really a form of homage to a leader. A famous Parisian example, of course, is the Place de l'Etoile, which above all else perpetuates the memory of Napoleon.

Others are veritable political and historical theatres. Those who have been there say that Red Square in Moscow is one of the most impressive and elaborate. It is in the centre of the city, with the Kremlin, the former religious heart of Russia where the tsars were crowned and now the seat of Soviet power, surmounted by the Red Star, marking off one side of it. Lying in his marble mausoleum guarded by soldiers, Lenin gives it the solemn atmosphere of a part of the Revolution caught and fixed for all future ages. In niches in the wall lie the illustrious dead who protect the square and form a link between the living mass outside and the supreme hierarchy enclosed within. The area is a synopsis of history and offers a whole concept of the assembly of the people.

At certain times, and particularly in the evenings, such animated places create a psychological state of communion and of waiting for one particular man. There is a keen and exalting sense of the exceptional, and everyone is eager to be part of what is taking place. The grandiose, when it is present, restores the order of things, for the leader is above the crowd. He is alone, but visible to everyone; the crowd is legion, but invisible despite its size. He has a name, which is shouted by all those assembled; it is anonymous. The crowd is hidden in its huge numbers, the leader parades his solitude. Even before he has arrived, before the first word has been spoken, everyone seems to be totally a part of the crowd and every eye is fixed on one particular point. No-one is there yet, but it is marked out by the likeness of the man who is to occupy it.

## III

Ceremonial turns a meeting into a *missa hypnotica* during which the leader makes full use of his charisma. The various elements come together in a veritable festival of symbols. The meeting of the leader and the crowd and its attachment to him and the idea he incarnates (the nation, the army, socialism and so on) are celebrated by flags, allegories, images and singing. Each symbol and the order of its entrance are directed towards renewing and stimulating the emotions, towards heightening the atmosphere, as the phrase has it, and they bring the process of blending the mass together to its peak. Everyone has to take part, either in the parade or by singing or shouting slogans. It is a necessary condition if there is to be a movement to action.

Demonstrations, military parades, protest meetings and political meetings which precede any crowd mobilisation also show that if there are no symbols to respect or overthrow, there are no living masses or indeed any masses at all. This can be seen during revolutionary uprisings, when the masses kill the prince after they have first burnt an effigy of him as a symbol and repository of oppression. Or they might attack the banks, the temples of money, or police stations, the centres of repression, and so on. Prison doors are smashed in, like those of the Bastille, the symbol of that arbitrary royal power which could lock someone away for life on the basis of a mere *lettre de cachet*.

Such actions may seem pointless or absurd, and there is always some opportunity to ridicule the stupidity of the crowd. Perhaps it is always pointless and absurd to attack a symbol when the real power is elsewhere. But symbols are of supreme use in that in acting thus the mass takes cognisance of itself and commits itself in front of its leader. However irrational he finds their acts, he for his part is forced to take charge if he wants to retain his authority and be master of events. As Le Bon points out, 'It is not from the rational but from the irrational part of our nature that great events are born. The rational part creates science, the irrational produces history' (Le Bon, 1910: 141).

As the ceremonies progress, they make the entry of individual cells into the mass, the getting under way of large-scale unconscious psychic movements and their functioning together in unison. Just as the shining object in the hypnotist's hand ensures that the subject will move from the waking to the sleeping state, so the festival of symbols prepares individuals for their new destiny. Then it is the turn of music to play the major role, maintaining a trance

rather as an electric current will keep the same vibration as a tuning fork if it is set at the same frequency. Here, however, the agreement is not simply at the physical and motor level. It is also, and to a higher degree, of a psychological order, for its essential feature consists, as it were, of putting into phase the individual who lives out his transitory identity and the crowd that sees it in him or imposes it on him. (Rouget, 1980: 441)

At the same time, the movements of the crowd are being orchestrated. One group after another, each with its own character and distinctive signs, moves to the appointed place. An example is the May Day celebrations at the site of the Bastille, when every human line converges on the stage at the edge of the circus which encloses them all in a network of common memories.

This mass choreography and the music that goes with it and greets the arrival of each group (a delegation from a particular town, a trades union, a party or an individual personality) approaches a peak. At the psychological moment, the leader, who represents them all, appears. This is the crowning point of the ceremony, and various music-hall tunes stimulate the crowd and put it in a frame of mind to welcome the star for whom it has turned out and to be *his* audience. This gradual raising of the psychic temperature also weakens conscious control and the critical sense and gradually brings to the fore automatic thinking and the forces of the unconscious. The crowd is ready to listen to what is said to it and to do what is demanded of it. It is the primary moment of suggestion and hence of seduction. The individual has broken his ties with external society and the only society he has is that of the mass around him. There is a universal communion of simple and strong emotions, and everyone is plunged into a state of the kind Stendhal described:

There was a *Te Deum*, clouds of incense, an endless firing of musketry and artillery and the peasants were drunk with happiness and piety. A day like that undoes all the work of a hundred issues of the Jacobin newspapers. (Stendhal, 1952: I, 317)

Such ceremonies are a kind of mass in which the leader is both the celebrant and the god, but they are hypnotic and not religious in inspiration. To the sceptical mind, the distance between them is not so great. They are indeed mass hypnosis sessions of the kind Le Bon dreamed about. Regarding totalitarian propaganda, the German philosopher Adorno has said that its format is that of the visible leader addressing the masses, based on the model of the hypnotist and his subject (Adorno, in Roheim (ed.) 1951: III, 279–300).

## IV

Once the scene has been set and the mass gathered together and plunged into a state of collective hypnosis, the centre of all attention is the person of the leader. His gaze holds them fascinated, in that mixture of attraction and fear that the ancients attributed to the eyes of demigods, certain animals such as serpents or basilisks, or monsters like the Gorgon. Once the mass has been subjugated, it is more receptive to words, which become the main vehicle for fascination. Everything depends on the leader's intention: he can refer the mass to its own desires, dictate a clear solution to complex problems and, his supreme achievement, address the crowd as if he were speaking to each member of it individually and in confidence. Le Bon saw language as the great lever of power. 'Words and formulas are the great creators of opinions and beliefs. They are powerful forces and have killed more men than cannons have' (Le Bon, 1911: 232). And, unlikely as it may seem, his disciple Hitler followed him, writing in *Mein Kampf*: 'The force that started off the great historical avalanches in the political or religious fields was from time immemorial no more than the magical power of the spoken word. The great mass of a given people always submits to the power of words.' This he proved himself on many occasions, as did his exact opposite, Gandhi, who used words as the most effective means of bringing peace to men's minds and fighting violence.

What changes ordinary words into fascinating ones? Certainly the charisma of the man uttering them before the crowd. How effective they are depends on the precision and imperiousness of the images evoked. 'The multitudes are never impressed by the logic of a speech, but they are by the emotional images that certain words and associations of words create' (Le Bon, 1910: 122). 'They are uttered with solemnity in the presence of crowds, and as soon as they have been pronounced an expression of respect is visible on every countenance, and all heads are bowed. By many they are considered as natural forces, as supernatural powers' (Le Bon, 1952: 103).

We need only think of certain slogans ('Liberty or death!', 'Long live France!') or of the magical powers that primitive peoples ascribe to formulas or names. They all have the mobilising power of images and memories. Crowd psychology puts a trust in language which is almost as unlimited as that which the Christian puts in the divine word, believing firmly that if it is used appropriately it can persuade men to believe what we believe and do what we want them to do. The grammar of persuasion is based on affirmation and repetition, its two sovereign rules.

The basic condition for any propaganda is that a unilateral position or a dominant idea should be clearly presented in a way that brooks no retort.

Its informational content may well be slender, and it could even be said that a public speech does not need to contain anything that those hearing it do not know already. As there is a kind of complicity or even identity between the crowd and the leader, which puts both on the same level, the latter must not try to play the teacher or show any kind of pedantic superiority.

In fact it is better not to innovate as far as content is concerned. With regard to the style of the speech or harangue, however, constant innovation and surprise are necessary. The phrases used have to be pithy and striking, like Cæsar's 'I came, I saw, I conquered', or, from a time nearer our own, 'France has lost a battle, but she has not lost the war'. De Gaulle's appeal of 18 June 1940 impelled his confused and helpless compatriots to action.

The lassitude of crowds and the erosion of words by long usage must constantly be taken into account, for over a period of time the latter acquire a rather well-worn look, and ones like 'liberty', 'equality', 'fraternity', 'revolution' or 'internationalism' may seem very threadbare. At times of danger, in a different context, they sound quite different. We mechanically repeat the words of the *Marseillaise*, but when the enemy is at our frontiers, '*Aux armes, citoyens!*' rings out like a bugle-call and becomes once again an image from the past we share. A call like that, minimal in content but imperative in form, can say everything with no need for logic or truth.

Affirmation generally reflects a clear-cut attitude, making a distinction between the strongly-held view the orator is defending and the opponent he is attacking. When a politician says that the rich are in power or calls for action rather than a wait-and-see attitude, he is expressing clear left-wing views and cursing the right. Every affirmation must also follow others, be based on them and confirm them. The human mind tends that way, as Bacon maintained in the *Novum Organum*, pointing out that once a proposition has been uttered, either as a result of a consensus or a general belief or because of the pleasure it procures, our intellect forces all others to bring fresh support and confirmation.

The more concise and positive its form, the more authoritative an affirmation is, since it seems to offer proof of the conviction and rightness of the person making it. Goethe expected this of anyone talking to him: 'If I have to listen to the opinions of others, they must be expressed in a positive form. I have enough problematical elements within myself.' Assertion demands the short and commanding tone of the hypnotist giving an order to the subject, and one that he is not free to contradict. It must be 'brief, energetic and impressive' (Le Bon, 1911: 194).

In a speech, to affirm means to refuse all argument, for a man or an idea open to argument loses all credibility. It also means that the audience, the crowd, is expected to accept the idea unthinkingly, to take it as it is without weighing up the pros and cons, to answer 'yes' without reflecting. There is the example of Goebbels at a rally after the defeat at Stalingrad:

'Do you believe with the Führer and us in the total victory of the German nation?'
Response from the body of the hall: 'Yes!'
'Do you want total war?'
(Ditto): 'Yes!'
'Do you want the war to become, if necessary, more total and radical than we can imagine at present?'
(Ditto): 'Yes!'

Such pseudo-questions are of course affirmations. They guide the mind of the crowd in a single direction. The pseudo-replies merely reaffirm what the orator says, since repetition is the strongest form of affirmation.

The magical effects of approved and repeated formulas and words come into operation and spread by contagion with the speed of an electric current. The crowds are magnetised. The words used evoke precise images of fire or blood, uplifting or bitter memories of victory or defeat and strong feelings of hatred or love. The following fragment of one of Ayatollah Khomeini's speeches gives a precise idea of the power of language in action:

You who are disinherited, stand up for yourselves! Israel has occupied Jerusalem, and this very day Israel and the United States have plotted to occupy the Al Karam and Al Nabil mosques. . . . Stand up and defend Islam, for it is our duty to do so. Put your trust in the Almighty and go forward! Victory is at hand! Victory is certain! (*Le Figaro*, 25 November 1979)

By using short sentences and referring to the sacred places that everyone has seen or heard of and by naming the enemies alleged to have desecrated them, the orator paints a picture that each of his listeners can easily see in his mind's eye – dark and diabolical forces are invading the sacred mosques. He explains briefly why fighting is necessary, calls upon everyone to come forward for battle and assures the people of victory.

Repetition is thus the second condition for propaganda, giving a greater weight of conviction to affirmations and transforming them into true reflex obsessions. They are heard time and time again in diverse forms and connected with the most varied subjects and are finally totally absorbed. They are unconsciously repeated and become a kind of linguistic and mental tic. At the same time, repetition erects a prohibition against any contrary belief or affirmation by irrevocably changing the words, images and positions in question. They thus acquire a weight and an obviousness which mean that they have to be accepted *in toto* and serially, like a chain of reasoning that finally proves what it set out to prove.

Once we have appreciated that fact, it is no longer surprising that the speeches of a dictator like Stalin or Hitler are so self-repetitive. The orator simply keeps churning out the usual themes, scarcely bothering to change the way they are expressed. The very repetitiveness shows how totally convinced he is and to some extent 'proves' his obsessive faith. All leaders, Le Bon observes, are 'generally very limited but highly tenacious men, who repeat the same things in the same way but are often willing to sacrifice their personal advantage and their lives to ensure the success of the ideal that dominates them' (Le Bon, 1910: 361).

Repetition has a twofold function, for it is both an obsession and a barrier to divergent or contrary opinions. It thus minimises the part played by reasoning and rapidly changes an idea into an action to which the mass has been conditioned like Pavlov's famous dogs.

This rapidity made Napoleon say that repetition was the only effective form of reasoning, and Le Bon, who admired Bonaparte, considering him and Robespierre as outstanding manipulators of the crowd, saw the process as of crucial importance in the psychology of persuasion:

This power is due to the fact that the repeated statement is embedded in the long-run in those profound regions of our unconscious selves in which the motives of our actions are forged.

He adds, however, this extremely subtle observation:

At the end of a certain time we have forgotten who is the author of the repeated assertion, and we finish by believing it. To this circumstance is due the astonishing power of advertisements. When we have read a hundred, a thousand, times that X's chocolate is the best, we imagine we have heard it said in many quarters, and we end by acquiring the certitude that such is the fact.   (Le Bon, 1952: 125)

This perception was confirmed by wartime research on propaganda.

By frequent repetition, slogans and formulas become independent of the person of the leader and acquire their own life and autonomous reality, like a prayer or an incantation. They burrow into the unconscious and become part of collective belief. This is strengthened by the fact that the crowd is often called upon to respond to the leader in the manner of a congregation responding to the celebrant at mass. The words are declaimed, then repeated in unison by the crowd of thousands like a huge echo. This repetition separates the idea from its source and transforms it into a self-evident truth independent of time, place or person. It is no longer an expression of the speaker, but of what is spoken. Repeat,

repeat, and something will remain, even if it is only a whisper. And whispers, like slanders and prejudice, are a force.

Repetition also serves to make ideas coherent. By the frequent association of declarations and scattered ideas it creates the appearance of logical connection and the sense that behind the phrases and the frequent conjunction of irreconcilable ideas there is some sort of system. If unusual collocations of words such as revolution and religion, nationalism and socialism, Marxism and Christianity, Jews and Communists are repeated often enough, the audience is surprised (or at least this used to be the case). But you are also convincing your listeners that the two ideas go together and that their juxtaposition has a hidden meaning. Human nature is attracted and fascinated by a unified representation of the world around it. Discussing totalitarian propaganda, Hannah Arendt justly notes that:

What convinces masses are not facts, and not even invented facts, but only the consistency of the system of which they are presumably part. Repetition, somewhat overrated in importance because of the common belief in the masses' inferior capacity to grasp and remember, is important only because it convinces them of consistency in time.                    (Arendt, 1967: 341)

She is wrong about one thing at least. The masses are capable of remembering. In one sense, they remember too much.


## V

The result of affirmation and repetition is mass suggestion. They come together in a current of beliefs that spreads with the speed of an epidemic. The contagion is even more rapid when the more powerful emotions have been roused and reflection has been short-circuited by action.

Le Bon sums up the matter in these terms:

Ideas do not compel us because they are correct but only because by means of the twofold mechanism of repetition and contagion, they have taken over those unconscious regions where the motives that create our behaviour are shaped. We do not persuade people by simply showing that arguments are correct, but by making them act in terms of them.                    (Le Bon, 1911: 22)

What is in many ways striking, and little understood, is the importance of words in crowd psychology. They receive power not from what they say but rather from their 'magic', from the man who utters them and the atmosphere that carries them. They are like embryonic images, the germs of ideas, almost like living beings rather than particles of discourse in the way they must be treated. An orator who evokes no memory evokes no response. When words exert their fascination, the crowd succumbs to the power of the things they evoke and the actions they demand and obeys the leader who has fascinated it. He offers grandiose but vague prospects, and the very vagueness which shrouds them increases their mysterious hold.

Many modern – and ancient – books have something to say about each of the three strategies of representation, ceremonial and persuasion, but crowd psychology related them to a common factor, hypnosis. When they are all orchestrated and combined in a unity of time and space, they become a single whole, the strategy of mass suggestion. The leader who has the gift and the vocation uses it to transform the most disparate gatherings – and the more mixed they are the better it is – into a homogenous mass, implanting beliefs whose kernel is a passion and whose aim is action. Since its discovery, the strategy has been applied everywhere. Its procedures have usually been examined and explained individually. I have presented them together to show the reason for their existence and their unity.

# 6. *Conclusion*

---

I

L ET US take one last look at hypnosis. All the cluster of ideas and hypotheses that we have discussed so far is based on it. Suggesting an idea or an action, for example, like a belief in one's own immortality or putting one's hand into a flame, is done in terms of an automatic mental life and owes nothing to reasoning or logic. The act is immediately produced by a firm suggestion that countenances no argument, and between the order and its execution, between the brain and the body, there is a direct line. The idea dislodges and replaces everything that the individual thinks and believes in the waking state. When it spreads from one individual to another by a kind of contagion, like influenza, it produces in them conformity and uniformity, creating in this way a collective reality peopled by shared beliefs and illusions, a world of the joint imagination which Le Bon describes in these terms:

If we look at history from a point of view lofty enough to enable us to see it whole, it is apparent that it is a process of bringing together peoples in order to create ghosts. Politics ancient or modern is merely a battle of ghosts. (Le Bon, 1910: 60)

In that battle, suggestion creates and undoes relationships between human beings. It is to psychology what exchange is to economics or consensus to society: the link between individuals and between the individual and the group. It creates the law of their mental unity.

When the hypnotist is replaced by a leader imposing his will on a collection of persons, suggestion makes them obey as if some internal force were involved. Each individual easily becomes someone else, carrying out actions that are normally voluntary and conscious like an automaton, and becomes a member of a compliant crowd fascinated by its creator. Mass and leader look at each other as if in a mirror, each constantly seeing the image of the other. Take off the mask of the leader, and there is the crowd. Take off the mask of the crowd, and the leader appears. In the age of the crowd, that relationship has assumed the form of the solar model, which dominates it from every point of view. In the centre is the leader. He is the incarnation and the vicarious representation of an idea such as the nation or freedom, the eponymous hero who thus alone has a name and gives it to others. At a distance, there is the collection of anonymous people surrounding the hero and ready to receive his suggestions, the crowd. The whole power of fascination radiates towards it and returns to the leader, reflected by the shared power of admiration. Freud represents this diagrammatically, showing all the individuals in the crowd as parallel arrows which finally converge at a notional point I, the leader or the idea he represents:

This seems indeed diagrammatic, but has been put into practice very effectively in assemblies and processions in Shanghai and Peking. The crowds processed before Mao, the adulated leader, the little red book raised towards the skies by millions of arms, millions of voices repeating the words of wisdom, the precepts for action and the political slogans contained in them. There as elsewhere, the magic formula showed how successful it was. The eponymous leader gathered the anonymous mass around him.

## II

If crowd psychology has shaped and still shapes contemporary history, it is for a reason that cannot be stated too often. It is because it removes hypnosis from the medical and psychiatric domain and places it foursquare in the social and cultural milieu as a paradigm of normal social relations between human beings. It is a paradigm which explains them as gravity explains the relationships between physical bodies. My object here is not to see what consequences this transfer has had in literature, sociology and philosophy, but it must be admitted that, as was its aim, it has changed the face of politics as radically as plastic surgery. Essentially, it has scientifically codified the use of mass suggestion (and propaganda) in terms of the rhetoric used to convince an audience and shape its opinions. It has shifted our view of the relationship between the leader and the mass, taking it out of the context of the power of the representative over those whom he represents (the prince's over the people or the master's over his slaves) and put it into that of the influence and suggestive power the hypnotist exerts over a mass of hypnotised subjects. It has tirelessly put forward the fact that in a mass regime the

151

practices evolved for an elite regime, in the *agora* of Athens or the parliaments of Europe, have reached their operational limits. In short, in a world in which revolution and counter-revolution are the rule rather than the exception, government by discussion is disappearing of its own accord in the face of government by suggestion, or by mass communication, which amounts to the same thing.

There are many convincing indications that this paradigm derived from hypnosis is pervading all quarters and becoming the framework of a political method today as it did in the recent past. I will give only the example of two very different leaders. The first, as you have probably guessed, is Hitler. Speaking to Rauschning, he said, 'What you say to the people collectively in that receptive state of fanatical abandonment remains in their mind like an order given to someone under hypnosis, which cannot be wiped out and resists all logical argument. But just as individuals have their own neuroses which are not to be meddled with, the mass also has complexes that must not be aroused.' At the other end of the political spectrum, Trotsky described the tactics adopted by the Bolsheviks in their struggle against the existing power in October 1917 thus: 'Applying the tactic of "peaceful penetration" consisted of legally breaking the enemy's bones and paralysing by hypnosis whatever will he had left' (Trotsky, 1950: 496).

If it is true that crowd psychology has turned the theory and practice of hypnosis into a model of our culture, initially of the relationships between crowds and leaders and subsequently of collective activity, then it has clearly created history. There is nothing particularly new about one science taking over and adapting the findings of another, after all, as chemistry did with culinary recipes or the study of electricity with the practices of those chemists who liked to play with electric sparks. But when the subject that is taken over and adapted becomes an integral part of society and culture it receives from it a sort of truth of a historical kind, rather as Marxism and psychoanalysis have done in our day. It remains 'true' even if a scrupulous examination ultimately leads us to the conclusion that it is not based on observation to any great extent. We know that it works – which some may think rather a good thing – and that is enough. Crowd psychology is by no means a unique example of this.

## III

Our contemporaries have given an almost unanimous verdict on the theories of crowd psychology, finding them unacceptable. We should not pay too much attention to that judgement on the part of scholars who know nothing about it and of ideologues who gain from knowing nothing about it. The most it can do is obscure the verdict of history. It cannot reverse it. One can, however, raise the following objections to the discipline. In the first place, however difficult the task might have been, there has been no attempt to bring together its ideas sufficiently to check them against possible empirical data. They have simply been rather loosely enumerated, with an occasional attempt to find a fact or so capable of offering intuitive support for this or that point of view. The risk has been that the discipline might become merely a collection of explicative anecdotal material and that the most that could be said about it was that it might not be true, but at least it was interesting.

Crowd psychology has also rather cavalierly dismissed the conscious and rational aspect of the life of groups in general and crowds in particular. Historical writings and laboratory observations, however, both indicate the great importance of this side of psychological life, particularly when groups have a joint task to carry out or belong to the same class. The problem is not whether crowds are rational or irrational, a question to which by definition there is no short answer, but what ties and relationships exist between rational and irrational mechanisms and how they combine in a concrete situation.

As Sorel did right from the start, one can also raise the following objection, which is still completely valid:

The major part of the volume [*The Crowd*] deals with the popular masses, their feelings and their ideas, but here M. Le Bon is on the wrong track, because he does not see that research of this kind must be based on economic conditions and class distinction.[1]                    (Sorel, *Le Devenir social*, November 1895: 769)

Because it does not take account of these conditions, it is based on the quicksand of analogy. No doubt it always has shocked and still shocks the sensibilities of those – the majority – who still believe in the ideal that has been dominant since the English and French Revolutions, that of the democracy of citizens. This happens even though we are tougher-minded now, less demanding and less frequently shocked by reality, all of which has happened since it became commonplace for peoples to elect dictators by universal suffrage and democratically abolish democracy by a solid ninety-nine point something of the votes cast. On behalf, of course, of another version of the same ideal: mass democracy.

Crowd psychology, at least as Le Bon saw it, opted for democracy alone, despite all its constitutional fictions and weaknesses, for as Le Bon wrote:

In spite of all the difficulties attending their working, parliamentary assemblies are the best form of government mankind has discovered as yet, and more especially the best means it has found to escape the yoke of personal tyrannies.
                    (Le Bon, 1952: 200)

And yet we know that they are threatened in a society with fragile institutions and anaemic beliefs. But there has been no society so limp and desperate as never to produce a group of men who would oppose oppression and affirm the rights of freedom and justice. There always have been and always will be men for whom absolute power is an insult and who set their hearts and minds to fighting it. Nothing has ever been able to put an indefinite stop to the growth of the seeds of their revolt. In the fight for freedom, no-one knows in advance who the victors will be, but the battle is unbelievably fierce.

PART IV

# The leader principle

---

## 1. *The paradox of mass psychology*

---

### I

THE MASS OF MATERIAL that I have consulted all indicates that in an age of optimism and reason mass psychology appeared as a science dealing with disturbing phenomena. And with unreason. It obstinately concentrated on things at once exotic and ephemeral and not forming part of the general picture of society: crowds, beliefs, mass suggestion and other matters of that ilk.

But it takes more than that to create a scandal. It needs a ground tremor that will overthrow established convictions. These were dealt a tremendous blow by crowd psychology since, despite economic and technological progress and the feverish destruction of past traditions, it claimed to reveal a human nature rooted in something beyond the troubled waters of history. It even declared that the past exerted an invincible force on the present and was of great political and cultural influence. Those who thought that they were changing human nature, abolishing the family, leaders, the hierarchy and religion, it seemed to say, were mistaken. Such things were still there and functioning. Anything that was truly real would not die or fade away.

That did not mean that there was no change of any kind. What crowd psychology was basically saying was that human nature, even if it did not progress at exactly the same rate as other things, was nevertheless influenced by them. It was adapting to change and surviving breaks with the past, which showed its extraordinary power of resistance. Language like that was of course unacceptable, offensive to the deepest-rooted ideas.

Into a society that was characterised by extreme attitudes and high political feelings, Tarde introduced those very qualities that were lacking, an analytical disposition and a love of clear ideas. He certainly shared Le Bon's fears about the state of French society and the same class anxieties about the rise of the masses. That, however, did not prevent him seeing that society was both in a crisis and expanding, following the bourgeois pattern of industrialisation, urbanisation and increasing wealth. It was as if the unrest and conflict, the revolutions and counter-revolutions were the price to be paid for continuous modernisation and visible scientific and technological change. Crowd psychology had to take this into account and adapt its ideas accordingly.

Tarde advanced along the road that Le Bon had opened up. Obviously, his starting point was crowds, those spontaneous, natural and anarchic groupings that are a general datum of social life. They seemed to him, however, to be in the last analysis less important than the artificial, organised and disciplined crowds encountered more or less everywhere (in political parties, firms or the apparatus of state, for example). The army or the Church could be seen as prototypes of them. A real qualitative leap, from an amorphous mass to created ones, was involved.

The change in perspective was considerable. So far, the masses had been seen as the result of a crumbling and settling of the normal structures of social life. They were the result of institutional collapse and represented a hiatus in the regular course of events. The inevitable conclusion seemed to be that the family, the Churches, social classes, the state and so on, which had all been seen as basic and natural collectivities, were really artificial and derived ones. They should, in fact, be seen as so many forms of mass, just as electricity, coal and plants are different forms of energy. It had been said that man first created society and then the masses appeared. The current view had to be that men were first part of a mass and then created society.

This was a radical change in the way of seeing things. The most refined and civilised social institutions, such as the family and the Church, the great historical movements, such as trades unions, nations and parties, were all metaphors for the simplest form of association, the crowd, and shared its psychic characteristics. This meant that the task of science was no longer to explain the properties of the mass from the starting point of society but rather the other way round, since any society was the product of the mass. This is, of course, a simplified picture, as I am restricting myself to essentials. What followed from it was this. From being a study of important but specific phenomena, crowd psychology became a study of society in general, since crowds were ubiquitous. Consequently, just as the laws of chemistry, electricity or biology were subject to the laws of energy, the laws of politics, sociology and even history were subject to the laws of psychology. The latter were therefore wider in their application. There were variations in them, but no exceptions to them.

## II

But this raises a major difficulty. Crowd psychologists see crowds as incapable of being intellectually creative or taking any historical initiative and as never leading artistic, scientific or political revolutions. They could not do so, as when individuals congregate in crowds their intelligence is weakened and their sense of reality becomes blurred. And yet institutions such as armies, firms and so on do make progress. Arts, sciences and technologies are created. Means of production and communication that change the face of societies are conceived and discovered.

This is a crucial paradox of crowd psychology that cannot be resolved by abandoning its basic principle, namely that the individuals making up a crowd are less intelligent and creative than when they are alone. As things stood, there was only one way out for Tarde. The alternative solution, which he quickly adopted, went as follows: in any crowd, there is a separate class of individuals who draw the others together and command them. They are the political, religious, scientific and other leaders. They are the source of all change, all inventions and all the social forms that create history. Their power of suggestion makes the majority copy and follow them, as subject to them as children to their father, apprentices to their master and hack artists to the true creative genius. In so far as the intelligence of such people and the discoveries they make are mutually stimulating and induce progress and consequently entail an advance on the past, the crowds imitating them also make progress and rise above the level of crowds in the past. Examples would be the present-day schoolboy solving a problem that baffled the genius of a Newton three hundred years ago, the psychiatrist daily and routinely treating his patients with a method that Freud himself left incomplete, or perhaps leaders of the middling sort who incorporate into themselves, their attitudes and their gestures those of a prototype such as Stalin or Mao. It was by hoisting itself up to such peaks that, in Tarde's view, humanity advanced and transformed itself.

Tarde's way of resolving the paradox was a particularly unprepossessing one. The only way of escaping from the vicious circle of trying to find out who the exceptional people were and where their power came from was to refuse to acknowledge the paradox. The nature of the solution, however, was less important than the three consequences arising from it. These were:

1. The centre of gravity of crowd psychology shifted from the mass to the leader. His own actions offered an explanation of his properties.

2. Imitation (a form of suggestion, it should be remembered) became the basic mechanism of social life. It was supposed to explain the leader's

hold on the groups of those imitating him, their uniform thought and behaviour and the spread of feelings and beliefs, and hence to explain why we conform to a common model.

3. Tarde's view was that there was on the one hand an initial direct suggestion from one individual to another and on the other an imitative and indirect one operating over a distance (by means of newspapers, for example). This meant that communication was seen as a kind of suggestion and made the journalist's work comparable to that of the hypnotist. This was another kind of generalisation, introducing quite properly into crowd psychology the rapidly-growing area of communication phenomena. Since the invention of the book, telegraphy and the press, the field of communications had continually restricted that of conversation, persuasive speech and rumour. The whole shape of culture was changed. Tarde outlined with astonishing precision a theory of communications for which nothing at the time had prepared the way and which still has not been disproved.

He described the way in which they made their way into every home and changed isolated individuals peacefully reading their papers, for example, into that kind of invisible crowd, the public, the readership of a newspaper or the membership of a party. The messages provided by the press suggest the capricious and momentary beliefs which are opinions, like waves coming into being and dying on the surface of the sea. The growth of the means of communication does indeed affect every section of society, determining what is said and thought and the scale of action.

That now seems self-evident to us, even though we have still some way to go. But it was a hundred years before MacLuhan's prophecies that Tarde expressed the principle later to be encapsulated in the Canadian scholar's famous dictum that the medium is the message. He also predicted its ultimate effect, mass culture. He did not, of course, use those words, but that does not mean that he did not study the phenomenon they referred to. As one English expert writes:

In so doing, Tarde made a vital initial contribution to the body of literature that today goes under the name of the 'theory of mass culture'. . . . Yet this has been consistently ignored, which is somewhat surprising, to say the least, as Gabriel Tarde's contribution to sociology is far from unknown.      (Giner, 1976: 60)

The essential fact is that the part he played was a pioneering one. Its basic argument was the primacy of the means of communication over all the instruments of social life.[1] It therefore saw them as those elements which would produce a complete upheaval in politics and the framework within which a new culture would come into being. It is not his forecasts that are important, but the analyses he used as a basis for them, and what he said about the press applies equally to the radio and television. Everything that theorists and critics of the media have written since is there in embryo.

# 2. *Natural crowds and artificial crowds*

THE GREAT SOCIAL MASSES provide for our observation a multitude of actions and reactions, people in a state of change themselves and also changing others and groups coming into being and disappearing before our eyes. If we look at them over a long enough period of time we observe not only variations but also repetitions, contrast and homogeneity, similarity and dissimilarity, the two categories, in fact, of basic data. In organic nature we talk of mutations and heredity; in social nature we are dealing with inventions and imitations. An inventor disturbs the order of things, an imitator re-establishes it. The former has produced successive waves and hence a development, the second repeated uniformity and hence a tradition or fashion.

If a child amuses himself by shuffling around the parts of a sentence, a stockman by selecting a new variety of animal, or if I do so by speaking of crowd psychology as if it were a coherent science, we have three situations that introduce the possibility of change. If what the child, the stockman or I engage in produces a response that is copied and repeated, we immediately have a new form of language, a new species or a new stream of research. As we know, the typical rhythm of social life is extremely simple. First there are individual creations and then waves of imitation, and the cycle is endless.

Everything follows naturally from this. If imitation proceeds from invention, then every group and society proceeds from an individual multiplied many thousands or millions of times. As their name indicates, Christians copy Christ and Stalinists are facsimiles of Stalin. Similarity within a group could be seen as arising from the fact that the members of that group imitate the thoughts, feelings and behaviour of one of their number who is at once their spiritual model and effective leader. The extraordinary simplicity of the idea explains why it has been so successful. It is so easy once you have thought of it that it would be nice to have done so just once in a lifetime.

Why do we imitate? Why do we immediately rush to copy a person, an idea or a garment? Probably for two reasons: instinctive tendency and economy of effort or, to put it more crudely, reversion to ancestral type and idleness. The instinctive tendency corresponds to the fact that imitation is a universal means of repetition and expresses the biological impulse of every living thing to reproduce itself indefinitely. A consequence of it is the mimetic desire in all of us to behave like someone else, as a child wishes to be like his father, a sister like her brother, or a servant like his master. Repeating or seeing others repeating ideas, acts, words and so on that we find particularly pleasing gives us great satisfaction.

We also do as others do to save our energy and effort. There would be no point in discovering or inventing again for ourselves the things that others have already discovered or invented. Replying to one of his critics, Tarde said:

I may be reminded of the fact that although imitation is a social thing, the tendency to imitate in order to avoid the trouble of inventing, a tendency which is born of instinctive indolence, is an absolutely natural thing. But although this tendency may, of necessity, precede the first social act, the act whereby it is satisfied, yet its own strength and direction vary very much according to the nature of the existing habits of imitation.                           (Tarde, 1962: 50)

In other words, in each of us there slumbers a sheep-like creature who avoids the sufferings and risks of the inventor and so, at a smaller cost to himself, repeats an invention that has already claimed a great deal of someone else's energy. It is not hard to imagine such docile creatures being led by anyone claiming to govern them. He hypnotises them, by means of his charisma amongst other things. Society itself is a hypnotic milieu, an area of images in which automatic behaviour can come into play, and it is bathed in the illusions that history has deposited in its memory. Tarde, summarising his own ideas on the subject, declared that:

The social like the hypnotic state is only a form of dream, a dream of command and a dream of action. Both the somnambulist and the social man are possessed by the illusion that their ideas, all of which have been suggested to them, are spontaneous.                           (Tarde, 1962: 77)

By means of this arresting comparison he reminds us that man is beyond a doubt a social animal, but only because (and when) he is open to suggestion. Conformity is the prime social quality and the very basis of suggestibility, bringing to light thoughts and feelings originating on a lower plane that waking consciousness knows nothing about. Both nature and the way society is organised encourage this conformity, which brings individuals together and plunges them into the dark world of dreams. They imitate like automata, obey like sleepwalkers and mingle in the great tide of humanity.

All this is said in one short sentence: 'Society is imitation and imitation is a kind of somnambulism' (Tarde, 1962: 87). I am aware how hard it is to reconcile all that, but cannot discuss it exhaustively. I hope instead that studying its consequences will help the reader to see more clearly how it all fits together.

## II

Man is a thinking sheep, credulously and impulsively rushing towards things which he neither sees nor understands. Depending on the orders he receives, he bends or stands, immersing himself body and soul in the multitude until he is indistinguishable from it as an individual. Tarde was convinced of this, as is clearly shown by his descriptions of crowds. Indeed, he incorporated all the features of what was now the classical picture. In his view, crowds lived in a kind of waking dream, constantly harassed by the movement of urban life and torn between simple but violent feelings. Consequently they were unable to establish serious and prolonged contact with reality or to escape from their illusion-ridden world. But, he declared:

However diverse they may be in origin and in all other ways, crowds are all alike in certain characteristics. These are their enormous intolerance, their morbid susceptibility, their grotesque pride, their delirious sense of irresponsibility arising from their illusion of omnipotence and their complete loss of any sense of moderation resulting from their overweening and reciprocally exalted feelings. For crowds, there is no middle way between horror and enthusiasm, between the cries of 'Long live . . .' and 'Death to . . .'. (Tarde, 1910: 36)

The major missing element was, of course, reason. It was missing because it belonged with a sense of measure and compromise and a recognition of the limits to what each of us can do. If this is lost, the future is fraught with danger. Thus, crowds in their normal state exhibited all the absurd and unreasonable characteristics visible in individuals when they were in the abnormal state of madness. They shared so many characteristics with 'the inmates of our mental asylums' that when, as in 1789, they ran forward at the slightest rumour, full of heroism or panic, it was impossible to make any judgement as to whether they were credulous or mad. 'They suffer from real collective hallucinations. Men in a crowd think that they see and hear things that as isolated individuals they would not see or hear, and when they think that they are persecuted by imaginary enemies their faith is based on the reasoning of madmen' (Tarde, 1910: 55).

Obviously, Tarde did not mince his words. In his view the persecutions that crowds in their fear 'imagined' themselves to be the victims of pushed them to the worst excesses and produced in them extreme swings of mood from excitement to depression. Sometimes, in their megalomania and intolerance, they had the impression that anything not forbidden was permissible. The rigidly consistent way in which he put forward the masses as a collection of sleepwalkers, disturbed and deprived of reason and any of the sense of responsibility proper to the civilised adult white man, was truly extraordinary. Caught up in the chain of stereotyped associations, he slipped from the 'crowd/madness' analogy into that of the 'crowd/woman':

In short, in its permanent capriciousness, its upredictable veering from fervour to tenderness and exasperation to laughter, a crowd is a woman even when, as is almost always the case, it is almost entirely made up of men. This is very fortunate for women, whose way of life means that they have to stay at home and are relatively isolated.                                             (Tarde, 1910: 195)

He believed that he had discovered several characteristics in crowds – emotional instability, collective hysteria, fits of mania and melancholia and a lack of moderation in all things – that he saw them as sharing with the inmates of mental asylums. Try to visualise in concrete terms what he was suggesting: thousands of men instantaneously changed into women, thousands of strict uniforms and tight trousers transformed into a sea of skirts floating in the wind and you will see not how absurd the fear discharged into this notion of the crowd was, but its secret explanation. It was at once a fear of the sex war and the loss of (male) sexuality. The (male) reader is implicitly warned that if he wants to stay a man he must avoid crowds, for any man who mixes with crowds becomes one of the leader's women.

For Tarde, saying that the crowd was female meant that it consisted of subject, obedient men ready to lose their manhood and be possessed by the leader, the only one to 'wear the trousers', as the popular phrase has it. One should, in fact, be quite blunt and say that the relationships that leaders have with the masses are homosexual ones. The comparison with women merely hides the obviousness of the act of renouncing individuality, the equivalent of losing characteristics seen as specifically masculine – castration, in short – and union with another man, and hence a union which goes against both reason and nature. For Tarde, the nature of crowds was ultimately female, and the individual stood out in contrast to society, as the male principle does to the female.

## III

Tarde adopted Le Bon's description of crowds almost to the letter, but maintained that they were spontaneous and transitory associations which could not remain perpetually in turmoil. They were destined either to break up and disappear as quickly as they had formed, leaving no trace, like a crowd of idlers, a meeting or a short-lived mob, or to develop into disciplined and stable bodies. Between the first and second kinds there was a chain of transformations that produced a new and distinctive character.

To see this clearly it is enough to observe the contrast between groups of individuals experiencing the same emotion or under the control of the same man during an earthquake, a football match or a pop festival and those formed deliberately and developing into a church, a political party or a firm. The difference, as can easily be seen, arises from the existence of an organisation based on a system of shared beliefs and operation in a hierarchy recognised by all its members.

That then is the charcteristic that separates natural from artificial crowds and improvised, spontaneous associations from controlled and formal ones. There is a logical development between the two. A striking event of any kind will spontaneously produce:

that first level of association that we call a crowd. From that rudimentary, transitory and amorphous aggregate, a series of intermediate stages lead up to the kind of organised, hierarchical, durable and regular crowd that can be called a corporation, in the widest sense of the word. The most intense form of a religious corporation is a monastery, the most intense form of a secular one is a regiment or a workshop. The largest forms of them are respectively Church and State.

(Tarde, 1910: 168)

We need not spend too long on something we are perfectly familiar with. What we perhaps ought rather to be concerned with is the nature of the transformation. From what we know, spontaneous crowds always come into being under the stimulus of a psychic factor or external conditions such as traffic jams, wet or fine weather (they are always popular in summer!) the time of day and so on. They are formed by a series of impulses and maintained by a quasi-mechanical series of actions and reactions such as shouting, processing and marching arm-in-arm.

Organised crowds, however, which are associations of a higher order, are formed and develop as a result of internal conditions and are moved by collective desires and beliefs and a chain of imitations which make their constituent individuals more like each other and their shared model, the leader. They are independent of variations in the physical milieu and immediate interpersonal stimuli. They also divide up time and space to suit their own convenience. Examples of this are calendars of parliamentary sessions, national or religious occasions, meeting-places, the arrangement of court-rooms or the positioning of platforms.

There are many instructive differences between the two kinds of crowd. The most important one, and the one that enables us to say that some are natural and some artificial, is the capacity that the latter have for imitation. This is what produces the much greater conformity visible in churches, political parties and the like, in which the individual is wholly caught up and shaped by a mimetic force for which there is no counter-weight. When they are organising themselves, crowds simply intensify that potential force and transform an almost physical pressure into social suggestion. In Tarde's words, 'an organisation of itself creates nothing, invents nothing and differentiates nothing. Its only function is to co-ordinate and to suggest inventions' (Tarde, 1895b: 227).

That provides the advantage that goes with replacing spontaneous masses by disciplined ones, a transformation that is always accompanied by an increase in general intelligence. As we have seen, anonymous, amorphous crowds reduce the reasoning power of individuals to the lowest common denominator, whereas those in which there is a certain amount of discipline oblige the inferior to imitate his superior, thus raising his faculties to a level perhaps higher than the average. Why should this be so? The answer is simple. Every member of an artificial crowd is always bound to imitate the leader who created it. It follows that his intelligence becomes theirs. Tarde, alluding to Le Bon, wrote:

And so we are right to see them as being generally of lower intelligence and morality than the average of their members. From this point of view not only is the social compound they represent, as is always the case, unlike that of its elements (of which it is the *product* and the *combination* rather than the sum) but it is usually inferior in value. That, however, is only true of crowds which come close to it. The opposite is the case when the *esprit de corps* is more dominant than the 'crowd spirit'. When that happens, the social compound perpetuating the genius of a great organiser is superior to its current elements. (Tarde, 1910: 180)

Just as every logician can learn the rules of Aristotelian logic and reason like the great philosopher, every member of a political party or every officer in an army can acquire the political or military intelligence of the leader who founded the party or raised the army, whether he be a Lenin or a Napoleon. In other words, it is as if individuals, after having regressed and lost their own intellectual faculties in natural crowds, acquired, once they had become organised and made up to resemble each other through the discipline of imitation, social and intellectual faculties and raised themselves to the level of the leader of the artificial crowd they had joined.

We can take the police as an example. Their methods of seeking out criminals, procedures for enquiries and set forms for compiling state-ments have all, in principle, been worked out by people of above-average intelligence. This means that every policeman applies rules and reason-ing processes that he would have been unable to work out for himself, since to do so would be beyond his natural ability. This fact drew the following humorous comment from Tarde:

If, according to the Latin proverb, it is true that 'the senators are good men, but the Senate is an evil beast', I have had many opportunities to note that policemen, although they are usually intelligent, are less intelligent than the police force.

(Tarde, 1910: 180)

The irony of the phrase reverses its meaning, and the police force becomes more intelligent than its individual officers. The same would be true of any body of people. Professors and students would be less intelligent than the University, priests and people less virtuous than the Church, the secretary-general and members of the Communist Party less politically conscious than the party itself, and so on. That is why the University, the Church and the Party would always be right.

To sum up, what differentiates between crowds is the existence or otherwise of a system of organisation. Natural crowds obey mechanical laws, artificial ones the laws of social imitation. The former reduce the level of individual intelligence, the latter raise it to the level of a social intelligence that the leader shares with everyone. The great superiority of artificial crowds, and hence of corporations, comes from the fact that they embody the achievements of a superior and unusual man and reproduce thousands or millions of copies of the characteristics of a single individual like de Gaulle, Einstein or Jesus Christ. From the social point of view, the existence of these reproductions, these groups of leaders, the essential transmission belt between the individual and the crowd, is the hardest and the most important thing to achieve. In one sense they are more necessary than the mass itself, for they can act and invent without it, whereas the mass can do little or nothing without them. The mass is the dough, and they are the yeast.

This idea has also been very clearly expressed by Gramsci, who saw such people as being the motive element in a party, the main cog that effectively and powerfully harnessed a range of national forces which left to themselves would achieve virtually nothing. In itself, of course, this element would not form a party, but it would form one much more surely than the average mass, given the right conditions. They would, he said, be generals without an army, but in fact it was easier to create an army than to create generals. It was also true that an already existing army would be destroyed if the generals disappeared, while the existence of a group of generals trained to work together, in agreement among themselves and with common aims, would soon create an army where none existed (Gramsci, 1953: 24). I am not suggesting that the great Marxist theorist followed Tarde's teaching or was inspired by it, although such links cannot be ruled out. It is simply that he very clearly expresses the essentials of the latter's ideas, and his words show just how far they had spread.

## IV

Once it included and distinguished between the two kinds of crowd, the field of mass psychology widened considerably. Along with street phenomena, the passing eruptions of the'populace', it now included all those varied and at first sight dissimilar institutions which include the Church, the army, political parties and the apparatus of the state, and which had hitherto not been part of it. They had seemed so distinctive in nature that no-one would have been bold enough to claim that all these laboriously constructed social edifices and all these regular and properly instituted social, national and economic bodies were indeed crowds, or that they were fuelled in the same way as those unconscious conglomerations of unaware and emotional people. All that it could mean was that beneath these organised and seemingly normal, unemotional and virile social bodies there lurked an emotional, mad (and, to boot, female) mass that surfaces as soon as it is given the chance, and that 'spends its historical existence oscillating between one type and the other, sometimes creating the idea of a large crowd, like the barbarian states, and at others that of a large corporation, like France at the time of St Louis' (Tarde, 1910: 168). Most psychologists, and, as we shall see later, Freud in particular, followed Tarde on this point.

But taking articial crowds into consideration had consequences, and perhaps even causes, of a political nature. On this point there is a contrast between Tarde and Le Bon, and I shall need to say something about it to illustrate these causes. Basically, Tarde said to Le Bon, we are in agreement. The masses and revolution are a danger that democracy in France cannot face up to. But I begin to dissociate myself from you when you claim that the greatest threat comes from what they do as unruly proletarian crowds. In my view, such phenomena are frightening rather than evil. Such crowds are transitory and ephemeral and come and go and rise and fall like dough. In the last analysis, they have no power. They are spontaneous associations of individuals, subject to random events in the physical milieu and tossed by fits of fury and enthusiasm. No doubt they are impressive. But however striking they may be at times of fusion and collective excitement, they are correspondingly wretched at times of dislocation and depression, when there is no stable structure to receive what is left of them, to preserve their experience or to ensure their continuity. This can be seen immediately after violent or heroic riots, when all their individual members go home, as sad and alone as on the morning after a major celebration.

Crowds begin to get really dangerous when they reproduce themselves at increasingly regular intervals and change into artificial crowds, sects or political parties. Previous trends are reversed. Sects or parties are the seeds of a crowd that they lead and inspire to intelligent action:

When a body of strikers concentrate on doing exactly what needs doing and destroying exactly what needs destroying (such as the tools of workmen who are not on strike) as a means to their ends, then there is a union, a combination or some kind of organisation behind them. Demonstrating crowds, processions, funerals that have the air of a triumph, are all the product of fraternal or political bodies. The Crusades, those enormous warrior-crowds, sprang from the monastic orders at the call of a Peter the Hermit or a St Bernard. The mass levies of 1796 grew out of clubs and were officered and disciplined by the remains of the old military corps. (Tarde, 1910: 197)

This is because sects or parties are organised and disciplined and gather men of varying talents and courage to the same idea. In such bodies a dominant will can establish itself much more successfully and very easily spread through shorter and more certain channels to the furthest recesses of society. Movements and orders orginating at the centre are carried out in a much more uniform way when organisation is more rational and the mimetic process more guaranteed.

Therein lies the danger of sects. Left to their own devices, crowds would never be very harmful, but a sprinkling of mischievous yeast is enough to make a large amount of stupid dough rise. It is often the case that if a crowd and a sect are kept separate neither can engage in criminal activities, but when they come together the combination can easily become criminal. (Tarde, 1910: 198)

Substitute 'revolutionary' for 'criminal' and you will see at once what Tarde meant. Up to a certain point, a determined minority and a turbulent majority (the Socialist Party and the working-class masses, for example) are both unable to endanger the existing social order. Once they are united, however, they have a serious chance of doing so. To take things a step further, if things happen thus, then the leader, however great his charisma, however great the hope put in him, cannot avoid the threat alone. It is not enough for him to fascinate a natural, sporadic crowd. Once it has been assembled, he still has to organise it and change it at least partly into an artificial one, into a corporation – party, army or church – of disciples who will imitate and follow him. When those conditions are met, a social order can be defended or overthrown.

The major organisational role in such a situation is also obvious. The leaders' room for action must be increased by spreading their ideas and instructions in a more disciplined way and long-distance suggestion facilitated. It is generally wrong to maintain that this leads to a better distribution amongst individuals, that it is necessary for their co-operation or indeed that it avoids disorders or corrects collective errors. These things follow, but remain of secondary importance. Superiority of organisation comes essentially and mainly from a smoothly-functioning machinery of imitation of superiors by inferiors, of a faithful downwards reproduction of inventions and of universal conformity to one model. As Tarde said:

> It is especially in fostering the spread of example that a social hierarchy is useful; an aristocracy is a fountain reservoir necessary for the fall of imitation in succesive cascades, successively enlarged. (Tarde, 1968: 330)

When we say that an organisation is more efficient because it ensures better co-ordination between individuals or avoids mistakes while action is in progress or work taking place, we are not really telling the truth. As Tarde says, it is more efficient when it ensures regular imitation and makes it easier for the leader to create the mass in his own image, and ultimately it is as good as its leader.

That observation is of capital importance. If the basis of a disciplined and organised crowd is its leader, then it is the leader we must now consider.

# 3. *The leader principle*

I

L ET US BE MORE EXPLICIT. Crowd psychology sees the masses as incapable of true spiritual creativity or social initiative, and every important invention and significant change in history as being the work of individuals. Behind every collective appearance an individual essence is hidden, and not the opposite. The cult of the masses and the glorification of their role in society is seen as a tissue of high-flown declarations emanating from demagogues and used to cloak their inordinate ambition and perhaps their hypocrisy. The masses, intelligent? Then why are they regularly taken in by men they have put their trust in, and why do they even want to be? Full of talents and virtue? Then why have they so little control over the authorities that they sometimes manage to set up, and why do those authorities draw them along with them to extremes sometimes of good but most often of evil? Those who love the masses betray them and only really love themselves. Tarde puts the point crudely:

So we should note that those famous men who only admired multitudes and at the same time despised all men in particular were monsters of pride. No-one more than Wagner, except perhaps Victor Hugo, and earlier maybe Chateaubriand and Rousseau, expounded the theory of the people as the effective force of the work of art and the single individual as incapable of creating anything or being able to do more than make a collective invention his own. Such collective acts of admiration, which cost no-one anything, are like impersonal satires that offend nobody, as they are directed against everyone indiscriminately. (Tarde, 1910: 60)

These observations were made long ago, but are still valid. It is painfully clear that so many people who achieve even minor power see themselves as great historical figures shaping events, even though they say the opposite in their speeches. In order to keep power, they persuade the crowds to think like them. With some success too, if we judge by the staying-power of even the most democratic party leaders. It is an extraordinary sight, even if it happens frequently – the leader throwing down his tributes to the crowd and the crowd throwing back up to him wave after wave of praise and allegiance, assuring him that he is unique and that no man of his stature has been seen on earth for many years. Both sides hear what the other says without daring to say it, since neither side is in its proper place. The man above should be below and the crowd below should be above.

But there is one respect in which the observations are out of date, and that is in their denial of the creativity of human groups, which has in fact been clearly demonstrated by history and ethnology in the fields of religion, language and economics. Is there any discovery more fabulous than agriculture or more wonderful than poetry or music, all of which we owe to the genius of peoples? In my *Essai sur l'histoire humaine de la nature* (Moscovici, 1968) I have demonstrated the popular origins of the arts, technology and the sciences. If a group or social milieu has provided at least the initial stimulus, an individual emerges and completes the communal task. That condition, however, must be fulfilled.

Simply by looking at the thinking behind the glorification of the individual proposed by crowd psychology, we see that only one real reason is advanced, that of his inventiveness. Whether he be a scientist, a statesman, a general or the chairman or secretary of a political party, the leader – the epitome of individuality – has his prototype in the inventor. Their aims and discipline vary, of course. On the other hand, they have identical characteristics and the same primary talents. There is a universal distinction between one category of men whose vocation is to invent, and hence to direct, and another, the majority in fact, whose destiny is to imitate and hence to be directed. This can be seen in the fact that they bear the name and model themselves on the image of the man they follow. Christians adopt the model of Christ, Darwinians that of Darwin, Communists that of Stalin, psychoanalysts that of Freud, and so on.

Calling a leader a kind of inventor or an inventor a kind of leader is both a commonplace and an exaggeration, but it contains a grain of truth, as I shall now try to show. If a leader attracts a multitude and influences it by suggestion, it is by means of some extraordinary and original action from which he derives status. He fascinates all those of us who are urged to imitate him. We all jointly take this need to imitate and interiorise it. The leader first attracts and rules our ego and then devours it. Since he occupies the same place in the psychic life of thousands of people, or perhaps even millions, the similarity of their reactions, the uniformity of their feelings and the kinship of their thoughts create the impression of a collective consciousness, of belonging to a group, of sharing a common ideology with an autonomous existence. What is really happening of course is that there are many copies of the consciousness, spirit and ideas of just one individual, the leader, just as there are many identical copies of a single book or record. The only difference is that in the first case we are dealing with the products of the social machinery of imitation and in the second with those of a physical printing machine.

Tarde, our guide here, expresses this succinctly:

Imitation is the basic force in military organisation, but what is imitated in armies? The will and ideas of the leader which are spread throughout the army as a result of obedience and exalted faith and turn a hundred thousand men into a single entity. There is nothing mysterious or enigmatic about the collective soul in such circumstances, for it is simply the soul of the leader.     (Tarde, 1895b: 171)

This hypothesis is, of course, a general one and does not only refer to the army. It is easy to see that what it really does is eliminate the idea of collective consciousness that Durkheim used and that of the 'crowd soul' that Le Bon abused. That soul, Tarde maintained, was intangible and had no real existence; or rather, it was simply a copy of the leader's. The 'crowd soul' and its mental unity were the ideal leader whose image each member carried within himself (Tarde, 1895a: 98).

But in Michelet's synthetic phrase it is the soul of 'the leader who concentrates within himself the honour of the people, whose colossal type he becomes'. He is to some degree the founder of the human collectivity and the model it resembles, once it has been created, as a child resembles its parent, and just as

the germ of basic order was implanted in the nascent mind by the appearance of the self, the prime germ of social order was implanted in primitive society by the appearance of the leader. The leader is the social self destined to undergo infinite development and transformation.[1]     (Tarde, 1895a: 98)

In short, he is the principle behind the existence of any crowd, and, as people never tire of repeating, men cannot do without a master any more than they can do without food, drink or sleep, and are political animals who need organisation; that is, order and leaders (De Gaulle, 1944: 64). 'It is a law of nature that when men come together in a group, they instinctively submit to the authority of one of their number' (Sighele, 1898: 71). 'In every social sphere, from the highest to the lowest, as soon as a man ceases to be isolated he speedily falls under the influence of a leader' (Le Bon, 1952: 120).

Each in his idiosyncratic way, de Gaulle, Sighele and Le Bon are all saying substantially the same thing, namely that when they are alone men are free, and when they are part of a group they seek a leader, surrender to him and follow him. Uttered with as much conviction as if it were a mathematical axiom, this principle[2] strikes home like a self-evident truth, even if we find the way in which it is expressed brutal and shocking. But as we know, crowd psychology never sugars its pills or justifies its sharp statements. It draws its proofs wholesale from shared popular traditions and trusts commonsense experience to verify them. If you want further proof, it invites you to open your eyes and look around you, for it is crystal-clear that most people accept the law of a living or dead leader. There is no-one without someone above him and below him in any of the societies we know. Such is the hierarchy of an enslaved humanity.[3]

## II

Kant saw man as an animal who, once he lived amongst others of his own kind, needed a master, and that master as also being an animal who needed a master. As you know, this idea of the master's master was one that he had discovered or that had taken possession of him. It served as a solid foundation for the view of the world that he adopted and of his own place in it, a view from which he could not deviate, as he had no other. He was caught up in a view, an ideology, and the prisoner of a mission from which there was no escape, just as the artist is caught up in his art, his perception of forms and colours, in a reality that he paints as he sees it and cannot paint in any other way.

The leader seeks to dominate men as much as his idea dominates him, and he is the first link in any effective form of domination. He is only tyrannical and exclusive when the domination is tyrannical and exclusive. It makes him superior to others, especially in an age when the masses are thirsting for certainty and hope. Once more it was Le Bon who made this point:

It is certain that men of immense, of almost supernatural insight, that apostles, leaders of crowds – men, in a word, of genuine and strong convictions – exert a far greater force than men who deny, who criticise, or who are indifferent, but it must not be forgotten that, given the power possessed at present by crowds, were a single opinion to acquire sufficient prestige to enforce its general acceptance, it would soon be endowed with so tyrannical a strength that everything would have to bend before it. (Le Bon, 1952: 153–4)

That is why the psychic characteristics of the leader, which both captivate us and make of him a born hypnotist, are similar to those of the inventor, a strong and asocial individual absorbed in what Balzac called 'the search for the absolute'. They indicate his singleness of purpose, which is proper to a man with a single passion and hence to the man who is illuminated, stubborn and a monomaniac. Tarde describes such a man in these terms:

The personal ascendancy of one man over another is, as we know, the basic phenomenon and is only a shade different from that of the hypnotist over his subject. In its passivity and docility, of which it is unaware and which it cannot correct, the crowd of imitators is a kind of somnambulist. On the other hand, the inventor and initiator is, given his strangeness and monomania, *his solitary and unshakeable faith in himself and his idea,* of whatever kind he may be, a kind of madman, as we have already said. His faith is in no way diminished by the scepticism around him, for it has social causes. Madmen leading somnambulists. What kind of logic can we expect from that? And yet both contribute to the achievement of the logical ideal, and seem to have shared out the work between them, with the sheeplike gregariousness of some keeping and levelling social faith and the boldness of others raising it and enlarging it.    (Tarde, 1895a: 127)

A description like that throws a harsh light on what could be thought and written less than a century ago about the masses and collective life, and that in a scientific work. The least one could say is that there is no pretence of impartiality, since the author makes no attempt to clothe his prejudices in learned language. But let that pass. The text contains in essence all the elements of these *Führernaturen*, as Max Weber called them when he investigated them further and combined them in a different way in his own theoretical work. Everything is there: the superiority of the individual to the crowd, the primacy of the act of inventing over that of imitating, the monomaniac inflexibility of the man predestined to fascinate and hypnotise masses of spectators and the gifts of the ideal hypnotist, that very rare bird indeed.

But what are leaders looking for in the crowd? What desire pushes them and attracts them towards it and forces them to act on it? A desire for power, personal ambition, class interest? All those things of course, but crowd psychology suggests just one reason more powerful than all others: the desire for prestige aroused in them by the enormous power of beliefs which are being transformed into an aim. It is marked by a name when it is a question of persons (Napoleon, Stalin, Jesus Christ, Karl Marx) or by a title, when it is a question of function (general, professor, emperor, president). The desire for prestige is reflected in the will to fame from which no man can escape, hence the leader's passion for baptising individuals, the party, towns, sciences and so on with his own name. Hence too that rapid switching around of names when the leader goes into exile or dies.

One might well wonder whether there could be such a thing as an anonymous leader. The answer is clearly no, for a leader is not really in power if no-one can put a name to his face. If that happens, he has neither name nor face. That is more or less what happened with Tito's successors. After the great leader's death, power, party and people all lapsed into anonymity. As soon as a leader commands, he tries to make everyone repeat his name. Canetti says that they are expected to utter it frequently and wherever there are large numbers of people, in a community in short, so that many people learn it and adapt to saying it (Canetti, 1973: 421).

Being a name and making a name gives no intellectual satisfaction, but it does provide a considerable emotional one. It means that we shall last, that glory or immortality will be ours, and is the most concrete indication that we hold power and act on others, for whom we have become a model and a focal point. In short, we have penetrated their ego and govern their imagination. Michels says of party leaders that they often acquire a kind of aura of sainthood and martyrdom, asking only one reward for all the service they have given: gratitude (Michels, 1971: 57).

Without that recognition from the people and the masses, no king, crowned or otherwise, is of any significance. So every leader depends on the crowd, and this shapes his power of suggestion, for he has to believe what the crowd believes and see what it sees if everyone is to identify with his decisions and understand them at once and unhesitatingly. He becomes a perfect mirror for the crowd, which becomes his image and is as much at ease in this role as in its own existence. Hence the leader may experience solitude, but never isolation, for he can never remain outside the crowd he emerged from without being seen as a cynical sham furthering his own ambitions. His strength is to be genuine and act genuinely. If he acts genuinely without being genuine, his strength evaporates and he falls into the illusion of being a master without a master. He then loses all his power to fascinate and all the trust the crowd has invested in him.

As long, however, as he remains that mirror, the crowd sees its own image in him. The masses recognise in him the charisma of collective belief, to which both are slaves, and in admiring him they are admiring themselves. Tarde concludes that when a crowd is admiring its leader or an army its general, it is in fact admiring itself and appropriating the high opinion the man is acquiring of himself (Tarde, 1895a: 114).

Admire yourself and the crowd will admire you. Such seems to be the advice that the leader should receive. In imitating the leader, the crowd is stimulating its self-esteem, its social ego, which is thereby strengthened. In his innermost depths, everyone feels that he is becoming a little de Gaulle, a little Einstein or a little Napoleon and sees himself with new eyes. It would appear that a strong leader strengthens and heightens the personality of his associates and followers, whilst a weak one enfeebles and diminishes it, rather as if the self-esteem of the individual Frenchman hit a peak or a trough depending on whether M. Barre or M. Mauroy was in power or that of the individual American varied according to whether Mr Carter or Mr Reagan was president.

That was seen as explaining why people demand strong and energetic leadership from time to time (but not too often!). Once again Tarde has something to say:

In fact, every time a nation goes through one of those periods when what it desperately needs is not only emotional power but also intellectual ability of a high order, personal government of republican form or parliamentary colouring is required.                                                                    (Tarde, 1910: 165)

Nevertheless, it should be pointed out that apart from one or two rare and exceptional cases, that is a very dangerous illusion. Personal governments have succeeded in raising a flagging national pride, but this has been achieved at the cost of bleeding the people's dignity white, or simply bleeding them. They were proud, and that was all.

## III

Why do the masses obey their leader like a flock obeying its shepherd? The question has always been asked, and more urgently since the Second World War. In the world we now live in, we have witnessed a phenomenon that appears to be an inexplicable survival, namely, that a daily reign of terror has been the concomitant of the authority of certain leaders. That authority has demanded the sacrifice of millions of individuals for reasons of class or race on a hitherto-unprecedented scale, and as we all know, the power of such leaders has its origins in the will of the people. In spite of their inhumanity, they have been and still are surrounded by boundless veneration and indeed love. In many cases love and veneration have gone hand in hand with terror and almost reached fever-pitch.

And yet things which have to be called crimes were known to all except those who did not want to know about them and covered their eyes, stopped their ears or remained silent instead of denouncing them. The popularity enjoyed by a Hitler or a Stalin is therefore deeply disturbing. As Hannah Arendt writes:

What is more disturbing to our peace of mind than the unconditional loyalty of members of totalitarian movements, and the popular support of totalitarian regimes is the unquestionable attraction these movements exert on the elite, and not only on the mob elements in society. It would be rash indeed to discount, because of artistic vagaries or scholarly naïveté, the terrifying roster of distinguished men whom totalitarianism can count among its sympathizers, fellow-travelers, and inscribed party members.                                    (Arendt, 1967: 318)

It is more than that. With regard to Stalin, when we remember how relentlessly he hunted down his enemies, it is literally stupefying. Their every deed and action was monitored. No-one escaped the terror. And that terror was only made possible by the spontaneous participation of the masses. Nor did it stop Stalin being very popular and worshipped like a god, in proportion, in fact, to the terror he inspired, which in this respect was more effective than any well-being that his regime might have brought about. The Soviet philosopher Zinoviev, who lived through the period, wrote that in his opinion the Stalinist purges did more to make a god of him than his stubborn policy aimed at bringing food prices down by a few kopecks (Zinoviev, *Le Monde*, 22 December 1979).

This did not only happen inside Russia. Abroad, too, he was glorified by poets and writers adding their praises to those of politicians. Nor was there any dearth of pens in France to produce declarations of love and admiration. 'How many hundreds and hundreds of thousands share the same clear-sighted love for Marshal Stalin,' wrote André Wurmser (Wurmser, *Nouvelle Critique*, 1949). The same year, Paul Eluard dedicated a poem to him containing the line, 'And today Stalin dispels unhappiness, trust is his razor-sharp mind.' At the time of his seventieth birthday, do not forget, every family and factory had to take part in a collection of presents that were sent by the wagonload to Moscow from the whole of France. That was how we honoured him whom Henri Barbusse described as 'the man with a scholar's head, a worker's face and a simple soldier's uniform'.

The masses wept in the streets when he died. With despair in their hearts, they looked anxiously towards a future without him, feeling themselves to be fatherless. Louis Aragon gives an account of this sorrow: 'Every time I shook hands with someone, whether it was Tom, Dick or Harry, both of us were afraid of looking into the other person's eyes and seeing the tears that would make it impossible to hold back our own.'

It was certainly not the first time that the death of an adored and despotic leader had produced reactions of that kind. Caligula himself was adored, and the people almost revolted when he was assassinated. If I briefly mention such events – and Stalin's death is still fresh in all our memories – it is in order to show that what is astonishing is not the subjection of the masses and their passive submission to such leaders, but the intimate affection they feel for them to such a degree that they are inconsolable when they die. How can men love their tyrants and follow them with no thought for their freedom or their lives? It would seem that they find any power vacuum, the real or imaginary emptiness around them when the leader is dying, impossible to bear. Mao, Franco and Tito have all died in our time, and we have seen the desperate and inhuman efforts their doctors have made to keep them alive and delay the inevitable, as if such men had no right to die.

Such machinations, and the fact that the true date of death has been hidden in order to maintain the illusion that the leader was ill or dying when in fact he was already dead, have another side to them, that of the real or supposed reactions of the crowd to the death. Do they panic or start a period of terror? Social ties are broken, cohesion collapses, there is anarchy and perhaps excessive manifestations of grief (although suicides are usually the work of the fans of movie stars). But there is also the fury of a crowd that turns its grief into violence against those who were close to the great departed. All the lesser men who cannot replace him are held responsible for both his crimes and his death. This emptiness left by his disappearance is only filled after much mourning and a long period of dethroning. In a sense, the latter never finishes, even in the most tightly-controlled societies.

This whole series of facts shocks the intelligence and conscience and defies scientific explanation. To crowd psychology, however, which to some extent foresaw them before they became large-scale phenomena, there is nothing exceptional or mad about them. What it does see as surprising, on the other hand, is that human nature had been so little understood.

## IV

How was crowd psychology able to forecast and describe them before they had occurred? As long as the political problem is seen in the classical way, it is taken for granted that all men are equal. We wonder why some command and others obey. If reason or self-interest induces the majority to obey, one can accept that. But if such motives no longer hold good, it is no longer comprehensible. And if in addition the majority actively collaborates in or passively consents to its own subjection, we cannot avoid the feeling that it does so freely and willingly.

Crowd psychology sees the enigma not as lying in the fact that some command and others obey, even in a despotic regime. The opposite is almost the case. If all the leaders commanded and all the crowds obeyed, there would be no major political problem or even any problem at all. It arises precisely because the former hesitate and follow instead of leading, whilst the latter hesitate between two extreme courses of action, sometimes imposing their will, sometimes foundering in apathy. It is then, says Tarde, that there comes into being:

a morbid distrust of the master on the part of the democratic crowd, and fear, whining and servility on the side of the so-called master. All he does is issue decrees incorporating his inferiors' orders. This is quite logical on both sides, for the crowd's distrust and the leader's fear both imply a judgement on the latter's weakness. There is also an agreement about ultimate aims, since the distrust increases the fear and perhaps *vice versa*. There is unfortunately a lack of agreement, however, in that the combination of fear and cowardice leads a people to the brink of the abyss. (Tarde, 1895a: 297)

In other words, the need for a strict hierarchy is so compelling that, remarkably, when the minority above obeys and the majority below commands, the balance of power is disturbed. A serious problem then arises, and the only way out is to re-establish an order of obedience. Those leaders who manage to achieve it receive gratitude of the kind awarded to an Atlas for standing up with his head held high and supporting a world that threatens to topple.

We can see that crowd psychology considers that in such conditions it is natural for the majority to be docile. What causes this docility? There are two answers to the question, and these are summed up in the two words *repression* and *admiration*. If we adopt the first solution, we invoke external causes: the naked force of the apparatus of the police, of parties and administrations, or that of wealth and money, which are all violent and corrupting. They sow the seeds of fear and humiliation and suppress all liberty of thought and movement and any will to resist authority. We could lengthen the list, for in such cases the worst is always certain to happen.

The second solution is the opposite of the first, just as in Mozart's *Don Juan* seduction is the opposite of force and the psychological means the opposite of the physical. It presupposes an internal cause, a psychic need to love, imitate and obey a superior being from whom we hope to receive direction and protection. This propensity makes us receptive to his suggestions, and we wish to receive them. It induces us to put our feelings, possessions and sometimes our lives at his disposal. In short, there is in human beings a need to admire that is not long in appearing. We admire our father, our teacher, our elder brother and then great artists or scientists, all those auspicious or inauspicious figures, in short, who have their place in the imaginary Pantheon of the peoples. Le Bon declares roundly that 'the need crowds feel to be admired very soon makes them the slaves of individuals whose charisma they obey. Their worship of those who admire them is frenzied' (Le Bon, 1911: 136).

This need to submit and admire is not an individual psychic need. When the individual is alone, he neither has it nor shows it, and very often rebels against what reminds him of it. In practical terms he is born free, in the general sense of the word. When he is part of a mass, however, the need does manifest itself.[4] It would appear that each one feels constrained to obey the collective side of himself, to submit to that part of his being which from the collective point of view, is him. There are several ways in which this need makes itself powerfully felt in the masses.

There is, firstly, the veneration with which they surround their leader. They watch him and listen to him, and his very name is uttered with respect. Secondly, there is the vehemence with which they reject any attack or criticism directed against him. Even when leaders contradict themselves or commit crimes, the crowds refuse to believe it. They think that others, the leader's entourage for example, must be responsible, and thus keep their image of him intact. We know that many Soviets and Germans were convinced that Stalin and Hitler knew nothing about the persecution and execution of opponents or Jews. Thirdly, satisfied docility is a phenomenon that has often surprised observers. It is conducive to obedience to decisions or orders without the use of great force or excessive constraint. In this connection Robert Michels felt entitled to say in his study of political parties that the masses feel a profound need to accept both great ideals and the individuals who in their eyes represent them (Michels, 1971: 62).

The two solutions – repression and admiration – are diametrically opposed. In the first case, the leader is obeyed because he commands, in the second he commands because he is obeyed. Most of the social sciences favour the first explanation, seeing repression as a type of violence arising from a relationship of force and hence from a social constraint. Crowd psychology prefers the second. In its view, the need to admire a remarkable and impressive man they can trust leads the masses to submit to the leader. He may dominate them and make them obey his orders, but it is done with their consent. That consent is sometimes so extensive that the point is reached where that man declares himself the sole and sufficient leader.

# V

So the mass is a despotic animal. It is clear that as soon as one accepts that it needs to submit and admire, a single individual wielding strong and unremitting power can satisfy it. But where is this need shaped and where does it come from? It probably originates from the same cause as the characteristics of the leader. If not, how could leader and crowd fit together like hand and glove? To save time at this point – we shall return to the question at length later – I suggest that the family is where we learn submission and is consequently the base on which power rests. Our parents, and particularly our father, prepare us for it.

It is they who teach us what to do and what to imitate, what we might call the know-how of conformity. More importantly, the family gives us a desire and a need for it, so much so that we fall at the feet of the first person marked out by his charisma as an example and a leader. Such unthinking, mesmerised and robot-like haste irrefutably suggests the presence of a need to obey that must be satisfied. And we derive pleasure from it. The truth of the matter is, declares Tarde, that most men take an irresistible pleasure in obedience, blind belief and indulgence where their leaders are concerned (Tarde, 1895b: 25).

We can reject the tenor of such statements, but it is harder to reject their logic and the reality of experience. We cannot avoid wondering whether there is any man who does not experience the temptation of admiring and obeying and feel it secretly at work within him. If our desire for freedom had been stronger, the world would be a different place. Submission and the family therefore belong together. Accepting one means accepting the other. Once it had established this link, crowd psychology took it to its logical extreme and turned the father into the prefiguration of every category of leaders. It was not Freud, but Tarde, who wrote the following lines:

Even in the most democratic societies, the one-sidedness and irreversibility in question always exists at the basis of social imitations, i.e. in the family. For the father is and always will be his son's first master, priest and model. Every society, even at present, begins in this way. (Tarde, 1962: 78)

If the masses sometimes defend themselves against the works of mass suggestion and profoundly distrust advertising and propaganda, it is not because they are afraid of being subsequently dominated or controlled by force or violence. They know that they can meet such a threat with greater force and violence of their own. What they really fear is that the demon which from time immemorial has urged them to adore and obey is stirring again. They are like a man who has stopped drinking or taking drugs for some time. He is not afraid of starting again, but of *wanting* to do so. He is afraid that the desire will make him go back to his vice, and against that desire he has no power.

That is why in the long term purely psychic means of persuasion and fascination are so much more effective. A single well-coined phrase is often better than a well-armed division. As Napoleon said, there are only two powers in the world, the mind and the sword, and in the long run the mind always wins.

That, then, is the attitude adopted by crowd psychology in the ancient and uncertain debate about the causes of servitude. Whenever men come together, they unpremeditatedly begin to obey one of their number, and that leader is always the one whom they all want to admire. This means that, visibly or invisibly, the distinction between the leader and the masses is always taking new shape as an interior need. This need is perverted and turned into oppression when the state manipulates it and provides it with a compulsory external means of satisfaction. In this debate, there is no doubt that most branches of knowledge have adopted a contrary and nowadays universally-held theory.

## PART V

# Opinion and the crowd

---

## 1. *Communication is the Valium of the people*

---

I

COMMUNICATION is the outstanding example of a social process. Change its forms and means, and it will immediately change the nature of groups and the way power is exercised, as history shows. It would be wrong to see it simply as a tool in the hands of men who set out to win the hearts and minds of crowds. The truth is that it imposes its rules on them, and they are indeed forced to obey them. As an illustration of this, one needs only to consider the profound transformation of political and cultural life under the influence first of radio and then of television. Over a single generation, the tone and style of discourse and the competition for time between words and images have totally changed.

Tarde had glimpsed this. Each type of communication, he said, had its corresponding type of sociability. Traditional communication from speaker to listener had the crowd; modern forms of communication, starting with the newspaper, have their public. Each also has its specific leader. The press created its own, the publicist.

It is possible to object that this is rather a narrow way of looking at things. Indeed, there is no mention at all of the social and economic conditions of these relationships. Perhaps in one sense the whole thing is a little superficial for someone who claims to examine the field exhaustively and we can no longer find it satisfactory. On the other hand, it is clear and can be expressed succinctly: the development of the means of communication determines that of groups and the way in which they are made susceptible to mass suggestion. There is a history of communications just as there is a history of technology and labour. It provides us with a veritable psychology of exchanges, ways of speaking and persuasion.

## II

We shall try to give an outline of this way of seeing things. It can be instructive without being complete. As you can imagine, everything starts with conversation, which of all the actions and reactions between individuals is the basic social relationship most of our opinions arise from. Knowing that nowadays in sociology and psychology conversation has become a fashionable subject and that it has taken so long to overcome indifference and arouse interest in this essential and elementary phenomenon, we can see even more clearly just how commendably precise Tarde's thinking was! Trying to study conversation in total isolation makes his ideas seem even madder, and hence more correct. He did not merely indicate the subject, of course, but also drew up the project. And first of all we must know what is understood by conversation. What, Maupassant wondered, was conversation?

A mystery! It is the art of never appearing boring, of being able to say everything in an interesting way, of being pleasing on any topic that comes to hand and fascinating when talking of trifles. How can we define this way of touching things gently with words, of gently tossing supple words around, that kind of gentle smile with an idea or two that conversation must be?     (Maupassant, 1979: 123)

One thing is certain. Talking is not conversing, or *vice versa*, for the conversationalist has to make use of a whole arsenal of skills – looks, inflections of the voice, pleasingly effective body language and so on – and surrounds himself with a particular atmosphere that we call charm. Like Tarde, therefore, we should restrict the word 'conversation' to indicating those dialogues in which we talk to others to interest and amuse them, sometimes out of politeness, sometimes out of pleasure in each other's company and most frequently for the pleasure of talking. This rules out all those discussions which are not disinterested and gratuitous, but have an ulterior motive beyond that of the enjoyment of those engaged in them: diplomatic or military negotiations, for example, or legal cross-examinations or scientific discussions. Tarde made an exception in the case of flirting and social talk, for the fact that their aims – to flatter and charm and so on and so forth – are so transparently obvious does not cut out the play and the pleasure involved in them, and in fact does quite the opposite.

In his view, engaging someone in conversation meant holding his attention and influencing his mind. No other social relationship could produce deeper interpersonal penetration or greater influence on their thoughts than conversation. This is what he has to say on the matter:

In bringing them into contact it causes them to communicate with each other by means of an influence that is as irresistible as it is unconscious. Hence it is the most powerful agent of imitation and the propagation of feelings, ideas and modes of action. A speech that carries its audience along with it and is applauded is often less suggestive simply because it is clear that it sets out to be persuasive. People talking together influence each other in close proximity by means of the tone of voice they adopt and the way they look at each other and not only by the kind of language they use. We are right to call a good conversationalist a *charmer* in the magical sense of the word. (Tarde, 1910: 85)

Quite calmly, as if the whole thing were self-evident, Tarde declares that conversation owes its whole effectiveness to its ability to produce effects similar to those produced by hypnosis. That would make it in many ways like interpersonal direct suggestion.

The other characteristic of conversation, that it is egalitarian and recreates equality in a universe of recrudescent inequality, has consequences at the general social level. In one of Tarde's posthumous notes we find these words:

In doing so, it synthesises all the forms of influence of one mind on another. Because of the complex nature of its influence, it can be seen as the embryonic form of social relationships. Its reciprocal influence makes of it the least-noticed and most powerful agent of social levelling.

Suggestion, equality and pleasure are the three words which spell out the characteristics of conversation. But monologue comes before dialogue. We must suppose, Tarde says, that in the early days of the human race, in the first family or human group, a single individual (and who could he be but the father?) would speak and the others would imitate him. After a long period of imitation, everyone learned to speak and converse. That is why we see vertical monologues, downwards from the ruling leader to the group and upwards from the obedient and acquiescent group to the leader.

It was not until later that communication between superior and inferior and *vice versa* became reciprocal. Parallel monologues changed into dialogues. In short, language was in the first instance the leader's language, ordering, warning, threatening and condemning. Later, copied and imitative, it also became the language of followers, approving, applauding, repeating and flattering. Finally, in dialogue, it was transformed into language for speaking. Aiming at neither condemning nor obeying, it was language given to others.

Tarde examines and describes in great detail all the circumstances leading to the development of conversation, noting, too, that the tone and content of our talk are reflected in the physical positions we adopt. In his view, conversations held while the participants are seated are the weightiest and most serious, but the 'lounging conversations' that the

by the influence of written language. Correspondence has provided a direct form of extension and philosophical dialogue; the theatre and the novel have created new forms. The groups of those 'talking to each other' have multiplied and currents of opinion now circulate on an enormous scale. This second stage is the one in which newspapers and their mass effects were the most outstanding phenomena. A possible analogy would be artillery replacing archery.

They regularly increased their readership and from being a mere tributary became the major river into which all the others flowed, carrying the essence of all the other means of expression – the novel, the theatre, political speeches and so on – with them. They nevertheless remained, from one pole of society to its other, merely an instrument of communication. Tarde saw them as being initially simply an extension of talk and correspondence and finally virtually the only source of them (Tarde, 1910: 157).

In modern society everything is against conversation, which presupposes uncertainty, divergence and the possibility of changing other people's opinions. We use this as a justification for the pleasure we take in arguing, and it brings its own satisfaction. Unfortunately, opportunities become fewer and fewer, for rules and objective information are more convincing than disputing debaters. Let us take as an example unorganised and colourful haggling between buyers and sellers. As soon as a fixed price is introduced, there is no more room for it. The going price for a pair of shoes is so much. You either buy them or you don't, and that's the end of the matter. The seller does not try to convince you, and you have nothing to say to him. Talk which was the result of ignorance or self-esteem is killed at birth, in so far as statistics or specialists provide us with an objective, or allegedly objective, conclusion. Tarde maintained that each new piece of information dries up an old source of argument, and wondered how many such sources had disappeared since the early days of the century (Tarde, 1910: 109).

We have perfected the system. Nowadays, everything is do-it-yourself, read-the-instructions-and-get-on-with-it. The press, for its part, imposes its compulsory list of topics, produces its peremptory solutions and makes correspondence, that cultivated form of conversation, or daily discussions almost pointless. It multiplies by a factor of $n$ all the results of printing, which enables the extraordinarily rapid long distance transmission of thoughts rather than men. 'Carrying force over a great distance pales into insignificance at the side of doing the same with ideas. Are they not a long-distance social force?' (Tarde, 1910: 7).

This is not a difficult picture to accept. When many thousands of people read the same newspaper and books and feel that they are the same public, they acquire that feeling of omnipotence proper to the crowd. One might think that the reader of a newspaper is freer than a member of a crowd, has the time to think about what he is reading and, most importantly, can decide which paper he will read. In fact, he is in a permanent state of excitement, and the journalist, by pandering to his prejudices and passions, makes his reader credulous and docile and manipulates him as he wishes. This turns the mass of readers into a mass of obedient automata, exemplified by hypnotic subjects who can be made to believe and do anything. The power of the journalist and the press to mobilise the public in great causes was noted by Tarde in a specific set of circumstances:

It is not because we have universal suffrage in France but because we have news-hungry and avidly-read newspapers that the Dreyfus affair divided the whole country into two parties, or rather into two violently opposed *publics*.

(Tarde, 1895b: 154)

In this connection Marcel Proust, that infallible chronicler of times past, describes how one of his characters, the Prince de Guermantes, had wanted to have a mass said for Dreyfus and had learned that another Catholic had made the same request. That other supporter of Dreyfus, that other *rara avis*, was his own wife. Every morning her personal maid slipped out to buy *L'Aurore* for her! (Proust, 1978: II, 711).

At times of crisis the press seems to have almost unlimited power. When danger looms on the horizon, every citizen becomes a reader avidly awaiting what the journalists will have to say. At such times, Tarde writes:

One sees the outstanding example of the social group, the nation, change like all others into a group of fevered readers eagerly awaiting each new report. In wartime, there is nothing left of social groups such as classes, professions, trades unions or parties in France apart from 'the French army' and 'the French public'.

(Tarde, 1910: 103)

Since it came onto the scene the press – to which can now be added the radio and *a fortiori* television – has constantly made the opportunities for meeting and discussion less frequent. It makes people turn away from public to private life and drives them from open places such as cafés and theatres to the closed ones of their own homes. It eliminates private associations such as clubs, circles and *salons* and leaves large numbers of isolated individuals ripe for incorporation into the mass, which shapes them as it will. Only then does the press gather them to itself and make itself their common denominator. Having removed the opportunities for personal and quarrelsome exchanges, it puts in their place the spectacle of bogus polemics and the illusion of uniform opinions. Tarde wonders whether:

If, for the sake of argument, all newspapers were suppressed and their publics along with them, would the population not be much more likely than it is now to form larger audiences at professional lectures or even at sermons, to fill public places, cafés, clubs, salons, reading-rooms and theatres and to behave everywhere more noisily?                                        (Tarde, 1910: 27)

That dislike of public places is very well known to us nowadays. Anyone passing through a town or village notices that the seats outside the houses are empty, the cafés deserted and the squares have nobody in them, as at a given time all the inhabitants are at home watching television. The rash of aerials sprouting on the roofs is the most striking sign of the change. Everyone knows how hard it is to drag people away from their sets to a political meeting, a religious ceremony or a local demonstration.

## IV

The natural history of communications has still to be written, and a comparative study of them has not yet reached even the drawing-board stage. We do, however, know enough about them to perceive certain trends in the light of what I have just been saying. They are what persuades us that crowd psychology, as made use of by Tarde, immediately saw the importance of mass communications. And the basic characteristics of the discipline became evident from the time of the birth of the press. One hesitates to talk of laws here, as the word is so hackneyed and misleading, and it seems better to talk of three trends that are constantly being confirmed. The first is concerned with the reversal of the respective roles of conversation and the press (to which we should add radio, television and the media generally) in creating public opinion. Before the advent of mass society, discussion groups and individual exchanges were the major element in the process. Since its arrival, ideas and feelings have reached and penetrated ever wider circles, and newspapers have extended and accelerated the process in much the same way as trains and aeroplanes have affected passenger transport.

With mass society, the press became the source of opinions travelling directly to the four corners of the land and even out into the whole wide world. Since it had partly replaced conversation, it also partly dominated it. This meant that its public was not created and influenced by it directly, but rather through the medium of the discussions that it stimulated and controlled to use as sounding-boards. As Tarde pointed out, it needs only one pen to set a million tongues wagging (Tarde, 1910: 76).

We can thus say that there are two stages in the way mass communications work. The first is when the influence of the press is directed towards basic groups of people who like discussing things. The second is when it is directed towards the interior of such groups in which each member is open to the suggestion and influence of the others. The aim is to change opinions and behaviour – the way people vote or their attitude towards a political party, for example, so that 'ultimately, the very acts of political power are ground up by the press, further chewed over in conversation and play a large part in the transformation of that power' (Tarde, 1910: 135).

This two-stage concept is the one adopted by most specialists, after fifty years of research (Katz and Lazarsfeld, 1965). In themselves, the mass media have no influence on the individual, and change neither his opinions nor his attitudes. By penetrating elementary neighbourhood, family and acquaintanceship groups, however, they do eventually influence and change him by means of the personal communications involved. In short, a press, radio or television campaign that does not operate through personal contact and discussion amongst neighbours and friends is not likely to have much impact. In Tarde's words, 'Shops, cafés, clubs, salons, anywhere where people talk, are the real causes of power' (Tarde, 1910: 132).

Even if we do not share his view of society or his trust in the power of conversation, we can recognise that at a certain level such observations have the ring of truth and stand up to the test of experience.

Let us turn to the second trend, the tendency for successive means of communication to make crowds more dispersed. This process loosens the ties between their individual members, isolates them and makes them more accessible to those wishing to influence them. There is a remarkable alternation between movements of association and dissociation, which is produced by technical processes and involves mental and social consequences. At first, a small group of people meets in a particular place to see and talk to each other. The press then separates them and turns them into so many individual readers. The cinema brings together a number of different individuals in a place where there is a direct process of intellectual and emotional contagion, and television scatters them once more into their individual homes, where they are glued to the box and in restricted contact even with members of their own immediate family.

This means that there is an alternation between real communication between people close to each other and a purely notional one within a correspondingly abstract group. What we might call a first-degree crowd becomes a second-degree one with, in the latter case, an increasingly diffuse but by no means less effective hold over its members.

The third trend is for communications in every society to become polarised. It has been said (wrongly, but perhaps ostensibly rightly) that

191

they have been developing towards greater democracy and increased participation on the part of their public. If we look at them in detail, however, the opposite is the case. Let us recapitulate. We said that in thousands of individual face-to-face discussions, individuals exchanged opinions and questioned and answered each other, with everyone having the same chance of influencing his fellows. Such discussions were so many scattered centres of decision and power in a specific milieu.

As the media developed, they displaced conversation and eliminated the part played by discussion groups. Each individual was alone with his newspaper and set and reacted alone to their messages and suggestions. The two-way relationship between people talking to each other was replaced by a one-way relationship between the reader and his paper or the viewer and his set, in which he could see or hear but had no opportunity to answer back. Even when he is directly involved the conditions in which he can use his right of reply always put him at a disadvantage. Applauding, booing, denying, correcting or replying to the paragraph in the newspaper, the image on the television screen or the voice on the radio all became impossible. All this has meant that we are now passively exposed to their control and subject to the authority of printed matter or projected images, all the more so since the isolation of the reader, listener or viewer means that he cannot know how many people share or disapprove of his opinion. The inequality gets greater, and the imbalance means that although readers sometimes have an effect on the press, the press always has an effect on readers (Tarde, 1910: 17). There may be one or two exceptions, but the general rule is that communications have become polarised and are increasingly one-way rather than two-way processes.

These three trends – the reduced importance of conversation, the scattering of the crowd and the polarisation of the media – are similar in nature, cause and effect. They all combine to play a part, though not an equal one, in delivering those nicely sweetened messages which, like pills, can often soothe but also, when the need arises, stimulate as well, and can go on doing so until the patient cannot do without them. The need for these means of communication is like the addict's need for his drug. Perhaps they are easily achieving the mental domination their masters expect of them. I have no intention of making moral judgements in an area where too many have been made already. I am simply reporting a fact that has never been refuted since it was first stated.

## 2. *Opinion, the public and the crowd*

### I

I F W E A R E T O H A V E a proper understanding of the effects of the development of communications on our society, we shall have to analyse its effects more closely, starting with those relevant to the subject of this chapter, the nature of crowds. Looking forward to what I shall have to say later, I shall indicate the most remarkable one first. That is that, instead of crowds being drawn together at the same place and time, we now have scattered ones or, in other words, a series of publics. The means of communication we have now obviously make it pointless that people should come together to exchange information and engage in a process of mutual imitation. The media penetrate every home and seek out every individual to change him into a member of a mass.

It is the kind of mass, however, that is seen nowhere because it is everywhere. The millions of people who quietly read their paper and involuntarily talk like their radio are members of the new kind of crowd, which is immaterial, dispersed and domestic. We are dealing with what I have called the public, or rather publics, that is newspaper readers, radio audiences and television viewers. They all stay at home, but they are all together, and all seem different, but are similar.

Tarde saw them rather than the 'colourful' crowds as the really new feature of our age, suggesting that

The modern age, since the invention of printing, has produced a very different and ever-increasing kind of public, a public whose indefinite extension is one of the outstanding features of the age we live in. We have studied crowd psychology, and now we need to study the psychology of publics.

(Tarde, 1910: 2)

Here he has been proved right, for opinion polls and analyses of the media are meeting this wish. We need to know why.

### II

Organisation changes natural crowds into artificial ones and communications change them into 'publics'. Organisation heightens the intelligence of the individual in the mass and communications lower it by making him part of a mass audience at home.

The implications of this are obvious. Whether we are scattered or concentrated, meeting in a stadium or in a square round a leader or alone in our flats reading our papers or glued to our television sets for the latest speech by the president, our psychological state is a similar one. We are ruled by our emotions and not our reason and are susceptible to suggestion. Even when we are separated, we still share the same illusion of omnipotence, are still subject to the same exaggerated judgements and feelings and still prey to the same emotions of hatred and violence as if we were taking part in a mass demonstration in the street. In short, we are still 'sleepwalkers' fascinated by the charisma of our leaders and ready to obey and imitate them.

If the first case, however, we are brought to that state by suggestion operating at close quarters and in the second by long-distance suggestion from the mass media, which are free of any spatial limitation. It is rather as if a doctor, instead of hypnotising a patient by verbal and visual contact, did so by means of letters and photographs of hundreds of patients whom he did not know and who did not know him. From a mass influence exerted by leaders (who will always be with us) performing on the spot, we have moved to one exerted by leaders who, like gravity, perform when they are not there. And, of course, 'if that long-distance suggestive influence on individuals forming part of the same public is to become possible, they will have engaged in it over a long period, which means being accustomed to an intense social life, urban life and suggestion at close quarters' (Tarde, 1910: 5).

This is what the newspaper does. The setting-up and presentation of topics and the particular colouring given to articles must all help compel the reader's attention. It may appear to be varied and to contain all sorts of things, but there has to be a focal point, a theme or headline that will capture the interest and hold on to it. This 'bait' is 'increasingly highlighted and holds the attention of the whole readership, who are hypnotised by the single brilliant point of light' (Tarde, 1910: 18).

The difference between the two modes of suggestion explains the differences between crowds and 'publics'. In the case of the former, physical contact is always there. In that of the latter, there is a purely *mental* cohesion. The mutual influences produced in physical crowds by bodily contact, the sound of a voice and the excitement and hold of a gaze are brought about in other forms by the communication of feelings and ideas. This means that crowds are quicker to act and react, to be carried away by their emotions and to show excessive enthusiasm or panic. A 'public' is slower to move, finds greater difficulty in committing itself to violent or heroic movements and remains, in short, a great deal more moderate. A crowd is an occasion of sensory contagion, a 'public' is subject to a purely intellectual one which is encouraged by the wholly abstract and yet very real grouping of individuals. Tarde notes that

publics are different from crowds in that the proportion of publics based on a faith or an idea is much higher, whatever their origin may be, than that of those based on passion and action, whereas there are very few believing and idealistic crowds in comparison with the number of passionate and agitated ones.

(Tarde, 1910: 37)

In short, a crowd is to a public as the social body is to the social mind. One might wonder how people who neither see each other, come into contact with each other nor affect each other can be associated. What link is established between people when they are at home reading their paper or listening to their radio and all spread over a very wide geographical area? The answer, of course, is that they form a public and are subject to suggestion, because each one of them, at the same time, is convinced that he is sharing an idea or a desire with a large number of his fellows. Has it not been said of the readers of a major national daily that the first thing they see when they unfold their paper is the circulation figures? They are influenced by *the thought of the regard of others*, the totally subjective feeling of being scrutinised by people very far away:

Merely being aware of it, even if he does not see the people themselves, is enough for him to be influenced by them as a mass, and not only by journalists, who have an effect on both sides and are all the more fascinating because they remain invisible and unknown. (Tarde, 1910: 3)

The crowd and the public, like all kinds of human groups, also have the common feature of being created and led by a leader. Anyone observing meetings of people simultaneously sharing an idea and striving and directing themselves towards a goal can immediately see that the leader is the instigator and orchestrator of their actions. In the case of crowds, the instigator is most frequently hidden, invisible because he is totally immersed in the anonymous mass and is anonymous himself.

There is certainly a lot about Tarde's ideas that is banal, but revealing the nature of 'publics' and foreseeing how they would behave in the age of the masses now suggests a deep sense of reality.

## III

And that is not all. Tarde inaugurated one of the most important chapters in the social sciences when he perceived that the chief feature of a public was the current of opinion it gave rise to. The great German sociologist

Habermas said of him that he was one of the first to make a pertinent analysis of public opinion. To appreciate this fully, we need only bear in mind that this analysis was the starting point for the study of social attitudes and survey methods. The latter, after a North American detour, have come back to France in an enormously improved and universally-accessible form. What is certain is that the opinion polls newspapers use and abuse (to such an extent that almost every day that passes produces a new crop of them) were more than embryonically present in the theories of the professor at the Collège de France.

But how can we define opinion? It seems difficult to do so without recourse to contrast and analogy. Perhaps we could say that it lies between the pole of tradition, prejudices and beliefs on the one hand and that of logic and personal feeling on the other, like the bourgeois between the ordinary people and the aristocracy, and is a more or less coherent cluster of reflections on and responses to current problems. Opinion is in fact a statistical system dominated as much by logic as by feeling and shared by anything from ten to ten million people.

For that statistical system to exist, the first essential is that each person must be aware of the similarity between his own judgements and those of other people, between, for example, those judgements I make about abortion, the President of the French Republic or nuclear energy and those that a large number of French people make at the same time. The second essential is that those judgements should be about the same thing – abortion, the President of the French Republic or nuclear energy – and that we must know about it, for if we do not know about it, it has no social meaning and obviously cannot be the object of an opinion. Tarde had this to say:

Opinion, in our view, is a momentary and more or less logical cluster of judgements which are made in response to current problems and are the same when made by persons living in the same time, the same country and the same society. (Tarde, 1910: 68)

You might well ask how we can achieve such an awareness of the similarity of our opinions. Tarde's answer would be that there is nothing simpler. Opinion originates from an individual who has uttered it or written it and then gradually spread it through the whole of society. In that way, he would say, it has become the property of everyone, and thus it is that linguistic communication, nowadays largely through the medium of the press, produces public opinions. The press also makes you certain that you share them with most other people.

In addition, communications have developed in a parallel way to opinion. We did not invent opinion, and it has always existed. In the clan, the tribe and the city, when everyone knew everyone else, the collective judgement formed by conversation in which everyone took part or by the speeches or orators in the public square still had a personal nature. It was associated with a particular face, voice or known member of the group, and everyone had had a share, however small, in creating it. This gave it a living, human and concrete character, which meant that for a long time its role in the government of the tribe or the city was that of a commentator, rather like that of the collective voice of the chorus in ancient tragedy punctuating and emphasising the words and actions of the protagonists by means of questions and exclamations of horror, pity, surprise or indignation, even though the chorus played no part in the action itself.

In feudal states, which were small and limited to one particular area and in which public life was restricted to the territory of a town or region, opinion was made up of a myriad fragments with no visible or permanent link between them. They were parochial, operating within a narrow horizon, rooted in a tradition and of concern to only a very limited number of people. Travelling merchants, journeymen, soldiers, monks, students and a number of other itinerant folk certainly acted as vehicles for news and opinions, but it is difficult to know what trust the settled population put in such migrants or to what extent they adopted the opinions and judgements of a wandering and certainly deviant minority.

First books and later newspapers provided the missing link and re-arranged all these fragments into an enormous whole. Such printed material and means of transmitting ideas served to replace local mentalities by a single public one and close, unanimous and primary groups of individuals by secondary ones composed of individuals who were closely associated but did not know or see each other. This meant, said Tarde, that

> There would be differences, and amongst them the fact that in primary groups opinions are *weighed* rather than counted, whereas in secondary and much larger groups where there is no visual contact, they can only be counted and not weighed. The press has thus unwittingly helped to create a situation in which *numbers matter* and to destroy one in which character, or even intelligence, was more important. (Tarde, 1910: 71)

During that development, which saw the victory of the many over the few, books and newspapers broke the barriers of space, time and class. Writers and journalists pumped in the modern age, channelling all the rivers and streams of particular opinions into the vast reservoir of a single public one, which increased in size as its waters were constantly renewed. After modest beginnings as scribblers or hacks expressing the opinions of a local parliament or court and reporting the gossip and foibles of the powerful, they finally became manipulators 'by imposing on speeches and conversations most of their day-to-day topics' (Tarde, 1910: 76). Balzac was already comparing them to the rulers of states: 'To be a journalist is to be a pro-consul in the republic of letters. A man who can say anything can do anything. Napoleon's maxim is understood' (Balzac, *Les Illusions perdues*).

The result of their labours was that opinion constantly increased its hold on European societies at the expense of tradition and reason. Whether it attacked customs, moral habits or institutions, no resistance was possible. If it attacked persons, reason hesitated and stumbled. We, too, have recently seen the extreme lengths a press campaign can go to. Things would be much better, in Tarde's view, if the fourth estate simply acted as a means of diffusing the works of reason and changing them into tradition, in which case 'what is reason today would become opinion tomorrow and tradition the day after' (Tarde, 1910: 65).

The likelihood of such a thing happening is obviously slender in the extreme. Instead of an *alliance* between opinion and reason, there is a constantly increasing and ever more complex rivalry. Extrapolating this, we might see a time when tradition has been eaten away and defeated and scientific thought has been threatened and reduced until they are no more than branches of opinion. When we reach that stage, a class of men – politician-journalists, philosopher-journalists and scientist-journalists – will duplicate and, in the eyes of the public, replace politicians, philosophers and scientists. Could such a thing happen? Many people think that it already has and that the power of the means of communication and that of public opinion are one and the same thing.

## IV

We have just touched upon the development of publics and of opinion. Perhaps we should look at what the general significance of this has been for mass society. Obviously, although great prudence is called for, one thing is clear: the mass media are constantly modifying the relationships between social groups. Economic and professional divisions based on particular interests – such as those of workers and bosses, peasants and traders – are losing their traditional character. They are transformed by the press, which attenuates them and envelops them in a public opinion which goes beyond them. They are being replaced by new dividing lines shaped by 'theoretical ideas, ideal aspirations and feelings, all of which are visibly stressed and emphasised by the press' (Tarde, 1910: 24). In other words, division based on opinion.

Once this stage was reached, individuals tended to belong to a public rather than to a social class or a church:

Hence, whatever the nature of the groups a society is divided into, whether they have a religious, economic or even national character, the public represents to some extent their final state and, so to speak, their common denominator, since it is to that wholly psychological and perpetually shifting group of states of mind that everything is reduced.                                     (Tarde, 1910: 28)

Interests do not of course disappear, but remain hidden in the background. The press, however, presents them in the guise of theories or passions capable of being shared by the great majority. We must accept the fact that crowd psychology anticipated the trend towards turning nations, social classes and so on into masses, in the form of either crowds or publics, it matters little which. This process means that all class conflicts are transformed into mass conflicts and hence into passions or ideologies. This changing of the class struggle into a mass struggle that could be won by psychic means was the aim of all the theories of crowd psychology, amongst which mass communications had pride of place.

That was not all. In Tarde's day the press, and since then radio and television, have been changing the nature of politics according to the same principle. Let us consider only the press, which dissolves everything it touches, unmaking stable and traditional groups such as clubs and corporations and remaking them as various publics. It provides the constant thrill of excitement and news, constantly shifting the attention of its readers from one topic to another, jumping from a strike to an assassination, a war to a royal marriage and so on.

If they are to follow the welter of events, create their own event and keep in contact with their members, political parties have to make use of the press. This puts them in a position of dependence and means that their planned activities and the make-up of publics are constantly being modified. In the past, political parties were less active and colourful but more durable and tougher. Now, they are in the position of accelerated self-creation and re-creation. Parliamentary parties like the Jacobin club had the basic characteristic of

being based on assemblies in which there was close physical and visual contact and immediate mutual personal influence. This characteristic changes when a party unwittingly turns into a *public*. A public is an immense dispersed crowd of indefinite and constantly changing shape in which the wholly psychic links consist of long-distance suggestion operated and experienced by publicists. Sometimes one party comes into being, sometimes several merge. In every case, however, this public increases at their expense, enlarging them and re-arranging them, likely to assume dimensions that what might properly be called parties, that is, parties based on a crowd, could never achieve. In other words, parties based on crowds tend to be replaced by those based on publics.

                                                            (Tarde, 1895b: 159)

The description may be a little vague, but the first group recognisably contains parties built up round a leader or group of leaders who are militants and capable of mobilising a mass around themselves, and the second consists of parties whose leaders and directing groups are capable of forming revolving coalitions amongst social categories as and when temporary conditions make it expedient to do so. In terms of French politics, it would be tempting to classify the Communists and Gaullists as 'crowd' parties and the Radical-Socialists, Christian Democrats, the UDF (*Union pour la démocratie française*) and so on as parties based on a 'public'. The Socialist Party sometimes comes near one of these types and sometimes near the other.

In Tarde's view, the media weaken mass and militant parties and favour those of 'publics' and publicists. Or, what is worse, they transform militants into the motive power of the media and the masses into the raw material for their public. This gives rise to an instability 'that is not really compatible with the workings of the parliamentary system in the English manner' (Tarde, 1910: 25). This is a valid judgement even if it is based on wrong reasons which we are far from accepting.

To sum up, the greatest change brought about by the press (and later by other discoveries in the communications field) has been the substitution of 'publics' for 'crowds', the replacement of a quasi-physical sociability by a scattered but cohesive one. This process has very quickly taught us how to make the individual part of a mass and has sought him out, as an individual, in his home, at work and in the street. Radio and television have since been even more successful, bringing to his home and re-creating especially for him everything that previously he had to go and find in the café, in the public square or in a club. This means that what they are really engaged in is a kind of large-scale hypnosis, the consequence of which is that we all belong to a more or less visible but omnipresent mass. In the last analysis, the individual is a residue. He only ceases to be a member of a public when he becomes a member of a crowd, or *vice versa*, or only ceases to be a member of one public when he becomes a member of another.

# 3. *The law of the polarisation of prestige*

## I

IN MODERN TIMES, prestige is to violence what the soul was once to the body. Power represents their union and is inconceivable if either of the elements is missing. The defenders of mass communications declare to those who will listen, and even to those who will not, that the technical progress following in the wake of the media means a move towards a greater equality of prestige in our societies, or in other words towards a bringing together of leaders and led. For almost a century, they have been telling us that its most outstanding result will eventually be total democracy. To back up their prophecies, they maintain that an ever-increasing majority of people now read newspapers, listen to the radio and watch television and are thus increasingly able to resist any manipulation of the media by the ruling minority at their expense.

Crowd psychology, as represented by Tarde, believes not a word of this zealous defence. Its mistrust is based in particular on the existence (which I have already pointed out) of a gradual polarisation of communications, which are increasingly becoming a concentrated and one-way phenomenon. We certainly cannot claim that men are born free and equal before the media.

Unless – which is unlikely – there is some radical upheaval, developments in the means of communication may well soon put them into the hands of an increasingly small number of leaders. These developments constantly increase the distance between leaders and led and the inequalities in matters of prestige. The law of polarisation indicates that the number of persons controlling them is tending to decrease. Conversely, the number of people they can influence is increasing out of all proportion.

Let us be quite clear about one thing. The point at issue is not the fact that some of the population cannot have access to the means of communication. Indeed, the fact that everyone has the possibility of access to them is what gives rise to inequality and widens the gap between leaders and led. To take present-day France as an example, it is as if, paradoxically, the discrimination against the left on radio and television was a safeguard for the degree of democracy still subsisting there. If things changed and it received favourable treatment, the left would undergo a quickening of the rate of development of a court or star system and could expect to be subject to the cult of personality as experienced here and there. It would be its turn to accept the democracy of 'publics', which is not a republican one, in which bombardment of the media takes the place of crowd meetings.

For crowd psychology, the opposite view of things would merely be wishful thinking. This would be for the very good reason that just as in the past we needed a greater number of workers to produce by hand the garments needed to clothe all our population, we also needed a greater number of leaders to keep the population accessible, to influence every citizen by their gaze, to win him over by sound of their voice and to control him by continuous physical proximity. And just as nowadays a worker at his machine produces a thousand times what his counterpart produced a hundred years ago, we also have leaders who, in their newspaper offices or in front of their radio microphones or television cameras, mesmerise a thousand times as many individuals as their predecessors.

A few hundreds or thousands of listeners were hypnotised by eloquence alone; many more were then influenced by hand-written books; and now incalculable numbers of human beings are fascinated over unheard-of distances by the press.
(Tarde, 1895b: 14)

The result has been that communications have been a field of extra-ordinarily high productivity. Symbolic capital, the mass of events and images that the media bring to us and all those voices and faces separated from us by the microphone and the screen, as well as ordinary capital, has been accumulated in immeasurably greater quantities than in the past. Society has been profoundly affected and has entered a new and decisive stage of its history. We have lived through the age of industrial and financial capitalism and are now in that of a symbolic capitalism based not on machinery or money but on communications. Reflecting on such quantitative speculations in crowd psychology, Tarde repeatedly con-cludes that

There emerges through every variation the outline of a kind of general law, that of the increasing difference between the number of leaders and the number of led. In classical times, for example, a town of two thousand citizens could be governed with twenty orators or leaders of *gentes*, a ratio of one to a hundred. Now, with twenty zealous or bought journalists, up to forty million people can be governed. This is a ratio of two hundred thousand to one.
(Tarde, 1895b: 14)

And if we want to be quite clear as to who those forty million are, the following passage will tell us:

And we have seen that the difference in size between the group of leaders and the mass of the led increased as a result of the greater resources made available to rulers by improvements in armaments, communications and the press. It may have taken thirty orators to move the twenty thousand citizens of Athens, but we now need no more than ten journalists to arouse forty million Frenchmen.

(Tarde, 1895b: 218)

That indefinite extension of the area of operation of leaders and their journalistic servants means that fame and prestige rotate more rapidly. It brings people and things quickly into the limelight and then just as quickly relegates them to obscurity. In the field of governing men, the effort of creation is just as intense and the period of enjoyment just as fleeting as in that of the production of goods. In other words, the media are enormous consumers of prestige.

When the means of communication work on such a scale and at such a rate, the productivity of systems of imitation and conformity does not lag behind. Where only ten or twenty thousand copies of a leader were once produced, we can now easily produce ten or twenty million. Ancient Greece manufactured perhaps ten or twenty thousand little Hitlers in one generation; contemporary Germany produced several million in less than ten years.

We can also easily demonstrate that the spread of communications and the intensity of imitation bring with them a monopoly of prestige, and often violence. It is confined to a restricted circle and concentrated into very few hands and indeed into those of one man. Whatever principles are involved, everything in the end becomes personal.

More quantification. The quantity of passions, beliefs and interests invested in a single man is increasing, like the population, geometrically. To get an idea of what I mean, think for a moment of all the passions that could be invested in a Pericles in Athens or a Socrates obliged to go through the markets to talk to the cobblers, joiners or painters of the city, or in a Robespierre, and compare them with those invested in a Roosevelt speaking to the American nation on the radio or a de Gaulle using television to harangue the people of France. The language of figures points to one kind of future only, in which there will be increasing anonymity below and accelerated personification above:

It is thus safe to predict that the future will see personifications of authority and power that will make the great despotic figures of the past, Cæsar, Louis XIV and Napoleon alike, pale into insignificance. (Tarde, 1895b: 219)

They have certainly paled since 1895, when those lines were written, and we would now see such people almost as wise and well-behaved monarchs, dictators who respected the law, if we compared them with the despots of our own age. If the value of a theory were judged on the basis of the correctness of its forecasts, this would be a credit entry for crowd psychology.

## II

The means of communication, as we have just seen, enormously increase the power of the leader by concentrating prestige at one extreme and admiration at the other. At the same time, they create another kind of leader, the publicist, the leader who has mastered the art of the press. Any leader or statesman must have his own talents and also those of a journalist if he is to be able to create a public, transform it into a party and stimulate it into following him. Nowadays, of course, he must have a good radio voice and television presence. The only difference is that the political publicist had to have a certain literary gift and a certain amount of imagination to complement his culture (and here we think of Zola and his *J'accuse*) whereas today's political stars need only the right personality for television or radio. The latter presupposes neither culture, nor literary gifts nor imagination, merely a smattering of acting ability. Tarde – to come back to him – therefore saw in the appearance of the publicist a major historical event. Newspapers took the place of speeches and journalists with their readers in mind that of orators swaying crowds. Such was the phenomenon that the 1789 Revolution established and intensified to a hitherto unknown degree:

Each of those great – and odious – publicists, Marat, Desmoulins and Duchesne *père* had his own public, and the murderous, incendiary, loot-crazed mobs that devoured and ravaged France and the French in every corner of the country can be seen as excrescences or malignant eruptions of those publics, whose evil cup-bearers poured them daily draughts of the heady and poisonous wine of empty and violent words and were conducted to the Panthéon in triumph after their death. (Tarde, 1910: 10)

In a single sentence he both settles scores with the firebrands of the Revolution and pours his own venom onto the people who rose against a regime that had oppressed them for centuries, that had shamelessly pillaged and humiliated from north to south and east to west. What he was doing here was once more expressing his hatred for those who had enabled him, the descendant of a Third Estate family, to write and think freely and even to insult their memory. His hatred and scorn led him to see Marat, Desmoulins or the elder Duchesne as the prototypes of the modern leader and to perceive their principal role, that of being at the origin of major currents of opinion and of being the instigators of social

ideas which, without them, would have remained chimerical and inar-
ticulate, like, by way of proof, socialism and anarchism,

before certain famous publicists such as Karl Marx, Kropotkin and one or two
others had stamped them with their own image and put them into circulation. It is
easy to see from this why the individual imprint of the person promoting it should
be more noticeable on a public than its national characteristics, and why the
opposite should be true in the case of a crowd.          (Tarde, 1910: 16)

Publics reflect the genius of those who create them, a crowd only the
collective unconscious of their culture or ethnic group. Thus, far from
lessening the historical weight of individuals in favour of that of peoples
or democracy, the press and opinion increase it and spread it much wider.
They are vast sounding-boards, an extremely extensive network of
imitators who are all the more ready to follow their directives and adopt
their fashions as there is no tradition to hinder them. The man of old was
imprisoned by local boundaries and protected by custom. Modern man is
free, and hence a prey to passing fashions.

There is a question that cannot be avoided. What is the source of the
power of publicists? It lies no doubt in their gifts as long-distance
hypnotists, but also in their intuitive and informed knowledge of the
public. They know its loves and hates and satisfy the shameless joy it
takes in the display of the most unseemly subjects despite the respect-
ability of the individuals who make it up. They flatter its partiality for
being excited by envy and hatred. Tarde sees the public's need to hate
someone or lash out at something, the search for a whipping boy or a
scapegoat, as a desire to act on that someone or something. Arousing the
public's benevolence, enthusiasm or generosity is not very productive
and will produce no startling effects. What really arouses it, on the other
hand, and gives it an opportunity to act, is stimulating its hatred.
Showing it a tasty morsel in the form of an object of aversion and scandal
lets it give free rein to its latent destructiveness and that aggression which
seems only to be waiting for a sign to unleash itself. This means that
focussing its attention on an opponent, either a person or an idea, is the
surest way of taking command of it and leading it. Since they are well
aware of all that, publicists do not hesitate to play on such emotions,
hence Tarde's statement that 'in no country and at no time has apologia
been as successful as slander' (Tarde, 1910: 59).

As a publicist, the statesman must also be aware of the respective
strength of opinions in the various kinds of public he addresses himself
to. Tarde was thus the first to advocate what we might today call political
marketing as a means of taking the nation's pulse:

But for statesmen, who have to handle what they call opinion, that is, the sum total of ideas and perceptions, it is much more important to guess in what class or group within the nation (which is most frequently a purely masculine group, and in that respect the comparison is a legitimate one) the most intense impressions and ideas and the most energetic (in the sense of either the most vital or longest-lasting ones) are to be found. (Tarde, 1895b: 263)

It goes without saying that in a scientific age like our own guessing is no good. We have to calculate, estimate and arrive at a precise evaluation of that energy. As political opinion polls show, however, that does not mean that there will never be any errors.

With regard to strategies of persuasion and the art of suggestion, they are the same. A newspaper has to be able to capture and hold its readers' attention by means of revelations, scandals and exaggerations, in short to 'attract attention by some sort of sensation' (Tarde, 1895b: 234). It must also state its ideas firmly and if necessary be dogmatic, for human beings in a crowd or a public have an irresistible need for dogma; and last but not least it must go on repeating the same ideas and arguments, since as Tarde said, 'with regard to arguments, one of the best is still the commonest: ceaseless repetition of the same ideas, the same calumnies and the same fantasies' (Tarde, 1895b: 236). It is not by chance that both Le Bon and Tarde proposed the same strategies of suggestion. Both adopted hypnosis as a model and drew the same conclusions from it, and there is thus no need to search for an alternative explanation.

A general observation arises from these last few chapters. The means of communication are a determining factor in any society. They modify the nature of groups (we have seen how a crowd becomes a public, for example), transform the relationships between the masses and their leaders and shape both the psychology and the politics of a period. The nineteenth century produced by means of brawn and machinery. The twentieth communicates and in doing so consumes little grey matter and intoxicates many media. Crowd psychology was the first disipline to see their role and understand their laws. I hope that I have managed to illustrate this.

## 4. *The Republic in France: from a democracy of the masses to a democracy of publics*

*Power comes from above, trust from below.*                    Sieyès

## I

IN ORDER TO SHOW how crowd psychology has developed, rather than to deal with its theories at length, I propose to glance at the present-day situation as we know it. This choice is justified by the fact that for both Le Bon and Tarde the only passion and the only world of realities was France. It was not that they were not seeking a universal truth or that knowledge for its own sake had no appeal for them, but in both their cases these things were subordinated to a vital concern and an obsessive reality. On reading their books one has the impression that the one history they felt they had to understand, their favourite images and the characters who inspired them all belonged to France. More exactly, it was the history, images and characters that since the Revolution of 1789 have haunted the minds of the French people. For Le Bon and Tarde, the rest of the world was a storehouse of examples and analogies, arguments and rhetoric. They could happily have written with Michelet that in comparison with their own, any other history was incomplete, Italy lacking its most recent centuries, England and Germany its earliest. France's history was that of the world (Michelet, 1974: 288).

At no time did they try to dissociate themselves from that history or reject the prejudices it had planted in their minds. There can be no doubt that these were class prejudices, but they were not those of a class existing simply anywhere. They were localised, part of the stock of a particular memory and formed by a specific language and culture. Those prejudices were specifically French ones, and posed a clear question for Le Bon and Tarde: in view of the sequence of revolutions from 1789 to the Paris Commune, what was the likelihood of seeing a democracy in France capable of maintaining social order? Neither of them thought it was possible or desirable to return to the *ancien régime*, and the only thing about it that produced any nostalgia in them was its durability.

In reply to the question, both men imagined a political system in conformity with human nature and in principle stable. They based their investigation on psychology, just as Durkheim and Michelet based theirs on sociology and history respectively, and crowd psychology certainly formed the background to it. The ideas of both of them deserve consideration both in and for themselves, especially since over the last twenty years they seem to have been visibly coming into effect. Indeed, if we make a conventional distinction between a Le Bon system on the one hand and a Tarde system on the other, General de Gaulle's presidency would illustrate the former and M. Giscard d'Estaing's the latter. But there is a small difference, for whereas de Gaulle had read Le Bon and adopted some of his ideas, it is pretty certain that Giscard d'Estaing knew nothing about Tarde. It should not, of course, be assumed that I am claiming that the two psychologists provided an inspiration, and that the two presidents simply received and adapted their respective ideas. All that I am saying is that the solutions they offered did correspond to a certain historical reality. Let us now look at this in greater detail.[1]

## II

Labels clarify ideas. Le Bon wanted a democracy of the masses grouped around a leader, in which plebiscites in the form of votes and demonstrations would confirm the link of sovereignty welding them together. Tarde argued for a democracy of publics that the press, and more generally the media, would make and remake in terms of current issues. He called, in fact, for a multitude of publics centred around a hierarchy of leaders (in the form of administrations, parties and the like) ranging up to the supreme office, referring to the image of the assembled nation, and with collective virtues as the dominant ones. A democracy of publics would recognise a diverse nation, each part of which would follow its own traditions and be based on the consensus of the individuals comprising it. Both kinds of democracy, however, were based on the principle of a leader, a non-discussing and non-discussable authority, since no other could carry out his task. Discussions of pros and cons would hinder action and eliminate what the authority of a Cæsar conferred.

De Gaulle, the concept and as it were the effect of his own will, had long ago described the conditions in which he would take power. At times of disorder, he maintained, in a society whose structures and traditions had been overthrown, the habit of obedience grew weaker and the personal prestige of the leader became the sheet anchor of authority (De Gaulle, 1944: 66).

This soldier who had broken with his caste, lost his rank and been court-martialled, this politician who had broken with his class and for whom the ability to say no was a sign of character, twice usurped the headship of state. As is the case with all great leaders, he based his whole power in the classical way on charisma. Many challenged him, but no-one hoped to succeed him. No-one – except the people – could make him resign.

He was a man of tremendous ideas and uncompromising choices. His total command of others earned him the personal allegiance of individuals and the unconditional loyalty of groups. Both gave him exclusive love and boundless admiration, which he inspired and kept in people who were seen as his opponents. Jean Daniel, the director of the left-wing daily *Le Nouvel Observateur*, described his meeting with him in emotional terms: 'When my turn came to shake de Gaulle's hand, he told me that he had already had the pleasure of meeting me at Saint-Louis. I felt as if I had been at Austerlitz' (Daniel, 1979: 173). In other words, he felt like an old soldier rather than a political enemy. The man of 18 June perfectly possessed the uncommon gift of arousing admiration and impressing admirers.

The network of allegiances and loyalties produced in the most varied levels of society was reflected in the creation, at various times, of a combination of crowd and party. He set up a whole series of such gatherings, which were associations aimed at stirring up his followers, but always refused to let them become permanent organisations. The image he projected every time and wanted to keep was one of masses meeting at a respectful distance from a single leader, an image that he fixed once and for all when he said that he would go to the Arc de Triomphe, that he would be alone and that the people of Paris would be there and remain silent.

He always had such an assured air that it was almost impossible to imagine him having recourse to expedients and ruses or to the opinion of others, and yet there was something intangible about his power to inspire confidence. He was surrounded by an invisible aura that came out in his inscrutable gaze. It is probable that the passionate devotion so many people felt for him, which amounted to a quasi-religious ecstasy, was a stimulant he could not do without. It helped him overcome the disillusionment to which he was inclined.

Like all politicians, de Gaulle interpreted the ideas of our times in his own way and in terms of his own idea of himself and his role in the state. He vigorously resuscitated a whole range of beliefs connected with the nation, the genius of the land, the independence of France and her place in the world. The famous slogan 'Honneur et Patrie' brings together all the memories of the past. These beliefs de Gaulle, appealing to the force of conservation in crowds, combined with essentially socialist ideas that were revolutionary in origin and entirely orientated towards the future, ultimately blending them with a total faith in the sovereign and powerful state. That state created around its leader an atmosphere of majesty he knew to be fleeting and a stability he occasionally suspected of being fragile. All the more so since his power, despite constitutions and referenda, lacked a certain legitimacy, as does everything which is based on charisma. To many people – and particularly the left – his accession to the supreme office has always had something of the *coup d'état* about it.

But de Gaulle, who was a past master in the art of fascination, filled that gap by becoming the powerful and meticulously orchestrated myth every Frenchman could believe in. He was a man alone and showed it, the sorcerer of the arcane and said so, and successfully established that respectful distance from the individual – rather than from the function – that ensures ascendancy and facilitates devotion. He was an artist in language and faithful to Le Bon's precepts who revitalised words with a highly affective connotation such as 'France', 'the Resistance' and so on by investing them with a solemn value. He also gave a fresh edge to meanings and images by giving them an extra sense, like the famous 'chienlit' (havoc, shambles) to denote the 'disorders' of May 1968 or his 'la hargne, la rogne et la grogne' (aggression, fits of temper and moaning).

His own conviction ws unshakeable, and he knew how to communicate it piecemeal and in his own time, and this was something he always managed to do whatever means of communication he used. The public, a 'powerless enchanter' in Malraux's phrase, needs a *powerful* enchanter, and that is how he always appeared on the radio or television. However, although he used the media with undoubted talent, dominating his audience with a gaze that betokened total conviction, he seemed particularly at ease on those hieratic occasions when he made patriotic journeys or took part in patriotic ceremonies. At such times, when everything was calculated, the simple but effective setting enabled him to exert an immediate fascination by his presence and his living words, which captured and held the crowd of the day. The strength that he drew and renewed in so doing enabled him to do without parties or to rise above them and make them all bow to his will and submit to his function and his person. Within this framework, his journeys abroad and the ceremony that accompanied them, the people he chose to talk to, the sonorous speeches he made and the masses he drew to him, made up of both the curious and the faithful, were events. In a world in which France was no longer in the first rank of nations, they represented the success that was necessary if he was to remain undisputed leader. There too he played his heroic and paternal role to a captivated audience.

His extraordinary charisma meant that he could use the referenda and regular plebiscites that a man without it would have had to avoid. Each such occasion involved ample ceremonies that recreated at a level above that of parties, classes or regions the invisible and yet ever-present scene of the crowd around its leader, of de Gaulle and the French. There was a feeling that outside that particular place, the embodiment of France, there was nothing. When the final referendum that followed the events of May 1968 showed how his charisma had waned, he gave up power of his own accord. Many people were astonished, but he, who was wiser than they, knew that in a democracy of that kind failure receives its deserts at once. When a leader has failed and lost his charisma, or even a part of it, he can no longer retain power.

## III

Between de Gaulle's assumption of power and Giscard's election the gap is as great as that between an elopement and a marriage. If the French had deliberately tried to find a head of state of the Fifth Republic diametrically opposed to its founder, there could have been no better choice than Valéry Giscard d'Estaing. An oustanding student at the Grandes Ecoles, a senior civil servant and a young minister responsible for an important section of the national administration, he ran up the ladder of success without experiencing frustrated ambition, the anxieties of failure or the problems and uncertainties involved in many careers. One knowledge-able observer describes him thus: 'This aristocratic patrician, born into an influential, wealthy and very conservative family, married into the aristocracy and blessed with every gift and opportunity, represents the most symbolic product of the governing class' (Duhamel, 1980: 245).

He thus possessed everything that fits a man for the prestige conferred by office and at the same time deprives him of that personal charisma that raises one man above all others. But since he was elected in a period of relative calm after the storms of decolonisation and student riots by a country divided and even torn between right and left, but which had nevertheless solved its colonial problems, modernised its industry, wren-ched its agriculture out of the routine of centuries, incorporated the Resistance into its historical memory, licked the wounds inflicted by the Algerian war and wiped out the memory of the abortive revolution of 1968, he seemed to some to be a kind of French Kennedy and to others to represent the return of politicians and technicians to the affairs of state. The time of a passionate and metaphysical approach to power was over and that of a rational and physical one had arrived. The greatness of France was still the backdrop, but the emphasis shifted from the collective to the individual. Giscard himself wrote that French society is based on self-fulfilment (Giscard d'Estaing, 1976: 3).

The substance of discourse changed accordingly. Vast historical panoramas, the evocation of images and appeals to age-old beliefs disappeared, and their place was taken by the grey but effective lessons of science and rigorous and astringent economic and sociological analysis. The solid logic of statistics was preferred to the uncertain one of emotions, and a republic of pretenders became a republic of intendants. The dramas of history, which can never be solved, became problems in economics, which by definition can. Those exercising authority were both leaders and organisers, each wielding authority over his subordinates and being competent in his own field. All, whether they were leaders of a party or directors of firms, top administrators or union bosses, were part of the circle of redistributed power and diminished responsibilities. They fought or haggled and made and unmade coalitions amongst themselves as circumstances dictated, with the head of state happy to act as umpire in the disputes of his minions.

The president still kept the machinery of authority in both general and specifically presidential areas in his own hands, but unlike de Gaulle no longer held it in that essential way that commands at once respect for the office and admiration for the holder. In this new context, the art of government was no longer that of fascination but the art – or the science? – of communication, in which the media played a decisive part (Debray, 1979). It was not by chance that along with participation, de Gaulle's motive idea of communication became a primary and basic notion. Giscard himself declared that French society had to be based on these two ideas (Giscard d'Estaing, 1976: 45).

Control of the press, the radio and above all television, became one of the stakes in political battle and social debate. Rightly or wrongly, each controlling group, government or opposition, thought that whoever had access to them would thereby gain a decisive influence on public opinion. Whether they were aware of it or not, they both accepted Tarde's idea that in order to establish and control their publics, modern leaders needed the media and the talents to use them. Pierre Emmanuel, in an article entitled in fact *Gouverner par la Télévision* (Government by Television) maintains that the French are governed by the media and for the most part have no idea that they are (Pierre Emmanuel, *Le Figaro*, 20 December 1979).

He then goes on to describe, quite appropriately, how the single individuals who make up the nation are incorporated into the viewing public, that form of crowd, and simultaneously receive the same images and information and hence the same ideas. Programmes are devised to that end and are in accordance with 'the mentality and current prejudices of the greatest number, and it is hard to say whether programmes flow from these or create them. There is no doubt that there is a mutual influence leading to increasing uniformity. This process of (to re-coin a phrase) "mass production" takes root in the most stagnant and inert part of the mind and enables the politics of those currently in power to hypnotise the awareness of all of us by a process of reassuring repetition' (Pierre Emmanuel, *Le Figaro*, 20 December 1979).

In this setting, all the personal loyalties, networks and journeymen of all kinds who in de Gaulle's day worked on crowds and mobilised them in ceaseless direct contact, using all their skill in personal persuasion to instil the spirit of Gaullism into them, have become, as Tarde predicted, quite superfluous. It only needs a handful of publicists to achieve the desired result, which is to make the president's thinking known and to impose his will on the whole country. Emmanuel has understood that this is not a question of chance or the mere application of perfected communication techniques and clearly sees that it is the result of a system. This is what he has to say about the president:

He is alone but not alone, for he represents a system of thought, an idea of the state and a concept of the citizens and the people which are obviously shared by a whole class of the technicians of political power.

(Pierre Emmanuel, *Le Figaro*, 20 December 1979)

It could not be put better, and his words are reminiscent of one or two of Giscard's most Tardean lines: 'The overwhelming majority of French people live in the hubbub of towns. Radio and television transmit their agitated messages everywhere' (Giscard d'Estaing, 1976: 152).

The only thing to add is that these messages come from one or more minds that are part of the star system subtly analysed by Edgar Morin, which is no longer restricted to the entertainment industry and now covers politics and literature, art and science.

## IV

From the point of view of crowd psychology, there seem to me to be two particularly significant differences between the two personalities. The first of these was particularly striking when Giscard travelled. Crowd scenes, with their characteristic warmth and fervour, were rare, and it was primarily leaders of opinion and civil servants, deputies and journalists that he addressed. Through them he sought to affect the country and win over the various publics. His speeches were always planned and always contained a lot of figures, indicating a desire to convince rather than sway. He was also better at handling his opponents than enclosing them against their will in a collective belief that he embodied. This was perhaps a matter of temperament, but it was also

213

purely and simply a limitation, for he did not govern on the bais of a contract with France, merely receiving his mandate from the votes of the French people.

Like any president of an important nation, he was obviously surrounded by a court. His person was honoured and everyone sought to please and charm him, especially as, in Duhamel's words, 'France is governed by an elected sovereign, a republican monarch, almost an enlightened despot' (Duhamel, 1980: 24).

But a cult of this kind could not arouse the admiration and devoted veneration that the leader of Free France had received and which alone draw crowds to their leader like iron filings to a magnet. Despite constant efforts, an excellent highlighting of the office and stage-management of great events, Giscard lacked the one thing, charisma, that could transcend them.

The other difference had to do with his attitude. De Gaulle always appeared as a war leader and prophet, and people saw in him a representative of the leaders of crowds and the founders of nations. He saw himself as both, whereas Giscard was at ease as a statesman and teacher. It was obviously in those capacities that he wanted to shine and, the times being what they were, he shone. When we talk of a military leader, we say that he is a leader of men, meaning that he draws them on to battle, to glory and to death and manages to say something brilliant and inspiring at exactly the right time. When we talk of a teacher, however, we talk of illumination, meaning that he enlightens his pupils and inspires in them perhaps not the same degree of knowledge, but at least a desire for it.

His characteristics were distinctive. He transmitted rather than created. Free of the torments of invention and the doubt that questioning raises, he knew only the satisfactions of being imitated and the peace of mind that comes from having an answer. And he had an answer for everything. Dogged persistence was characteristic of him. He was faithful to one school of thought, one textbook and one philosophical system. Once he had made up his mind on something, he was unwilling to change it. It was not simply a refusal to see the other person's point of view or a different side to a question. For him, such things did not even exist. His own reasoning had led him to the opposite conclusion, and there was no cause to reverse it or take a fresh look at the problem. This meant that dialogue was impossible. He only heard the sound of one voice, his own, and did not understand the questions he was asked, since they assumed a different system or doubts about a basic premiss, neither of which had any existence for him. Thus, teacher-like, he delivered a monologue. He did not take kindly to objections, but liked to digress and repeat, reiterating word for word what his audience knew already.

Nowadays, economics is a favourite subject. All language, all thought, and in short all public discourse, is stretched out on the Procrustean bed of that branch of learning – liberal economics, of course – and to such an extent that if there is disagreement or conflict with the opposition the talk is now no longer of the great choices of history, but of the nature of things. Those who dare to contradict are assumed to be unaware of things as they really are, to suffer from unbridled idealism and to lack a sense of responsibility. Whether or not that judgement is a true one, we are beginning to think and talk like Tarde: 'In their game of ups and downs, *governments* and *oppositions* are like *bulls* and *bears* on the stock market. Governments like a bullish market in public affairs, oppositions a bearish one' (Tarde 1895b: 144).

What makes the comparison even more apt is the fact that the stock exchange is a barometer of opinion and reacts in the direction indicated. Tarde saw that as a law. It is indeed a law, but one established from the point of view of a minority that commands and imposes its will, not from that of a majority that obeys and resists.

It is clear that in Giscard's public speeches and appearances there was a pedagogical dimension, hence the language of philosophical argument, lit up here and there with a touch of chaste feeling. Hence too the abstract vocabulary suitable for senior civil servants and the observations packed with figures and further details. The purpose of the whole apparatus was first to teach and then to convince. That might work in peaceful times within a uniform political class, once the rebels have been thrown out, but it would only need the arrival of another leader capable of turning publics into crowds to shake the carefully-constructed edifice and draw France once more towards a democracy of the masses.

These and other differences indicate the direction the Fifth Republic has taken. It is quite clear that the ways in which it has developed have had less effect on the bases of society and, for the moment, on the economy than on the nature of the forms of groupings, action and political power. I have merely tried to highlight those psychological aspects which are always omitted from concrete analyses (Todd, 1979). There is nothing surprising about such an omission, since it is forbidden to take them into consideration and since one could write a best-seller by using historical and economic arguments to justify the prejudice. One can even be taken for a progressive by contributing to such a regression of knowledge and falsification of current political practice.

## V

One thing is certain. Over the last ten years or so, the political parties have been changing. In Tarde's phrase, 'crowd' parties are becoming 'public' parties. There are three indications of this. The first is the competition they engage in to have access to and control the means of communication. Measuring their impact on viewers, audiences and readers (and also on citizens) is a preoccupation they all share. This is why they love surveys. The pulse of public opinion is taken, percentages listening to a programme are calculated, likely voting intentions are listed, attitudes to specific questions such as abortion, inflation, immigrant workers or Jews are measured, to say nothing of the ups and downs of the popularity ratings of political figures. The results are published in the papers every week, replacing public debate and taking our decisions for us. In short, opinion polls, directed at the various publics, have taken the place of those solemn and passionate plebiscites that only a leader with charisma can risk. We could see such surveys as a simple statistical exercise and the tables of results as merely information about what people are thinking. Giscard's book *Démocratie française* reminds us of their real significance: 'public opinion provides stimulus and penalty, deciding as it does where freedom stops and disorder starts' (Giscard d'Estaing, 1976: 158).

Political marketing is spreading, as predicted and urged by Tarde, and determines the presentation and choice of candidates. The judgements and preferences of a sample of individuals are used as the basis for an analysis of their opinions, which have to appear in the manifesto of every party. There is a sketch of the ideal deputy, whom every aspirant must resemble if he is to be credible. This means submitting not only to intellectual modifications, but also to physical operations. Mitterrand's teeth and Chirac's and Debré's glasses were changed, to mention merely those items reported in the press.

Launching electoral poster campaigns is, as we know to be the case with the Socialists and Gaullists, a matter for advertising specialists and entrusted to agencies once in-depth market studies have been carried out. A whole image industry has come into being as a result of the frequency of elections, to enable candidates to address themselves to even larger and more varied publics, and this in the knowledge that the citizen is a reader or viewer and will react as such before he reacts as a voter. Candidates are chosen on their likely performance. Let us have a look at the UDF list for the European elections. We have what *Le Figaro* of 22 April 1979 described as a 'scientifically established order of merit'. Personal rivalries, conflicting trends and differences of opinion, the article goes on to inform us, have been settled without difficulty, 'as the UDF has decided to rely on marketing techniques to make the choice when negotiations were clouded by hesitancy or ambition. The first twenty-five candidates have all been tested by public-opinion polls, and the results of these have influenced their order of preference in the list.' 'Influenced' seems to be a euphemism for 'dictated'. We know that the strategy paid off.

Finally, following the example of communications, prestige is becoming polarised in the state, the parties and most institutions. The organised masses are everywhere becoming indistinguishable from their leaders, with each one seeming to become the leader's personal property. It is becoming usual to talk of M. Marchais' party rather than the Communist Party, or M. Chirac's party rather than the Popular Republican Party. The electoral system, particularly the presidential electoral system, shows clearly that it now takes only one individual to interest and convince fifty million viewers or listeners where in the past it took several hundred and even thousands.

In fact there is no longer any room for more than five or six major pieces on the political chessboard if we are to go through the motions of direct democracy. The rest are pawns and are quickly eliminated from the game. Observers describe this development in terms which, in a more modern and necessarily more abstract language, take up the themes of crowd psychology and in particular those of Tarde, that infallible foreteller of the future:

The primacy of the candidate or leader over the political grouping he belongs to is a trend towards the personalisation of power visible in all politicians and can be explained by the fact that political communication is increasingly based on the system of exchanges of images and symbolic values. The image created and propagated by the media turns the electoral field into a veritable universe of signs in which the sorcerer's apprentices of hidden meaning have taken over from Cartesian logicians. (Noir, 1980: 71)

These somewhat less than sorcerer-like apprentices conscientiously apply the strategies that have proved their point. They are not asked to take part in a confrontation of ideas or human beings so much as in a confrontation of images, with all that that implies of ceremony and ritual, and this is largely due to the media, for they suggest great dreams and convert the masses without, however, inducing them to act. They ask a single individual, a gifted leader and publicist, to persuade them, which means to fascinate them.

The passage from a democracy of masses to a democracy of publics could be described in much more detail. Between them there is a continuity and a transformation of political psychology. They offer many analogies with the theories of Le Bon and Tarde and this gives them a flesh-and-blood quality, as if they were part of the same soil that gave birth to those theories and an inescapable part of the reality that they glimpsed and to some degree anticipated.

We can now close this list of examples and prepare for the next stage of our investigation. With his description of crowds and his brilliant analysis of the 'crowd soul', Le Bon created a new kind of psychology. By means of his study of imitation and communication and his concept of the role of the leader, Tarde extended it to cover the whole of society. The machinery was in place, the inner structure built, the parts fitted and adjusted, the raw material to be worked on chosen. Like the Golem, that clay man built, so legend tells us, by a rabbi of Prague, all that it lacked was the vital spark, its own motive power. Crowd psychology now needed to be set in motion and its how and why explained. That was to be Freud's task.

## PART VI

# The best disciple of Le Bon and Tarde: Sigmund Freud

---

## 1. *The black books of Doctor Freud*

---

### I

THERE ARE TWO KINDS OF GENIUS, university ones and universal ones. The first kind, men such as Durkheim, Weber or de Broglie, belong exclusively to the world of learning. They, and their disciples, are scholars. The second kind, men such as Marx, Darwin or Einstein, belong by virtue of their ideas and personalities to the world in the widest sense of the term. They are men of vision who at some point join the gallery of our cultural heroes, the Moses, Aristotles and Leonardo da Vincis and all the legendary figures of history. Freud was one of them, and that is why there has grown up around him a school of disciples which is also a band of the faithful, a group of enquiring minds who are also priests prostrating themselves before the image of the creator of their system of beliefs.

All of them have seen their task as propagating his ideas and keeping them as free of heresy as a faith, and the means to this end has been a zealous commentary on the texts of the Master. This commentary embodies a tradition and maintains a legend, uniting the servants of a cult of a saviour of humanity once they have undergone due initiation. Truth has thus become faith and finally ritual, and the latter has obviously been at its strictest when the veneration for the great man has been most marked. This is because no-one can give up his freedom of thought or his desire to be another cultural hero without depriving others of that freedom. In short, Freud's followers ensure that there can be no other man of his calibre. There will be no Freud but Freud, just as there will be no Marx but Marx, no Christ but Christ, merely disciples and the faithful.

This extraordinary cult of the man, however, does not alter the fact that certain of his writings have a special place in his work and are condemned by both Freudians and anti-Freudians. These writings deal with the origins of religion, social institutions, political authority and, in general, mass psychology. The works in question are *Totem and Taboo, Group Psychology and the Analysis of the Ego, The Future of an Illusion, Civilisation and Its Discontents* and *Moses and Monotheism*. Together with *The Ego and the Id*, an essay which develops a new vision of the personality, they form a whole that has been, and still is, seen as compromising. As Marthe Robert writes:

In no other field did Freud put his scientific reputation at greater risk than in that of religious psychology, where both intellectual curiosity and the general line of his research led him to venture several times. *Totem and Taboo, The Future of an Illusion* and *Moses and Monotheism* were the three stages of a compromising adventure which was seen as intolerable by those it concerned, caused him to lose some of his supporters and is still a thorny problem for a certain lineage of Freudian psychoanalysts. (Robert, 1964: II, 145)

It is even thornier if we add to Marthe Robert's list the other titles I have just mentioned. We can see that we are not dealing with carriages that have come uncoupled from the engine and just got lost, but with a whole train solidly coupled up and taking an unexpected direction. Because the unity has been missed and the link between the 'religious psychology' and crowd psychology (which you will shortly see) has not been understood, the whole picture has become confused and worrying. Freud is no longer Freud, and to hide our confusion we have had no recourse but to seek explanations of the most far-fetched kind.

One reaction has been to see them as the work of an old man and of no scientific value. Just as Marx's early writings were long excluded from his work because of their philosophical nature, Freud's later ones were ignored on the pretext that they were a kind of mythological hangover. Marx's youthful writings were excluded because it was claimed that he produced them at an age when he was too young for serious science. Freud's later writings remained hidden (for how long?) on the nicely symmetrical grounds that at that stage in his life he was too old for it. This is like thinking that economics and psychology are like physics and that in their case we can see exactly where science starts and finishes, or like imagining that scientific fertility, like female fertility, can be placed within strict limits.

It has also been said that the reason why Freud produced such work is to be found in the difficulties psychoanalysis encountered in the treatment of neuroses, and that Freud tried to restore its prestige by writing a series of non-scientific works on topics of current interest for a non-specialised public. Such writings would ensure continuity and success outside the inner circle, but would be of no direct relevance to psychoanalysis or interest to psychoanalysts.

In addition – and this was an accusation rather than an explanation –

each of them has been seen as an inappropriate and dangerous attempt by psychoanalysis to encroach on the fields of other disciplines and in particular to reduce social problems to individual ones and politics to psychology. In short, they were considered to be a form of intellectual imperialism and pre-eminently as an attempt to take over the territory of Marxism. Psychoanalysis was seen as having its own territory, that of psychology and hence that of the individual and of neuroses, and as having no other.

The reason for this narrow concept, for standing an entire body of work on its head, was that the historical and scientific context in which it was produced had been ignored and that it was seen as impossible and unthinkable that at a given moment it had turned its back on individual psychology and faced up to the problem of crowd psychology. Once this kind of social psychology is ignored, all Freud's writings on it belong to the old man's secret world and the dark side of his nature, rather like what alchemy was for Newton or astrology for Kepler, although the analogy is not an exact one. And the less said of that world the better.

I have absolutely no intention of discussing and refuting these explanations, which seem to me to be aimed rather at getting rid of embarrassing facts than at accounting for them. One cannot criticise them for their tenuous intellectual content. It is a fact of life. What they can be criticised for is the ignorance they show and their unseemly haste to sever the relations that were established at a particular time between psychoanalysis and crowd psychology in the work of Freud and his disciples. Purists hate the links between intellectual heroes and jobbing intellectual historians like Le Bon, Tarde and McDougall. For unavoidable reasons of intellectual snobbery and political colouring, they obviously prefer nobler links with the likes of Nietzsche, Kant and so on. But Freud had not read them, although he had read, discussed and paraphrased Le Bon and Tarde. Those who condemn them without having read them remind me of the eighteenth-century aristocrat who had fought fourteen duels because he thought that Tasso was a greater poet than Ariosto and then confessed on his deathbed that he had never read a line of either of them.

So I shall not spend any time on the mass of studies devoted to these various explanations. I mention them only in passing, so as not to seem to be ignoring them. In science, too, the tip is useful. It is better to go straight to God than to his saints. Or to his interpreters.

## II

Let us take a look at the obvious facts. It was in his essay *Group Psychology and the Analysis of the Ego,* published in 1921, that Freud made his first official incursion into social psychology. When he had completed and extended his analysis of the individual ego, he seemed to have found the mark of the social. This was not only in the form of the other, or the Other, in the neutral and abstract sense we now use to hide his concrete identity, but also in the form of organised and non-organised masses and leaders. This social dimension was all the more fascinating and disturbing as the leader, given concrete form by the masses, was on the same level as what the individual represses and brought out into the open that side of man that is so difficult to reach, the unconscious.

The unconscious made incarnate in crowds terrified Freud as much as it terrifies us, arousing in him the same fears as it had aroused, you will recall, in Le Bon. In Marthe Robert's words:

That fear of crowds, which it would not be too much of an exaggeration to call a phobia had always, it seems, been present in him and he had always explained it in a curious way by means of an analogy which much later was to provide the theme of his essays in sociology. This was that the masses are on the same level as the depths of the psyche and between them and the human unconscious there are relationships of connivance, and almost of complicity, that threaten the highest values of consciousness and all that individuality has acquired.

(Robert, 1974: 81)

Whatever the reasons for Freud's phobia may have been, the study quoted here incontestably sets out a new scientific position which, from the point of view of crowd psychology, can clearly be seen. Le Bon had merely described them, Tarde merely analysed them and said what they were. In *Group Psychology and the Analysis of the Ego,* Freud tried to explain them and say why they were what they were. This step is a major one in any field of knowledge. Seen in this light, the continuity is so striking that one commentator, who never makes unfounded assertions, sums the matter up very tellingly:

Le Bon's theory was considered as indisputable scientific truth by many. One may wonder that Freud took it as starting point for his own theory. As shown by Reinwald, Freud's theories, while contradicting Le Bon, show noteworthy similarities with those of Tarde. What Tarde had called imitation, Freud called identification, and in many regards Freud's ideas appeared to be those of Tarde transposed in psychoanalytic concepts. (Ellenberger, 1970: 528)

That is true both in its broad sweep and in detail. Each of the three thinkers made his own particular contribution to the description of the same class of phenomena. Each helped set up a reasoned system of concepts and a search for those causes of which a knowledge strengthens the outline of a science. That is a fact of history that can be seen as important or unimportant, as one wishes, but that it is difficult to deny.[1]

## III

So far, I have explained nothing that you did not know already. My aim, however, is not so much to instruct or astonish you as to remind you of the facts of the matter. While reading, you will certainly have wondered how Freud came to be interested in crowd psychology, which seems a thousand miles from his concerns as a doctor treating neuroses. But when we think about it, we can see that he came to it quite naturally for several reasons, all of which conspired to force him to look increasingly outside the four walls of his consulting-room. It is as if, at a given moment, he no longer asked his patients how they were, but how the world was.

We can place that moment – and this is the first of the reasons for his interest in crowd psychology – at the end of the First World War. No doubt there have always been wars, but they follow one another without being alike. The countries they affect are not ravaged to the same degree. The 1914–1918 war came after a long period of peace that lasted long enough for many men to cherish the hope – or the illusion – that science, industry and an international outlook would push back the passions of earlier centuries. Murderous clashes and struggles between nations were seen as things of the past. As we have seen, the socialists thought they could mobilise the workers against war. The philosophers and scientists thought that the growth of knowledge and the development of the human conscience would show it for the absurd thing it was and eliminate it. In addition, there were all those people for whom wars were neither just nor unjust but simply horrible. They said, with Maupassant, 'And the most amazing thing is that people do not rise up against such governments. What difference *is* there between monarchies and republics? The most amazing thing is that the whole of society does not rebel against even the word war' (Maupassant, 1979: 61).

Neither optimism nor pacifism nor indignation prevented the war. With the victory of the Allies came the disappearance of two empires, Germany and Austria-Hungary, and a whole chain of national and social revolutions. Only one of the latter, the Russian Revolution, succeeded. The rest were bloodily crushed. For his part, Freud was immensely disappointed in them. His world was split asunder. The war and revolutions seemed to him to provide a blindingly clear demonstration of the invincible power of the masses driven by hate.

Scarcely had the gunfire stopped – and this is the second reason – than other movements of the oppressed masses broke out. They did not give power to the people, and the hoped-for democratic society yielded to the pressure of totalitarian movements. Millions of men were taken in by the words and ideologies of demagogues, and those who put their faith in reason and good sense were cruelly disappointed. Right was crushed by might. Free men accepted slavery and sovereignty imposed by violence (Lederer, 1940: Newmann, 1965). And amongst all this upheaval sharp ears, pricked up like those of a hare and for the same reason, the sensitive ears of Jews, first began to pick out the sound of antisemitism and then that of the jackboots of Nazi parades. From a cellar in one of the most civilised countries in the world, Germany, in full intellectual power and bursting with scientific, artistic and literary genius, the vestiges of barbarity were arising, thrusting against the foundations of a fragile democracy and undermining them. The last hopes that could be put in liberal politics and a rational vision of history were destroyed by this unleashed savagery. The sound and the fury of these hordes aroused ancestral fears in Freud and those like him. Even when such fears are ill-advised, they do not augur well, for they reawaken the memory of excited crowds moving in mobs from pogrom to pogrom.

Freud was a Jew, the Nazis were antisemitic. He had drawn in his fears with his mother's milk, and he had only to look back into his memory to recognise in what was happening a dress rehearsal for massacres and to realise that there was no hope that the Nazis would disappear as a party (Robert, 1974: 81). Like all the intellectuals of his type and time, he was steeped in German culture. Putting his full trust in the powers of reason and science, he wanted to be assimilated into the surrounding culture and to be indistinguishable from it. For him, the constant rise of antisemitism meant a door slammed in his face because of his racial origins and a proof that once a Jew, always a Jew.

This Freudian version of Swann's Way does not of course explain everything, nor do I intend to restrict myself to it. On the other hand, playing down the importance of this element and ignoring it as if all cases were indistinguishably similar would be worse than frivolously pretending that it was the only explanation. Freud never denied that he belonged to a singular race and a singular history. Unlike Marx, he did not want to settle the Jewish question. Unlike Einstein, who once half-jokingly remarked that he had become a 'Jewish saint', he did not see himself as entrusted with a particular mission. For Freud, being Jewish was simply a datum of his biography, a fate that he had to accept without mysticism, and to try to sever the thousand invisible links that attached a man to his Jewish roots would make him even more a product of them.

In a preface to the Hebrew edition of *Totem and Taboo*, Freud wrote that if he were asked what there was left in him that was Jewish when he had abandoned everything he had shared with his compatriots – religion, national feeling and so on – he would reply that there was still a great deal, probably the major part.

He certainly did not deal with such questions joyously or willingly. Who would have done? But it is clear that constrained, forced and with bitterness in his heart he devoted himself to them with all the strength that his illness left him. This is made clear in a letter he wrote to Zweig in 1930, in which he said that he knew too little about the will to power in men since he had after all lived as a theorist and that he was astonished that the upheavals of the last few years had drawn him so far into the events of the world around him. I would scarcely have attempted to write this book or wondered why Freud had devoted his last years to crowd psychology if our present-day history were not copying, although not repeating, that of his time.

The third reason is of a strictly scientific order. As you know, the major turning-point of Freud's career was his discovery of hypnosis while he was in France. At the time, it was the only effective form of treatment for neuroses in general and for hysteria in particular. Freud was fascinated and deeply impressed by the results Bernheim and Liébeault were obtaining and became its champion and defender. German medical circles, however, were hostile to hypnosis, which they saw as mere quackery. Freud also used hypnotic suggestion and paid homage to its inventors. Then he made his own discovery, the 'talking cure', in which the patient, stretched out on a couch, relates everything that is passing through his head. This free-association method marked the beginning of psychoanalysis as an original therapy for psychic disorders. However, in his struggle to impose his theories and techniques, Freud repudiated hypnosis, replacing it in all circumstances with the procedures and ideas he had discovered himself.

He became aware, however, that in one important area of psychology – crowd psychology, which was very popular at the time – suggestion was still the process of explanation.[2] And the ideas contained in it are still current in that area. Better than anyone else, Freud knew that psychoanalysis had never come to terms with what it owed to hypnosis and fascination. (Today as then, one has only to look at the setting in which psychoanalytic treatment takes place to establish the truth of this – the analyst's office, the way his words are ritualised and his verbal exchanges and relationship with his patient are turned into a ceremony.)

Suggestion, after being in eclipse for twenty or thirty years, thus returned to the scene. Freud could not but take account of this fact. He described how continuous his reflection on it had been and reminded his readers that the opinion he had formed of it in 1889 was still valid in 1921:

We shall therefore be prepared for the statement that suggestion (or more correctly suggestibility) is actually an irreducible, primitive phenomenon, a fundamental fact in the mental life of man. Such, too, was the opinion of Bernheim, of whose astonishing arts I was a witness in the year 1889. . . . Now that I once more approach the riddle of suggestion after having kept away from it for some thirty years, I find there is no change in the situation. (There is one exception to be made to this statement, and one which bears witness precisely to the influence of psycho-analysis.) (Freud: XVIII, 89–90)

And so the fight was resumed on new ground. Facing and being able to stand up to one's old demons is perhaps a way of regaining one's youthful vigour. Here, after all, it was a case of showing that psychoanalysis was the basis of crowd psychology.[3]

The fourth and final reason was of a personal nature, as Freud himself has testified. With no battles left to right, he had grown old, and heaven knows that his old age provided more than one of his skilful detractors with an opportunity for denigrating what he had written before 1920. Some attributed his views on the crowd to the proverbial conservatism of old people and his pessimism to the suffering his cancer caused him. All those who provide explanations of that pessimism would do well to see it as an effect of his objectivity. One could say of him what Jacques Rivière said of Proust: 'Proust looks at life without the slightest metaphysical interest, the least bias towards a constructive view, the least inclination to offer consolation.' They would also do well to remember that only a superstitious philistine thinks that it is enough to close one's eyes to the reality of the world for it to be a better place. Freud could never adopt the ostrich's policy or see things in a different way, and his words have proved to be tragically prophetic.[4]

Other critics have maintained that his intellectual powers were failing. Both groups are ignorant of the kind of freedom with regard to social constraints and the serene indifference to the opinions of the living that the approach of death gives to lofty minds.

At every age there operates a kind of balance between the power of the mind and the moral strength to resist the pressures and snares of society. With the coquetry of the old who know that they are the equals of younger men, Freud complained of a hardening of his scientific arteries. But age did bring one particular blessing. In the hope of being listened to, he repeatedly stated that his medical career and clinical work had been imposed on him by outside circumstances. He had suffered the servitude they inflicted on him and borne the yoke that had frustrated his passions and stifled the deepest instincts of his youth. The world he came from had disappeared and he had finished his work and successfully completed his task. With all these restrictions removed, there was nothing left to stop him going back to the ideals and preoccupations of his young manhood (Shorske, 1973). At the time, he had thought of becoming a barrister, going into politics or devoting himself to social and cultural questions (Fromm, 1962: 100).

It is never too late to make good. In the postscript that he added to his *Autobiographical Study* in 1935, Freud noted that over the previous years a 'significant change' had been observed in his writings. This he explained as follows:

Threads which in the course of my development had become intertangled have now begun to separate; interests which I had acquired in the later part of my life have receded, while the older and original ones become prominent once more. [. . .] My interest after making a lifelong *détour* through the natural sciences, medicine and psychotherapy, returned to the cultural problems which had fascinated me long before, when I was a youth scarcely old enough for thinking.
(Freud: XX, 71)

In other words, he was now interested in the currently-fashionable crowd psychology.

Each of these reasons – the disappointment brought by the war, the rise of totalitarian, antisemitic parties, the persistence of hypnosis as a model and the recrudescence of his personal interests – explains why he turned towards that branch of science. His bourgeois origins also inclined him towards it, which is so obvious as to need no further discussion. It could not, however, be the only reason at a time when the dark night was closing in on nations once more sliding into war.

## IV

If what I have said is true, then I am not taking his name in vain when I link it with crowd psychology in order to add fresh lustre to a science which experienced a blaze of glory and then a no less sudden eclipse. Despite all the reservations you may have, I would like you to accept the hypothesis that Freud's interest in crowd psychology was a radical turning point and a real revolution in his research and hence in psychoanalysis. After considerable reflection, I have reached the conclusion that once this new step had been taken there were two distinct theories and not, as is usually believed, an extension of the original one.

The only way I can think of to provide a quick illustration of this hypothesis is by comparing it with Einstein's two theories. The first, that of restricted relativity, in fact solved known problems and was the high point of classical science. The second, that of general relativity, set out to explain the laws of the universe by bringing together electricity and gravity. It is still an intellectual breakthrough that nothing had prepared us for and that few things confirm. Its only result (but what a result!) has been to give a new impetus to a somewhat faded science, cosmology, and provide it with the whole of the starry skies to investigate.

In the same way, *before* the break we are looking at, one could say that there was a restricted psychiatric theory that dealt with the individual and the family and neurosis and dreams and marked the high point of the development of classical psychiatry and psychology. On its first contact with hypnosis, it had introduced three key ideas. These were the libido, which explained the universe enclosed within the individual; the unconscious, which offered an analysis of his mental life: and the Oedipus complex, which defined the area of conflict arising from father/son rivalry and attempted to show us ways of being a human child. The technique of free association became the emblem of this new discipline.

*Afterwards*, there was the second encounter with hypnotic suggestion, this time in mass psychology. From this was born general psychoanalytical theory, for which only one question is worthy of interest: how can one be a father? From it, however, a number of others flow. How can one create a group and govern a nation? What is the origin of culture, indeed of humanity? Without warning, it shifted attention from the world of the individual to that of the masses. The transfer revealed the unknown and terrible transformations of the human psyche.

And thus we see Freud disengaging himself from the study of family problems before all the hurrying philosophers and already drawing the profile of an anti-Oedipus at the level of the whole of civilisation. That the profile should be one of a prophet (Moses, in fact) and not of a king is another problem and a vast and complex one. The whole of the domestic drama with a cast of daddy, mummy and baby was now only of value as an image or analogy. Only the political and cultural tragedy was of value as an example. It was the tragedy of the death of the leader and the inexpiable struggle, with no real reconciliation, between him and the mass.

From the day Freud put forward the hypothesis of the slaying of the domestic tyrant by his sons, everything that had gone before swung in a different direction. He himself knew this and wrote to his favourite disciple, Ferenczi, that he had only wanted a passing affair and yet found himself, at his age, obliged to take a new wife. And what a wife she turned out to be! She made him take a hard look at religions and adapt rather uncertain ideas – those of identification and the super-ego, for example – to them: ideas that came to him from the times he lived in, and those times gave him neither confidence nor the desire to spare them. He dealt with things as they came, and on the whole they came badly rather than well, in a procession of uncertain revolutions, lost freedoms and the shadow-graphs of war. He saw no glimmer of hope in the mighty social sciences which, like the politicians of the time, were cultivating Weimar-type theories and dead ideas, maintaining that salvation came from the unplumbable essence of humanity at a time when men were sinking into the barbarity in which they would ultimately perish.

These 'as if' theories occupied him greatly in *The Future of an Illusion*, *Civilisation and its Discontents* and *Moses and Monotheism*. One feels that each time, in each book, something finishes and something new comes into being. They are inhabited by some hard and desolate presence and an obstinate determination to explore all the hidden mysteries of human nature in spite of the unpleasant truths that will certainly be found there. Despite his anguish, Freud applied his genius to a full and remorseless account of our psychic wretchedness. In those works, we only escape the Scylla of the neuroses to plunge into the Charybdis of religions. Freud certainly hesitated to go any further. As he himself admitted, 'We find ourselves here in the field of group psychology, where we do not feel at home' (Freud: XXIII, 70).

However that may be, the area of mental life gave way to that of religious life and the beliefs that mark it out. Here, time itself takes on an Einsteinian quality. We are no longer in the linear and absolute time of the first theory, divided up into phases (from birth until the age of five, from five to twelve and so on) but in the relative and cyclical time of human development, where men sometimes submit to their master and sometimes revolt against him, and the sequence goes on.

In order not to spend too much time on this point, we can make the rapid observation that in moving from the restricted to the general theory of psychoanalysis we change from one universe to another. We feel that we are leaving astronomy, the study of isolated planetary systems, and moving into the field of cosmology, the study of the life and death of the hosts of stars and galaxies that we can see on a clear night. It would be extremely interesting to pursue this historical parallel, but history is not the sole object of this book.

## 2. *From classical to revolutionary mass psychology*

### I

IN SHORT, all things were working together to consign crowd psychology to indifference and oblivion, and with it Freud's studies. These we no longer understand, and they seem to us simple and repetitive. There is an obvious explanation. Unlike his pupils and successors, Freud was writing for a readership of men and women who, far from being won over, were downright hostile to his ideas. This explains the sometimes elementary nature of his analyses, the abundance of familiar and everyday examples in his work and the burning need to convince that can be sensed behind the thread of logical argument. It does not, however, in any way diminish their novelty or importance.

These qualities are wasted on us. Since his disciples are addressing themselves to an initiated public, they now seem pointless. Present-day Freudians simply seek to strengthen the certainties of readers who are already converted. Their linguistic brilliance, their intellectual artificiality and the outlandish situations they choose to study are all intended to flatter the sensibilities of the true believers. Psychoanalytical works written exclusively for psychoanalysts and those philosophers who, so to speak, read over their shoulders are overloaded with conniving winks, esoteric formulas and gnostic shibboleths. *We too shall have to return to basic things and the painful task of analysis couched in universally accessible language. The simplicity of concepts must be maintained, and things that are normally veiled in artistic obscurity must be expressed plainly, for the crowd psychology of both Freud and his precursors is still unknown to us. We are suspicious and consequently ignorant of it, and the only way we can move towards an understanding is by means of the elementary and the familiar. This will preclude neither a critical approach nor a recognition of those new things that this book will enable us to discover.*

To start with, we must accept a basic fact: Freud shared with Le Bon and Tarde the conviction that everything depends on and is explained by psychic factors. To speak plainly, only one science, psychology, reaches the heart of reality. When reflecting on the great social problems, on world religions, on social movements, he was thinking of the various categories of crowds. We might ask what part sociology played in all that. For Freud, sociology was simply a form of applied psychology:

For sociology too, dealing as it does with the behaviour of people in society, cannot be anything but applied psychology. Strictly speaking, there are only two sciences: psychology, pure and applied, and the natural sciences.

(Freud: XXII, 79)

This much is clear. Psychology is not a discipline sharing the cake of truth with the other branches of knowledge and trying to grab the lion's share. It embraces the whole of human reality, including history and culture, and no part of that reality is alien to it. This means that, contrary to what is commonly thought, Freud's various studies are not contributions to this or that branch of knowledge. *Totem and Taboo* is not a contribution to anthropology, *The Future of an Illusion* is not a contribution to the study of religions, *Moses and Monotheism* is not a contribution to history, *Group Psychology and the Analysis of the Ego* is not a contribution to sociology and so on. He certainly studied the evidence amassed by these disciplines and discussed current interpretations of it, but only with the aim of relating it to psychology and in particular to crowd psychology, of which each of these disciplines was a facet.[1] One American writer on Freud concludes that with Nietzsche, Freud declared that the master science of the future was not history but psychology, and that history would become *mass* psychology. With regard to the neurotic phenomena of religion:

The only really satisfactory analogy, Freud thought, was to be found in psychopathology, the genesis of human neurosis; that is to say, in a discipline belonging to individual psychology, whereas religious phenomena must of course be regarded as a part of mass psychology.          (Rieff, 1979: 210)

All the works I have just mentioned belong to that kind of psychology for historical and, primarily, *logical* reasons. They are mysterious and superb creations which narrate the birth of a work, the story of a novel of the mind which has several different beginnings and which, like *Finnegans Wake*, never reaches the conclusion which it can of course never have. Nevertheless, as if we were listening to some final symphony or watching the last burst of an elaborate display of fireworks, we can see in it all the major themes of crowd psychology – the fusion of individuals into the mass, the power of leaders, the origin of beliefs and religion and their preservation in the 'unconscious' of the tribe, the enigma of the submission of men and the art of ruling them. For us, and by that I mean all those who are interested in that kind of psychology, they are worth a complete treatise. That is the perspective we must see and understand them in, even if they are twilight works.

## II

The function of mass psychology is to explain all past and present political, historical and cultural phenomena. This was known. It is, however, the first time that its task has been so clearly defined. As long as it remained inside its original setting, its sole concerns were political ones. It was liberal and conservative, and its task was to preserve the existing social order, not because it was the best, but because it was the most tolerable one. In spite of his fierce criticism of repression and his denunciation of the conditions imposed on the mass of humanity, and in particular on those who were most humiliated and exploited, Freud is still associated with that tradition. He seems to have expressed the kernel of his political thought to Zweig, who admired him in those early days:

In spite of all my dissatisfaction with present economic systems, I have no hope that the road taken by the Soviets will lead to any improvement. Indeed, any hope of that kind that I had has disappeared in the ten years since the Soviets came to power. I am still a liberal of the old school.

His own words express the truth of his position with regard to the historical situation. Taking that into account, he saw that man experienced a hell on earth. His thought at that stage was quite naturally concentrated on theories and methods aimed at making man conscious of that hell and at helping him to free himself from it. It was not aimed at re-awakening the illusions that he had had from time immemorial and which (so he believed) helped to make his earthly misery bearable, but at destroying them. Men were to be drawn out of their waking dreams, made aware of their own strengths and abilities and enabled to transform reality so that illusions would no longer be necessary.

It was in order to destroy illusions that Freud, in the best atheistic tradition, made *The Future of an Illusion* into a pitiless indictment of religion and the fictitious solutions that it proposes for the problems of human existence. In that book he showed the similarities between religion and obsessional neurosis, which, through its rituals and repetitions, blights the lives of individuals and cuts them off from reality. It should not be forgotten that for him as well as for Le Bon and Tarde, religion was the first structure of all collective beliefs. In denouncing it he was, it can be justly claimed, denouncing all views of the world, whatever their particular content might be.

Several texts, of which the earliest was *Group Psychology and the Analysis of the Ego*, seem to be devoted to the task of exposing the reality of the link between the leader and the crowd. The leader is generally evil, a manifold and yet entirely naked force distinguishable behind the hypnotist, who is his prototype. Hypnosis is a violent form of attraction used against the individual, and the regression so evident in the crowd is the price that has to be paid for it. In Freud's view, the great seducers were not Don Juan or Casanova or their imitators (seducing a couple of hundred women was no great achievement) but leaders of the calibre of Napoleon, Stalin or Mao, who could move whole crowds to flights of amorous folly, diverting them, as swindlers divert funds, to their own use. Enormous masses of people gather to acclaim such men, go into ecstasies when they hear them speak, try to be like them and kill or are killed on their behalf. During their lifetime such leaders are objects of worship, and even when they are dead they continue to arouse passions and to play havoc with the emotions and memories of all of us. Freud was right, for what is involved here if not stolen love?

In all Freud wrote at this period there is a spirit of merciless revolt. Ideas and realities are uncompromisingly swept aside. Crowd psychology, which had been an apologetic discipline, suddenly became a critical weapon. Like all his earliest followers, Freud was perhaps an 'old-fashioned liberal', but in his iconoclastic attitude to all the intellectual complacency of the times he represented the most coherent form of that view, decanting the ideas of crowd psychology into a different social milieu which was critical of society and preoccupied with revolution.

An earlier generation, that of Le Bon and Tarde, had stressed the streak of conservatism in the masses, seeing it as a bulwark against revolution. Those who succeeded them had affinities with Freud and were concerned about that same conservatism since in their view it was a hindrance to revolution. They set out to explain it and to discover why the masses could not be caught up in revolution even when social and economic conditions were ripe for it. Their conclusion was that the explanation must be of a psychological nature (Korsch, 1970).

There grew up here and there a mass psychology, initially inspired by Fromm and Federn, which was revolutionary or leftist in nature and set out to analyse the nature of this obstacle.[2] Paul Federn, a disciple of Freud, wrote a book with a title that itself sets out a whole programme: *Contribution à la psychologie de la révolution: la société sans père*. Its argument was that an authoritarian, patriarchal structure of the kind found even in socialist parties ensured the survival of bourgeois societies. If this structure, which the family perpetuated in us, did not collapse, the chances of a real revolution were small.

The book fervently pleads the case for workers' councils ('soviets' in short) which create a new fraternal ethic (Glaser, 1979). All previous mass organisations had been constructed from the top downwards. This pyramid shape provided an ideal model for the father/son relationship. The new organisation, however, grew from the masses, upwards from the base, whence it drew the appropriate impetus and psychic system, that of fraternal relationships. Federn, however, was pessimistic and saw the family as the greatest obstacle to a lasting victory for workers' councils.

It can thus be seen that, even before Freud's studies of crowd psychology had appeared, the discipline had already come to the notice of his circle, bringing with it several new themes which were to be continually developed. A number of the more creative of his disciples were attracted to it in their search for better ways of dealing with political and cultural crises. Their writings and their actions prove that psychoanalysis includes crowd phenomena amongst its legitimate concerns and is not restricted to what takes place in individual clinical situations.

Outside Europe, in America and even in England, intellectuals were not obliged to take an interest in such questions. In Germany and Austria, however, poised between a socialist regime and the Nazi threat, the distance was less great.[3] Not only had revolution failed; counter-revolution was under way. Everywhere in Europe the masses were howling approval while their leaders were binding them hand and foot. Wilhelm Reich was perhaps not the first intellectual, but he was certainly the most passionate, to try to achieve the aim of psychoanalysis within the framework of the political left, and he asked those questions already raised by crowd psychology in connection with other leaders:

How is it possible that a Hitler, a Dzhugashvili (i.e. Stalin) could reign supreme over eight hundred million individuals? How can it be possible? It was in 1927 that I raised this question on a sociological level. I talked at length about it to Freud.
(Reich, 1972: 46)

This two-way traffic is worth noting. Reich (like Fromm, Broch or Adorno) immersed himself in crowd psychology to understand Hitler and the Nazi movement. He was, of course, not aware that Hitler had mastered the subject in order to create his movement, to become Hitler, in fact. Reich was interested in it in order to understand social reality, Hitler in order to apply it to that same reality. The former soon saw that the marriage of psychoanalysis and Marxist economic and political theory would provide an explanation, as the two systems were complementary:

Hence, the line of questioning of mass psychology begins at precisely the point where the *immediate* socio-economic explanation hits wide of the mark. Does this mean that mass psychology and social economy serve cross purposes? No, for thinking and acting on the part of the masses contradictory to the immediate socio-economic situation, i.e. irrational thinking and acting, are themselves the result of an *earlier* socio-economic situation.
(Reich, 1975: 54)

Breaking with his teacher's theory, he showed that the family, itself the product of economic conditions, creates a type of character-structure through the process of bringing up children of the very type to support the political and economic order of society as a whole. The result is the repression of sexuality, physical discipline and conformity to the forces of order. By the time we emerge from childhood we are ready to conform and expect to be commanded by a leader.

It must be admitted that in one sense what Reich maintained is also present in one way or another in the work of Le Bon or Tarde, and even more clearly in that of Freud. But the ingredients of the mixture he concocted and his vigorous assumption that the triumph of Nazism in Germany cannot be explained solely by Hitler's charisma or the machinations of German capitalists but were also the result of the psychic complexion of the German masses mean that the mixture is an explosive one.

There is at the very least one other level at which we must understand and explain the tyrannical and authoritarian phenomena of our time. Reich's assertion that 'fascism is to be regarded as a problem of the masses and not as a problem of Hitler as a person or the politics of the National Socialist party' (Reich, 1975: 131) has remained engraved in the minds of several generations down to our own day. We can also see reflected in it the flames of the *autos-da-fé* and the many sombre ceremonies that he himself witnessed. In fact, most of Freud's close pupils saw sexual repression as one of the main mechanisms of political domination and the family as the producer of authoritarian ideology and conservative character-structure (Robinson, 1970).

Their ideas bring us to Herbert Marcuse, who took up these themes and modernised them. He moved in the opposite direction to Reich, moving from Marxism to psychoanalysis, largely via the famous Frankfurt School, which saw as its task the combination of the notion of the class society with that of the mass society. It attempted to criticise the former from the point of view of the anonymous and solitary masses and the latter by pointing out the facts of its exploitation and class content as shown in Marxism. This meant both infinite variety and a very wide horizon. In any case, Freud's *Group Psychology and the Analysis of the Ego* was the work most often quoted by the Frankfurt School (Jacoby, 1975: 44) and provided the framework for what its members wrote. All their work expressed the same idea, namely that mass psychology was one of the major issues of our world.

That critical and revolutionary wing stressed the possibilities of liberation and of resistance to authority by the masses. They were seen as capable of overcoming all sexual and economic repression, a power which had been denied them, and of smashing the bolts on the door blocking the way to a revolt against the social order, an ability which had seemed doubtful. The leader, especially when his name was Hitler or Stalin, was not the answer to their psychological wretchedness: he *was* that wretchedness itself.

Adopting this point of view meant that crowd psychology was changing direction and declaring itself to be of the left. It legitimised mass society and then became its critic and its teacher. But that was not all. As a result of the combined influence of Freud's creative disciples (of whom Reich was the most vital) and of those subtle minds he inspired (of whom Adorno and Marcuse seem the most aware) and their influence on recent social movements in Europe and the United States, crowd psychology once again made an impact on history, showing that it could serve not only leaders but also the masses. Freud's work is at the root of these changes. As one of those who brought them about was to write, 'In the end it was modern depth psychology which finally purged the findings of Le Bon's mass psychology of their political equivocation' (Horkheimer and Adorno, 1973: 77). All this, of course, happened without Freud intending it and even against his wishes.

In the last analysis, most of the human sciences – and one has only to look at economics, history, sociology or anthropology – have undergone similar changes. They started as branches of study concerned with order and became disciplines concerned with revolution. Nevertheless, in each case this change of direction was taken without distorting the fund of classical ideas that had been accumulated.[4] If we want to trace these ideas in their entirety in the field of crowd psychology, we shall have to return to Freud. That will be the last, and the longest, stage of our journey.

# 3. *The three questions of mass psychology*

THE NAMES of Le Bon and Freud have often, quite rightly, been
linked. The two were of course separate planets, but nevertheless
part of the same solar system, as Freud recognised from the start. In
his description of crowds, he used the palette and paints provided by 'Le
Bon's deservedly famous work *Psychologie des Foules'* (Freud: XVIII, 72).
The major characteristics are already familiar to you. In a crowd, individuals lose their own opinions and intellectual faculties, can no longer control
their feelings and instincts and begin to act in a way that surprises both
themselves and those who know them. To recapitulate, the main features
of their conversion into a human mass are the disappearance of the
conscious personality, the guiding of thoughts and emotions into a single
direction by means of suggestion and contagion and a tendency to
actualise the ideas suggested.

All observers are agreed on these phenomena, but they nevertheless
raise three questions. What is a mass? How can it have such an influence
on the individual? What is the nature of the transformation he undergoes? It is the task of a theoretical group psychology to answer these three
questions. Freud (XVIII: 73) begins by dealing with the last one: how does
an individual in the presence of other individuals change his way of
thinking, feeling and acting? The order in which they are dealt with is self-
imposed, since the first step must be to establish symptoms and describe
effects. Only when that has been done is it possible to move to causes. But
I am jumping ahead. In brief, it can be said that such symptoms reflect a
psychic regression on the part of the individuals in the mass. This
manifests itself in many ways. Within the crowd, the repression of
unconscious tendencies diminishes and moral inhibitions disappear.
Instincts and affectivity are more intensely expressed, and simultaneously fairly archaic values and customs take the place of reason in
determining how each person will act. Since these are shared, however,
behaviour becomes uniform. Individuals act in unison with no effort on
their part, like clocks set by the same watchmaker all striking the hours at
the same time. Mass man acts like an automaton with no free will under
the control of unconscious forces and thus goes down several rungs on

the ladder of civilisation. The mass is impulsive and irritable. It is also credulous and has no critical mind. It knows neither doubt nor uncertainty and is dogmatic; hence its intolerance and its blind trust in authority.

A mass is of necessity conservative and has a deep aversion to novelty and progress and an unlimited respect for tradition. Besides, they

> have never thirsted after truth. They demand illusions, and cannot do without them. They constantly give what is unreal precedence over what is real; they are almost as strongly influenced by what is untrue as by what is true. They have an evident tendency not to distinguish between the two.      (Freud: XVIII, 80)

If we wanted to paint a complete picture of social life, we should have to subject all Freud's observations to reflection and commentary. Reading any one of them in isolation is like unwinding one thread from the whole skein. Separating them out means reducing their combined ring of truth. But Freud's analogies should not be pushed too far. Seen in a certain light, what he is plainly saying is that, to use the traditional vocabulary, masses are primitive, childish and mad. But we understand fairly readily that the primitives he is speaking about are not somewhere else, a thousand miles away. They are not Indians or Africans, and they are *here*, scorning the works of civilisation and the laws of reason. We ourselves are the primitives he studies and knows.

It is clear that the purpose of all these analogies is to show us that masses illustrate affective and intellectual and sometimes even moral regression on the part of mankind. Beyond consciousness, when the barriers are down, there is a dark and ancient world that has left its trace in our bodies and our memories. The slightest weakness is enough to let it wreak its vengeance and topple the normal mental and social order.

Upheavals of this kind usually occur at the height of a national festival, a riot, a religious procession, a war or a patriotic ceremony. On all such occasions, one feels that the unconscious is loose upon the streets and that the masses are its physical body. It uses them to shout, gesticulate furiously, overthrow prohibitions, insult superiors and broadcast disorder and protest and to indulge in all kinds of excesses and incredible violence. Reality is abolished, and the masses live in a crude dream.

> Indeed, just as in dreams and in hypnosis, in the mental operations of a group the function for testing the reality of things falls into the background in comparison with the strength of wishful impulses with their affective cathexis.
>
> (Freud: XVIII, 80)

## II

It is hard to imagine that Freud did not know what he was doing when he paraphrased Le Bon and to believe that he was not aware of the relationships between his theory and the views of the masses that it entailed. Comparing them is only of limited value, but it does highlight the still mysterious kinship between their two apparently unrelated disciplines. That kinship lies in the fact that they both discovered the unconscious. Did not Le Bon write that 'intellectual life can be compared to the small islands that are the peaks of enormous invisible mountains beneath the sea. The huge mountains themselves are the unconscious' (Le Bon 1911: 36). And Freud himself saw this as the thing that really drew the two men together:

> We have made use of Le Bon's description by way of introduction, because it fits in so well with our own psychology in the emphasis which it lays upon unconscious mental life.
> (Freud: XVIII, 82)

From the point of view of dates, however, he could just as well have written that he came close to Le Bon's. But that is not very important. At this stage, there is something that matters a great deal more and to which we should pay attention. Le Bon was obsessed by his social hatreds and unwittingly rather negligently made use of them and his intuitions without always making a distinction between what was of major and what of secondary importance. Thus, when he was dealing with the unconscious, the pure gold of lucid and articulate hypothesis never emerged from the surrounding dross of platitude. We have already come across one aspect of this. Once the individual becomes part of a group, his conscious mind loses control of an increasing part of his images, thoughts and actions. In short, Le Bon was clearly aware of the hold of the unconscious. How does it present itself? Obviously, no longer as a hidden and invisible force or as a sort of collective unconscious made up of compelling archetypes and symbols overlaid by the reason of each individual. The variations in any stable mass are too great to allow such archetypes to persist. So the only way out was the one which fitted the facts of the matter, which can be summed up in the formula 'masses are the unconscious'. Mass psychology is the psychology of the unconscious, but in a different way. What can immediately be seen on the surface of masses is thrust into the depths of the individual, and that is where it is to be found. If there is a grain of truth in all that, then the unconscious is an idea that *explains* the psychic life of individuals but only *describes* that of masses. We can see that the idea has been to some degree avoided in concepts of theory, even in Freud, since theory tends to explain visible effects in terms of invisible causes.

After noting this similarity, Freud hastened to add that Le Bon's ideas were not entirely original, and that very many statesmen, thinkers and poets had had them before he did. There is nothing new about this, but accusing someone of not being the first to have an idea is not very original either. It has been a fairly common way of denigrating all researchers, including Freud himself. When their detractors are tired of calling them scandalous and weary of repeating that they are simply echoing common sense, they scorn them for having discovered nothing new and saying things that have been known for ages.

In fact, Freud broke with Le Bon at the very same point as with Jung, the thorny problem being, as you can imagine, the collective unconscious. And it was a thorny point, for as I have suggested, Le Bon cared very little for logic and rigour, which led to a welter of confusion and triviality at every level. Freud therefore assumed that for Le Bon the unconscious was a national or racial residue, drawing its power from a long sequence of generations, each of which had contributed something to it. In psychoanalytical terms, however, the unconscious chiefly contains repressed material thrust into it by each individual ego. This explains the considerable difference between the two kinds of reality designated by the same word.

A further disagreement hinges on the following point. According to Le Bon, the range of characteristics of crowds, which we have already examined, are not possessed by individuals, being acquired only when they are closely linked with other individuals in a mass. Freud however, as we have just seen, thought that this was not the case. Everyone had these characteristics, but in a repressed form. As soon as we are part of a crowd, a general slackening takes place and the individual regresses towards the mass:

The apparently new characteristics which he then displays are in fact the manifestations of this unconscious, in which all that is evil in the human mind is contained as a predisposition. We can find no difficulty in understanding the disappearance of conscience or of a sense of responsibility in these circumstances.

(Freud: XVIII, 74)

When individuals associate with each other, the effect is not, as Le Bon claimed, a dissolution of their individual consciousness. They return to a more primitive stage of psychic life, and on each occasion, 'all that is evil in the human mind' obscurely but inevitably takes over. This explains the intellectual regression and affective exaggeration observed in crowds.

The final disagreement has more to do with individual interpretation. In many ways, Le Bon is seen as the crowd psychologist who put most emphasis on the role of the leader and described it in great detail, devoting whole chapters of his books to the matter. In his view, the crowd could not act without the leader, and he saw the most tragic fault of modern societies as being that of lacking leaders and thus depriving crowds of an element essential for their well-being. Here, too, Freud followed Le Bon, but with a certain reticence, seeing the latter's analysis as not quite complete. In his view, the explanations concerning the leaders of crowds were not quite clear and offered little to help an understanding of the laws governing the phenomenon. That is why:

Le Bon does not give the impression of having succeeded in bringing the function of the leader and the importance of prestige completely into harmony with his brilliantly executed picture of the group mind.                    (Freud: XVIII, 81)

It is not literally true that his description of crowds was more brilliant than his description of leaders. Freud's criticism of Le Bon could pass for homage nowadays in comparison with the faint praise and insults that usually come his way. But that does not make it any more appropriate. It is clear that Freud was announcing what the real basis of the new theory was to be, and in this sense his criticism was justified. In the crowd psychology that Freud worked out, the crowd was very soon to disappear from the field of investigation, to be replaced by the leader, who occupied the dominant, central and ultimately exclusive position on the horizon. One thing is clear. After studying the family and making the father its pivotal point, psychoanalysis had more to say about authority and the leader than anything else.

# III

If Freud criticised Le Bon's concept, it was thus to a specific end, a clear definition of the framework of his own study. It would therefore be pedantic to look at his objections in detail. Except one, which will enable us to see what that framework was. Like others before him, he was determined to find out whether crowds were as much inferior in intelligence to the individual and as sterile as Le Bon claimed. Perhaps it was the case as far as great intellectual creations and the inventions of art and science were concerned. In such cases, Freud thought, the major advances had only been made by solitary individuals. But that did not also mean that crowds had not played a creative role, as indicated by our language, our arts, or folklore and the like. It was also quite clear that in the past collective works had come before individual ones. Popular oral poetry had been the forerunner of cultivated poetry and the model for it. Popular religions also came before those spread by an inspired man such as Christ, Mahomet, Moses or Buddha. Between Le Bon's assertions and what is seen in reality there was a glaring contradiction. How could this be resolved? Were crowds sterile, or were they creative?

To solve the problem, we need only see that Le Bon's affirmations applied merely to certain crowds. There were others with obvious

241

intellectual capacity which were creative and had a different mentality. This meant that Freud could take over the distinction (that we are already aware of) between natural and artificial crowds. This is what he himself says:

A number of very different structures have probably been merged under the term 'group' and may require to be distinguished. The assertions of Sighele, Le Bon and the rest relate to groups of a short-lived character, which some passing interest has hastily agglomerated out of various sorts of individuals. The characteristics of revolutionary groups, and especially those of the great French Revolution, have unmistakably influenced their descriptions. The opposite opinions owe their origin to the consideration of those stable groups or associations in which mankind pass their lives, and which are embodied in the institutions of society. Groups of the first kind stand in the same sort of relation to those of the second as a high but choppy sea to a ground swell. (Freud: XVIII, 83)

After adopting Le Bon's description of masses, Freud now took up Tarde's classification of them. Like the latter, he reached the conclusion that it was necessary to distinguish between organised masses on the one hand and non-organised ones on the other. The study of the former would be of the greater interest. By a series of independent intellectual processes, he reached the position that Tarde had adopted with regard to the function of hierarchy, tradition and discipline. In short, with regard to the function of organisation,

The problem consists in how to procure for the group precisely those features which were characteristic of the individual and which are extinguished in him by the formation of the group. (Freud: XVIII, 104)

He was, of course, talking about intelligence.

The difficulty was therefore resolved. One could say that spontaneous and natural crowds must always be sterile, whereas artificial and disciplined ones, such as a village community or a political party, were fertile and culturally productive. Where the former regressed, the latter progressed. *Freud set himself the task of studying, as a priority, the psychology of artificial crowds.* They were stable and durable and usually directed by a leader. The features they had in common with the family meant that an analogy between psychoanalysis and crowd psychology could be established, permitting movement from one to the other. That was the real reason for Freud's choice, which had nothing to do with what have been seen as gaps in Le Bon's works.

Amongst artificial crowds, those most like the family are the Church and the army, and both are closely modelled on it. They are like it even in its tiniest psychological detail and claim to do on a large scale what the family does on a small one, namely to be the protected world of father and son. Like the family, the other two institutions submit their members to external constraints. Membership is compulsory, whether desired or not:

As a rule a person is not consulted, or is given no choice, as to whether he wants to enter such a group; any attempt at leaving it is usually met with persecution or with severe punishment, or has quite definite conditions attached to it. It is quite outside our present interest to enquire why these associations need such special safeguards. We are only attracted by one circumstance, namely that certain facts, which are far more concealed in other cases, can be observed very clearly in those highly organized groups which are protected from dissolution in the manner that has been mentioned. (Freud: XVIII, 93)

By virtue of his choice, Freud definitively made the field of crowd psychology co-extensive with that of society and culture. But we are not over-surprised at this. The opposite would have been a great deal more astonishing. Of the real world as seen by Freud, one could say what Borges said of the imaginary one of Tlön:

It is no exaggeration to state that in the classical culture of Tlön, there is only one discipline, that of psychology. All others are subordinated to it. I have remarked that the men of that planet conceive of the universe as a series of mental processes, whose unfolding is to be understood only as a time sequence.

(Borges, 1962: 24)

The reference to Freud is transparently obvious. And even if there is no reference, the description is still exact and truthful. We shall shortly see what he bore courageously.

# 4. Crowds and the libido

I

THE POINTS MADE in the preceding chapter are of a preliminary nature. Their import is that most of the changes colourfully described by various observers really only amount to a single one, the regression of psychic life in crowds. We have seen how this manifests itself: the conscious personality fades and affectivity becomes dominant. Crowds tend to move on to action as an expression of an idea that has taken possession of their minds. The ideas and feelings of every member are channelled in the same direction, and the crowd is psychologically united.

We can accept that. But the next step is to find an explanation for it. What are the reasons for the profound changes that human beings undergo when they are surrounded by other human beings or become part of a group? Why do we unknowingly and involuntarily adopt the opinions or emotions of our friends, neighbours, leaders or fellow citizens? Why do we, who are diverse and dissimilar people, tend to become uniform and similar mass-men when we are part of a crowd?

So far, crowd psychology had explained such various manifestations of regression by means of suggestion. The Russian psychologist Bechterev wrote that:

Once a mass has gathered and a common psychic impulse has united all those composing it, suggestion and reciprocal suggestion become the decisive factor with regard to subsequent events. (Bechterev, 1905: 130)

But can suggestion be seen as an explanatory notion? Is it a basic and irreducible phenomenon producing psychic reactions in all human beings? We know for certain that it is a determining factor in hypnosis. Why is this? Simply because most individuals are more or less suggestible. That is obviously what gives rise to their propensity to let themselves be influenced, carry out the orders they are given and move from the waking to the sleeping state. Facts are facts, whether it be a question of clinical observations, laboratory experiments or statistics. And facts allow us to say one thing only, which is that suggestibility is a quality of all social beings, just as a tendency to fall is a quality of all heavy bodies or the capacity to reproduce themselves is a property of all living beings.

Noting that a property is general is an important discovery. It does not, however, explain it, but simply describes it. Discovering that all bodies have a tendency to fall rather than rise or move to the left or right defines them as being heavy, but does not explain why or in terms of what law they do so. To reach that stage, we have to understand gravity and be able to formulate Newton's law. Freud, approaching the puzzle of suggestion, specifically noted that no-one had done more than describe it and show that it was widespread.

But there has been no explanation of the nature of suggestion, that is, of the conditions under which influence without adequate logical foundation takes place. (Freud: XVIII, 90)

My aim in quoting this passage is to remind you that in the period between the definition of suggestion and the establishment of its proven efficacy and Freud's interest in mass psychology it had been in common use without any understanding of the way it worked. In other words, no progress at all had been made, and in scientific matters repetition means losing ground. In those circumstances, suggestion became a word suggesting a magical power like the sleep-inducing quality of opium. It could be dispensed with, and Freud immediately proposed the concept of the libido to explain the links between individuals in a crowd and also the psychic modifications they undergo.

Since it is more concrete and is centred on sexual love, the term is better known. It covers and combines all those varieties such as self-love, love for one's offspring, those close to one, for one's ideas and so on. Both the word and the thing frighten us, particularly when used to express the nature of the links uniting individuals in a crowd and the binding quality of social relationships. Tarde, as you know, had had the same intuition and saw that love, sexual or otherwise, one person's liking for another, lay at the basis of every association. Freud, however, proceeded systematically and made libido one of the explanatory principles of collective psychology.

He had no intention of giving in to the opposition he expected to meet. Nor did he resort to doubtful compromises and replace plain words by decadent and distinguished ones, as did one or two other investigators who avoided the proper term and advised him to do the same. He remarks that:

I might have done so myself from the first and thus have spared myself much opposition. But I did not want to, for I like to avoid concessions to faintheartedness. One can never tell where that road may lead one; one gives way first in words, and then little by little in substance too. (Freud: XVIII, 91)

Probably very few people expected to see the word *libido* escape so quickly from current psychoanalytical language and lose and dissipate itself in so many low Latin or higher mathematical paraphrases.

To take up Freud's idea again, it is love which provides the impulse that creates ties between individuals. In every relationship, which is apparently as neutral, abstract and impersonal as that between soldier and officer, believer and priest, student and professor or worker and worker, there are hidden strong emotions – rightly called disorders – which act without our knowledge, being most powerful where we are least conscious. The libido is the very matter of the crowd soul, the force that unites it and gives it cohesion, since such a force must exist.

It is also at work in the hypnotist/subject relationship and the source of suggestion. Doctors and psychologists prefer to ignore and draw the seemly veil of science over it. 'What would correspond to them [love relationships] is evidently concealed behind the shelter, the screen, of suggestion' (Freud: XVIII, 91).

This is in fact a very strange reversal. For over a century, from Mesmer's time onwards, those who were first opposed to animal magnetism and then hypnotism claimed that these techniques were really no more than the trickery and mumbo-jumbo of charlatans. They also accused hypnotists of using their therapeutic methods as a cover for sexual relationships between physicians and their male or female patients and of abusing the amorous credulity characteristic of women, all the time claiming that such techniques were useless in themselves. Those using them defended themselves vigorously against accusations of this kind, stressing the impersonal, objective and asexual nature of their methods.

And on the one hand Freud said that the opponents of mesmerism were right, that suggestion was of little account and erotic relationships were everything. He insisted too that there was no room for defence and secrecy. Yet the same Freud, on the other hand, would have no truck with such critics. What he was saying to them in fact was that instead of censuring the libido or asking him to censure it, they should rather admit that it was necessary, fundamental and of scientific value. It enabled the doctor and the psychologist to act. In that relationship, as in all others, it made it possible to establish a social link.

## II

In order to understand how the libido operates, we have to go back to a specific scientific context. It is generally accepted that man is essentially a social being with a natural tendency to unite with his fellows to satisfy his needs, work and create. Crowd psychology, however, did not see things in this way, but pictured man rather as subject to antisocial tendencies working against such a union. Every group and crowd had to overcome these if it were to establish lasting social ties. There were two antisocial tendencies.

The first was narcissism, self-attachment, the exclusive love for the ego and its own body. This made the individual resistant to the desire of others and intolerant towards everything outside himself. How was this to be understood? The individual kept his libido for himself, refusing to share it or to transfer it to any object. Self-esteem and self-admiration swelled up and became vanity. By extension, this exaltation by the subject of his own ego and his own body developed into an exclusive love over a wider area, such as that of the inhabitants of a town for their place of residence, that of a football team for their club, that of citizens for their country, of the French for France, or militants for their party or their leader, and so on. The active and passionate fellow-feeling experienced for one's compatriots or clansmen or for those sharing the same idea had as its counterpart a no less active and passionate antipathy for the nationals of other countries, the inhabitants of a neighbouring town, those with a different religion or for foreigners, blacks, Jews and the rest.

The combination of fellow-feeling for 'us' and antipathy for 'them' had the corollary of a feeling that 'we' were superior. Men are frequently prepared to recognise as fully human only those individuals belonging to their own ethnic, linguistic or national group and to treat outsiders as less than human. The names of many Amerindian tribes simply mean 'men', 'flesh' or 'people' (the Navajos, Apaches and Utes, for example) and the Greeks were kind enough to call all foreigners barbarians.

Such disproportionate pride on the one hand and parochialism, racialism, xenophobia and class prejudices on the other are the poisonous fruits of narcissism. They smack of aversion and scorn and prevent the formation of social links. Exclusive love necessarily entails rejection of all that is different:

We are no longer astonished that greater differences should lead to an almost insuperable repugnance, such as the Gallic people feel for the German, the Aryan for the Semite, and the white races for the coloured.          (Freud: XVIII, 101)

Where self-love stops, hatred of others begins.

The immediate satisfaction of desires and instincts, particularly sexual ones, was the second obstacle to the creation of social ties. It is true that sex drives attract individuals to one another and unite them. Once desire is satisfied, however, they separate again and subsequently change partners. The problem is clear. If there was a change of sexual partners each time desire had been satisfied, no stable link would be possible, and

247

the resulting crowd would have a purely momentary existence. Freud notes:

those instincts which are directly sexual incur a loss of energy each time they are satisfied, and must wait to be renewed by a fresh accumulation of sexual libido, so that meanwhile the object may have been changed.　　　(Freud: XVIII, 139)

The fluctuations of desire are contrary to the stability that institutions and collective life demand. The only way of diminishing the scope of such fluctuations is to divert desire and refuse to fulfil it and hence to encourage individuals to set up a lasting crowd, organised and based on a higher ideal. That is the logical conclusion to be derived from these observations.

## III

It can thus be seen that narcissism and the direct satisfaction of impulses are major obstacles to the emergence of any collectivity worthy of the name. Let us try to see how they are overcome, dealing first with the direct satisfaction of desire. For this, we must return briefly to the nature of the libido. The hypothesis that it plays a major part suggests a widespread duality. It is clear that on the one hand we have an introverted *narcissistic libido* which is attached to our own ego and body like an inseparable shadow. It springs up in the midst of the *erotic libido*, which is constantly in search of others, constantly changing objects, and hence partners, in the attempt to achieve satisfaction. Love covets love, as a Spanish proverb has it. That is indeed the law of the erotic libido, which can only develop through the succession of objects, and hence of partners. It can move outside the boundaries of the concrete and extend to all women or men, to a star whose fan one is or to a leader whose follower one is. A man declaring himself ready to lay down his life for his leader is making a declaration and carrying out an act of love. There is much that suggests this ability to acquire substitute objects. These are part of a current of love of which the sexual kernel is a first sketch.

One it has been awakened, the erotic libido, the desire for union, overcomes the narcissistic libido. Here, as in many other cases, love enables us to bypass the obstacle posed by narcissism and to check the antisocial and hence egoistic tendencies which we experience as individuals. In Freud's words:

By the admixture of erotic components the egoistic instincts are transformed into social ones. We learn to value being loved as an advantage for which we are willing to sacrifice other advantages.　　　(Freud: XIV, 282)

For Freud, of course, love was not a spontaneous sentiment nor, like good sense, was it the most widespread thing in the world. Every single one of us finds it as hard to love as to be loved. We put up strong resistance to other people's feelings. Either we despise those who show affection for us, or we despise ourselves, seeing ourselves as unworthy of it. Most human beings thus expect from their fellows something they know they cannot accept, and this inability makes the relationships between them very fragile. But there is no other way. Their inclination to love forces them out of themselves and creates the first atom of sociability:

And in the development of mankind as a whole, just as in individuals, love alone acts as the civilizing factor in the sense that it brings a change from egoism to altruism. And this is true both of sexual love for women, with all the obligations which it involves of not harming the things that are dear to women, and also of desexualized, sublimated homosexual love for other men, which springs from work in common.

If therefore in groups narcissistic self-love is subject to limitations which do not operate outside them, that is cogent evidence that the essence of a group formation consists in new kinds of libidinal ties among the members of the group.
(Freud: XVIII, 103)

This is a very strange declaration coming from Freud when we remember how little faith he had in spontaneous generosity and the milk of human kindness. But we must be clear about the words used. In the last analysis, love equals sexuality, and all the changes within and the relationships between individuals are marked by it. They are not, as had been thought, the product of some mysterious and ineluctable suggestion, but are brought about by a state of inamoration that drags us from solitary self-contemplation in the mirror of our own body and our own self. That is the very state that defines the crowd:

If an individual gives up his distinctiveness in a group and lets its other members influence him by suggestion, it gives one the impression that he does it because he feels the need of being in harmony with them rather than in opposition to them – so that perhaps after all he does it '*ihnen zu Liebe*' [for love of them].
(Freud: XVIII, 92)

The moral of history is a simple one. Men live in society not because they are sleepwalkers but because they feel love. In both cases, however, they lose their heads. We have certainly seen the effect, but so far we have been mistaken about the cause.

# IV

The observations we have at our disposal are more informative about the part played by the libido in artificial crowds such as the Church or the army than in natural ones. Nevertheless, there is some difficulty in making a definitive assessment of that importance. Other material factors, such as force and interest, come into play and cannot be ignored. But what is attractive about research, and psychology in particular, is that it is never finished, All we are really doing is imaginatively reconstructing something on the basis of a relatively small number of facts, rather like palaeontologists bringing prehistoric civilisation back to life from a few bones, tools and the stratigraphical analysis of a site.

Artificial crowds seem to us to be disciplined collections of human beings. At one extreme there is the leader, at the other, the mass. They show us – which is of interest here – a *dramatis personae* built up on the hierarchy of two categories of feelings of love, self-love and the love of others. In terms of the reading suggested in outline here, the leader is someone who loves, and in extreme cases can only love, himself, which probably explains the exclusive confidence in his ability and ideas and his own feelings of superiority. In him, narcissism stands firm in the most difficult circumstances. His great self-love means that he can even do without that of others, if it is not obvious. What Freud wrote about the leaders of archaic crowds is valid for leaders in general:

His intellectual acts were strong and independent even in isolation, and his will needed no reinforcement from others. Consistency leads us to assume that his ego had few libidinal ties; he loved no one but himself, or other people only in so far as they served his needs. (Freud: XVIII, 123)

An independent individual and a being apart, the leader does not need the approval of others to act nor their opinion in order to admire himself. He has no care for that reassurance that we lesser mortals constantly seek from our fellow men. Whether we have a serious decision to take or are simply wondering which film to watch for our evening's entertainment, we find it difficult to ignore what other people think. The leader does not live in fear of losing the love of others, be they friends, colleagues or fellow citizens, for in the words of the writer Raymond Radiguet they are 'Narcissuses hating and loving their own image, but indifferent to any other'.

A crowd on the other hand is made up in theory of individuals for whom the affection of their fellows and being loved as much as they themselves love is a major need. Such people in fact admire and accept themselves to the extent that others admire and accept them and constantly depend on the shared erotic libido. In its extreme form, this contrast means that leaders love themselves but do not love others and that mass individuals love others but cannot love themselves.

When statesmen – amongst others – talk of the tragic loneliness of power and the need for a distance between themselves and the people, they justify it by seeing it as a sacrifice made in the interests of all, but they are seeing things the wrong way round. It is because of their self-sufficiency, their ability to do without and even to despise others that they have reached the top. Once they are there, they isolate themselves and keep their distance in all circumstances in order to be in a position to make even greater use of this surplus of affection in their privileged position. Tito's former companion, the Yugoslav writer Djilas, carefully observed that leader's relationship with his entourage, which seems to have been an excellent example of this phenomenon:

In mortal danger Tito kept a certain distance, became impenetrable and inaccessible. Between him and his friends, and his wives, there was always a movable barrier. A movable barrier, not a gulf! The barrier was moved instinctively. You could see it closing whenever anyone got too close – a certain hardening in his expression, a flicker of malice in his eyes. (Djilas, 1981: 122)

We know, or think we know, why Tito refused any emotional commitment, any reciprocity of feeling and all risk of intimacy with others. His own narcissism demanded this. Indeed, since he was only capable of loving himself, how could he reach their level and love them? But there is nothing exceptional about a barrier of that kind, and we encounter it every day when we have dealings with narcissistic – or, in ordinary language, egocentric and egotistic – individuals.

We come back to a current idea with perhaps little-known consequences, for if it is tenable we encounter this paradox. Crowds are made up, in principle, of individuals who have overcome their anti-social tendencies and sacrificed their self-love in order to be part of them. And yet at the centre of them is someone who is the only one to have retained and even exaggerated these tendencies. By a strange but explicable effect of the link that binds them to each other, the masses are not disposed to admit that they have given up what the leader has kept intact, the thing that becomes their focus, that is self-love itself.

In short, they are not inclined to recognise that that is precisely the source of a state of dependency that would cease as soon as they were able to keep what they had become accustomed to doing without. That is perhaps the real meaning of Robespierre's statement that in order to love justice and equality, the people needed no great virtue and it was sufficient that it loved itself. All leaders are a symbol of the paradox of an anti-social individual at the pinnacle of society, for he who is without narcissism is also without power.

## V

All these observations complete what we already know about mass psychology, which is that the leader is the keystone of artificial crowds and that the members of those crowds have an amorous attitude towards him. According to Freud, every member of the army and the Church has a libidinal attachment to the supreme head, Christ, on the one hand and to every individual member of the crowd on the other. But these ties are constantly threatened, and we know where that threat comes from. In the first place, it is the risk that the paradox we have just described might be perceived and that the fact that the links are not reciprocal might be discovered. Secondly, there is the fact that the crowd begins to suspect that the leader shows greater favour to some members of it than to others and loves some more than others. Morality, which warms and sweetens reality, is not enough to calm its fears. Individuals see themselves as equals and want to be treated as such. That shared aspiration gives rise to the illusion of being loved in return without distinction. Every individual loves the leader, who loves every individual and favours none:

In a Church (and we may with advantage take the Catholic Church as a type) as well as in an army, however different the two may be in other respects, the same illusion holds good of there being a head – in the Catholic Church Christ, in an army its Commander-in-Chief – who loves all the individuals in the group with an equal love. Everything depends upon this illusion; if it were to be dropped, then both Church and army would dissolve, so far as the external force permitted them to. (Freud: XVIII, 93)

Love, the libidinal link, is thus what holds crowds together and gives them vitality. The Church knows this, and puts forward the Christian community as a vast family in which the faithful are brothers in the love which fills Christ, and he or his representatives bear witness to that love in return. His relationship to every Christian making up the crowd is that of an elder brother taking the place of his father, and this is what unites the faithful. In the army, too, the leader is supposed to be like a father who loves his soldiers equally. This provides a reason for the ties of comradeship. It is quite clear that the same thing could be said about a party, where the ties between each member and the leader – Lenin or de Gaulle, for example – can also be seen as ties amongst the members themselves.

The libido thus provides a way of explaining the major phenomena of crowd psychology, and we have seen what that way is. In the first place, it is the unity that includes all the individuals and holds them together and is to varying degrees erotic in nature. In the second place, there is the submission of the crowd to the leader, arising as a result of its renunciation of self-love and the consequent predominance of love for others. That submission remains fragile and threatened, however, since the leader receives from the crowd a freely-given affection that he refuses to return or is incapable of returning. In order to palliate that drawback, a real non-reciprocity between the two extremes of the social hierarchy is transformed into an illusory one. The individuals involved thus imagine that they are receiving the equivalent of what they have given, just as a workman or labourer imagines that he is receiving a wage equivalent to his work. In the emotional economy of society as in an ordinary economy, unequal exchange takes on the appearance of equal exchange. Everyone thinks that he is receiving the same as he gives and drawing a fair wage for his emotions, whereas in fact that is by no means the case. The domination exerted by leaders entails an increase in value, a surplus of love without any real counterpart. But what maintains this illusion of a fair exchange of affection? The nature of the erotic libido itself, for it has the feature of reciprocity which contrasts with the egoism typical of the narcissistic libido.

Even to-day the members of a group stand in need of the illusion that they are equally and justly loved by their leader; but the leader himself need love no one else, he may be of a masterful nature, absolutely narcissistic, self-confident and independent. We know that love puts a check upon narcissism, and it would be possible to show how, by operating in this way, it became a factor of civilization.
(Freud: XVIII, 123)

The twofold and yet single nature of the libido, that is, of love, enormously increases its power. In a crowd, individuals are so to speak submerged by the superabundance of affective links between themselves and with the leader. As long as they are alone and tranquil and secure, they can reason and show independent judgement. As soon as they are overwhelmed by these emotions, their intellectual activity decreases. Excessive credulity and extreme movements come into play, and their fluidity is a material expression of the intense and contagious nature of amorous impulses. Any untimely outflow of the latter takes on a violent aspect and arouses fear. And it is not surprising that crowds frighten us, since they bring back an archaic past. As Freud says:

Some of its features, and similar features, which we find so impressively described in Le Bon, show an unmistakable picture of regression of mental activity to an earlier stage such as we are not surprised to find among savages or children.
(Freud: XVIII, 117)

But there is also clearly a step forward, for we now have an explanation to help us understand that description. We have seen the *how* and now have an idea, even if it is a very rough-and-ready one, of the *why*. A more or less direct sexuality seems to be the force that easily obscures consciousness, makes light of the bolts and throws open the door to the most ancient and anti-social impulses. But in the last analysis it proves to be the only force capable of overcoming egotism and attracting very different people, fusing them into a crowd where everything, as in lovers' quarrels, ends in an embrace.

# 5. *The origin of affective attachments in society*

## I

IN THE LAST CHAPTER we noted that the immediate satisfaction of needs and drives is the second obstacle to the creation of a lasting social link in the crowd and that a more or less desexualised love in particular is a force capable of drawing individuals out of their narcissistic egotism, just as a large quantity of energy can pull electrons out of their orbit in an atom and set them in motion. But that force is not enough to guarantee the stability of social atoms. What hinders it is simply its own nature, which has its own peaks and troughs, the prelude and postscript to the sexual act, and its own periods of affective charging and discharging. There is also the possible sequence of different partners from one occasion to another. Eros is the enemy of repetition and repetition the enemy of Eros, as experience shows. Theory has to draw a conclusion from this.

But no society or culture could be based on something as vague as the whims and amorous caprices of its members. Yet societies have been established and continue to be established, and this is because they have found ways of turning people away from the immediate satisfaction of their erotic inclinations and fixing them in a stable relationship. The monuments of culture are so many altars on which love has been sacrificed. We can say in its defence that it does not try to dupe people about this.

What methods does society use? One is repression. The libido is denied and treated as if it did not exist. The initial basis of such repression is one of prohibitions prescribing how and with whom people may associate, with a female cousin but not with a daughter, with someone of the same religion or social class but not of a different one, and so on.

A second method is that which leads to giving up the satisfaction of the desire for a given object, such as a father or mother, for higher reasons. This presupposes that the individual has internalised a prohibition or external repression and thus voluntarily accepts something which was once involuntary. In other words, a rule imposed in social life is now incorporated into psychic life.

We call an attachment of this kind for a person such as a father, a friend or a teacher *identification*. It replaces amorous desire for that person. The desire is internalised and the being of the lover becomes like that of the beloved. Imitation brings control, and the willing sacrifice enables us to master ourselves and our relationships with others in terms of Goethe's precept that we only possess what we have renounced. The consequence of applying this austere piece of wisdom is that the atoms of society become stable. We must fully absorb and accept the idea that the *libido*, which limits narcissistic egotism, and *mimesis*, which consolidates an affective relationship, are both indispensable to the creation of a human mass. In one of his admirable commentaries on the Bible, Maimonides declares that two safeguards are better than one. Both forces carry out their respective tasks in their own way, one lighting the fire and the other stopping it going out or burning the house down.

## II

What we now have to understand is how we acquired them. Here too I shall follow Freud, but his writing on this matter was never finished. This means that I shall have to extrapolate from what he said and prune his writings to make them more precise. In doing so I shall take into account the continuity between the two concepts of identification and imitation which a Swiss writer sums up in the observation that there is a striking kinship between Tarde's theory and that of Freud (Fischer, 1961: 24).

Everyone has heard of identification. The word may be familiar, but the meaning escapes us and we are faced with the most demanding mystery of depth psychology. That discipline has accustomed us to obscure ideas that we seem to understand only because we misunderstand them, because we are curious about them or because we associate ideas. From this point of view, identification breaks all the records. Neither detailed clinical accounts nor those numerous commentaries which take no account of its role in crowd psychology can clear away this cloud of unknowing.

Nevertheless, I shall still try to separate the concept, as far as is humanly possible, from its vague context, even if this entails painful simplification. The hardest thing is to know where to begin. In order to clear our minds, I propose to distinguish between a *general identification* free of all ties to the libido and instinctual drives and a *restricted libido* which is linked to those areas. The first is manifest in large human masses as a whole, the second is connected to the family. To some extent, the distinction can be seen as Freudian, since he considered that in a 'particularly frequent and significant' number of cases,

It is noticeable that in these identifications the ego sometimes copies the person who is not loved and sometimes the one who is loved. . . .

it may arise with any new perception of a common quality shared with some other person who is not an object of the sexual instinct. The more important this common quality is, the more successful may this partial identification become, and it may thus represent the beginning of a new tie.(Freud: XVIII, 107 and 108)

If you accept the distinction I suggest, we can get to the heart of the matter. Let us start with what is most visible, which is what the theories and facts deal with. We know intuitively that general identification is expressed in the act of imitating, of reproducing a model. It also includes a feeling of attachment, a communion with the person imitated and reproduced. The basis of this attachment is what is called identification, which is 'the assimilation of one ego into another one, as a result of which the first ego behaves like the second in certain respects, imitates it and in a sense takes it up into itself' (Freud: XXII, 63).

At the same time, this process widens out our range of sensations from the tactile to the visual, for looking plays an important part. The imitator scrutinises and spies out the fine detail of his model, traces it out and fills himself with it. Like an actor practising a part before a mirror, he checks that he has copied all the characteristics he has observed, that he has imitated his model successfully and become his double. That examination of oneself might even bring pleasure. Vision is the sense of identification, the outstanding social and artistic sense. 'Seeing' and 'wanting to imitate' are one and the same thing, said Proust, writing of that kind of visual identification.

Let us take a closer look at the various aspects of it, and in the first place at our way of purely and simply repeating the gestures, words and actions of other people. We have an unconscious propensity for reproducing a movement, a sound and so on as soon as an individual or a group makes that movement or utters that sound while we are there. Bechterev, the Russian psychologist, writes that imitation, which Tarde had cast so much light on, is the natural consequence of reproducing one's own or someone else's act, the carrying out of an act and leaving of traces in the nervous pathways which will make repetition easy and encourage it (Bechterev, 1957: 167).

Tarde has indeed written of the criminal's tendency to relive his crime in his imagination or to return to the scene and repeat it. He also pays particular attention to the more widespead tendency to repeat, consciously or unconsciously, acts and situations from our own history (Tarde, 1890). In a letter of 1907 to Jung, Freud speaks of the general human tendency to constantly make new copies of the photographs they carry inside them. This was one of the major lines of his theory, and he came back to it time and time again (M. Moscovici, 1980: 71–101).

In fact the function of repetition is to restore a shattered harmony by taking up again a sound uttered or a movement carried out by other people, or even an idea. It strives to return to a real or imagined previous state the subject has inhabited. The difference between him and others is wiped out. He takes possession of what was formerly exclusively theirs and in doing so has the impression of controlling them. When a group of children is playing at imitating the strange attitudes and words of a newcomer – as in Flaubert's famous *Charbovari* scene – it is orchestrating a return to the *status quo*, when they were all experiencing and doing the same things.

Repetition also always has the value of confirming and perfecting a link. This is the case with festivals, commemorations and celebrations. The same words, songs, gestures, parades and so on are repeated year after year to strengthen the permanence of the Republic or a local tradition. Those who follow a particular school of thought repeat the same idea, crowds shout a slogan a thousand times. This is a way of recognising continuity and controlling group membership, and also of providing protection from the fear of separation, which is always a possibility. The stubborn and tireless repetition observable in adults can already be seen, a thousand times more marked, in children:

> Nor can children have their *pleasurable* experiences repeated often enough, and they are inexorable in their insistence that the repetition shall be an identical one.
>
> (Freud: XVIII, 34)

This means that they make them permanent and make use of them several times over. They also feel that they are springing the traps that diversity sets for them and discovering a uniform order in the shifting morass of disorder. The world bears the marks of their stereotypes and they therefore recognise it as their own. When they are older, the rituals of society simply need to take over and deepen the grooves that can already be traced.

Identification is also a simulatory ploy, aimed at driving away danger or the hostility of human beings or the elements. You have often noticed how someone coming into a room or a meeting instinctively looks for a particular group, such as his own age-group or people who have the same job or opinions as himself. Birds of a feather flock together, as both proverbial wisdom and laboratory experiments confirm. But why do people behave in this way rather than go up to others at random? On the one hand, by looking out for familiar faces and carrying out the ritual gestures of recognition, the individual is clearly economising on effort.

On the other, he is protecting himself against possible rebuffs, the hostility of people he does not know and perhaps even against his own hostility towards them. The fact that he looks like others and shares an identity with a group is a protective mask for him.

Camouflage is an art used by the whole animal kingdom. Certain insects look like twigs and lizards change colour according to their surroundings. Some mammals are spotted, in order to blend in with sunlight and shadow. Certain crabs 'disguise' or 'decorate' themselves so well that we do not notice that they are there until we have sat on them. Human beings also dissimulate when they rightly or wrongly see other people as a danger. There is always a sword of Damocles hanging over the subordinate, the child or the outsider.

The foreigner's tendency to assimilate and even exaggerate the characteristics, linguistic expressions or customs of the country he is living in, to be more French than the French, more American than the Americans, more royalist than the king in fact, corresponds to a need for defence. It is a precaution against the danger of being excluded. The same is true of the social masks we wear. In identifying with others, the individual is always seeking a way of disarming them and putting them off the track. His aim is to deflect from himself the hostility originating in their self love, that of exacerbated narcissism.

We can go further. A whole series of mimetic ploys and imitation games serve a similar purpose. The clown – and which of us is not a clown at some point in his life? – turns a tense or even tragic situation into a comic one. The jester fends off blame, jokingly uttering truths that courtiers dare not even whisper. With a cruel twist of the pen, the cartoonist amusingly reproduces an idea or a person that it would be impossible to mock in any other way. The man who laughs is the strongest of the strong, says Sartre about 'The Boy', another clown, a character invented and embodied by Flaubert to react to the scorn of his family by making himself more grotesque than he really was (Sartre, 1971: 1223).

All forms of masques, parodies, travesties and fancy dress occasions and all humour belong to this category and are directed against individuals with authority within a group. The same is true of children's games. Freud writes:

But mimicry is the child's best art, and the driving motive of most of his games. A child's ambition aims far less at excelling amongst his equals than at mimicking the grown-ups. The relation of children to adults is also the basis of the comic of degradation, which corresponds to the condescension shown by adults in their attitudes to the life of children. (Freud: VIII, 227)

This selection of examples from amongst many others shows the extent to which identification removes the danger of group rejection or

259

aggression, from either our superiors or our fellows. Being like others, in anonymity and synonymity, is often a form of life insurance. Sometimes it helps us to save appearances, at others to create them, it matters little which. The fact that those appearances are there is the main thing. Without them, social life would be impossible.

Identification also frequently takes the form of a real appropriation of the other person, serving at such times to control both him and the relationship with him. Its most immediate and adaptable expression is the desire to incorporate and fuse him into one's own being. To eat him, in fact, so that we can say that we *are* the other, we are the father, the breast, the right arm; as Louis XIV said 'The State? I *am* the State.' This is perfect identification. Love sometimes creates the illusion of it. Sometimes hate does too, and many public and private assassinations have no other motive than this impossible substitution, as we saw in a recent example, that of John Lennon's killer. First he tried to imitate the star by making music and collecting his records. Then he wrote Lennon's name on his work clothes instead of his own. Like Lennon, he married a Japanese woman. Finally, he lay in wait for him one afternoon and killed him.[1]

A less crude and immediate expression is the possession of things belonging to the other person: wife, house, car and so on. In the wish to be desired, we take what he desires. By becoming like him and possessing what he possesses, we are indeed, or imagine that we are, the other person. Similarly, the person who has a rich man's house or a sports car imagines that he himself is rich or sporty, provided at least that nothing destroys the illusion, and he covets a still more sumptuous house or an even more powerful car.

This aspect of the relationship between human beings is a fundamental one and determines the object of our choice. Most of the time we prefer one thing to another because that is what our friends already prefer or because that object has marked social significance. Adults, when they are hungry, are just like children in that they seek out the foods that others take. In their love affairs, they seek out the man or woman whom others find attractive and abandon those who are not sought after. When we say of a man or a woman that he or she is desirable, what we really mean is that others desire them. It is not that they have some particular quality, but because they conform to some currently modish model.

Of all writers, none has described better than Proust the 'intermittencies of the heart', the alternating passion and coolness, the need for a woman to love, or whom one thinks one loves; tortured by suspicion and torn by jealousy when one knows that others are looking at her, touching her, loving her, yet feeling terrible indifference when she is actually there.

We plan and degrade ourselves to have her with us, and once she is present we no longer want to see her or talk to her and are bored in her company. If we get rid of her, the suffering will start all over again. . . . You remember Swann's admission that he had spoiled years of his life and wanted to die, that his greatest love had been for a woman who did not please him and was not his type (Proust, 1978: I, 382). Should we then conclude that we are jealous because we love? No. The precise opposite is the case. We love because we are jealous.

From another point of view, unconscious imitation as a way of reproducing from other materials the gestures or situations created by a friend, parents or a schoolfellow is another way of appropriating and controlling a person or an object that escapes us. In this connection, Freud gives the example of the child throwing a bobbin and then pulling it back and playing the game over and over again. This indicated that he was staging and playing the going out and coming home of his mother using something, a simple bobbin, that he had to hand. His actions were like those of a magician who believes that he can make rain fall by means of a song or a dance. In this way, the child made the absence of his beloved mother bearable:

In the case of children's play we seemed to see that children repeat unpleasurable experiences for the additional reason that they can master a powerful impression far more thoroughly by being active than they could by merely experiencing it passively.                                                                                           (Freud: XVIII, 34)

In a less polished, or more elaborate, way we finish up resembling the other person we try to appropriate. Copies are never enough for long. They rapidly become part of our second nature and hence our real social one.

These different aspects – repetition, simulation and appropriation – are present in every identification with an individual, a group or an idea. What are the consequences of this? Identification certainly gives us a chance to avoid stressful or unpleasant situations. In so far as the repetition of a gesture, the copying of a feeling or an object or the recognition of traits that we habitually share with other individuals are agreeable, they change displeasure into pleasure. Freud writes that 'it seems to be generally agreed that the rediscovery of what is familiar, "recognition", is pleasurable' (Freud: VIII, 121).

Virgil was aware that the memory of past pain is sweet. *Haec quoque meminisse juvabit*, (These things too, it will be sweet to remember) are the words he gave the hero of the *Aeneid*. We must suppose that such a pleasure can take the place of others, particularly sexual ones, and can in fact overcome them. If the substitution principle is based on resemblance to a shared object, it is not surprising that those involved should be submitted to a pressure to identify. Each is led to produce as exact a replica as possible of a model and to desire in the same way what the other desires. The end result is that both free themselves from the object, which thereby ceases to be the goal of an action or need and becomes a means of relating to an individual or group.

As in economics, what determines the choice of object is its value on the market, its trade value, what a being or an object is worth for others. It is not its utility, i.e. the extent to which it satisfies a real need for itself. If we adopt the tastes, desires and opinions of our model, we choose the same objects and consequently have the same tastes, like the same things and the same people. We wait to be told what we should appreciate and like before we want and acquire such things, whether they be big American cars or little English minis, seaside or mountain holidays, slim women or nicely rounded ones.

We can sum this state of affairs up by saying that identification takes us back to a situation similar to the one we were in before we could recognise our desires and choose our own object, before we had acquired our own individuality and become different from other people. In that sense, it fights against any change or new creation that would upset the collective uniformity. It transforms every impulse into a reflex, and thus demonstrates the existence of an interior force which, after taking a long and roundabout path, reduces the individual to the social and obliges it to become part of others again and overcome its separation from them. In extreme cases, identification could lead to total conformity, with everyone loving what everyone else loved and having no preferences and passions of his own. No-one would be in any way different from the common model. There would be one single way of being a good son, a good patient, a good soldier, a good writer or a good believer. Individuals would be as alike as the proverbial two peas. There would simply be a crowd with the same name, the same face and the same clothes.

If, as we have just seen, identification tends to take us to an earlier stage than that of separation and individual expression, we might suppose that it would also take us back to the same partner of our desires whom we would otherwise wish to change. It does so because that partner is already familiar to us and hence a source of pleasure. Even when we do imagine ourselves to be making a change, identification leads us to make our initial choices again and seek a new partner who resembles the first. In short, if we can do nothing about the peaks and troughs of the libido – apart from repressing it – we can make sure that it has the same object and find a complementary satisfaction in regulating our relationships with it. This is enough to strengthen a stable social link.

It is true that there is constant tension between the libido and mimesis. Libido knows nothing about a return to the same thing; mimesis aims to regain and re-establish the *status quo*. All groups and individuals are engaged in a game of constant ruses and give and take, and in the end there is division and collaboration between them. The division occurs because the libido as it were defines the subject of desire and determines its intensity and identification determines which object will be desired. For example, it is certainly an amorous need that pushes us towards a man or a woman, but the fact that we prefer a maternal woman or a paternal man to a child-woman or a male teenager depends entirely on a pressure to identify with a mother- or father-figure inherited from our childhood. And unions of that kind always have favourable results. Thus Freud wrote of President Wilson's marriage:

the more his wife resembles his mother, the richer will be the flow of his libido in his marriage. (Freud and Bullitt, 1966: 46)

We now have a reasonable if not entirely clear idea of the general identification process, which leads to stable social links. If we reflect on its characteristics, we can see that they have much in common not only with imitation (without recourse to hypnosis) but also, and to higher degree, with the death wish described by Freud in his famous essay *Beyond the Pleasure Principle*. There is nothing surprising about that, and indeed everything that he said about that instinct had already been said about imitation. So much so, in fact, that in his essay the two words could be transposed without changing the sense as a whole.

We might conjecture that the death he is referring to is that of the individual returning not to inorganic but to social life. Destructive and aggressive tendencies are one result of it. Thus, from identification with a father, a master or a leader there might develop in the child, the disciple or the subordinate the temptation to get rid of him and completely take his place. But we are jumping ahead. That temptation is not fortuitous, and I shall try to show what its consequences are.

## III

Identification consists of choosing a model. It is a problem in society. It may be necessary to choose from among several people or objects, and in addition every individual belongs to several groups and is linked to them to varying degrees. A young man entering adult life, for example, may identify with his age group and class and adopt their ideas, way of life and thinking, and also with his nation, becoming chauvinistic and even a racialist in his dealings with other young people. It is partly because of this indeterminate quality and this problem that general identification attests to autonomy with regard to the amorous desires I have described.

Things are different with the family. There is no lack of determination here, and choice is fixed in advance. The family is the framework in which restricted identification takes place, and there is no problem here. It is grafted onto the feelings of love the child has for its father and mother. Here, we can follow Freud more closely than we have done so far and enter with him into one of those cells of society in which everyone begins his existence. We shall leave aside little girls for the moment and stay with a little boy. The curtain of birth is raised, and we can soon see how uncomfortable his situation is. On the one hand he desires his mother. On the other, he is still very attached to his father, admiring him and wanting to imitate him and become like him. This makes him want to do things he must not do, such as have intimate relations with his mother. At the same time, his flesh-and-blood father is also a sexual object for him, desired in rather a passive way by the feminine part of his libido. Here too the little boy wants what he cannot have. His desires are hemmed in and frustrated on all sides. He is caught on the horns of a dilemma, his attachment to his father and his troubled amorous feelings for him.

In the first case one's father is what one would like to *be*, and in the second he is what one would like to *have*. The distinction, that is, depends upon whether the tie attaches to the subject or to the object of the ego.          (Freud: XVIII, 106)

The little boy learns to his cost that his father is his rival, will not let him find any outlet for his incestuous feelings for his mother and will not take her place. He is not even consistent with himself. As an example to be followed, his father is someone he must imitate. As an all-powerful individual and a major opponent, he implies that the boy must not imitate him. The least one can say is that there is a major conflict between what 'father' in general asks of him and this particular father forbids him to do. In the face of so much injustice, his relationship with his father takes on a hostile colouring. If he could, he would kill him, and would then be able to take his place even with his mother. So even from the shaky start to our lives our relationships with our parents are to some degree ambivalent, a mixture of attraction and repulsion, love and hate. No feeling is ever present in isolation. It always hides another, its opposite and shadow.

But if our little boy, like millions of others, grows up normally, he will find ways – fascination and renunciation – of escaping from the dilemma that enfolds him. On the one hand, having failed in his attempts at amorous possession, he changes tactics. The little boy (or girl) seeks to fascinate his or her parents. In oriental erotic literature, imitation is reckoned to be one of the ways of attracting. The Sanskrit texts, for example, give an important part to the trick of the woman copying the dress, expressions and speech of her beloved. This kind of mimetic drama is urged on the woman who, 'being unable to unite with her beloved, imitates him to distract her thoughts'.

The child too, using the devices of imitating attitudes, dress and so on, seeks to fascinate, with a magical intention, the father or mother and thus to 'distract its thoughts'. Identification means that one is abandoning and not abandoning amorous desires. It is a lure which the child uses to capture his parents and which, it must be admitted, they fall for. The same is true of the masses, who imitate their leader, bear his name and repeat his gestures. They bow to him, but at the same time they are unconsciously baiting a trap to hold him. Great ceremonies and demonstrations are just as much occasions when the multitudes charm the leader as *vice versa*.

On the other hand, however, once the child is aware of the balance of forces and his own limits, he gradually gives up trying to have this particular father or mother in order to have *a* father, to internalise him and become like him. To that end, he tries his best to resemble him, to be his twin. The model of the father takes the place of the father himself, that object of love and hatred. Identification substitutes ideal parents for real ones, parents as he sees them as being and not as they really are.

Identification is therefore the most important tie that an individual creates in his life, inducing him to incorporate the figure imposed on him as a prototype. Through this process he learns to assimilate and obey all the various forms of the prototype, all the father- or mother-substitutes he will encounter throughout his lifetime.

In the family, identification is a two-way process, and this is what makes it so strong and deep. Freud ignored parental reactions and concentrated only on those of children. If parents have children, however, it is because they want to reproduce and perpetuate themselves. Reproduction was their joint aim and that of the species. They therefore tend to make their children into flesh-and-blood copies of themselves in conformity with a model in their own minds and that society demands of them. Even before a child has opened his eyes, we wonder who he looks like, and we shall always go on doing so.

If a little boy mostly imitates his father and is extremely powerfully attached to him, it is because his parents' aim has now become his own. Consequently, any sexual relationship can only be the result of a confusion that they find frightening. This is due to a disorder in their desires. The truth is that, consciously at least, parents do not wish to reproduce themselves *with* their child, but *in* him. The two are not at all the same thing.

Thus when a child is identifying himself, he is not only giving up his own desires. He is also achieving his parents' wish for self-perpetuation. If he assumes the characteristics of one or both of them, it is because he believes that the more he does as they wish, the more completely he will be accepted in the family. When, for example, his father makes it clear that he wants to be imitated, he is expressing something that goes beyond himself. To be sure of being obeyed, he will even cut the child off from the rest of the world, as Stendhal's father did. The writer tells us that he was loved only as a son 'whose duty was to perpetuate the family', and that this was a source of suffering for him. He tells us that at that stage of his life, 'such a happy one for other children, I was badly behaved, gloomy and unreasonable. In short, I was a slave in the worst sense of the word and gradually acquired the feelings that go with slavery' (Stendhal, 1955: 95).

In earlier days, many children suffered the rigours of such a confinement, and some still do. I stress this aspect of identification because it is important to appreciate that it is not only a substitute for the repressed desire of the child but also a manifestation of the exacerbated one of its parents. It is incontestably our earliest and most primitive tie, given its profound link with the reproduction of the social cell and the species. All the actions and reactions that I have just described come together to produce a single result: a decrease in our amorous desire for someone enabling us to identify with him.

# IV

It is not hard to show that the child's development puts him in a Hamlet-like situation in which he wonders whether to be like his father (or mother) and his father's ghost urges him to be like him and not to be like him. His whole personality is indeed determined by the fact that here are two answers to a question and not one single one, as there was to the riddle of the Sphinx that Oedipus managed to solve. Whilst he is hesitant and uncertain, the litle boy is assimilating the characteristics, opinions and orders of his father.

The latter appears within the psyche as an authority, the ego-ideal or super-ego, which represents him and which Freud clearly sees as the moral part of our nature, the judge and constant critic of deeds and actions, the eye and voice of our parents, leaders and even of society.

The ego is thus split into two contrasted parts continually at war with each other. One has been formed by our assimilation of the judgements and prohibitions of all the people we have identified with and hounds the other with its severe and disagreeable comments. It always addresses it in the curt, harsh tone of a prosecuting counsel, or even of a vengeful god forcing people to stick to the straight and narrow path. When they look as if they might stray from it, it reprimands them, telling them what they must not do and pointing out the evil of their ways. The voice of conscience lies in wait for us, cutting us off from all that we are spontaneously inclined to do and keeping us obedient to the models that have been impressed upon us. It occasionally approves of what we have done when we have followed its dictates. Then and only then do we receive any kind of satisfaction from our super-ego. Freud tells us that:

it gradually gathers up from the influences of the environment the demands which that environment makes upon the ego and which the ego cannot always rise to; so that a man, when he cannot be satisfied with his ego itself, may nevertheless be able to find satisfaction in the ego ideal which has been differentiated out of the ego.                                                                         (Freud: XVIII, 110)

It is the representative of our parents, approves of us, encourages us and gives us the same pleasure as we would have obtained from satisfying our erotic instincts. Our own experience tells us that we imagine such characters in our minds. And unfortunately, when they are not fathers, mothers or brothers, they are leaders. The despotic part they play was what made the sinister Hermann Goering declare that he had no conscience save the Führer. Nor do I personally find his words particularly surprising. They were uttered some time ago and have often been heard throughout history.

Having a super-ego of that kind is, as Cicero said, like having a master on our head. Like all masters, the super-ego scolds us continually and occasionally encourages us in the manner of a parent. When it is strong, it drives and harasses us.

It admonishes incessantly: You must make the impossible possible! You can accomplish the impossible! You are the beloved Son of the Father! You are the Father himself, You are God.                                      (Freud and Bullitt, 1966: 42)

Or at least it behaves like parents who are now middle-aged, for traditions fade and certain psychoanalytical accounts now look a little colourless and superannuated, rather like period photographs in a family album: a little boy in a sailor suit, smiling shyly and paling into insignificance at the side of a large gentleman with hat and stick, strict eyes and a moustache. Neither fathers nor super-egos are what they were, thank goodness. When the latter is indulgent and less exigent, it allows us to live like the humble mortals that we are.

We are getting near to the heart of the matter here. The super-ego protects and oppresses us as did our father, the god of our childhood. Like Providence, the god of our adult life, it holds the threads of fate in its

Sigmund Freud

hands. From that fact follow a moral and a political philosophy expressed by the divine Apollo in these terms: 'Understand your position as a man, do as the Father bids you, and tomorrow you will be secure.' Tomorrow, when you are grown up and have renounced enjoyment, when you too will be a father and able to impose your will on your son.

## V

There is probably more to be said about restricted identification, for it became a commonplace of depth psychology too quickly. It is true that Freud changed his attitude and position in these matters very considerably, which is troublesome to minds enamoured of clear hypotheses that can be illustrated with three neat facts. Like his predecessors, he had also said that the child was bound to follow and imitate his father, but he was not content to repeat the same old facts. He modified the idea and gave it a new dramatic character, while at the same time remaining faithful to the idea of a simple identification with either the father or the mother.[2]

All this nevertheless means that identification with the father takes place along with the parallel identification with the mother. Both play an equally important part in the child's psychic development, which means that he is engaged in a twofold process. He intellectually and emotionally rearranges the relationships between his father and mother, acting as judge and interested party in the case of a couple that already had a history before he became part of it. In short, he constructs 'family fictions' which more or less correspond to reality. While this is going on, his ego develops and becomes differentiated enough to assimilate the family group and take it in charge from a psychic point of view. This is what leads us to the concept of the super-ego as being formed not in the image of one dominant individual, the father, but in that of a social mini-group consisting of at least the two parental figures. When we listen to our conscience, we hear a dialogue for several voices, a conflicting din of opinions and judgements from the past, not just a single voice. The father's may often be the strongest, but it is not the only one.[3]

This would explain how individuals can at different times belong to different masses and identify with their ideals without experiencing serious collective disorders. Indeed, they might seek out these multiple relationships in order to combine and use them. Freud, writing of the man of today, said that:

Each individual is a component part of numerous groups, he is bound by ties of identification in many directions, and he has built up his ego ideal upon the most various models. Each individual therefore has a share in numerous group minds – those of his race, of his class, of his creed, of his nationality, etc. . . . . – and he can also raise himself above them to the extent of having a scrap of independence and originality. (Freud: XVIII, 129)

Let us sum up this development. At the origin of the social link lie very demanding identification processes that mark individuals for life. On the one hand they cause a regression in the desire for a sexual object. On the other, they entail a differentiation of the psychic apparatus by building external authorities into it. The latter is divided into a properly individual ego and a social ego or super-ego which dominates it. These ideas are important ones and will be used in the remainder of this study. This particular personality structure is interesting to the extent that it is supposed to explain both the similarity observed in crowds and submission to the leader. Freud declared that:

We are aware that what we have been able to contribute towards the explanation of the libidinal structure of groups leads back to the distinction between the ego and ego ideal and to the double kind of tie which this makes possible – identification, and putting the object in the place of the ego ideal.
(Freud, XVIII: 130)

From this point, the super-ego certainly became pivotal in the theoretical field.[4] It is the highest authority in human development and the guarantor of all humanity's social, religious and ideological functions, the voice which constantly reminds us that we are always responsible for the survival of our culture and refuses to cast onto scapegoats – the world around us, power or exploitation – everything that is due to our own nature. Like Edmund in *King Lear*, the super-ego forbids us to 'make guilty of our disasters the sun, the moon and stars; as if we were villains on necessity, fools by heavenly compulsion; knaves, thieves and treachers by spherical predominance; drunkards, liars and adulterers by an enforc'd obedience of planetary influence; and all that we are evil in, by a divine thrusting on – an admirable evasion of whoremaster man, to lay his goatish disposition on the charge of a star!' The man who refuses to scramble up the steep slope of reason.

# 6. *Eros and mimesis*

IN THE PRECEDING CHAPTERS we have seen that cluster of human relationships summed up in the words 'love' and 'identification'. They relate to two groups of desires, those of inamoration, whose function is to turn the individual away from himself and unite him to others, and the mimetic desires representing a propensity for identity and exclusive attachment to another person, a specific model. The first group leads us to associate with people we would like to *possess*, the second with those who embody what we would like to *be*. In principle, these ideas offer an adequate explanation of the phenomena of crowd psychology.

What effect does that have, you will probably ask, on what has been said so far? From the point of view of content very little, but from that of theory a great deal. So far, it has been assumed that everything could be explained by just one dynamic factor, the desire for inamoration. Identification was seen as merely a mechanism for deflecting that desire and for an internal repression of instinct. It was assumed that it was because we could not love someone – our father, our leader and so on – that we identified with him. Now, however, we see it as a second dynamic factor which is autonomous and irreducible. Our recognition that Eros is no longer any more explicable in terms of a mimetic model than mimesis is in terms of an erotic one is an indication of the way we should go.[1] Every human being tries to resolve the conflicts resulting from these areas, that is, those between the many desires of the libido and between the libido and the demands of mimetic desires in conjunction with the facts of the social world.

The duality of Eros and mimesis seems to me to introduce a great economy into our explanations of crowd psychology. Sometimes collective relationships show themselves to human beings in the guise of amorous passions, mixing and uniting them. At other times they show themselves in the form of repetitions and imitations, obliging them to resemble each other or contrast with each other according to whether they conform or do not conform to a model.

Strictly speaking, the duality separates us from Freud's theory, but it extends the area subject to its influence. It was his idea always to contrast two psychic forces, two instincts, in order to explain basic phenomena. That is the point I wanted to make. We are always and everywhere in the presence of two dynamic factors. There is, however, one difference. With regard to the individual, the erotic tendency is paramount over the mimetic one, whereas in the case of the mass, the opposite is the case.

Let us move on from these general considerations to specific questions, for this will show how important they are. How do the individual members of a crowd become equal? Why are crowds unstable and why do they move from panic to violent intolerance? Why do they move through cycles of exaltation and depression? These phenomena have often been described, but there have been few attempts to explain them.

I am telling you in advance that all the explanations we shall reach turn around a single formulation, namely that an increase in mimetic desires has as its corollary a decrease in the desire for inamoration. This means that in the end we always imitate rather than love. The permanent and ubiquitous law of crowd psychology is that mimesis finishes what Eros starts.

It is depressingly likely that the explanations based on this idea that I shall put forward will disappoint you. They take no account of the historical and economic conditions of the masses or of whether they belong to a social class, whether it be working or middle, rural or urban and presuppose observations that have never been rigorously carried out. This is a weakness that undermines everything described so far and still to be described. So why continue? Why claim to explain such sketchy data? To tickle the reader's curiosity about such striking phenomena? There is certainly some of that in it, but the only excuse I can really offer for providing such explanations is that there are no others. Short of closing our eyes to social realities or dismissing them as the prowling follies of history, as many investigators do, we cannot manage without either these occasionally imaginary hypotheses or the solutions.


## II

In crowds, there is a strong pressure towards equality, which is one of their universally recognised characteristics. Why is this? In social and family life, there are many people with whom we would like to have an exclusive relationship – a woman, for example, or our father or a famous artist. It only needs a friend, brother or neighbour to have such a relationship for us to be filled with envy. Throughout our lives we are tortured by the question of why it should be them and not us. We are a prey to uncertainty from our earliest childhood, continually wondering whether our parents and infant school teachers love us as much as our brothers and sisters or the other children in the class. But at the same time we want to be the only ones to be loved. When someone says that he likes Johnny or that Johnny is intelligent, we feel a pang of jealousy, as if he had said that he likes Johnny better than us or that Johnny is cleverer than we are, even if no comparison was intended. The tension between a desire for a unique and exclusive relationship and one based on identification and similarity never slackens. We would like to be different from everyone else, but at the same time no-one should be different from us or better than us.

Let us move on from these general statements and consider a more concrete situation. Imagine the reactions of the firstborn when a second child arrives. He will spontaneously feel jealousy and hostility towards the new arrival, who disturbs his exclusive relationship with his parents. He is no longer the sole focus of their attention and is obliged to share the love that was previously his alone, and all this in addition to the quasi-sexual envy he feels when his mother breast-feeds the baby. Think too of the earliest fans of a star who becomes increasingly popular. They too will feel only jealousy towards newer ones who steal their idol's affection. In both situations, the firstborn or the fans would like to get rid of the intruders, the spoil-sports, and keep the exclusive affective relationship with the loved one. What do they do? Throw the baby in the dustbin? Machine-gun the other fans? They cannot, for that would mean going against the parents' desire to have more than one child or the star's wish to have a host of admirers. Whatever their personal preferences might be, parents have obligations to all their children and stars to all their fans, and neither can single out one for special favours.

So, since they cannot get rid of bothersome rivals and remain in sole possession of their beloved or give free rein to their jealousy and hostility without endangering their own relationships with those they love (who could not tolerate such things), both children and fans are obliged to modify their position. We see a decline in mutual hostility and attachment to former rivals becoming dominant. Conflict becomes coalition. Some give up the idea of privilege and a past exclusivity, others the idea of achieving such things in the future. As a result, the distance created by distrust and hate is reduced and there is universal mutual identification, imitation and repetition, with everyone immersing himself in the same activities and receiving some degree of consolation from the pleasure of these mimetic exercises. As Canetti writes:

Only together can men free themselves from their burdens of distance; and this, precisely, is what happens in a crowd. During the discharge distinctions are thrown off and all feel *equal* . . . and an immense feeling of relief ensues. It is for the sake of this blessed moment, when no-one is greater or better than another, that people become a crowd. (Canetti, 1973: 19)

They nevertheless continue to keep a close watch on each other to make sure that no-one gets more or special favours.

This discharge is a sign that the amorous attraction has been replaced by mutual identification, which is the best means of cementing relationships within a crowd. This is indicated by the birth of the feeling of a common destiny and a community spirit whose first demand

is for justice, for equal treatment for all. We all know how loudly and implacably this claim is put forward at school. If one cannot be the favourite oneself, at all events nobody else shall be the favourite. (Freud: XVIII, 120)

It also becomes apparent in the admirers of idols of the theatre or popular singers.

Originally rivals, they have succeeded in identifying themselves with one another by means of a similar love for the same object. (Freud: XVIII, 120)

Crowds would thus seem to obey a principle of negative democracy or levelling down. If someone else looks as if he may be lucky or may benefit from something, their reaction is 'Why him? Why them? Why not me?' There are always grounds for envy. No-one ever gets everything or exactly what he wants, and so the universal reaction to other people's desires is always the same. Envy produces rivalry, and equality offers a way out of it, even if it means universal renunciation and general deprivation.

Public-spiritedness and *esprit de corps* are based on reversals of this kind. We give up hoping for the things we want and abandon our most cherished ambitions in order to oblige everyone to make the same sacrifice. This is often reflected in hypocrisy and fools' bargains. Whether we are happy or unhappy, the main thing is to be together, with no-one's fate being different from that of his fellow-citizens, neighbours or friends. In Freud's words:

This demand for equality is the root of social conscience and the sense of duty. It reveals itself unexpectedly in the syphilitic's dread of infecting other people, which psycho-analysis has taught us to understand. The dread exhibited by these poor wretches corresponds to their violent struggles against the unconscious wish to spread their infection on to other people; for why should they alone be infected and cut off from so much? why not other people as well? (Freud: XVIII, 121)

The pressure to conform becomes so strong and concentrated that the slightest divergence becomes a threat against the group, which sees it as a breach of the unspoken agreement its members have entered into, the spark that could cause a sudden outburst of long-contained hostility. We should remember that constraint is at work. We have surrendered our individuality for the sake of being like our rivals. The rewards for that difficult task of limiting ourselves are justice and equality. And transgression is a challenge that calls its utility into question. That is why they do us some degree of violence, and democracy presupposes a strict inner discipline, for everyone has an ambivalent attitude towards it and is ready to question it. There are still some who, in Orwell's phrase, would like to be more equal than others.

Seen from another angle, the equality operating within the crowd makes it a kind of haven of peace, a place of refuge where people feel that they are among their own kind. Individuals feel a sense of release, as if they had laid aside the burden of social and psychological barriers and discovered that men are equal. Being with other people is like being with oneself. Hence a certain lack of order. The crowd is filled with hundreds of incessant movements like those of particles suspended in a liquid and is perpetually milling and agitated.

In that sense, we can describe masses as libertarian, for their equality encourages anarchy. This positive democracy is powerfully attractive. It is given a new lease of life by every revolution and in every community, and each of them promises its earthly kingdom. What is the psychological driving force behind it? It would see it as lying in the pleasure derived from the mimetic desire to be like one's fellows, one's parents or one's children and the imagined lack of any difference. Usually this desire is not imposed without a struggle. It means that we have to make sacrifices and it causes discord. At this stage, however, we imagine that we can enjoy it without hindrance.

What we are dealing with is an imitative enjoyment rather like sexual pleasure. But there is a difference, for the former means that individuals are almost submerged by the crowd, whereas the latter produces isolated couples. Freud describes this phenomenon thus:

Two people coming together for the purpose of sexual satisfaction, in so far as they seek for solitude, are making a demonstration against the herd instinct, the group feeling. The more they are in love, the more completely they suffice for each other. (Freud: XVIII, 140)

When these two versions of equality are superimposed, the crowd is both a form of extreme constraint upon the human person and an unlimited field of freedom and individualism. Some people withdraw and resist it, keeping themselves aloof. Others, however, throw themselves into it and lead the life they have dreamed of. We are eternally at cross purposes here. There are those who urge a return to the old village community life. But the people in those very same villages are leaving them for the shelter of mass urban anonymity, to get away from the watching eyes of family and neighbours and the jealous tyranny of all those people who wish them well and do them harm.

There is one exception to these two versions: the leader. To put it differently, every group demands that its members should be identical and have the same lifestyle and future. Only one person is excepted. In Freud's words:

> Do not let us forget, however, that the demand for equality in a group applies only to its members and not to the leader. All the members must be equal to one another, but they all want to be ruled by one person. Many equals, who can identify themselves with one another, and a single person superior to them all – that is the situation that we find realized in groups which are capable of subsisting.                                    (Freud: XVIII, 121)

Crowds are therefore like solar systems with many planets revolving round a sun, their central point. If we are to describe their movements, however, we need to work out the relationship between love and identification in the same way as we work out that between attraction and repulsion in astronomy.

## III

We shall now describe another class of phenomena, those involved in the movement from panic to terror, or the oscillation between fear and violence. At one extreme their major cause is the loss of identification and at the other the over-identification of the individuals submerged in the mass. We shall keep to artificial crowds. For the sake of clarity, we shall take the leader to be the keystone of the whole system of relationships. What happens when the keystone fails and the whole system threatens to fall apart? There are two excessive reactions – by which I mean reactions which are out of proportion to reality – and these are panic and terror.

In an army, which we have taken as one of our examples of crowds, every soldier identifies with his comrades and the hierarchy. The commander-in-chief is invested with the love of his troops, and they share the illusion of being loved by him. Then something goes wrong. There is a break in tone or command. This may happen after a defeat, but a defeat in itself is not enough to produce panic, which only occurs when the leader withdraws. After the defeats of the Russian campaign, the French army did not begin to collapse until Napoleon suddenly left it to get back to Paris. As one of his biographers says, 'He had left the *Grande Armée* in a terrible state. Even in such a plight, however, it was still an army and capable of effort and hope. Once the emperor had gone, there was total disorder. It was a case of every man for himself and saving his own skin. Orders were no longer obeyed, and discipline broke down even amongst the higher officers' (Bainville, 1959: 401).

You are well acquainted with the symptoms. Individuals become isolated and look after themselves, neglecting the most basic rules and orders. Fear takes possession of everyone. It is the expression of the loss of an illusion, namely the discovery that there is neither love nor a mutual link. It also reflects a loss of identification with the crowd, though this may last only a very short time. The response to such a situation is a feeling of abandonment which produces behaviour like that of an anorexic child unable to find a target for his anger. 'He's looked after number one. What about me?' is the thought in everyone's mind. And so self-hatred begins to appear, or aggression is directed against other people, with whom the only unity was that of the common model. The temptation of individual and collective self-destruction prowls everywhere. This has been admirably described in Zola's novel *La Débâcle* on the subject of the Franco-Prussian War, in which the French collapse was largely due to the hopeless incompetence of Napoleon III and his military leaders. 'There was real despair amongst the troops. Many wanted to sit on their packs in the mud of that sodden, rainswept plateau and simply wait for death. They sniggered and insulted their leaders, and what leaders they were, brainless men who sauntered up and down when the enemy was not there and slipped away when he was, undoing in the evening what they had done in the morning. The last stages of demoralisation finally turned the army into a herd with no faith and no discipline sent out to be slaughtered by chance along the road' (Zola, 1965: 108).

When people no longer identify with their group, their comrades or their fellow-citizens, all these become strangers and hence enemies, and previously repressed fears surface. This has been seen on more than one occasion on battlefields, during street disorders and in fires in places of public entertainment, with the fire in the Bazar de la Charité being the prototype. Even if the danger is not as great as it was on that occasion, everyone becomes sensitive to the slightest rumour, every movement of the crowd is a cause of anxiety and a feeling of abandonment spreads. Everyone becomes suspicious of everyone else, which is a sign of mutual hostility and a tendency to turn one's back on one's fellow human beings and to trust no-one.

Many incidents from the flow of refugees in France and Belgium in 1940 lend support to this view. As the Germans advanced and political and military authority collapsed more or less completely, people began to distrust each other. Spies – that famous Fifth Column that we had been taught to fear for so long – were seen everywhere. Trepper, who organised an anti-Nazi spy network, writes as follows:

By some mysterious association of ideas that psychiatrists and crowd psychologists can perhaps explain, people suspected that Nazi spies might be disguised as priests. On 11 May, I saw an incredible sight on the Place de Brouckère in Brussels. A hysterical and uncontrolled crowd grabbed a young clergyman and lifted up his soutane to see if he was wearing a Nazi uniform underneath it.

(Trepper, 1975: 51)

A real spy would hardly have been wearing a uniform, but in defrocking, so to speak, the harmless priest, the crowd was probably mentally stripping neighbours or leaders to see whether they were really enemies.

In truth, panic creates nothing and merely brings out the fear and hostility latent in everyone. Once identification weakens, our familiar surroundings become strange and threatening, as if a child were suddenly plunged into darkness and thoroughly terrified. This is the desolating and extreme psychological misery of the masses that Freud describes thus:

Over and above the tasks of restricting the instincts, which we are prepared for, there forces itself on our notice the danger of a state of things which might be termed 'the psychological poverty of groups'. This danger is not threatening where the bonds of a society are chiefly constituted by the identification of its members with one another, while individuals of the leader type do not acquire the importance that should fall to them in the formation of a group.

(Freud: XXI, 115)

When individuals have firmly established themselves and then later withdrawn, completely, as was the case with Napoleon or the military leaders in 1870–71, the pressure to identify slackens. Social ties are deeply affected, and the mass even breaks up into its individual constituent narcissistic atoms. Freud writes that:

If an individual in panic fear begins to be solicitous only on his own account, he bears witness in so doing to the fact that the emotional ties, which have hitherto made the danger seem small to him, have ceased to exist. Now that he is by himself in facing the danger, he may surely think it greater. (Freud: XVIII, 96)

Faced with the collapse of the group and the setback to his desire for inamoration and imitation, he turns in on himself, returning to that exclusive self-love which, he believes, will enable him to survive.

Simultaneously and irresistibly, the most tenacious and uncontainable of anti-social forces becomes dominant, spreading like a virus. Self-concern drowns all other internal and external voices. Exclusively concerned with his own physical being and well-being, the individual becomes autistic, deaf and blind to the needs of others.

Nor do I believe it to be by chance that in times of intense panic caused by disasters or epidemics men are revolted by the way authorities, powerless to deal with such calamities, abdicate their responsibility and consequently abandon themselves to sensual satisfaction. Identification disappears so totally that Eros fills the vacuum it has left. The history of the great medieval plagues offers us an outstanding example of this. The desire to live was enormously heightened amongst those who fled the charnel-houses and the plague-stricken areas. Their appetite for pleasure sought satisfaction in feasts, dances (which were often dances of death) and sexual pleasure. Others could not tear themselves away from the stark fascination of ravaged houses, funeral pyres and common graves. That erotic masterpiece *The Decameron* was of course related by people who thought they could escape panic in eroticism.

Very occasionally, the mass wins again. Identification takes place once more, and everyone seeks a scapegoat for the universal misery, claiming to know who is the really guilty creator of panic or author of crime. It is not the defaulting leader who is pilloried, but his active and malevolent double. Universal impotence is replaced by the individual omnipotence of the guilty Jews, blacks, poor, rich, Bolsheviks or whatever.

Medieval paintings show such apocalyptic scenes. Jews are accused of poisoning wells and persecuted. They are tortured and their houses burnt while the crowd shouts its joy aloud, and the torturers use their weapons to thrust those trying to escape back into the inferno. The Second World War also brought such scenes of horror back to us, unleashed by an ever-present fear of which the holocaust was one of the signs.

All these elements lead us to believe that panic and the speed with which it spreads are basically a narcissistic infection. As in all infections, the virus and microbes are present but latent. While we are in good health and our physiological state is satisfactory, nothing happens. But as soon as our health declines as a result of a poor diet, overtiredness or bad living-conditions, the virus and the microbes emerge and proliferate. That is why one can see how hard it is to get rid of panic. It is no good merely reassuring people or giving them 'clear' instructions if we want them to behave reasonably. The only things that can achieve this are the re-establishment of an identity and the re-creation of the crowd by means of a firm order.

In a religious crowd identifying with a belief rather than a person, reactions are different. Since such a crowd is assured of the love of a leader – of Christ, for example – it responds to the threat of the loss of its identity with a strengthening of that identity. We do not detect fear in it, but observe that common elements are exalted and extraneous ones are excluded. Non-believers, for example, are expelled, as aliens are exiled or interned in wartime. Tolerance becomes intolerance and those individuals who endanger the link uniting the faithful are persecuted. Freud's view was that

Fundamentally indeed every religion is in this same way a religion of love for all those whom it embraces; while cruelty and intolerance towards those who do not belong to it are natural to every religion.          (Freud: XVIII, 98)

Intolerance takes the form of a campaign of terror directed against those who are seen as 'enemies' or those who no more belong to the flock than do the faithful of a different religion. And if they do not exist, they have to be invented, as Stalin once invented the enemies of the people to restore a fading cohesion. The aggression aroused by such so-called enemies has all the qualities of homicide, and circumstances alone prevent them from producing their full effect. Society suffers, of course, when such violence is unleashed and a wave of high feats of arms, hangings, drawings and quarterings, burnings at the stake, *autos-da-fé*, and tortures of all kinds washes through it, to say nothing of the trials, pillagings and sackings that go with it and all the other means of separating the wheat from the tares that are used under the banner of Christ, Luther and other holy religions. The Inquisition and the Counter-Reformation set up a model for Europe that was to be imitated time and time again.

We must believe that the churches of all kinds that dominate societies cannot do without such measures. In Freud's view, that would never happen. The fact that nowadays they are more tolerant, he warns us, should not be allowed to lead us into error, for that is not a sign that there has been any major change in crowd mentality. At most it can be seen as an indication of the weakening of religious beliefs and links with the Church. It is not that our ways have become gentler, but merely that our beliefs are not as strong.

If another group tie takes the place of the religious one – and the socialistic tie seems to be succeeding in doing so – then there will be the same intolerance towards outsiders as in the age of the Wars of Religion; and if differences between scientific opinions could ever attain a similar significance for groups, the same result would again be repeated with this new motivation.          (Freud: XVIII, 99)

That conclusion, dating from 1921, is really striking when we remember that at that time there was nothing to suggest the imminence of the ideological wars of Marxism nor any reason to foresee that Stalin was to become the Napoleon of the *gulags*. In any case, what Freud was suggesting was that we are more likely to predict the future correctly if we adopt the hypothesis that all social movements obey the laws of mass psychology rather than accept on the basis of their declarations of intent that they are the exceptions to them.

What connection is there between panic and terror? In the case of panic, the individual turns his fear against the crowd and blindly destroys it. This can be seen in fragmentary collective systems, those strips of human groups attached to their original tissue. They imagine themselves to be threatened and appear to flee the peril, but in reality they rush towards it in a mixture of fear and fury. In the case of terror, it is crowds that turn their fear round and direct it at individuals, spying out even those who deviate least and offering violence to those who resist. When it is in a state of exaltation, the crowd also sacrifices those who do not share its fervour once it has exterminated those who so far have been marginal and unenthusiastic. Whether violence is a reaction against one or more individuals, it has its origin in the misery of the threatened masses, either in their love or in their identity. Only curing that misery can stop violence and hold men together. For how long?

## IV

Crowds are like women, it was said, and both were lumped together and accused of being fickle and capricious in their moods and of swinging from one extreme to another. In fact, they obey a cyclical rhythm, experiencing alternating joy and sadness. Their moods change as suddenly as an individual's. Lenin, for example, was very sensitive to the ebb and flow of the moods of a crowd and often spoke of this (Porchnev, 1970: 27ff). In what follows, we shall abandon the doubtful analogy with female whims and use the more exact one with melancholia and mania.

Right at the start there is, of course, the division between the ego and the super-ego. The latter normally watches, admonishes and imposes its discipline, preventing any escapades and restricting the instinctual pleasures of the ego. Conformity, predictability and the pressure to identify procure certain satisfactions, but no-one can permanently put up with so many sacrifices or the separation of the ego and super-ego and the constant pressure of the latter on the former. In other words, the constant suppression of erotic tendencies by mimetic desires and the necessity to want what others want clearly result in a wearing tedium that can become depression.

When saturation point is reached, there is an attempt to escape, to change the situation. The ego, anxious for unity, attempts to effect a reconciliation with the super-ego. If they come together again, like a child once more joining his parents after a long separation, there is a honeymoon period of rejoicing for the psyche. The super-ego no longer harasses the ego and allows it both to love itself, identify directly with all the other egos in the crowd and become one with them. Things could not be better. The freedom goes to their heads, and they reach a point where all prohibitions are violated, all taboos are broken, and they become as feverishly excited as someone in a manic state. Carnivals and sometimes political or sports meetings are the occasions for such outbursts. Almost every barrier between individuals, classes and sexes is broken down, and promiscuity is tolerated and perhaps even required. The world is a violently-coloured place and the various channels for aggression and love are open to all. Societies which can look ahead and are concerned for the well-being of their members set aside certain times of the year – the Roman Saturnalia, for example – for this purpose and provide appropriate places for them. Disorder and protest beyond all measure and the waste of patiently-amassed wealth are the price paid for the peace of mind of everyone and a means of increasing subsequent toleration of routine and boredom.

But there may be other unforeseen manifestations, experienced in much the same way. In rebellions, riots and pillaging, festive and aggressive elements combine to form an explosive mixture that can sweep away constraints and smash existing laws. It has often been pointed out that the events of May 1968 saw a similar kind of mass exaltation, with everyone being free to talk when, where and as he liked. The various social categories, who usually ignored each other, came together and acknowledged each other with a profound sense of having become a community again. The slogans of the time – 'nothing is forbidden' and 'prohibiting prohibited', for example – became the very words of life.

For a month, ordinary society practically disappeared. Another society, and an extraordinary one, ruled in its place. Everything seemed unreasonable, but not inexplicable. Freud writes:

But the ego ideal comprises the sum of all the limitations in which the ego has to acquiesce, and for that reason the abrogation of the ideal would necessarily be a magnificent festival for the ego, which might then once again feel satisfied with itself.
(Freud: XVIII, 131)

But, as popular wisdom has it, all good things must come to an end. Passion spends itself, disenchantment sets in and the music stops. The world gets back to its repetitive and routine-bound rut. Identification with a social category, a job, family and class becomes the norm again. The super-ego dissociates itself from the ego once more and sets up a proper distance and an opposition. Once again, it begins its mole-like work of undermining pleasure. Depressive gloom spreads like an epidemic. The crowd is riddled with its virus, dislocated and dispersed:

Exaltation is swiftly followed by depression, which is that much deeper the more violent the collective fever has been, and which leads inexorably to the arousal of individual instincts of defence and self-preservation.           (De Felice, 1947: 14)

All these so-called instincts rear up and force the individual back into the boredom of everyday routine.

We could see this as a way of explaining the cycle that natural crowds are subject to. They move from a Dionysian exaltation to an Apollonian calm. The cycle is repeated with all the regularity of the ebb and flow of the tides. Days of brilliant sunshine and dull, drizzly days alternate with each other as the moods of the crowd shift and change. It would be a grave omission on our part if we were so carried away by Freud's powerful analogy with melancholia and mania that we forgot one basic fact. This is that at times when rules are suspended or reversed for some festivity, when children no longer obey their parents or servants their masters, there is an order behind the disorder, and it follows prescribed rules and well-established custom. The process is repeated at set intervals, thus meeting the demands of the super-ego. No-one imagines that he can avoid it and escape serious consequences. Like Sunday rest, festivities are compulsory.

None of this invalidates the theory of alternating peaks and troughs in the struggle between Eros and mimesis. The most we can say is that some societies have seen how important that struggle is and have decided to make methodical use of what had been a spontaneous phenomenon.

Since they are of such great practical importance, it is possible to imagine other explanations for the events I have touched on. We should try to test them against as many varied observations – of an economic and political nature, and so on – as we possibly can, but we must acknowledge that crowd psychology has made progress possible simply by imagining such an explanation and being able to account for the characteristics of crowds as described by Le Bon and Tarde. Whatever reservations we may have, we now have a more coherent view than we once had.

# 7. *The end of hypnosis*

---

O UR ACCOUNT is becoming clearer and covering more ground. It means that we can see the properties of the crowd, such as equality, or its movements, such as panic or terror, as the result of a conflict between two desires. We shall see later that a wider and deeper form of the same method of explanation will provide both a general and a detailed account of the psychology of leaders.

But what part should we see hypnosis as playing? So far, we have seen it as the mechanism that binds the individuals in a crowd together. We saw in the first chapters that it is based on a direct injection of the hypnotist's ideas and orders into the subject. Although there is little theoretical justification for it, its practical success gave it recognised authority, and it was seen as capable of influencing anyone to do anything. It was so impressive that Maupassant, who had seen the hold it exerted, said of the medical practitioners using it that they 'have played with that weapon of the new Lord, the domination of a mysterious power over the enslaved human soul. They called it magnetism, hypnosis, suggestion and many other names. I have seen them amusing themselves like thoughtless children with that horrible power. What wretchedness for us and for all humanity!' (Maupassant, 1924: 39). What would he write if he were with us now, when everything in civilisation confirms his worst fears? He would have seen, however, that just when it was beginning to produce its full effects in practice, hypnosis was becoming irrelevant to crowd psychology.

## II

The kinship between the amorous state and hypnosis is strikingly obvious.

There is the same submission to mesmeric fascination, the same renunciation of any judgement and the same over-valuation on the part of the person under its control. Nothing could be more normal than that he should do all that he is asked and have the feeling that he is acting or thinking for himself when in fact he is obeying suggestion. He acts like a lover who has adopted the feelings and judgements of the beloved and is obeying his or her orders. He abandons his own judgements and feelings and conforms to those of his partner. Nor is it in any way astonishing that the same individual should find himself in a dreaming or sleepwalking state. What happens in fact is that the hypnotist controls his access to reality and takes charge of his concrete experience. He sees and feels nothing except what he is told to see and feel by the super-ego embodied in the hypnotist. The latter becomes the sole object of his attention, a disturbing object who asks him to look into his eyes.

It is this gaze that transmits the man's power. Words charm, dissimulate and prevaricate for it and are the servant, not the mistress. The gaze directs itself here and now to the person and searches his consciousness and silently reaches the old and familiar sentiments, desires and inclinations. And it is also:

the *sight* of the chieftain that is dangerous and unbearable for primitive people, just as later that of the Godhead is for mortals. Even Moses had to act as an intermediary between his people and Jehovah, since the people could not support the sight of God; and when he returned from the presence of God his face shone – some of the *mana* had been transferred on to him, just as happens with the intermediary among primitive people.[1]          (Freud: XVIII, 125)

Hypnosis can also be induced by asking the subject to look fixedly at a brilliant object or by getting him to listen to monotonous sound. This method distracts his attention from the diversity of the external world and the hypnotist's intentions, transferring every thought and affect to him, as happened with his parents in the past:

By the measures that he takes, then, the hypnotist awakens in the subject a portion of his archaic heritage which had also made him compliant towards his parents and which had experienced an individual re-animation in his relation to his father; what is thus awakened is the idea of a paramount and dangerous personality, towards whom only a passive-masochistic attitude is possible, to whom one's will has to be surrendered, – while to be alone with him, 'to look him in the face', appears a hazardous enterprise.          (Freud: XVIII, 127)

Faced with such a powerful coalition of forces – those of his amorous feelings and his identification with the hypnotist and the image of his father that he creates – the ego realises that it cannot win. It does not, however, completely abandon all resistance and is still a spectator in the game that it cannot escape. Consequently, it attempts to secure the approval of the super-ego by espousing its desires and perceptions. In so far as any effective sexual relationship is excluded, the tendency to idealise the doctor and to be passively subject to him is greatly increased:

The hypnotic relation is the unlimited devotion of someone in love, but with sexual satisfaction excluded; whereas in the actual case of being in love this kind of satisfaction is only temporarily kept back, and remains in the background as a possible aim at some later time. (Freud: XVIII, 115)

Relationships of this kind are analogous to medical, pedagogical, religious and, of course, political ones. It is the fascination relationship described by Le Bon. We now know what causes it and gives it its strength. If the analogy is a valid one, we can assume that in all such cases the leader is forbidden to have sexual relationships with his followers, those whom he wishes to influence.[2]

If he does have such relationships, or lets the possibility of them be glimpsed, his influence will be diminished and his charisma lessened. This would hold true for professors, priests and doctors and clearly also for political leaders. That is the price they pay for making use of their ascendancy to transform amorous admiration into an erotic conquest. The real meaning of the saying that no-one is a hero to his valet is perhaps that no-one is a hero to a lover.

## III

Although he never stopped producing fresh arguments and was nearing the end of his undertaking and indeed of his life, Freud never stopped telling us in all seriousness that unfortunately he was more and more convinced that the mystery of hypnosis would never be completely solved. He would be right to see the hypotheses I have been putting forward as at most a rather dowdy branch of science that can do no more than enable us to think about it in less mystical terms. It underlies every action of man on man in both psychiatry and politics. And it is very useful, provided that we do not use it. From a psychological point of view, and disregarding the numbers involved, hypnosis is identical with the crowd.

We can say that it is a single section across the behaviour patterns adopted by every individual in the mass towards his leader:

Hypnosis is distinguished from a group formation by this limitation of number, just as it is distinguished from being in love by the absence of directly sexual trends. In this respect it occupies a middle position between the two.
(Freud: XVIII, 115)

Imagine ten, a hundred or a thousand such sections, a multitude of links like spokes in a wheel attaching the single hub to each of the points on the rim. As new recruits to the mass arrive, the number of one-to-one relationships increases. The central figure remains the same, but the relationships between peripheral ones, between the points where the spokes of the social wheel meet the rim, change. If we move from individual to collective hypnosis, we have the image of a crowd with its attention fixed on the leader, who occupies a place identical to that of the hypnotist in relation to his patients.

Tarde rightly said that

This plural is basically never more than a dual, and however large in number a corporation or a crowd may be, it too is a sort of couple in which now each individual is subject to the suggestion of all the others together, a collective suggestion, in which the dominant leader is included, now the whole group is subject to the leader's suggestion. (Tarde, 1910: 211)

But mimetic desire becomes more powerful than the previous erotic desire and is intensified. Everyone wants to be like his neighbour and the man who brings them together. Ultimately, everyone identifies himself as a member of a cult and an admirer of a famous man. By copying each other and their idol, the individual members of the crowd all acquire uniform postures and ways of speaking that enable them to recognise each other and to be classified by other people as members of this or that section of society.

We can now easily see the psychological make-up of the crowd. Vertically, there is a universal urge towards the leader. Horizontally, there is a mass of people orientated towards the same ideal of the ego and consequently identifying with each other. Amongst them, identification regressively takes the place of libidinal attachments. In a crowd, even disguised sexual relationships are absent and of minimal importance. Freud says that

The love relation between men and women remains outside these organizations. Even where groups are formed which are composed of both men and women the distinction between the sexes plays no part. (Freud: XVIII, 141)

That is the picture presented by an incorporated group, with everyone loving the leader and identifying with his neighbour. We should keep the idea of an asymmetrical distribution of human attachments. Every desire is preferably restricted to one of the terms, the erotic in the case of the leader, the mimetic in that of the crowd. The leader loves himself and is loved, the crowd loves him and imitates him instead of loving itself. That is what generally happens. The only exception is the Catholic, and hence religious, crowd. The Christian may love Christ and identify with other Christians, but the Church asks much more of him than that. What he has to do is love them as Christ loved them. But, as Freud points out, 'This addition evidently goes beyond the constitution of the group' (Freud: XVIII, 134). The picture we have chosen is the real one and shows us its essential features.

# IV

Hypnosis is not included in that picture, as it has become a pointless hypothesis. It may still be a hurtful enigma, but it is one that we can do without in accounting for the dynamics of the masses. Psychoanalysis has taken over from it and provides the necessary concepts and images for the crowd. In crowd psychology, we are no longer dealing with hallucination, somnambulism, a procession of waking dreamers or intelligent automata, but with the realities of desire and amorous, imitative individuals grouped round a leader. For each of them he is a consciousness and causes each to regress to a primitive state such as childhood.

The principle of the endless conflict between Eros and mimesis has been very explicitly formulated. That it has been insufficiently explained, I accept. But the change is of major importance. The complacently-perpetuated magical element in crowd psychology has been removed, as in the past gravity removed the Cartesian vortex from mechanics. In its place, we now have more observable and intelligible notions. That is the progress – and I use the word very hesitantly – that Freud enabled crowd psychology to make. That progress has been so great that a whole mass of earlier work and writing is now out of date.[3] Freud showed his aversion to all anti-rational thinking and rejected such ideas or combined them with others that were easier to handle. Although he took over Le Bon's descriptions and Tarde's analyses, he completely changed the current image of the masses. Their irrationality, i.e. their submissiveness and their strange indifference to reality, was a result of symbolic thinking, of the 'blind or still symbolic thinking' (*cogitatio caeca vel symbolica*) that Leibniz speaks of.

That is true, but it is now clear that it is now a matter of something other than automatic thinking. The almost amorous veneration that the crowd feels for the leader and the fact that the individuals making up the crowd identify themselves because of him are the ideas that that thinking expresses. Seen in that light, he is no longer a *de facto* phenomenon, something patched onto the situation, but the basic datum of the crowd. He seems to be its 'onlie begetter', but in fact is simply a part of it. We now know why the masses reign but do not rule.

In crowd psychology, the leader is the common element, the universal and indispensable super-ego and social ego around which men unite. That discipline simply repeats what Mao Tse-tung used to say, that there will always have to be leaders.

Choosing between the weakness of the masses and the strength of the leader (and hence of the Party, the Church, the army and so on) is, of course, not choosing between heaven and hell or truth and error. The choice is between two evils of which neither is the lesser, between the plague and cholera, since with regard to individual freedom every mass is irrational and every leader despotic. But for everyone who sees things clearly, that is the essence of any choice. If we choose that which gives strength, we overcome weakness and ensure the survival of our society. All the classical crowd psychologists, including Freud, adopted that position. Unlike others, however, the latter shored up the discipline with a coherent theoretical framework, hence his criticism:

But we shall venture, even now, upon a mild reproach against earlier writers for not having sufficiently appreciated the importance of the leader in the psychology of groups.                                                                           (Freud: XVIII, 118)

We should add that since everything is now explained in terms of love and identification, subjectivity has its place in crowd psychology. The puppets of Liébeault and Tarde, influenced by suggestion, have gone, stored away in the same cupboard as hypnosis. Their place has been taken by thronging, passionate hordes, the characters of ancient tragedy and the heroes of Shakespearean drama, as we shall shortly see. Our contemporary horror – American, of course – of the affective and subjective has hidden these changes.[4] But their impact on reality is a much deeper one than that of the whole of calculating cogitation. But why bother about it?

While such a transformation is taking place, the political equation, which is a form of rational exploitation of the irrational substance of the masses, follows quite obviously. Indeed, it could not be otherwise, since it is the strategies designed to handle the two major desires that give power now to one, now to the other.

## PART VII

# The psychology of the charismatic leader

## 1. *Prestige and charisma*

I

THE LEADER is to crowd psychology what squaring the circle is to mathematics. All those who have tried to solve the puzzle have been obscure and hesitant. Some have even gloried in it, making Pascal's words their own. ('Do not criticise us for obscurity, for we profess it.') This is a harmful and blameworthy attitude, since they have never attempted to explain the phenomena they have made use of and have consequently piled up one difficulty on top of another. Some of these have been pointed out in the course of this book. The time has now come to tackle the most troublesome of all.

When we examine the picture Le Bon, Tarde and Freud have drawn of the leader, we have a strange feeling. Looked at in a certain way, it has a certain verisimilitude. Seen from a different point of view, it is simply a dated, exaggerated caricature, reflecting the prejudices of a bygone age rather than the impersonal observation of our own. Indeed, there is such a variety of leaders, corresponding to a great diversity of forms of authority – compare Roosevelt and Robespierre, Gandhi and Mao, de Gaulle and Giscard d'Estaing or Léon Blum and Marchais or Mitterrand – that it is distasteful to try to lump them all together. How can we put them all into the same category without having first decided what their common feature is, if indeed they have one?

And so we remain puzzled. Do the leaders that crowd psychology describes correspond to a sociological reality or only to a crude fiction? If we could not answer that question, our investigation would be super-fluous. We should not know what the explanations were explanations of, since one cannot explain what does not exist, be it a monster, a chimera or whatever. A theory can be true or false, and most theories are sometimes one and sometimes the other. If it does not refer to something concrete, however, it is neither, and myths alone are not a sufficient basis for science.

## II

In the social world, there is a kind of authority that enables us to form an idea, in the psychic world, of a form of domination exerted less by virtue of anonymous physical power than by that of personal and spiritual influence, namely charismatic authority. In its traditional sense, charisma refers to a holy man or woman who explains the dogmas of a religion and suggests a grace that consoles the suffering, a light that fills the tormented mind of the believer and the living word of a prophet who moves men's hearts, in short, the interior harmony of the master and his disciples.

In our own time, as a result of the work of Max Weber, the German sociologist, this kind of grace is seen in those leaders who fascinate the masses and become objects of adoration for them. Churchill possessed the gift, and so did Mao, Stalin, de Gaulle and Tito. It has also been given to Pope John Paul II, whose hold over the millions who await him and listen to him fervently has struck observers. The *Figaro* reporter covering his visit to Poland wrote that his great strength lay in both the clarity of his speeches and his charisma, and *The Economist*, that austere British weekly, went even further, saying that such magnetism is power.

Nowadays, charisma has become such a popular word that even the large-circulation papers use it, supposing that their readers understand it. Its vogue owes a great deal to its obscurity and vagueness. It sets up mysterious echoes in our minds. The ideas of the man responsible for its current usage, Max Weber, are a great deal clearer, however. His view is that this type of authority 'is specifically foreign to economic considerations. Wherever it appears, it constitutes a "call" in the most emphatic sense of the word, a "mission" or a "spiritual duty" ' (Weber, 1968: I, 244).

In other words, the leader's ascendancy over the masses depends on neither wealth, industry nor the army, which from its point of view seem to be secondary concerns, mere matters of day-to-day management. Properly speaking, charisma denotes a gift, a certain quality of relationship between believers or servants and the master they trust and obey. This gift or quality – the ability to cure formerly attributed to kings, for example – is defined by a belief or a shared view of things.

Once it has been recognised and accepted, the gift acts like a *symbolic placebo*, producing the desired effect on those coming into contact with the person possessing it. It works just like a harmless palliative prescribed by a doctor, even though it has no intrinsic physical or chemical qualities. In spite of all the scientific progress we have seen, we are constantly being made aware that human beings cure each other and are the most universal form of medicine. Doubtlessly charisma is more closely linked to the beliefs of the mass than the personal talents of an individual, but the latter are not a negligible factor. Not everyone can be a witch-doctor. Otherwise why should there be so many called and so few chosen? However difficult it may be to define such talents, we all seem to understand at once that they are the mark of a leader. Shakespeare catches the moment admirably:

*Lear*: Dost thou know me, fellow?
*Kent*: No, sir; but you have that in your countenance which I would fain call master.
*Lear*: What's that?
*Kent*: Authority.

Like all primary and irrational powers, charisma is at once a grace and a stigma, conferring on him who possesses it the sign of extraordinary worth and also the mark of excess and intolerable violence. It offers analogies with the unusual power of African chiefs to radiate extraordinary strength and the 'triumphal talisman' of the Homeric kings, to whom *kudos* was supposed to give absolute magical superiority.

The common characteristic of such gifts is that they are at the same time attractive and threatening. They protect and strike fear into people. Charisma is beyond reason and, like the powers mentioned above, it arouses the contradictory passions of love and hate and is both challenging and repellent. Since time out of mind it has brought about an increase in affects. It snatches crowds from their torpor and galvanises them into action. I shall return to these ambivalent feelings towards it, for the matter is a basic one.

## III

The charismatic leader is believed to be endowed with uncommon and superior qualities. But the relationships people have with him are of a personal nature. They are certainly subjective, and based on an illusion of reciprocity, enabling every individual in the crowd to feel that he is in direct contact with the man he admires. To feel this, it is enough for them to have seen him, come near to him or approached him just once, perhaps on the battlefield or on some great crowd occasion. The individual comes back saying 'I have seen him and touched him' or 'He spoke to me', just as Napoleon's Old Guard told their stories: 'I was in Egypt, at Austerlitz, at la Berezina with him.' Max Weber stresses this aspect.

In its pure form charismatic authority has a character specifically foreign to everyday routine structure. The social relationships directly involved are strictly personal, based on the validity and practice of charismatic personal qualities.

(Weber, 1968: I, 146)

In other words, the leader's authority moves above all intermediate bodies such as organisations, parties and the mass media and above all those institutions in every state that change the state into a cold and impersonal monster. Around his person there is created a community of fidelity and hope that cannot be contained by hierarchical structures. Everyone can declare himself a disciple, partisan or companion without feeling in the least lessened or diminished.

An organized group subject to charismatic authority will be called a charismatic community (Gemeinde). It is based on an emotional form of communal relationship (Vergemeinschaftung). (Weber, 1968: I, 243)

The leader and his partisans seem to choose each other mutually. The former's good pleasure is hidden behind the arbitrary dictates of the emotions. He weaves the links that bind him to his men. They have faith in him and put their fate into his hands, totally identifying with him, and never knowing exactly why they act as they do. They justify abandoning themselves to him in terms of either a thought-out decision or a personal revelation, or a mixture of the two, like cardinals going into conclave to elect a Pope. The outcome is always identical, with the charisma of one individual being validated by all. Max Weber describes the situation as follows:

It is recognition on the part of those subject to authority which is decisive for the validity of charisma. The recognition is freely given and guaranteed by what is held to be a proof, originally always a miracle, and consists in devotion to the corresponding revelation, hero worship, or absolute trust in the leader.
(Weber, 1968: I, 242)

The other side of the coin, as you can easily imagine, is submission. It obviously originates from a common faith, since it consists of a pure and simple gift of oneself. The person subjecting himself expects neither reward nor payment for doing so. His gift goes even further, for he is putting himself at someone else's disposal and renouncing his own will in favour of that of another person, who by this gesture is made into a true master.

## IV

The circumstances in which authority of this kind comes into being are also exceptional. It appears when there has been a clear break in the existing social order, a serious erosion of beliefs and disappointment with moribund institutions. At such times, the masses feel that everything is crumbling around them, that mindless forces are threatening to crush them, and that the storm will drive them into unsure harbours. Daily life has an unusual quality, for there is neither peace nor war, but a state that has something of both. Day-to-day living, because of its very routine, no longer has a place. Men are ready to be carried away by waves of enthusiasm or fury and are inclined to find simple and definitive solutions to problems that have been made intractable by continual compromise, fiddles and swindles. They can see the colours of the rainbow gleaming through the grey rain.

You can see that we are talking of times of crisis and latent or acute disorder. The masses unconsciously seek someone capable of determining the course of events, welding ideals and reality and what can and cannot be achieved together again. Someone, in fact, who can overthrow the existing order, which is seen as a disorder, and bring the whole of society back to its proper purpose. There is a need for the kind of authority that can transform things from within, and charismatic leaders respond to that need. Who are they?

Usurpers, deviants and outsiders from other places or peripheral regions. Napoleon was from Corsica, Hitler from Austria and Stalin from Georgia. There is also the usurpation, which is often regicidal, of men such as Robespierre, Cromwell and Lenin, and that of the great resistance leaders like de Gaulle or Tito, condemning those legitimately in power to exile, death or imprisonment. There is that of the present Pope, a non-Italian elected to the traditionally Italian See of Peter. In one way or another, such men end the domination of former leaders, creatures of set habits who have turned an authority that can endure only as long as it keeps its brilliant colours and catches the imagination into something colourless and purely rational. The conditions for the emergence of charisma are thus a break in the social tissue and a recognition of the leader's authority on the part of those who submit to him.

Weber maintains that in its strongest sense charisma belongs to the prophet. Or perhaps to certain heroic warriors. Prophets formulate new roles for society. People venerate and obey them, recognising their exemplary merits. Everyone swears personal allegiance to those historical characters of whom Hegel said, 'They can all be called heroes, for they drew their aims and their vocation not from the regular course of events sanctioned by the existing order, but from the spring of that inner spirit which is always hidden beneath the surface and strikes the external world, forcing it to burst asunder, like a chicken its shell. Such were Alexander, Cæsar and Napoleon.'

As I have said, Weber thinks chiefly of prophets, particularly the Jewish ones, as leading their people and giving them a new belief, a new ideology and above all a new faith. As one American scholar has written, 'Even in the religious field, where there is most direct continuity with

Israelitish prophetism, on which the concept [of charisma] draws so heavily, new styles of leadership emerge' (Wilson, 1975: 1).

It can be objected that in talking thus of this kind of authority we are neglecting economic interests, which are real and not at all prophetic, and that those interests have used leaders, disposed of them and imposed them. There is a ready answer. Certainly such things can be taken into account. It is nevertheless true that the majority of military, economic and other kinds of interest have need, in order to achieve their aims, of a Napoleon and not a Fouché, of a Cæsar and not a Pompey, in other words, men with a particular gift, men who have mastered that art of crowd psychology.

## V

To take up the thread again. Spurred on by doubt, I had wondered whether the leader described by mass psychologists corresponded to a definite social reality. There were a good few reasons for thinking that this was not the case. But we have unexpectedly discovered that charismatic power does in fact cover that very reality. What has been said about prestige, its personal and symbolic nature, the effect of magnetism on the masses, spontaneous faith, unconstrained obedience and admiration for the leader, all apply to charisma as well. There is little essential difference between the two notions, except that charisma is more prophetic and prestige more affective, and this means that it is the source of all forms of power. Theories of prestige preceded those of charisma and indeed inspired them. What is important is that they both appeared at more or less the same time and tried to find a solution to the same political problem, that of government and democracy in a mass society (Weber, 1958).

Their similarity means that we can advance over less shaky ground and that we have a much wider field of observation at our disposal. We should now return to our chief concern, which is to explain the nature of the charismatic element. Why does it fascinate crowds? How do they come to follow a leader? What induces them to give up some of their resources, time and freedom and to break their social commitments and ties to help his vision triumph? What are the moving forces of his psychology? When are people inclined to follow him?

These are theoretical questions, but they are also practical ones. Far from seeking charisma in those who possess it, the mass media, advertisers, journalists and others are increasingly trying to create it and, in certain cases, they are succeeding.

If we look closer, we can see a difficulty. This type of leader is not only exceptional. He also seems archaic, belonging more properly to past societies and hence of purely anecdotal interest in those of our own time. And yet we see him subsisting and becoming more common, contrary to all our expectations. Obviously, we are not here to provide him with some magical aura that would protect him against the whole process of historical erosion. We have to see such men as a reality and examine them with the unemotional eyes of knowledge. I make this point because at the beginning of the age of the crowd and mass parties, mass psychology foresaw this rise and maintained with Le Bon that 'the type of hero dear to crowds will always have the semblance of a Cæsar. His insignia attract them, his authority overawes them, and his sword instils fear into them' (Le Bon, 1952: 54–5).

But most scholars thought and still think the opposite, namely that nowadays the charismatic leader is only to be found in that no man's land between socially stable phases, in those narrow, critical historical zones marked by spontaneous faith and unrestricted admiration. They also think that the growth of democracy, and of mass parties in particular, since it is linked to economic life, means that he will disappear. Gramsci, the philosopher and leader of the Italian Communist Party, felt certain that with regard to leadership collective organisations (i.e. parties) would take over from outstanding individuals, or 'charismatics', as Michels called them (Gramsci, 1952: 227).

These brave words have been proved false by the very Communist parties they referred to. When Gramsci was writing them in the Fascist prison he was to leave only to die, they were headed by those 'individual leaders' they were supposed to be making it possible to do without. The forecast that the part they play would diminish as modern societies develop has been categorically shown to be wrong by subsequent events. And what is even more astonishing is that no-one any longer shows much astonishment. Let us hope that in future scientists, and especially political ones, will pay greater attention to the reasons why crowd psychology was right in this matter. In doing so, they would be applying the basic rules of the scientific method.

## 2. *The postulate of mass psychology*

I

W E HAVE JUST GLANCED RAPIDLY at the matter we are dealing with to get an idea of how difficult it is. All we have done is to highlight the relationship between charisma and mass psychology. Now we must ask what makes that relationship possible. Only when we have done so can we begin to account for it. We should note that charisma is characterised by an evocation of the past, an awakening of memories hidden in the deepest places of the memory and the authority of tradition. It is by working with the world of remembered things that the leader immediately produces obedience. It is as if he needs only to speak, for the mass to perceive in him another leader who played a part on a different stage in different circumstances. He seems to awake in them some kind of internal dæmon, just as the hypnotist makes his patient aware of an archaic inheritance. That dæmon, memory, is the only real one that human beings have.

The link between charisma and the traces of the past has indeed already been established by Weber himself, who points out that 'in traditionalist periods, charisma is *the* great revolutionary force' (Weber, 1968: I, 245). Everything would be fine if we could imagine how this link is possible and how it manifests itself psychically. It is indeed extremely difficult to do so. If we are to overcome this obstacle, we shall have to accept a postulate and then suppose the existence of an appropriate mechanism, the third (erotic drives and identification being the other two) of those enabling us to explain the phenomena of mass psychology. This third mechanism, unlike the other two, is related to the development of collective relationships and time.

II

Let us be more specific. One of the reasons given to explain the reactions of the crowd – which are out of all proportion to the objective facts – and its lack of reason, is the persistence of thoughts and feelings from the past which, when they return, obscure men's minds. What the dead have thought weighs oppressively on the concerns of the living. This is the age-old truth that Valéry described so well when he said that the past, which is more or less fantastic, acts on the future with the same sort of power as does the present itself.

Perhaps nothing is lost in psychic life, and anything can come back at any time. We often say that the people have a short memory, quickly forgetting heroes and events. The exact opposite is in fact the case. They have a long memory and are constantly looking into the mirror of the past. Le Bon and Tarde were convinced of this and made no bones about saying so. So was Freud, but he found it very difficult to explain. The difficulty was twofold, for it was connected with both the survival of memories and traditions and the way in which they are transmitted.

It is a fact that everything that happens in an individual's life leaves a memory trace and is inscribed in his brain. But how can we talk of the memory traces of the masses? The problem becomes insoluble when we consider the transmission of memories from one generation to another. It matters little whether we are thinking of individuals or masses, for if there is no inheritance of acquired characteristics, there can be none of the memory of the group or the species. Here, since Darwin, we are up against the veto of genetics when we try to speculate on the problem. This means that there can be no valid analogy between individual and mass psychology or any transfer of ideas from one to the other. Freud thought that:

The second difference about this transference to group psychology is far more important, because it poses a fresh problem of a fundamental nature. It raises the question in what form the operative tradition in the life of peoples is present – a question which does not occur with individuals, since there it is solved by the existence in the unconscious of memory-traces of the past.     (Freud: XXIII, 93)

But certain obvious facts mean that we can get round the obstacle and escape the dilemma. Language seems to be an excellent vehicle for transmitting memory traces between generations. From earliest childhood we immediately recognise and understand the symbols it carries. In addition, anterior to language we have myths, religions that gather and preserve very ancient ideas and rituals for millennia. Posterior to it, we also have the monumental group milieu that includes all causes for celebration (Christ's birth, the Revolution, victory over our enemies etc.) and commemoration of the group itself, keeping the same load of emotions from one generation to the next. Our living records, which we call Earth, are an imaginary geography and biography. They create an illusion of continuity and a link uniting all those inhabiting our planet since time out of mind. What is based on such obvious facts can only be postulated and not proved.

The postulate is that *impressions of the past are conserved in the mental life of the masses as well as in that of individuals in the form of memory traces*. In certain favourable circumstances, they can be reconstituted and reanimated. In addition, the more ancient they are, the better they are conserved.

Scientifically, the postulate is obviously preposterous. It means that everything that happens in our lives now is determined by memories of the past and that the psychic and interior causes of our actions are more important than the physical and social ones. But however outrageous it may be, we have to accept it, for 'if this is not so, we shall not advance a step further along the path we entered on, either in analysis or group psychology. The audacity cannot be avoided' (Freud: XXIII, 100).

## III

Here is a very simple, but not unimportant, observation. It is not so much the possibility that the past is preserved in mental life that obliges us to subscribe to this postulate; rather it is its consequences, and particularly the most shocking of them. Namely, that history is a cyclical movement. Crowds also move through cycles, returning to places they have already visited and unconsciously repeating ancient actions. Charisma is one of these. We can see in it one of those materials subsisting from ancient times, periodically resurfacing when the wheel of society brings it out into the open air again and then disappearing once more. We must push our hesitation aside and ask how the process works. Beings and situations from the past take the form of an *imago* or figurative representation in our minds. Like old-fashioned pictures, they make present, in a simplified form, what is absent. It is usually a question of beings and situations we have identified with – our parents, our nation, a war or revolution associated with particularly strong emotions. As Laplanche and Pontalis point out, the *imago* can manifest itself in feelings and behaviour as well as in images (Laplanche and Pontalis, 1967: 196).

Most kinds of *imago* bear the mark of having been suppressed at one time or another for moral, political or cultural reasons. They come from a process of selection aimed at erasing them from the history of a people. The condemnation of Galileo or the execution of Louis XVI, the persecution of the Jews or the crucifixion of Christ were attempts to stop the people identifying with them or their ideals, which were to be eliminated once and for all. Far from disappearing, such forbidden and selected elements are grouped together and reconstituted in memory. With the insight of genius, Balzac has movingly described in *Le Médecin de campagne* how the scattered and secret members of the Old Guard lovingly reassembled the fragmentary memories of 'their' Napoleon and created the legend of the man whose name it was forbidden to utter during the Restoration.

With its terrible obstinacy, the memory first *conventionalises* both the smallest thought and the most insignificant detail of reality and every actor involved. By this, I mean that it removes everything that is incompatible and complex in them, stereotypes them and reproduces them in conformity with certain typical set forms. Heroes will always die a striking and tragic death, great leaders will always have the majestic face of the strict, calm father, prophets will always have a flowing beard and speak in angry and just tones, and so on. And they are made close to us and familiar to us, all alike. The process of identification always fixes characters in a vignette, and this they endure valiantly.

Memory then endows them with an all-pervading emotional strength. For want of a better term, let us call this *the charm of nostalgia*. By contrasting past and present, our memory contrasts the people and the reality around us with the image of their counterparts reconstructed by our minds. We remove all that is unpleasant, negative or unbearable from them and tend to keep only what is agreeable, positive and gratifying. And even when it is a question of history's bloodiest tyrants or the most lamentable periods of our own lives, we always recreate memories which are more satisfying and more in conformity with our desires.

In most cases, this charm of nostalgia removes all virulence from past conflicts, as when we think of our own childhood or the history of our country. It makes incompatible things compatible and even manages to make implausible ones plausible. It reshapes the *imago* according to the principle of the *coincidentia oppositorum*, the cohesion of opposing ideas, feelings and characters. The result is that things from the past never appear to us as they really were, but are filtered through the major themes of our own history or culture and are always more brilliant or more obscure than in reality. There is no such thing as memory. There are only memoirs, like those written by authors seeking to justify their existence, seeking to fascinate the reader with the story of their life and convinced that they are telling the truth.

The charm of nostalgia is all the more irresistible when more distant and more ethereal periods are involved. Freud notes that:

Long-past ages have a great and often puzzling attraction for men's imagination. Whenever they are dissatisfied with their present surroundings – and this happens often enough – they turn back to the past and hope that they will now be able to prove the truth of the inextinguishable dream of a golden age. They are probably still under the spell of their childhood, which is presented to them by their not impartial memory as a time of uninterrupted bliss.   (Freud: XXIII, 71)

What is transmitted from one generation to another with such slavish fidelity is thus a work of the imagination grafted onto a stock of indestructible psychic reality.

## IV

These types of selected and forbidden imago are preserved like memory traces. From time to time they emerge into our conscious mind. Together with thoughts and memories linked to a drive, they are, according to Freud, censored, deformed and stifled by the individual's desire to keep them in the unconscious. Despite being thrust back in this way, however, they tend to come back along the indirect road of dreams, neurotic symptoms and so-called psychosomatic disorders. When this happens, the unconscious content exerts, without the knowledge of the conscious mind, an obsessive and inescapable influence. This disturbing process is the return of repressed material. Strictly speaking, however, it is proper to individual psychology and difficult to apply to mass psychology.

In the first place, it presupposes the existence of an unconscious, which is not a mass phenomenon, and not admitted by psychoanalysis (Freud: XXIII, 259). In addition, the return of repressed material is primarily a matter of repressed erotic drives, and it is to these that the greater part of what is compressed and forgotten in the unconscious relates. But the psychic residues of times long past, the inheritance of the mases, is rather of a mimetic nature. It is a question of identification with one's ancestors, a great man such as Einstein or Napoleon, or with one's birthplace and so on. It returns in each generation. When Freud, in the closing pages of *Moses and Monotheism*, undertook his final account of the development of the human race, he declared that it could be seen as 'a return of the repressed'. But he immediately went on to add: 'Here, I am not using the term "the repressed" in its proper sense. What is in question is something in a people's life which is past, lost to view, superseded and which we venture to compare with what is repressed in the mental life of an individual' (Freud: XXIII, 132).

In order to avoid a rather dubious transfer from one branch of psychology to another, we can envisage a specific process, *imago-resurrection*. This is expressed in a sudden, almost theatrical, and at any rate total and vivid, recall of situations and persons from the past. There are several analogous situations. If the temporal cortex of an epileptic patient is stimulated, there is a total resurgence of the experiences, images, situations, actions and feelings of the whole of his past life. Similarly, when someone is in a state of emotional shock, he begins to speak in a different and forgotten kind of language and to react in an archaic way unseen for a long time. In addition, what has happened in the past and relates to the primordial identification of a group tends to be tirelessly repeated and to impose itself as a kind of coercive model. It is as if, for example, those participating in one revolution were reproducing and resuscitating another, as if we were seeing a recreation of the French Revolution in the Russian Revolution. Or again, as if a single emperor, a Cæsar or a Napoleon, were being continually reborn in every other emperor.

There is an important consequence. In everything to do with the present, we are not only seeing a copy of the past but reliving it with the feelings appropriate to the original events. Thus we can see the achievement of an archaic and perfect society in a future society, Christ in the Pope, Napoleon or Louis XIV in de Gaulle, and so on. We are reminded of the words of the great Arab philosopher Saada: 'Great is the number of women who in the shade of the tent and hidden by the veil are beautiful. But take aside the veil and thou wilt see the mother of thy mother.'

I have spoken of resurrection because the idea is a very ancient one. All cultures have beliefs connected with it and ceremonies to facilitate it and show its result, particularly when a charismatic leader is involved. Max Weber has pointed out that the possession of a magical charisma always presupposes rebirth. The rebirth is that of an image that the mass recognises.

In addition, identity with another person is always mentioned on such occasions. Especially with a dead person. Pythagoras' pupils pictured him as resembling the wizard Hermotines, and later Stalin was seen to resemble Lenin. The Romans made the process into a political formula, with the founder resurrected in each successive emperor, who therefore bore the title *redivivus*: Octavius Romulus *redivivus*, for example. The practice still continues. When the Soviets declared that Stalin was the Lenin of their day, they did so under the pressure of the same social and psychic necessities. All leaders hold on to power by recalling a multiple *imago* of the past which, once it has come to the surface, rekindles the feelings of days gone by. Baudelaire saw this clearly: 'Those phenomena and ideas that occurred periodically throughout the ages take on, each time they are resurrected, the complementary nature of the variant and the circumstance.'

All I have said here may well seem difficult and unconvincing. It is hard to believe that events and persons are stored in an immaterial form in the memory of succeeding generations, and that after an interval they are invariably reincarnated in a new physical and social being, or that even the smallest event and the most insignificant emotion of the masses have their causes in that past and their effects in the future that recreates it. In short, that the future is already part of the past. And so we shall consider the resurrection of *imago* as a hypothetical and perhaps even an imaginary process, rather like the ghost fields of physics. It does just make it possible for us to envisage the continuity of identifications in the course of history, but no more.

# 3. *The primal secret*

T HE MASSES PRESERVE and repeat the traces of their past life and of primitive times. What returns and is repeated – and this is what we really must be clear about – is the relationship of the charismatic leader with his people. In artificial crowds such as the churches, guilds and the *collegia* of ancient Rome, we can see that it is the same ceremonies that celebrate attachment to the common stock of beliefs and feelings. The ceremonies involved are, according to Tarde, essentially those in which a meal is shared and there is common worship of an ancestor. We should, he stresses, always bear these features in mind, for they explain why castes, corporations and ancient cities attach so much importance to 'commensualism', that is, to periodical fraternal and confraternal feasts and the accomplishment of funeral rites.

Such meals, which others have described as 'totemic', certainly commemorate the founding father of the crowd who is imitated by his disciples and whom they see as their model. He is canonised after his death and survives in their minds, like Christ in those of his earthly representatives and Pythagoras in those of the leaders of his sect. We can accept that and still pass as sane, but several questions are immediately raised. Why is the dead founder associated with his successors' charisma? How can he still influence them when he has in fact become an imaginary being? What is it that perpetually renews his control and prevents it ever fading? And how is it that this can still happen in a scientific and technical age? Freud's answer is a simple one and can be summed up in a few words. The meal taken together and the funeral rites commemorate a major event, the murder of the primitive father by his sons acting in conspiracy. All human development starts from that prehistoric event, which is still being expiated and is periodically recalled. One could almost say that it is the only thing in our mental life. It is the kernel of mass psychology. Freud declared that after this discussion he had no hesitation in declaring that men have always known (in this special way) that they once possessed a primal father and killed him (Freud: XXIII, 101).

That is the primal secret. We hide it and clothe it in our religions, the charisma of our leaders and our homage ceremonies. That is precisely what is contained in the postulate of mass psychology. In spite of, and perhaps because of, the rebuffs he received in the learned world, Freud remained convinced of its truth right up to the end of his life, and the last pages of his published work are devoted to it.

## II

Why was the crime committed? Freud thought that in prehistoric times men had lived in a band consisting of an all-powerful father and his sons and wives, holding them in constant terror because of his strength and intolerant of even the least impulse towards autonomy or any signs of a rival individuality. The vision and the wishes of a single man were binding on all, and individual despotism was the basis for a system of social customs.

At the same time, the father was respected and even loved by his children, for obvious reasons. He represented the zenith of power and was the universal ideal, and one can only imagine him possessing what Kafka called 'the mysterious character of all those tyrants whose right is based not on reason but on their person'.

He ruled by acting as he saw fit and by coercing everyone else. This father, who was probably a hunter, purely and simply repressed by the use of external physical constraints the slightest impulse in others to satisfy their erotic desires. It is easy to imagine the hatred that accumulated in such conditions. Rebellion smouldered beneath the feet of the ancient despot. Since unity creates strength, his sons joined together to kill him. In this they were certainly encouraged by the long-humiliated mothers, who had fed their enmity since they were children. They must have been part of the alliance, as they too wanted a degree of freedom, especially as it was about this time that women invented agriculture.[1]

The result of all this plotting is obvious. One of the brothers, probably the youngest, of whom least was expected, carried out the thankless task. The father must have fallen at his feet, calling out like Cæsar, 'And you too, my son!' In our history, Brutus is the image of the son who enters into a conspiracy and commits the liberating crime. Once the murder had been done, the sons all ate their father, sealing their pact with blood, for nothing binds men together more than a crime in which they have all played a part. Since then, the shared meals of totemic brotherhoods, guilds and other artificial crowds have been memorials of this primitive meal. The body of the father, however, is replaced by that of an animal, their totem.

That is how the first association of free and equal individuals recognising no god or master, the brotherhood, came into being.

One danger might have been that once they had broken the shackles of paternal domination, every individual could have given a free rein to his own instincts in a frenzy of mutual destruction. But conspiracy had already taught them how to create new links with each other and how to work together for the common good. They had also contracted a debt of active complicity with the womenfolk, their mothers, which was a further reason for not resuming previous relationships. This twofold factor obliged the sons to restrain their instincts and to unite with the women only under certain conditions.

In that way, what had been at stake in the conflict between the generations and the sexes, the apple of discord, that is, sexual possession, changed into a means of alliances between the men and with the women. The former gave up any wish to become the collective tyrant, the latter stopped being objects and became partners. Exogamy replaced common ownership of women and provided freedom of movement and the possibility of choice. Incest was still ruled out, but this was now the result of an interior renunciation necessary for collective life and no longer the consequence of paternal repression. The sign of rivalry with the father now became a contract of association with the mother. Sons could overtly identify with her rather than possess her, just as they identified with the ancient father instead of fighting with him. However that may have been, the fraternal union was changed. Relationships based on instinct and violence gave way to ones based on value and law. Thus 'we see that right is the might of a community' (Freud: XXII, 205).

Law put an end to the despotism and personal rule common when the father was dominant and gave everyone a share in the government of the community. However, it also obliged the brothers to let that share revert to the community, for both the brother and the citizen must, in Robespierre's words, 'hand back to the common mass that share of public power and the people's sovereignty that he holds, or else must be excluded by that very thing from the social pact'. It was in a situation of this kind that the first form of social organisation, based on the acceptance of mutual obligations, the renunciation of instincts, and legal and moral institutions requiring personal consent and voluntary adherence, came into being.

We can see that in place of a collectivity built up on domination, there arose a different kind of society, founded on discipline and entailing the prohibition of incest. This enabled men and women to marry, and to identify with the clan or fraternity, which paved the way for unity between men and generations. We can put forward the hypothesis that the idea of law was invented by mothers to channel their sons' instincts, put an end to tendencies towards tyranny and legitimise conspiracy against it. Indeed, who more than women had an interest in preventing unlimited violence and limiting physical power by means of an opposing psychic and social power? It is also probable that, since they were in control of the agricultural resources of the community, they would be able to ensure that the latter was respected.

Law, as you can see, is a sign of the absence of the father. Every time the latter reappears under the guise of a leader, he empties law and subordinates it to his own lawless rule. Moreover – and this appears to lend further support to the idea – the first code of law instituted after the filial revolt is a matriarchal one. As Freud says,

A fair amount of the absolute power liberated by the removal of the father passed over to the women; there came a period of matriarchy.　　(Freud: XXIII, 82)

## III

The revolutionary masses wrote on their banners 'Liberty, Equality and Fraternity *or Death*'. They would have done better to write 'Liberty, Equality and Fraternity *and Death*'. Far from disappearing once he had been struck down, the father, that loved and hated despot, returned to harrow the consciences of those who had murdered him. Since he was no longer *above* the crowd, he came back *in* it. None of his sons carried out his tasks, but each one assimilated, so to speak, a share of his power along with a part of his body. Since there was no longer anyone to be the father, everyone became him, and paternity became no longer an individual but a collective condition. As time passed, his brutality was forgotten and only his positive features and the good times of the past were remembered. A combination of a nostalgia for childhood and guilt appeased hatred and tempered criticism. People began to love the effigy and memory of the man they had hated in the flesh.

In the end, they turned him into a god, and a whole religion, or more exactly the whole of religion, grew up around him, hiding both the murder and its failure. For if sons have killed to take their father's place beside their mother, they have failed in their purpose, since they have been obliged to give up of their own accord the very thing that he refused them, sexual promiscuity, and forced to put in place of the violence born of the strength of one man a violence born of the strength of all. Thus, in order to satisfy their desire, they seek at one and the same time to hide the murder of the father and the futility of their revolt.

In brief, such is the lesson of all religion. Theirs then created the image of an ideal father, a god loved and, after some resistance, obeyed by all his sons. When he was alive, he had been a tyrant. Once he was dead, he became the symbol of the collectivity, the guarantee of morality and law.

> What had up to then been prevented by his actual existence was thenceforward prohibited by the sons themselves in acordance with the psychological procedure so familiar to us in psychoanalysis under the name of 'deferred obedience'.
>
> (Freud: XIII, 143)

The father became the voice of conscience, shot through with threats and reminders of a guilt that nothing could wipe out. When they proclaimed this, like Schiller's Swiss mountain folk who had just killed their tyrant and called out that they wanted to be a single people of brothers, the echoing response was that they were a people of conspiring sons and parricides.

This then is the probable explanation of the characteristics that Tarde and Freud attribute to artificial crowds and the reason for their submission to a venerated and deified leader. It follows that the relationships between their members, the fraternity, are based partly on a background of matriarchy, on which law reposes, and partly on a profane or sacred religion they have created round the father to hide their crime and appease their consciences. The split between the worlds of reality and illusion, custom and myth, law and power reflects the polarity of the two extremes from which culture has flowed, the patriarchal and the matriarchal. All organised masses – the Church, the army and so on – develop from one to the other, providing themselves with the necessary means for enduring the unbearable tension involved in that double alliance.

We have just made an important observation, which is that the murder of the leader by regicide or homicide is the factor that makes it possible to move from a natural to an artificial crowd in the same way that the murder of the father makes it possible to move from the primitive band to organised society. We still have to see why the resurrection of his *imago* shows us the nature of charisma. The third and final stage of the awakening of mankind will show us this.

## IV

It seems that society abhors the absence of the father as much as nature abhors a vacuum. Once he has been rejected, his sons miss him and all dream of replacing him. As time passes, the forces of disintegration are stronger than those of unity. This is what turns the conspirators into fraternal enemies and their rivalry into latent warfare until one of them has the courage to call for the return of the father and defend him with all the skill of a Mark Antony recalling the virtues of Cæsar to the Romans gathered around his remains. Speaking to the heart rather than the mind, he reawakens their attachment to the dead man, reminding them of their filial submission when they were children. At the same time, he proclaims the necessity of the father's return in the person of an heir, and he does so so persuasively that his absence is all the more cruelly felt.

That is precisely what the resurrection of the *imago* signifies. The murdered ancestor whose memory and representations are kept for a certain length of time in the galleries of memory returns to claim his place and his rights. This, however, he does in the form of one of his sons who, having taken part in the murder, has become a hero, and is seen by all as *his father's representative*. Once he is in his father's place, he makes all his brothers atone for that long-bygone murder in which they all shared, doing so with all the determination of a Mark Antony hounding Brutus and the other conspirators and the violence of a Stalin humiliating and then exterminating his revolutionary companions. In this way, he unloads his own guilt onto them and nips in the bud any impulse to kill him as the real father was killed. In Freud's words:

It must be confessed that the revenge taken by the deposed and restored father was a harsh one; the dominance of authority was at its climax. The subjugated sons made use of the new situation in order to unburden themselves still further of their sense of guilt. (Freud: XIII, 150)

They bow their heads – and some of them lose them – bound hand and foot in an alliance used by one of them against the rest. The latter, who like Cæsar, Stalin and Mao has become the master of his equals and *pater inter pares*, admonishes them thus: 'You know as well as I do what has happened. What use are such old stories to you? Do you think that the crowd wants to know them? Of course not. It needs to believe in our fatherhood and to obey the father that I represent.' Then, before all, he proclaims that the ancestor of all has been brought back to life in him, thus putting himself on display and assuming the features of the incomparable and unforgettable founder of the collectivity, Moses, Christ or Lenin, guaranteeing the past and tracing the outline of the future.

The new leader can now take back into his own hands the power previously shared out amongst all. He accomplishes his task and once again establishes inequality in a mass of men that has just fought its fiercest battle for equality. His task is like that of Napoleon, immediately after the Revolution, when he restored the titles and ranks of the *ancien régime*, or Stalin's immediately after the Soviet one, renewing the privileges and honours just held up to the obloquy of history. These examples are not intended to prove anything, simply to illustrate my point.

The course of evolution is not interrupted, however. Nothing comes back exactly as it was. Whatever advantages he had, the man who took the father's place was a usurper, stealing the power of the father and that of his brothers. But he has to accept the law of the existing clan and make his actions and his authority conform to higher demands. In order to meet that obligation, he keeps the form of that law but modifies its substance whilst still respecting its egalitarian nature, for the law is binding on all men. The resurrected father, however, gives it a prohibitory character and hence turns it into an external obligation. But the application of this prohibitory quality takes account of the power of everyone. Men are equal in the sight of the law, but not with regard to its rewards and punishments. What is allowed in the case of superiors is forbidden to inferiors. Incest, for example. Once it passes into the hands of sons who have become fathers, judges and parties to an action, the law is no longer the *fons et origo* of power and the binding force in society, but simply an instrument of that power and an instrument involving two standards, one for those who dominate and another for those who are dominated. This radical change is only possible because the sons now all share the same religion and see the true likeness of their father in the leader.

This recognition becomes the new source of authority and its avowed principle, legitimacy. It represents a reaction against egalitarian revolution and also overthrows a number of earlier ways of living and social forms. In short, the feminine invention of law is turned aside and transformed into a matrix for that masculine creation we call order. We are obviously dealing with a patriarchal order based on hierarchy and power that cuts short the endless deliberations and continual discussions between brothers or brothers and mothers and legislates or interprets the law, as appropriate. All those occasions for wasting time, for women's 'gossip' and for councils that need close watching, are swept away. Only what takes their place, the commands and decisions of the representative of the father, which are to be given immediate effect, are of positive consequence. Like all leaders, he thinks that nothing is as good as an order. What he says is an order and his silence, too, is a force. Thus there is a conflict between the legitimacy of his power of life and death and the legality of the clan, and the latter is vanquished. 'In the meantime', writes Freud, 'a great social revolution had occurred. Matriarchy was succeeded by the re-establishment of a patriarchal order' (Freud: XXIII, 83). Freud expressly states that paternal order succeeds maternal right.

At the same time, society is divided into large families, each headed by a father wielding an authority tempered by a small number of moral traditions. He is both an heir and a successor and combines in his person functions that had become separated over the course of time, being at once legislator, judge and uncontested leader. In him are blended the two incompatible sources of all order, rigorous legality and the legitimacy on which it is based. As master and domestic tyrant, he recreates the band, the natural mass in which everything began, in the form of an artificial mass, the family.

## V

How does charisma compel recognition? What is the sign that marks out the man who rallies others to him? What is the instrument of his power? Charisma meant the dead father resuscitated and reincarnated in one of his murderers, but it also meant that the murderer himself was a hero, since he was one of the sons who had opposed and overcome the tyrant. There are thus two characters in one: the deified imago of the father and the sign of a heroic individual, his son. The leader has that charisma, and the masses recognise him. He attracts feelings of amorous admiration for the dead father and fear in the face of the flood of cruelty and violence fraught with frightful consequences that the man who has both killed his father and subjugated his rival brothers is known to be capable of.

It is the twofold nature of his charisma that gives him his greatest strength. He seems to be at once above other people and like them. He is the representative of his father, *redivivus*, who now lives again in him, and also of the mass of his brothers who joined him in the conspiracy and have now yielded their power to him. This was the impression given by the Roman emperors – and we now know why – the fathers of the *patria* and the tribunes of the *plebs*. It is also that given by contemporary leaders who are the elected representatives of the people and hold all power. In short, charisma is the meeting of opposites in the person of one man. Hence its irresistible fascination.

This is where the real difficulty arises. As you probably feel, this reconstruction of human development is not in accordance with the observed data, and I am not the first to point this out. In my view, the strangest thing about it is not that it arose out of a flight of genius or that painstaking scholars have demolished it, but that instead of disappearing into an intellectual limbo, as one might have expected, it has survived and still attracts our interest. I therefore need to offer a convincing explanation of that interest and justify keeping this view of things as the central hypothesis in the rest of my account.

It seems to ring a bell, to strike a chord in us and to refuse to let us reject it out of hand. That chord is insistently audible in all Shakespeare's works. Every character in his tragic universe speaks to us of the death of the king at his son's hands and of his resurrection, when times have changed, in the guise of another person. It also echoes at the heart of our culture in Nietzsche's violent affirmation of the death of God, procured by us and still effective. To which Freud retorts that it is the father, our god, that we have killed, and that long ago, at the beginning of human time. Now all we do, he says, is repeat the ancient crime and remember it. Every revolt and revolution in modern times, which have not seen a dearth of them, is a reminder of it. Moreover, the association of death and resurrection is a feature of every culture, as if it expressed some indisputable psychic truth that our hypothesis reflects in our own. (One of my reasons for making a distinction between the process of the resurrection of the *imago* and the return of repressed material has been precisely the fact that the former is linked to this particular content of the killing of the father and to a pre-established cycle.)

In addition, the development defined by the hypothesis of the totemic cycle, as it should be called, is an attempt to explain the nature of the hold exerted by charisma on crowd psychology, which would otherwise continue to seem 'something gratuitous, miraculous and irrational' (Alberoni, 1968: 15).

So, is it a fruitful hypothesis? The rest of this study will tell us that. At this stage of the enquiry, we can at least see that it poses the problems of crowd psychology in a way unlike that of any other hypothesis, and this is certainly why it has an essential place in Freud's work in the field. Indeed, it is the major theme of that work. If we take it literally, this picture of the way mankind has developed from the age of the crowd to that of law and then to that of order (via band, matriarchy and patriarchy) intersects the admirable line of evolution traced by Vico from the age of gods to that of heroes and then that of man. At the same time, however, it tends to picture history as the result of *an attempt to idealise*.

In the beginning, constraint was imposed on men with the force of a raw reality that they overestimated, in the same way that paternal tyranny psychically repressed the sons' desires to unite with the women. There was then a period of trials and coalitions amongst them, during which they created a social counter-reality, initially to show their refusal to comply and subsequently their determination to win. That is the meaning of the killing of the father, for example. But the strength thus defeated in all finally came back in each individual, transformed into a psychic reality composed of memories and symbols. It was obeyed, of course, as reality was, or the tyrannical father, but to the extent that it represented its opposite, an ideal, the ego-ideal or the group ideal. There was no longer a direct reaction to the beings of the universe, or even to men's experience of it, but a reaction to beings idealised by thought, to the multiple *imago* presented by the universe. What man now had to

311

surmount was no longer the strength of reality and its effects on him, but the strength of the ideal in him. He broke free of the former only to become the slave of the latter.

The totemic hypothesis gives a meaning to this process of idealisation, defining the movement from the external to the internal world observable in both culture and politics. Over long periods of time, men brought about within themselves, in the form of psychic authorities like the super-ego, the renunciation of instinct and everything externally imposed. In the economic and technological fields the opposite happened, with development becoming external rather than internal and establishing a process of *materialisation*. In that process, there is a constant desire to reproduce, externally, prosthetically and physically, in the form of robots, tools and machines, the parts of the human body (arms, legs and eyes) and also internal ideas and sensations. On the one hand, we try to turn the world of things into a world of men, and on the other to turn the world of men into a world of things. Maintaining that that development springs from a remembered parricide is a simple, almost a too simple, idea. No-one had ever thought of deducing a hypothesis from it and introducing it into science. Now it has been done.

## PART VIII

# Hypotheses about great men

---

## 1. 'The Man Moses'

---

### I

O NE FACT ALONE is enough to cast light on the way we are about to go. It is that every time there is a major upheaval and a new type of political authority comes into being, what that authority teaches and how it looks is expressed in a myth. This means that the most abstract reasoning leaves its mark in the living tissue of culture. Think of Hobbes' *Leviathan* and Machiavelli's *Prince*, that still symbolise for all of us the monolithic state and the leader of men. The fundamental character of *The Prince*, Gramsci wrote, was that it was not a systematic treatment, but a 'living book' in which political ideology and political science were fused in the dramatic form of a 'myth' (Gramsci, 1953: 3).

Our age needed its own myth. It is certainly true that the leaders of the age of the crowd have a feature in common with those of all other times, for they are all men of power and government. But in order to draw along and govern the peoples of our day and age, they need specific character-istics unlike those of others. It is clear why. Their chief place of action is no longer the parliament, the chancery, the church, the cabinet or the court, but streets and public places and forums. They no longer have power because they have been appointed by a parliament or ordained by a Church. They have not been given it by a superior authority, but by the logic of an idea shared by the crowd. For them, the enemies on whom everything hinges are no longer superiors, representatives, monarchs or ministers, but the masses who give or do not give them a mandate. Almost everything is decided by that sort of contact. Thus the power of leaders can only be artificially supported by force or law, even when they are in a dominant position, if it is associated with a belief shaping actions, thoughts and feelings. If there is no such belief, or if the association loses its force, their authority has no more life than a fallen leaf or an uprooted plant.

Such a leader must therefore be at once a man of an idea, of power and of faith or belief. Only when such qualities are combined in a single person has he any chance of achieving his aim. What does that mean in his case? Basically, the ability to weld people together in a mass in the shape of a party, a movement or, more usually nowadays, a nation. He gives them the feeling of belonging to a particular human group with its own distinct life-style and its own task to fulfil. He persuades them that each individual can only be fully himself within a group characterised by its own shared customs and beliefs, language and artistic and philosophical means of expression and also the features of kinship, class and ethnic group. The individual has no real existence unless he shares these characteristics and features and the values and aims of the group. In Le Bon's view, as we saw when we were considering his ideas, every leader must have the passionate conviction of a Robespierre (the man made idea) and the seductive charm of a Napoleon (the idea made man). He must be that world soul before which peoples bow down, something equally admired by both philosophers and the Old Guard of Napoleonic times.

We could add many other uplifting or disgusting examples to the list, but it is impossible not to see their kinship with the kind of authority that Weber associates with charisma. The charismatic leader brings beliefs out of their lair to conquer the ideas produced by reflection. His gifts blend with the matter of power. That is why we unhesitatingly proclaim that the leader dominates. He only does so, however, because faith, his own and that of the masses, has made him the leader. All these facts lead us to create the image of prophecy and the prophet, and more precisely the prophet of Israel, portrayed by the German thinker from history, as Michelangelo portrayed him from memory. And who other than Moses could be the perfect example of such a man, since Scripture tells us that there has been no other prophet like him? The traditions relating to his gifts and what he did are shrouded in the mists of time, and it is very unlikely that any new documentary evidence will come to light. In any case, it does not matter whether we know him in detail or not. In his case as in that of every great man or woman, the main thing is the legends that have grown up around him. The basic fact is that he has never faded from the historical and cultural scene.

Le Bon, Weber and others can be given the credit for developing, even if in rough-and-ready terms, a systematic concept of the leader appropriate to the age of the crowd. What they accomplished was necessary, but it was not enough. What was still needed was to make him into a living figure and a dramatic presence that anyone could grasp. Freud was the one to do so. I want to discuss the work which he first called *The Man Moses*. Like all books of that kind – like that Renaissance masterpiece *The*

*Prince* – which give us a way of seeing the politics of their time, this book does so for its own time, the age of the crowd. That is basically what it is about, and that is what explains the apparently very bizarre details of the way it is put together. The digressions which seem to us superfluous or nonsensical and as having little to do with what the book is really about are in fact the direct outcome of the way the great prophet is studied throughout the work. In my view, *The Man Moses* is a *Prince* for our age. Instead of causing eyebrows to be raised, the suggestion should meet with wholehearted approval. The comparison might cause something of a stir, but it could be an extraordinarily fruitful one.

I shall not wish to claim that Freud chose his hero on purpose. During his lifetime, other characters filled his mind. Once he had penetrated the psyche of the masses, however, and seen that the leader was the crucial element in their mystery and their misery, he was led towards Moses by, so to speak, an invisible hand. In depicting him in simple and noble words, with undiminished vitality and all the power of his natural creative talent, Freud became the echo of a vanished world that comes to life again in his book. His immense popularity with both intellectuals and ordinary readers comes from the way in which he expresses the abiding truths about life in the most direct terms, like Descartes, Galileo, Machiavelli and Darwin before him. It is abundantly clear that in our times, the Man Moses is the archetypal mass leader. That is why he rose out of the past to become the personal tyrant of Freud, who circled around him as if he were circling around the mystery of his own being, risking both his life and his reputation in the venture.[1]

All the elements of the analysis and make-up of the archetype are taken from the man of power, the man of ideas and the creator of a people, from the prophet, in short, but not only from the venerated religious prophet. Freud tells us as much:

We must not forget that Moses was not only the political leader of the Jews established in Egypt but was also their law-giver and educator and forced them into the service of a new religion, which to this very day is known after him as the Mosaic one. (Freud: XXIII, 18)

Some instinct took Freud towards great causes and basic problems. Casting a lucid and unsentimental gaze over the contemporary scene, in which so many leaders of nations and crowds were emerging, he described their agitation and their fragility. Going back to the roots of their psychology and the distortions it had undergone in historical reality, he drew forth the brilliant model and ideal of which they were merely poor copies and proposed it as an example.

He never put himself forward as a teacher of morality or a righter of

315

wrongs. He was only too aware of the hardness of ambitious hearts and the arid nature of their reasoning and knew that the exclusive control of power in the midst of a roar of applause where even the mocking laughter of the jester had been silenced was not conducive to justice or the love of men. He was also convinced, however, that the psychic needs of the masses were not those that were presumed or exploited. Moses was the mirror in which those masses could see their true image.

For the man at the helm of government, there is no better example. Imposing and respecting an ethic ensured that the crowds would be loyal and support him in his political action. Their desire to believe in their leader's words has played more than one trick on them. That desire enabled Moses not to feed their illusions but to spread truth. That ethic served to forge and preserve a human character finely tempered to survive the storms of history in victory. He rejected cruelty, disdain for his fellow men, force and magic. He went even further and renewed the prohibitions on them. A few simple rules engraved in the minds of the people led to enormous consequences. In comparison with the meteoric rise and fall of a Hitler, a Mussolini or a Stalin, the continuous presence of Moses is a proof of this (Freud: XXIII, 54). Freud would no doubt have agreed with what Einstein said in 1935, that in the final analysis all human values rest on morality, that it was the unique greatness of Moses to have seen that clearly in ancient times, and that the people of their own time were far from moral.

Perhaps because of that, the book that Freud dedicated to him is the only one of his works that can be opened at any page. The dialogue has already begun, but the reader feels that he is welcome. And if the book is still readable after so many false starts, it is because the author gave himself the necessary time for reflection. Even death had to wait until it was finished.

## II

It is correct to say that great men do not make history. On the other hand, neither is it made without them. In mass psychology, they are the yeast, the active and creative fermentation agent, and the masses are the dough, the matter within which they operate. Mankind, Freud maintained, needs heroes, and just as the hero who remains faithful to his mission raises the whole level of human life, so the hero who betrays it lowers that level. This statement goes beyond the available historical and sociological data, and so far beyond the data and opinions we all share that it seems like a challenge to good sense. Contemporary theory has entirely abandoned the idea that great men play a part in the fate of peoples and are worthy of attention. In the last analysis the most important thing in its view is the action of the masses and events. History takes an irresistible course, and those who wish to ascribe its merits and responsibilities to a certain number of men are making a major mistake.

What we therefore need to know is the position of mass psychology on such matters. It fully recognises that external and objective factors such as technological progress, economic conditions and soaring population figures determine how human societies develop, but also sees internal human and subjective ones, and hence outstanding individuals, as playing a part. Such men are not simply minor actors in the drama of history. For most people, they are its heroes. The theory of the 'great man' in history can be rejected, but it has to be admitted that mankind as a whole has accepted it and continues to do so. The desire to believe in an inspired leader, an exceptional man capable of setting the course of events to rights, someone the crowd can tranquilly obey, is a well-attested phenomenon in ancient and modern societies. The basic desire to believe in him and his extraordinary gifts has had and very likely still has a considerable effect on social life. It is, of course, not the only factor to induce change and always goes hand in hand with general and impersonal ones. 'There is room in principle for both. . . . Thus we reserve a place for "great men" in the chain, or rather the network, of causes' (Freud: XXIII, 108).

That is how crowd psychology sees things. We could sum up that view in one sentence. The great man is the father of history, and the mass its mother. No doubt the description only applies to a handful of individuals in the very highest positions and acting at a universal level, a Napoleon, a Cæsar, a de Gaulle, a Roosevelt, a Mao or a Mahomet, for example – but it is valid for others too. Every nation, tribe and village has its great men, its 'big fellahs' as the Africans say. They have shaped it, given it a matter by bringing individuals and groups together and a form by enduringly impressing their own character and destiny on it. There is no people without its Pantheon, and none with an empty one. Even if the village Hampdens are not mentioned in the annals of world history, local chronicles remember their names and recall them with veneration. There are associations to keep their memory alive and scholars to write their biographies. Statues and plaques at street corners or on the houses they were born in celebrate their memory and express the admiration of their community.

All these phenomena are an indication that great men of varying degrees of brilliance are a group apart. What they have in common is the fact that they have fashioned the culture they come from and have endowed it with a focus and a super-ego.

## Hypotheses about great men

It can be said that the great man is precisely the authority for whose sake the achievement is carried out; and, since the great man himself operates by virtue of his similarity to the father, there is no need to feel surprise if in group psychology, the role of the super-ego falls to him. So that this would apply too to the man Moses in the relation with the Jewish people. (Freud: XXIII, 117)

Or at least as far as our own culture is concerned. That is why it is so important, if we are to understand men of that kind, to be aware of how he developed, shaped the character of his people for thousands of years and became great for their sake. But we must not aim too high. In such cases, scientific knowledge can give us a fragment of the truth, but it entails neither the necessity nor the possibility of a total one.

## 2. *The family romances of great men*

I

H OW, WE MIGHT ASK, is the psychology of great men different from that of ordinary ones? All the comparisons we have spent so long on have taken us no further, which is hardly surprising. Such men are not marked off from the ordinary run of mortals by either their intelligence, their eloquence or their strength. We shall therefore make use of the less specific and more social indicator employed by the anthropologist Marcel Mauss when contrasting *homo duplex*, the divided individual, and *homo simplex*, the united and whole one. The former's separate consciousness enables him to conquer his instincts and face up to the external world. The latter's reason and feelings intermingle, and his reaction is a total one in every situation. One the one hand, as Marcel Mauss writes:

Only the civilised persons of the upper strata of our own and a small number of other civilisations of earlier periods, eastern and less technically developed, are able to control the different spheres of their consciousness. They are different from other men, specialised and often differentiated hereditarily by the division of labour, which is also frequently hereditary. Above all else, however, they are further differentiated in their own consciousness and *are conscious*. This means that they can resist their instincts and, as a result of their education and upbringing, their ideas and their deliberate choices, can control all their actions.

(Mauss, 1973: 306)

On the other hand, however:

The ordinary person is split and feels that he has a soul; but he is not captain of his fate. Nowadays the average man – and to an even greater extent the average woman – and almost everyone in archaic and backward societies, is a *whole*, by which I mean that his whole being is affected by his slightest perception or the least mental shock.

(Mauss, 1973: 306)

Here we have a picture of two distinct human categories. The first corresponds to our culture's idea of the individual, of which Faust, torn between his two 'souls', is the outstanding example. The second relates to mass man as described by crowd psychology. For the moment, it seems scarcely possible to improve on the two definitions, but we can perhaps fill out the anthropological picture by adding a few psychological details.

319

We can suppose that the divided man has a sharply-defined super-ego and an ego with a high degree of self-esteem. His main concern is self-conservation and his own mental life is satisfying. He is also independent and self-confident. That is what we understand when we say of someone that he has will-power and the courage of his convictions. An individual of this kind is particularly apt to 'act as a support for others, to take on the role of leader and to give a fresh stimulus to cultural development or to damage the established state of affairs' (Freud: XXI, 218). There is an obsessional side to him and the kind of tenacity that reflects a predominant super-ego; hence the characteristic sense of mission that makes him a man of action (Freud: XXI, 84).

Looking at the united and whole man, we can also see that he too must have self-esteem and be self-centred enough to survive to hold his own in a highly competitive society where everyone has to resist the pressures he is subjected to. His predominant feature, however, is the erotic component of the libido. Attracting the love of others is his main concern and losing it what worries him most. This makes him dependent on those who can give him love or withdraw it and ready to conform to the dictates of his drives. Seeking satisfaction in that area colours his whole existence, and that combination of self-love and love of others, of the narcissistic and the erotic libido, 'is perhaps the one we must regard as the commonest of all. It unites opposites which are able to moderate one another in it' (Freud: XXI, 219). That is why even if such individuals are aware of a gap between consciousness and effects, they neither separate them nor see a clash between them.

We can also fill out our picture of these two distinct kinds of individual by using a general hypothesis concerning their psychic make-up. We could sum up Mauss's divided individual by saying that he is split between the two opposite forces of love and identification, or between Eros and mimesis, and is torn between extreme individuality and extreme sociability, each of which seeks to dominate the other. This tension arises from the fact that he has wholly identified himself with an idea, a group or an ideal person and is consequently, as Le Bon would have said, hypnotised by them. The voice of conscience constantly reminds him that it is his duty not to succumb to his instincts, urging him to pursue his goal exclusively. The voice 'produces a few great men, many psychotics and many neurotics' (Freud and Bullitt, 1966: 41).

Freud expresses his ideas as follows:

Fools, visionaries, sufferers from delusions, neurotics and lunatics have played great roles at all times in the history of mankind and not merely when the accident of birth had bequeathed them sovereignty. Usually they have wreaked havoc; but not always. Such persons have exercised far-reaching influence upon their own and later times, they have given impetus to important cultural movements and have made great discoveries. They have been able to accomplish such achievements on the one hand through the help of the intact portion of their personalities, that is to say in spite of their abnormalities; but on the other hand it is often precisely the pathological traits of their characters, the one-sidedness of their development, the abnormal strengthening of certain desires, the uncritical and unrestrained abandonment to a single aim, which give them the power to drag others after them and to overcome the resistance of the world.

(Freud and Bullitt, 1966: xvi)

However exaggerated or shocking this picture may be, we have to take it into account. It is a familiar one in crowd psychology, as we have already seen with Le Bon and Tarde, and we cannot be aware of it without seeing it there. It may be a fiction, but a fiction of that kind is not without some connection with reality, otherwise it would not be so effectively present in all cultures. However that may be, the picture does throw a certain amount of light on the crowds devoted to the man it represents.

The whole man, on the other hand, combines both aspects of one and the same force, the narcissistic and the erotic libido, just as attraction and repulsion are the two aspects of gravity in the same body. It is in this sense, of course, that he is simple, being made, so to speak, from a single material and obeying a single force, love. The other force, identification with a person or a collective goal, is only moderately strong in his case, and the result is that his conscience – his super-ego, in short – does not ask more of him than his love for himself and others demands. It is a gentle voice, 'an agreeable one for the person who harbors it: but it has the disadvantage that it permits the development of a very ordinary human being' (Freud and Bullitt, 1966: 41). But we should not imagine this man as being simple-minded or having an impoverished interior life.

That is the dividing-line we have been looking for. It presupposes that Eros and mimesis are sharply separated and mutually opposed in the divided man. If there is a conflict, mimesis always has the last word. The united and whole man, on the other hand, is filled with harmony. Mimesis always respects the primacy of Eros and takes care to avoid any excess or lack of due measure. That is why this kind of man can only expect to be obeyed by a crowd in proportion to the love he receives from it. We now have to perform the most difficult part of our task, which is to explain the origin of the division we have been discussing.

II

To that end, I shall introduce the idea, if it really is an idea, of what Freud calls 'family romances'. Normally, not much heed is paid to it, but in so far as it seems to play a bigger part in crowd than in individual psychology (and also because we have to use all means that come to hand) I have no hesitation in examining it. What is involved?

Psychoanalysis sees the child, and more specifically the male child, as desiring his mother and opposing his father. He even desires the death of his father, who is his rival in love. This rivalry shapes his life and determines how his personality develops. The search for a solution to the conflict with his parents is the mark of the family or Oedipus complex and shapes their subsequent relationships. At the same time, the child tries to escape from these painful tensions. Since he cannot do so in reality, he struggles to achieve release in the world of the imagination. That is why he creates a second family for himself, either providing himself with a second father and mother or becoming attached to his grandparents, as happened with Stendhal, who hated his father and adored his grand-father. But do not as many adults try to escape from their real surround-ings by creating ideal ones peopled by creatures of their heart's desire?

The child thus creates another world as a means of resisting the one in which he is imprisoned. From it he draws the strength to rebel against the commands of an authority that itself is the first to trample on them. In his famous *Letter to my Father*, Kafka tells us that his childhood world was divided into a number of areas including one 'where I, the slave, lived under laws invented for me alone and with demands that I, for some reason I was not aware of, could never meet'.

As the child reaches adolescence, this sense of injustice becomes more acute, driving him even more to reject his real parents and prefer borrowed and imaginary mothers and fathers. If he is going to have fantasy parents, they may as well be powerful and protective, kings, famous artists, people of genius or scientists of repute. Apart from the part they play in providing him with protection and escape, however, these borrowed parents both replace his own and shield him from the insoluble problems raised by his smouldering and forbidden desires for persons of the opposite sex. As Freud wrote to Fliess in 1898, 'all neurotics create a family romance for themselves (which becomes conscious in paranoia). It runs parallel to and is the double of the family complex, the weft of its true history. It flatters megalomania and is also a defence against incest. If your sister is not the child of your mother, no-one can accuse you, and the same applies if you yourself are the child of other parents.'

The child tends to invent a whole family romance with its source in the deepest part of his being and a parallel course to his real one. It mirrors the Oedipus complex, the framework of his real life history, just as in olden times the epic sung by poets mirrored the deeds and actions of warriors and kings and transformed them into heroes. This means that he has a double fight, struggling at both the real and the fictional level, and lives a double life.

The outline we have suggested is beginning to take on shape and substance. It means that alongside each 'native' family, that of the real parents, there is a 'superior' one which is 'foreign' and often 'aristocratic' and which the child imagines and imitates. The former is the locus of love and hatred for father, mother, brothers and sisters, and Gide has described its atmosphere in his famous (and notorious) apostrophe: 'Families, I hate you. Your homes are impenetrable, your doors closed, your happiness jealously guarded.' In contrast, the latter is entirely composed of admired and imitated people, with whom relationships are of a rather distant and abstract nature. This means that it largely meets the child's need to have the same kind of father as other children he identifies with, who often belong to a higher social stratum than he himself does. He compares his parents with those of his comrades and finds them less successful, foreigners, black, Jewish or poor, and hence not the 'right sort of people'. He would very much like to have the right kind of parents, like his friends. That is reason enough for the adolescent to be critical and even hostile and ready to sacrifice his 'native' family to his preferred 'nice' one, which in his eyes is perfection itself.

This enables him to widen his family horizon and interiorise the scale of relationships between social groups. The sometimes unbridled invention of a sequence of fictional fathers develops both an imaginary world of daydreams and his own critical awareness of adults.

But as intellectual growth increases, the child cannot help discovering by degrees the category to which his parents belong. He gets to know other parents and compares them with his own, and so acquires the right to doubt the incomparable and unique quality which he had attributed to them. Small events in the child's life which make him feel dissatisfied afford him provocation for beginning to criticize his parents, and for using, in order to support his critical attitude, the knowledge which he has acquired that other parents are in some respects preferable to them. (Freud: IX, 237)

This is rather like adults going abroad and coming back and seeing their own country with a new critical eye, discovering its defects and limitations. Some even go so far as to make the country they admire into a means of measuring their own, admiring for example only things American, English or German and becoming imaginary citizens of those countries.

In short, we can see each child as dividing his life between two families, his 'native' one in which Eros is all-important and the 'nice' one based on identification with a group, a person, a scale of social values or his idea of it. Not everything in it is imaginary, of course, for as in all fiction elements of real experience provide material. The 'native' family belongs to reality, to the child's life history as it is, the 'nice' one to the ideal world, to his life history as he would like it to be.

In his letter to Fliess, Freud[1] speaks in this connection of the romanticisation of their origins in paranoiacs, the heroic founders of religions. But no-one has described relationships of this kind more subtly than Proust. At the beginning of *A la Recherche du temps perdu*, the young Marcel is hostile towards Charles Swann, because when he comes to dine with his parents his mother does not come up to kiss him goodnight. Later, Swann's daughter Gilberte becomes his friend, and Marcel acquires a new ideal father. Everything in the Swann household, the house, meals, the servants, is just as it should be and everything the family does is just right, whereas everything in Marcel's home seems inferior, old-fashioned and contemptible. Subsequently, his love for Gilberte and the Swanns fades and he begins to admire the Duke and Duchess de Guermantes, who become his new parents and introduce him into the world of Society that he has always aspired to enter.

## III

The mental make-up of great men, if there is a specific one, has its origins in this situation. The two family histories come into conflict, perpetuating a kind of civil war between the family complex which is a datum and the family romance which is a fiction. Most of us probably opt for the easiest and most realistic solution when we are trying to reconcile these two factors in our attempt to regain our inner peace. This means assimilating the romance into the complex, for fiction, after all, is only fiction and a bird in the hand is worth two in the bush. Consequently, we prefer the love of flesh-and-blood parents to the gratitude of people who are not only distant but also imaginary.

We can suppose, however, that a minority of children are narcissistic or asocial enough to trust their strength and are absolutely determined to live out their fiction and achieve their dream. They either find life in their real family unliveable, as was the case with Flaubert, or think that having a borrowed one is the only way they can survive psychically, as happened with Kafka, for example. In their case, a very unstable unity is based on the family romance and the characters they have identified with. At the concrete level, this unity is expressed both by a weakening of the amorous attachment to the real parents and an interiorisation of the fictitious ones, amongst whom are numbered national heroes, artistic and scientific geniuses and the like. Indeed, the way in which the conflict between the family trees is resolved follows the usual pattern, with the libido regressing as identification advances.

We can see that individuals of that kind, unlike the majority of human beings, come very close to sacrificing the Oedipal emotions to their ambition of ruling, discovering or writing. Consider, for example, the extraordinary gift that statesmen have for giving up their dearest friends virtually overnight and forming alliances with new ones, or the ease with which men of genius neglect every family tie in order to concentrate on their work. Balzac's *La Recherche de l'absolu* makes this point very well indeed. The sacrifice they make very early in life is made again and again, for what they need is to be like and to equal those superior beings they have modelled themselves on. They want to enter the world of the elite, and in order to do so they separate themselves from everything else with the determination of the go-getter who hides his humble parents because he is ashamed of them. Such people have irrevocably removed the family they were born into and replaced it with one that they have chosen and thought up themselves. In the earlier stages of their lives, this fictitious family was merely a way of criticising and escaping from society. By the time they reach maturity, it has become the motivation for their actions and the source of their creation of reality, and they are living out their family romances.

When they are making this choice, the lives of exceptional men like Lenin or Napoleon, Marx or Einstein, Moses or Christ, play a decisive part, providing the plots, episodes and examples for what could be a successful family romance, the story of someone who has succeeded, someone they would like to be. They spur on future revolutionaries, prophets, scientists and artists, urging them to give up their normal surroundings and imagine prestigious ones for living and working in, encouraging them to see themselves in advance as the sons of these spiritual fathers and to reject their vastly inferior fleshly ones.

At a very early stage, all such men create a mental Pantheon in which they hope one day to occupy an exalted place. This can be seen in concrete form in those artists – Picasso, Vasarely or Chagall, for example – who have a gallery built for them while they are still alive, and political leaders whose every gesture and speech betrays a concern for what future historians will think. They even, while they are still alive, plan their own funerals. The fact that such men live with their memoirs and obituaries in mind and that their identity has a pre-established model, their legend, all goes to show how powerful the family romance is and how crucial a part it has played in their careers. They have striven successfully to change it into reality, to make a *historical* romance of it.[2]

And yet the psychology of those great men who are leaders of crowds keeps its ultimate mystery. We have, however, made some progress, since at the very least we are now in a position to explore it. As we have seen, it presupposes an internal division and the control of the opposing forces of the super-ego and the ego, that is, of identification and love, and arises from the separation of the family romance and the Oedipus complex, the profound duality in the life of the child and later the adolescent. The offspring of parents becomes the offspring of his own creation. I do not know whether we have arrived at any explanation of all those questions which have so far remained unexplained. All I can do is to ask the reader's indulgence and imagine what such an explanation might consist of. In knowledge too, to use a phrase of Jaurès, 'human progress is measured in terms of the tolerance the wise show towards the dreams of madmen'.

## IV

'If on the one hand we thus see the figure of the great man grown to divine proportions, yet on the other we must recall that the father too was once a child' (Freud: XXIII, 110). Legends tell us about this childhood, and what is striking is the fact that they follow the pattern we have just traced. Crowd psychology is the screen on which episodes from a family romance magnifying the stature of the hero and explaining how he has come to be what he is are projected. Moses is a case in point.

What were his origins? The Bible, as we know, maintains that he was the child of Jewish slaves. Freud, however, insists that he was born into a family of Egyptian pharaohs and was therefore not a Jew, and adduces the evidence of his name itself, which is undeniably Egyptian in origin. His main argument, however, is based on an analysis of the legend of his birth. The first observation we can make is that the latter conforms to an archetypal pattern occurring amongst all races, in which the hero is described as the child of a royal or noble couple. Just before his birth, there is some crisis, famine or war. His father, feeling that he is threatened by the arrival of an heir who could take advantage of the situation or in some way help his enemies, orders him to be abandoned, exposed or killed. Like the least of his subjects, he resorts to infanticide in an attempt to avoid his inevitable fate.

Other major figures who, according to legend, were abandoned in this way include Cyrus, Romulus and Hercules. Fortunately, however, the child is saved by a man of the people, suckled by a poor woman or a female animal (the she-wolf, in the case of Romulus) and survives. The goodness of humble people prevents the crime of the mighty and is an instrument of destiny.

The child is brought up in his adoptive family and grows in stature, strength and courage. His subsequent life is one of dangers and perilous adventures and reveals his heroic nature, and he is finally recognised by his real and noble family. He later revenges himself on his father and unites his country once again, coming to the throne that has been his since before he was born. It is precisely because he challenges and defeats his father that he becomes a hero. His family history is the same in all legends: 'In the typical form of the legend, it is the first family, the one into which the child is born, which is the aristocratic one, most often of royal rank; the second family, the one in which the child grows up, is the one that is humble or has fallen on evil days. This tallies, moreover, with the circumstances to which the interpretation traces the legend back' (Freud: XXIII, 13).

There are, however, two exceptions to the typical scenario: Oedipus and Moses. In the Greek tradition, the former is abandoned by his royal parents and taken in by an equally royal couple. Each episode of his tragic life – his incest with his mother and the banishment of his children – takes place within the golden circle of the demi-gods. The fact that the two families are of the same kind means that he undergoes none of the trials that reveal the exceptional being, set the imagination on fire and stress the heroic nature of the great man.

In the Bible, the contrast between the two families is inescapably there, but it is reversed. Moses is a son of humble Jews, born into a family of slaves. Since they cannot provide for him, they do what the poor have always done and abandon him. The baby is saved by an Egyptian princess and brought up as her own son. This is where the normal legend is changed, for it is not the first family that is noble and the second of lowly status, but *vice versa*. Moses grows up amongst the children of the Egyptian pharaohs and is an adult when he discovers his true parents. Instead of taking his revenge on them, he saves them and the whole Jewish people, whose prophet and leader he becomes, as is well known to us.

His birth and life are an exception to the rule, with events taking place in reverse order. If we simply make them conform to the rule and put them back in the right order, the truth that the legend hides becomes clear to us, Freud argues. He puts the biblical narrative back into the series of similar stories and comes to the conclusion that, like all great men, Moses must have been of royal parentage and hence Egyptian. In order to make him a Jew, the Bible had used the trick of inversion. In his words:

Whereas normally a hero, in the course of his life, rises above his humble beginnings, the heroic life of the man Moses began with his stepping down from his exalted position and descending to the level of the Children of Israel.

(Freud: XXIII, 15)

327

In substance, what really happened was not that the Israelites rebelled, but that they were liberated. Their revolt came from above, not from below. In maintaining that Moses was an Egyptian, Freud is in fact telling the Jews that they never really revolted against authority, but simply followed an Egyptian prince and fulfilled the destiny of their master, a pharaoh, succeeding where his own people had failed in adopting monotheistic religion.

There is no point stressing the fragility of Freud's argument or the data it is based on. That has been done many times already. He turns the sense of the biblical narrative, which is of a historical nature, on its head. Far from showing us the hidden truth of the legend, he creates a new one for the twentieth century. As Ahad Haam said, in each generation of Jews there is new meaning for Moses. It fell to Freud to create one for his own.

We can now offer our provisional conclusions. We first saw that in order to explain how heroes are created, legends follow the uniform pattern of a birth and childhood with two families, one 'native' and the other 'noble' and all the trials of a move from one to the other. It is as if, like a machine which works only when there is a difference between a hot and a cold source of energy, an individual creates the forces that will make him an exceptional being only when there is a difference in social level between the two families. In his real family, he is born; in his borrowed one, he is really or imaginatively reborn. Do the Hindus not maintain that high-caste people are 'born twice'?

We say the same about exceptional individuals, the only difference being that they are not born into the same milieu twice. The fact of belonging to two families makes the child great both in his own eyes and in those of others. In Freud's words, 'one of the families is the real one, in which the person in question (the great man) was actually born and grew up; the other is fictitious, fabricated by the myth in pursuit of its own intentions. As a rule the humble family is the real one and the aristocratic family the fabricated one' (Freud: XXIII, 14). The comparison is limited, but it does cast some light on what marks him out and makes him a divided being.

We must also reflect on the two exceptions to the general pattern of the legend, Oedipus and Moses. The former was born and brought up in two socially-equivalent families, both being royal. The latter, however, according to the Old Testament, was born of poor parents and subsequently adopted by people of elevated rank. The son of slaves was reborn into the world of his masters.

The two exceptions offer, in an imaginary form, solutions to which we can attribute a general psychic significance. One consists of dissolving the family romance in the Oedipal complex and bringing fiction back to reality. The other involves the opposite process, in which the created individual becomes dominant, shaping character and real life and tending to become true.

By analogy, the first solution makes Oedipus the very type of the whole man, the *homo simplex*, and the second makes Moses that of the divided man, the *homo duplex*. Oedipus underwent severe trials and was punished for having sinned against social taboos in committing incest with his mother and killing his father, but he did not experience the tragedy of alienation and the opposition of men and cultures. He was an heir, and re-established the order to which he belonged with every fibre of his being. Moses lived out that alienation and opposition, shaping his own being in revolt and the struggle between the top and bottom of society. Whether or not he was of noble birth, his destiny was to be a rebel, a usurper and a stranger amongst his own people. As we know, a usurper takes the place of the man he has usurped, with the young man replacing the old and the slave replacing his master, freeing himself and mankind. Moses founded nations and created symbols. He was not an Oedipus, for in his case another factor came into play. When the family romance defeats the family complex, there is a triumph of spirituality over sexuality, for the latter is an immediate datum and empirically known, whereas the former is a creation of the spirit, the result of observation and deduction.

# 3. *Creating a people*

FAMILY ROMANCE might explain the 'something extra' in great men. There is nothing anti-rational about such a hypothesis. Without in any way prejudging what analysis might really tell us about individual cases, we can say that the hypothesis certainly represents a cultural datum. If we grant that, the questions we ask will take us a little further. What particular conjunction of circumstances makes an individual into the leader of a people? How does he influence that people? Why do they follow him to the extent of making him their hero?

All these questions imply that the 'great man' has the power of changing a natural mass into an artificial and disciplined one and thus have the following sense, as formulated by Freud:

> How is it possible for a single man to evolve such extraordinary effectiveness that he can form a people out of random individuals and families, can stamp them with a definitive character and determine their fate for thousands of years?
>
> (Freud: XXIII, 107)

We could ask that about Lenin as much as about Moses, Mahomet, Franklin, Mao or Christ, and we are on more familiar ground here. This is because the hypothesis that emerges in response to it is that of the totemic cycle begun by the murder of the father and closed by his resurrection in the son who takes his place. We have traced it far enough to be able to see where it might lead us. It helps us order reality and reflect on it. What it does not do is provide us with a detailed knowledge of things as they happen. We should admit once and for all that the empirical content of the conjecture we are making is about as great as that of Descartes' vortices. It does, however, correspond to a certain psychic truth about what the masses do and how they are operated on, which is that the visible force of the living produces no result without the invisible one of the dead. It is as if, in order to make history, every reality had to act within it in the form of a memory of those claws no-one can ever escape. This is true at least as far as Moses and his creation of the Jewish people are concerned.

## II

Let us come back to him and accept Freud's statement that he was an Egyptian. He would have been born at the time of the pharaoh Amenophis IV in the fourteenth century before Christ. The king had been converted to the monotheistic cult of Aten, taking the name of Akhenaten in his honour. He set about wiping out polytheism and the ancient deities and idolatries, even outlawing the word 'gods' in the plural. A new capital, Akhetaten, 'the horizon of Aten', was built for him far from Thebes and the traditional priesthood of Amun. Many other sanctuaries were built in Egypt and its empire. After a brief initial success, however, the attempt failed, and his successor Tutankhamun re-established the cult of Amun, whose name he bore, in all its splendour, along with the authority of his priests. Nevertheless, one of those loyal to Akhenaten – Freud identifies him as Moses – a man of deep faith and devoted to his master, would not yield and return to the religion of the majority. This meant that he was exiled from his class and his country, and as Freud says, 'he could remain in Egypt only as an outlaw or as a renegade' (Freud: XXIII, 60).

He was in a minority amongst his own people and perhaps even in a minority of one, but he was tenacious and stubborn and consistent both in what he thought and in what he did. These were qualities that Akhenaten had lacked. In a study of the influence of active minorities, I have shown that it depends on two things: their ability to occupy a forbidden position in society and the consistency of their behaviour in all circumstances (Moscovici, 1976a). As his modern chronicler tells us, Moses met these two conditions fully, as he was an aristocratic and prominent man and, unlike Akhenaten the dreamer, an energetic one (Freud: XXIII, 28).

An outcast amongst those of his own race, he sought another people to evangelise with his religion, thus making up for the losses it had suffered. The people he turned to were foreigners, the semitic Hebrew tribes who had emigrated to Egypt several generations earlier and were now living in slavery in the outermost parts of the empire.

Moses, an outcast himself, revealed the contents of the new religion to these other outcasts, plotting with them and agreeing to leave the inhospitable land of Egypt and find another where they could live in freedom. Together they took the road of exodus. In short, Moses succeeded where Akhenaten had failed. No doubt the Hebrews projected onto this foreign prince and his equally strange religion all their hopes of regaining their lost freedom and saw in him a leader and in his faith a doctrine justifying their revolt. In his turn, he found himself 'at home

331

with the plan of founding a new kingdom, of finding a new people to whom he would present for their worship the religion which Egypt had disdained' (Freud: XXIII, 28).

We should see a logical pattern in all that. Founding a new nation presupposes a combination of deviant, outcast individuals and a collectivity that is oppressed but willing to unite around new teachings and ideas. When all those ingredients are present, an active minority is certainly formed, the masses are drawn along with it and ideas are put into practice. All the great creations and transformations of history are the work of such minorities or such men, who are outside or above existing societies (Moscovici, 1968).

And all these conditions, according to Freud, were met when Akhenaten died. There was a stubborn and fanatical leader, the discovery of a monotheistic religion, something so far unheard-of, and a string of rebellious tribes on the edges of the empire. That was no doubt what made Moses *choose* them as the human material he would fashion his people from. 'Moses had stooped to the Jews, had made them his people: they were his chosen people' (Freud: XXIII, 45). With them, he fused these scattered factors into a creative whole.

I wish particularly to stress this view of active minorities as the means by which history is changed and peoples created. It could be reduced to simply the murder of the father, who has often been the only figure to emerge. In fact, however, that murder is part of the whole explanation and one of the things resulting from it, for the father has also been a rebel after all, and in this particular case it is the father who teaches his son's people to rebel. In a first phase, a leader or group of leaders establishes as a task the propagation and imposition of a new doctrine within a group. This could be called the phase of *revelation*.

Moses revealed to the Jews a religion that would make them the people of a single god. But like master, like man. They were no more made of a nobler metal than the Egyptians were and balked at the strict morality and prohibitions of monotheism. Nor were they anxious to give up their idols and magic or to see why their leader wanted to keep them permanently separate from other peoples, by circumcision for example, or why he wanted to impose a teaching stricter than that of his master Akhenaten on them. For Moses had broken every link between Aten and the sun god. Their whole physical, rational and emotional being cried out against the commandments of a religion that took so little account of human nature and against the god described by Schönberg in his opera *Moses and Aaron* as 'inconceivable because invisible, immutable, permanent, eternal, omnipresent and omnipotent'.

And that was not all, of course. But when a doctrine is in its revelatory stage, by which I mean when it is externally imposed on a collection of individuals, it is a matter of the head only, for it is imposed on them by a kind of coercion and does not really convince them at any deep level. Not only do they resist it, but they have no difficulty in rejecting it and get rid of it under the pressure of contrary affects and beliefs. Moses, however, 'deriving from the school of Akhenaten, employed no other method than did the king; he commanded, he forced his faith upon the people' (Freud: XXIII, 47). This was exactly what Lenin was to do two thousand years later, thinking that he could implant a socialist conscience into the workers from outside. Moses thought he could coerce the Jews into monotheism. The rigours of religion and the limits to its propagation, however, encouraged a whole series of rebellions described in the Bible, such as the Golden Calf and the breaking of the tablets of the Law. During one such revolt, the Jews are said to have killed Moses. Freud writes quite simply that both he and Akhenaten met the fate that awaits every enlightened despot (Freud: XXIII, 60). The Jews had a father and killed him. In doing so, they thought that they had put a stop to everything, but in fact it was merely the beginning of a long, and indeed over-long, history.

## III

Like the original primitive father, Moses dead was infinitely more power-ful than Moses alive. His violent end made a martyr of him. What greater proof can a man give of his identification with a doctrine than laying down his life for it? The sacrifice itself is universally seen as a witness to the value of his belief. It is true that the mass of men understand very little of the ideas of Bruno and Galileo, but the fact that the former was burnt at the stake and the latter condemned by the Church makes their ideas exemplarily attractive. The same holds true for Moses, even if 'everything in the Mosaic god that deserved admiration was quite beyond the comprehension of the primitive masses' (Freud: XXIII, 63).

The fact that the believer is put to death is a testimony to the man and his greatness. In a more general way, the action of a minority, whether it be a question of a group or a single person, is aimed at creating a conflict with the majority and bringing that conflict to term (Moscovici, 1976a). The persecution and suffering endured by such a religious or political minority or by a single person, an artist who has created a new kind of art or a scientist who has revealed a new truth, are inherent in the conflict. They are vital if such people are to overcome the emotional resistance they encounter. Actions speak louder than words. Writing of cultural heroes, Freud has this to say:

In many instances the analogy goes still further, in that during their lifetime these figures were – often enough, even if not always – mocked and maltreated by others and even despatched in a cruel fashion. In the same way, indeed, the primal father did not attain divinity until long after he had met his death by violence. (Freud: XXI, 141–2)

The same applies to Moses.

Once the murder had been carried out, the Hebrews turned away from monotheism. 'Moses is dead, who would not die,' is the conclusion of a liturgical elegy turning the crime into a natural death. They recreated a tribal society, worshipping several gods of whom Jahweh was the chief one, and took up the magical practices of the peoples around them. Perhaps they even returned to a matriarchal society. Whether that was so or not, they had no outstanding leaders with paternal authority. They were led by mouthpieces, elder brothers in charge of communal tasks, placatory men who said only what they were asked to say and what people wanted to hear. The figure and the teachings of Moses were in eclipse during this period, thrust into the background and seemingly forgotten by all and sundry. What had seemed so important when they were leaving Egypt now seemed cloaked in complete silence. Freud declares that 'there was a long period after the defection from the religion of Moses during which no sign was to be detected of the monotheistic idea, of the contempt for ceremonial or of the great emphasis on ethics' (Freud: XXIII, 68).

He believed that the masses are in a state resembling that of the individual who is about to leave childhood behind and is going through a period of latency. Most of the events and desires of early childhood have been thrust down into the memory and appear to have been forgotten. In reality, they remain in the unconscious, waiting to return to the conscious like a submarine about to resurface after a long underwater journey. Here, however, we must once again take care to avoid any inaccuracy arising from a possible confusion of the individual and the social levels. Analogy is not identity, and we cannot move from one to the other.

Let us then say that once they had been revealed, the character and religion of Moses underwent a phase of *incubation*. The latter is well-known to anyone engaged in research. It is the essential prelude to discovery and invention. Mathematicians, who were the first to describe it, depict it as a period in which an idea or solution they are working towards is silently and invisibly taking shape below the surface without their knowing it and suddenly erupts when they least expect it. They sometimes realise that they have already had it and forgotten it and that it comes back to them later. In exactly the same way, the religion and character of Moses spread through the mental life of the Hebrews without their realising it or wanting it.

The ideas sown in their minds certainly did not wither and die. They remained ineffaceably inscribed in the records of the people, carved in the hearts of its sons and indestructible. Ideas and feelings took a conventional form in a kind of collective memory, combined with other more familiar notions and feelings expressed in popular language. The most striking thing is not that the incubation process lasted a long time, which is to be expected, or that the religion of Moses underwent a hidden selection and rearrangement in order to bypass Jewish intellectual and emotional resistance, or that it was handed on from generation to generation in restricted Levitical circles.

What was much more remarkable was the consequence of this period of incubation. The prophet's precepts and ideas were transformed into belief and tradition: 'And it was this tradition of a great past which continued to work in the background, as it were, which gradually gained more and more power over men's minds, and which finally succeeded in transforming the god Yahweh into the god of Moses and in calling back to life the religion of Moses which had been established and then abandoned long centuries earlier' (Freud: XXIII, 124).

We know why this period that the tradition spent in purgatory was so important. Crowds are not influenced by the purely ethical or intellectual content of a doctrine, of whatever kind. What happens is that during the incubation period, every doctrine acquires psychic and affective weight. Unknown to them, it becomes part of their concrete experience and opinions, acquiring an internal obviousness and clarity of the most straightforward kind. It takes root in the collective memory and becomes a belief in the strictest sense of the word, all the more powerful because it is ancient and has had time to mingle with others that still persist in the conscious mental life of human beings.

The Mosaic teaching never in fact fell into total neglect. It was still propagated by certain people, and there were still a minority of disciples ready to bring it back, speak on its behalf and renew the sacrifice their master had made. There was no immediate response and no clear influence on the people as a whole, but such disciples, like all minorities, continued to exert a hidden and unperceived influence (Moscovici, 1980). Amongst the Jews, it was the prophets who took the lead in this tireless work. They 'revived the fading tradition . . . renewed the admonitions and demands made by Moses and . . . did not rest till what was lost had been established again' (Freud: XXIII, 111).

Their efforts overcame countless rebuffs and were eventually crowned with full and lasting success. In short, every doctrine (and that of Moses was no exception) finally 'dies' like a seed in the ground. Thrown down and half-forgotten, it germinates and bursts forth, emerging as a tradition and being reborn as a belief. What is first rejected by reason and scorned by the emotions is preserved in the memory and finally accepted by faith.

## IV

After the ebb comes the high tide. Nostalgia begins to exercise its charm and embellish the past. The image of Moses as a repository of every virtue drew the Jews closer to the man who had brought them out of slavery and whose single-mindedness of purpose had revealed to them both their faith and themselves. It is the privilege of every father, founder and ancestor of a dynasty to mark a watershed. Before him, there was nothing. After him, anything is possible. Like the inventor of an art or science, the man who creates, or at least regenerates, a people is a point of departure, as were Romulus, Robespierre, Lenin and de Gaulle. We can move away from them and flee them, but sooner or later we have to come back to them, particularly when, like the Jews, we have a feeling of guilt and want to make amends for our crime.

As the centuries passed, the figure of Moses loomed increasingly large in their memory and was more and more present in their imagination. The remorse they felt because they had forgotten him also became increasingly bitter. The stage was thus set for someone to give flesh-and-blood form to the absent leader and gather to him all the available stock of love. Putting new masks on old faces is not something anyone can do. Nevertheless, someone was there when he was needed, a Hebrew this time, with enough talent to presume to take the place of Moses the Egyptian. He was determined to complete his work. Such a man had to be possessed of immense pride, uncommon strength and extraordinary confidence at a time when there were so few exceptional personalities. One of the corollaries of the hypothesis of the murder of the father, it should be stressed, was that the first leader was a foreigner who chose the mass, and the second a 'native' emerging from it. Its feelings had run through him for his whole lifetime, and in its atmosphere he saw what concerned, affected and moved it. We must also see him as being a man whose ideas were luminous, simple and profound enough for him to talk of them without encountering the old resistance to them. When all these conditions are met, the image of the founding father can come to life again in the person of the son who reincarnates and replaces him.

We can suppose that amongst the Jews the first Moses, the Egyptian prince, was reborn in the form of the second, the Hebrew priest. Much later, the Bible created a composite figure combining the two, thus wiping out the traces of the murder of the father and resuscitating him in the man who took his place, as if there had been one single Moses. This removed any reasons for guilt feelings towards him in the Jews and freed them from their remorse. That is what the Old Testament concealed and what Freud thought he had disclosed.

We also know that when the image is resurrected, the old and forgotten one works on the new one. This is done in terms of the *coincidentia oppositorum*, which mingles and joins together two beliefs, two emotions, two persons or two conflicting gods that have come into being in very different circumstances and are linked to two dissimilar forms of social life. In more specific terms, everything imposed by the unlimited authority of the father and everything instituted by the alliance of the brothers and the law of the mothers they associated themselves with.

There is nothing surprising in the fact that the monotheistic teaching of Moses incorporated, when it was reintroduced, some elements of the cult of Jahweh that the Jews had adopted after the murder and during his long eclipse. Freud expresses the firm belief that the duality he found behind the recreated unity of the Jews and their religion is a decisive proof of his interpretation:

Our findings may thus be expressed in the most concise formula. Jewish history is famous to us for its dualities: *two* groups of people who came together to form the nation, *two* kingdoms into which this nation fell apart, *two* gods' names in the documentary sources of the Bible. To these we may add two fresh ones: the foundation of *two* religions – the first repressed by the second but nevertheless later emerging victoriously behind it, and *two* religious founders, who are both called by the same name of Moses and whose personalities we have to distinguish from each other. (Freud: XXIII, 52)

A very flimsy case is argued with a great deal of conviction. It was clearly the second Moses who overcame idolatrous beliefs, welded the people together around its leader and as it were legitimised subversive underground teachings. Without the fear, remorse and authority that emanated from his person he could not have succeeded where his predecessor had failed. In order to succeed, however, he had of necessity to rely on the teachings that had now become traditional. He no longer had to overcome the people's emotional resistance to the religion of Moses. What he had to do in fact was control the rise of the tradition and channel the strength it gave to all, a force stronger than that of logical arguments and the constraints imposed by Moses. He also needed to make the entire people realise that their real beliefs had changed in the intervening time. On this point, Freud says:

It is worth specially stressing the fact that each portion which returns from oblivion asserts itself with peculiar force, exercises an incomparably powerful influence on people in the mass, and raises an irresistible claim to truth against which logical objections remain powerless: a kind of *'credo quia absurdum'*.

(Freud: XXIII, 85)

The mass of Jews, like any other mass, were less resistant now because they were more a prey to guilty memories, those pernicious and debilitating viruses of the soul. They yielded without a struggle and zealously accepted what they had once violently refused. The whole people moved from polytheism, which was now seen as a false faith, to monotheism, the true one. This was the third and final stage of this particular development, *conversion*. Religion had been imposed from outside by a single man and adopted by a minority. Now, in short, it welled up again from within.

Over a certain period of time it had circulated like an idea in the mind of a scientist or artist, changing minds in a hidden and unnoticed way. On its rebirth, it operated openly and exerted a total hold (Moscovici, 1981). Every Jew openly identified with Moses, the father who had come back to his people, declaring himself his son and his faithful follower. When we say that a race has risen from its ashes, we really mean from its memory, or more exactly that it has recovered from the memory of a crime that has shaken it at every level. But without that crime there would have been nothing. Chekhov very aptly says that there is nothing good on earth that has not some infamy at its source. In mass psychology, that infamy will always be parricide.

## V

With the return of Moses and the conversion of the mass of Jews to his religion, the cycle of their prehistory is complete, and their history begins. In their enthusiasm, they renounced the rule of the instincts and no longer wanted to make man an idol for men, for that was at the root of servitude. Their god reigned in the human soul, invisible, nameless and with no likeness. They were proud of their control of their instincts and saw themselves as a chosen race in the sacrifices they had accepted – the Golden Calf, ikons and the other props of religion. As part of their heritage and their obedience to their god, they were henceforth reluctant to pay too great a reverence to the signs of power. If they were stiff-necked, as the Bible describes them, it was because they had identified with the intransigent character of Moses and were afraid of lapsing from grace in his eyes.

There are one or two conclusions to be stressed. It is important to remember that we have sketched in an idea of how history changes and how we ourselves change in terms of the totemic cycle we proposed as a hypothesis. More particularly, we have looked at how a people creates itself and how its leader creates it. This seems to be the particular task of 'great men' and active minorities. In the case of the Jewish people, the example we look at if we follow Freud, this was achieved in three stages.

The first was that of the appearance of a new doctrine, a new vision and an energetic, consistent and determined man, whom we shall call Moses. He chose a mass of men who were outcasts like himself, just as Mao is said to have chosen the Chinese workers and peasants, who saw him as an outsider, letting them see his vision and imposing it on them. Once he is their leader, they take the road of revolt. The law of the land declares them outlaws or renegades and forces them to go into exile. Everything that is new, however, arouses resistance within the very mass it sets out to win over and in the end it is rejected along with the man who was the source of the scandal. The Jews were no exception to the rule and rid themselves of Moses by killing him and of his doctrine by reverting to their idolatrous beliefs.

In the second stage the Jews, who were now united by their crime as the primitive brothers had been by theirs, apparently became a people like any other. They were nomadic, of course, and moved around, creating their customs and renewing their code, which was probably matriarchal, and adding one or two local gods, including Jahweh, to their religion. On the one hand, the majority reverted to the magical beliefs and practices of the Hebrews. On the other, a minority remained faithful to Moses, following his example and continuing to spread monotheism and contrast it with the dominant polytheism around them. Like all minorities, they did not avoid conflicts but provoked them and kept them alive, as the prophets prove. Even if at the obvious and superficial level the great mass of the Jews followed popular opinion and met the requirements of the established religion, at a deeper and hidden level the ideas of Moses penetrated and infiltrated the collective memory until they achieved the status of a tradition. Individuals changed within themselves. Externally, they were polytheists; internally they became monotheists, aspiring to the lost unity imposed by Moses and longing to make up for the loss they had endured.

The third stage was that of his resurrection in the second Moses. Disturbed by internal divisions and tortured by remorse, the mass rallied to him completely, embracing his religion and accepting the prohibitions he imposed. The majority identified with the minority, adopting its beliefs and way of life and primarily its one god. Both were welded into a single people, giving full allegiance to a single religion and recognising a single great man or founding father.

We could say that initially he chose the Jews, as an artist chooses his raw material of wood, iron or paper, imposing a form on them and welcoming them as his people, his creation. As Freud writes:

And since we know that behind the God who had chosen the Jews and freed them from Egypt stands the figure of Moses, who had done precisely that, ostensibly at God's command, we venture to declare that it was this one man Moses who created the Jews. It is to him that the people owes its tenacity to life but also much of the hostility it has experienced and still experiences.          (Freud: XXIII, 106)

Moses can be seen as having created the Jews, rather as Robespierre can be seen as having created the Jacobins, Lenin the Soviets and Washington and Franklin the Americans. But why do the Jews owe so much of the hostility they have aroused to him? Moses is a special case, for he demanded that they accept a profoundly rational ethic and forbade them and their leaders to have any recourse to idols and magic, and this shaped a very special kind of power situation. Max Weber writes that the rejection of magic meant that, unlike what happened elsewhere, the Jewish priests could not use it systematically to control the masses (Weber, 1980: 304). Moses also ordered them to keep themselves separate from other peoples and to maintain their difference. In obeying his demands, they absorbed his character, that of the member of a minority, an outcast, in the view of some, dominated by the interior tyranny of his aim and ideal, indifferent to the fate of solid majorities and not afraid to create a conflict if necessary. In other words, the mentality he created for them was that of the active minority, which is also that of the leader, tenacious, uncompromising and ready to say no. For thousands of years people have been saying of the Jew what Stalin said about de Gaulle: that he was a very stiff and stubborn man.

In a general way, he was able to stamp this personality on them because, like the Americans in modern times, they were exiles who chose their own country, creating there the tradition of their religions, whereas other peoples created a religion conforming to tradition. Some Jews, however, the Christians, were unable to meet those demands and face up to the consequent hostility. For good reasons, they decided to mingle with the mass of men, like ink in water, to change their religion and receive the love they lacked. These changes meant, in Weber's view, that they lost those characteristics peculiar to the Old Testament ethic, particularly those which determined the particular position of the Jews as an outcast race (Weber, 1980: 622–3).

This was a difficult and painful task, demanding many sacrifices. In so far as it achieved the conversion of peoples on their home ground, so to speak, and became the religion of pagan kings and vast multitudes of human beings, Christianity inevitably had to incorporate a great number of polytheistic beliefs and magical and idolatrous rites, just as socialism, in similar circumstances, annexed religious and nationalist ideologies. This meant that Christianity, a form of monotheism for the masses, was in opposition to Mosaic beliefs, a form of monotheism for a minority, with all the tensions that that contrast implies. In a civilisation steeped in Christianity, antagonism of that kind has been enough to fan every deadly hatred for thousands of years.

The story of Moses and his creation of the Jewish people is no doubt very much *sui generis* and has long flouted reason. Nevertheless, it is not so unique that what we learn from it cannot be applied elsewhere. The phases a doctrine goes through – revelation, incubation and the final conversion of a people – on its way to becoming a religion are sufficiently general to fit any history. But there is no need to spend any more time defending a hypothesis that I have consistently described as flimsy and that is irrelevant outside the context of mass psychology.[1]

# 4. *Mosaic and totemic leaders*

L EADERS WIELD THEIR POWER because they have exceptional gifts and an idea, a view of the world, that they proclaim. It becomes the major passion of a class, a party or a people. We sense the presence of these gifts, which are truly charismatic, in an individual most frequently when words that would seem ridiculous in anyone else's mouth and actions that would appear bogus if anyone else performed them are far from being laughable or out of place when they originate from him. Coming from him, they make a strong impression on us and we see them as signs of a man at one with his ideas and his mission.

But let us consider the variety of modern leaders. We can distinguish two main kinds, the *Mosaic* and the *totemic*. Under the first heading, we immediately think of prophets, founders of republics (as in the United States, for example) and the creators of social and religious movements such as Mahomet, Marx or Gandhi, and under the second of tyrants, mob orators and the wizard-kings or shamans of so-called primitive societies.

Putting them into categories is not enough, however. We also need to know what crowd psychology has to tell us about the basis of such selection. There can be no doubt that the main one, which we are often unaware of but which subsumes all the others, is the prohibition against making images. This means opposing any recourse to rituals, magical procedures and teachings which create a concrete representation of their gods and leaders. With Moses, it was a question of the principle of authority: 'Thou shalt not make unto thee any graven image, or any likeness of any thing that is in heaven above, or that is in the earth beneath, or that is in the water under the earth.'

Whoever follows and respects this prohibition is turning his gaze away from transitory figures and towards invisible realities, and his ears are tuned to catch the sense of words and not their sound. For the important thing is still what is said, not how it is said, and what men must admire and respect is higher ideas and not the men who embody them, who are really no more than flesh-and-blood idols. With this commandment, Moses wanted to prevent the return of those he had driven out, the magicians and worshippers of fetishes who create illusions and hypnotise peoples.

Among the precepts of the Moses religion there is one that is of greater importance than appears to begin with. This is the prohibition against making an image of God – the compulsion to worship a God whom one cannot see. In this, I suspect, Moses was outdoing the strictness of the Aten religion. Perhaps he merely wanted to be consistent: his God would in that case have neither a name nor a countenance. Perhaps it was a fresh measure against magical abuses. But if this prohibition were accepted, it must have a profound effect. For it meant that a sensory perception was given second place to what may be called an abstract idea – a triumph of intellectuality over sensuality or, strictly speaking, an instinctual renunciation, with all its necessary psychological consequences.

(Freud: XXIII, 112–13)

By making the forbidding of likenesses a measure of the progress of culture and intelligence, Freud makes their glut of images, adulation and splendiferous homage the sign of a regression towards an enslavement to the instincts, which can be observed in a substitution which takes place. Instead of impersonal obedience to the religion, god, social teaching and so on that the leader represents, there is a personal one to him and his name. These are the snares and delusions masses and leaders alike must reject if they are to recover part of the lost ground of reason. Only if they do that can they look forward to living one day in the world as it should be, the world of which the Zohar says that 'it will be a world without images in which there will be no comparison between the image and what it represents'.

## II

I now propose to develop further the brief outline of the division between the two kinds of leaders with the aim of showing more clearly its concrete nature and widening the scope of the contrast between them. The first and most important aspect of that contrast lies precisely in their propensity to either ban or encourage the representation of themselves in the form of images, which they can either reject or use as an instrument of their power. By virtually refusing to use it in this way, Mosaic leaders tend to control the radiant strength of the 'great man' and reduce the temptation that others feel to imitate them and see reality through their eyes. In doing so, they hope to prevent religion becoming superstition, charisma a magic amulet and their own person a false god and an object of adoration. It is not by chance that the Mosaic prohibition has frequently been renewed throughout history. Indeed, Marx did precisely that in modern times, writing to one of his comrades that when he and Engels joined the Communists, they did so on the understanding that everything connected with the superstitious adoration of authority would be banished from its statutes.

343

Totemic leaders, on the other hand, do all that is in their power to encourage a cult of their personality, trying unceasingly to establish a visual, metaphor-laden legend around themselves and the idea supporting them. They do the easiest thing, which is to draw on traditional customs and ways of thought. This allows them to keep an ancient and familiar content, the Golden Calf of the imagination, beneath the attractive trappings of the new. To this, the crowd submits very rapidly.

This is what the fathers of the Christian Church did, assimilating a whole baggage of pagan customs and local divinities (who underwent baptism and re-emerged as saints) when they set out to win over whole peoples. And to establish its power it instituted glittering and splendid ceremonies, the magic rituals and pomps of the world it had conquered and which it had the chance of controlling by such means. As Max Weber observes, 'mass religion in particular is frequently and directly dependent on artistic devices for the required potency of its effects, since it is inclined to make concessions to the needs of the masses, which everywhere tend towards magic and idolatry' (Weber, 1965: 244). The Chevalier de Jancourt had made the same observation much earlier:

Those who have governed peoples in all ages have always made use of paintings and statues, the better to inspire in them the feelings they wished them to have, both in religion and in politics.

Once they take this path, leaders set up a living Pantheon as a receptacle for the signs of their authority in which they occupy the chief place. They make themselves into idols to capture the crowd's attention, stage-managing their person and their function in order to increase their hold over it. They tell the whole world to create a likeness, their likeness, and to have faith in it. Their personality is imposed on the crowd by the sea of portraits and emblems the crowd carries everywhere, which are to be found in homes as well as in public places.

At least, that is what happens unless they have the unusual gift of changing the crowd itself into their image, as happened some years ago in Peking when the huge crowd in Red Square formed a portrait of Mao, who was watching them from the stage and could see himself in them. When there is this mirage, individuals are gathered from all sides, caught up in the mirror the leader offers and dominated by sensations, losing their critical powers. The leader who knows how to make himself into an idol enjoys the absolute sovereignty of one man over all others, since he is in direct control of their memory.

The second difference between Mosaic and totemic leaders is that the former want to identify the mass with a religion or an idea and suppress themselves to that end, whilst the latter seek to identify the mass with themselves and become its central preoccupation. Mosaic leaders therefore try to abolish the external signs of power, seeking to affirm, by the modesty of their attitude, that they are part of ordinary humanity, as if they were afraid of offending the ideal they serve. Their attitude is always one of sobriety and their power is always discreet. They try to diminish their own stature and are aware of the fragile nature of what they have accomplished. They have no illusions about the chances of success of any human undertaking. The Bible says of Moses, 'Now the Man Moses was very meek, above all the men which are upon the face of the earth'.

This characteristic has become the criterion by which we judge the calibre of a great man. It is an indication of maturity and the renunciation of the pleasures of power. It reassures and meets the crowd's longing for purity, reconciling it with authority. It is even stressed in Khrushchev's famous secret report on the harm done by the cult of personality: 'The great modesty of Vladimir Ilyich Lenin, the great leader of the Revolution, is well known.' As all the accounts tell us, the latter was unostentatious and sober in speech and extremely polite in all his dealings. Trotsky relates how, during mass demonstrations, he would collect his notes as soon as his speech was finished and leave the stage quickly, to escape the inevitable sequel of the cries and cheers of thousands and wave after wave of tumultuous applause. He had little in common with those who came after him, for they were and still are applauded to order.

The words 'humility' and 'modesty' evoke a simple idea when they are applied to leaders. The man has sacrificed his ambitions to the cause, and not the opposite. We all see that as the true sign of real faith and genuine wealth. As the poet Rumi says:

Thus a branch laden with fruit is bowed down towards the ground, and a branch without fruit holds its head high, like the poplar. When there is a great abundance of fruit, there are supports to stop the branches trailing on the earth. The Prophet (be he blest) was very modest, for all the fruits of the world, from its beginning to its end, are gathered in him. Therefore he is the most modest.

Totemic leaders, however, make a show of their extraordinary qualities. In order to attract mass attention, they create an aura of personal omnipotence and infallibility in all their deeds. They want everything they are and do to be matchless and recall these things incessantly. Their self-confidence is visible and contagious. They start by persuading the crowd that they are not like other men and hence come to believe it themselves. The crowd tells itself that its leader can do great things and even perform miracles. The man who has been marked out in this way seems to have been designated by God, history or nature. This makes him, like Stalin, an outstanding example of this kind of leader,

345

a superman endowed with supernatural qualities like a god. Such a man is supposed to know everything, to think for everybody, to do everything and to be infallible. (Lazitch, 1976: 53)

It goes without saying that the two kinds of leader can only be understood with reference to each other. We cannot, of course, judge how important they are in the life of a society or say which is better suited to which kind of crowd. Questions of that nature will be answered one day, if there is need of it. It is easy to see, however, that Mosaic leaders take a loftier road, for they primarily and principally ask the masses to give up any immediate satisfaction of their desires and instincts. This is not done for the sake of authority or abstinence, but only as a means of confronting the external world and the constraints of work and social life. It is by recognising the limits of the world and interiorising them in terms of an ideal that we become masters of ourselves, for in so doing we become the masters of our instincts and desires. Consequently, since it is for their sake that we have made these sacrifices, we identify more closely with our community and its aims.

In short, such leaders ask of others what they ask of themselves and dominate them to the extent that they dominate themselves. This means that their authority has an ethical origin, as Freud writes:

But ethics is a limitation of instinct. The Prophets are never tired of asserting that God requires nothing other from his people than a just and virtuous life – that is, abstention from every instinctual satisfaction which is still condemned as vicious by our morality to-day as well. (Freud: XXIII, 118–19)

But this sacrifice, far from diminishing individuals psychologically, enhances them and gives them self-confidence. Why should this be so? Because the leaders who ask it of them play for each individual the part of a strict but fair super-ego of the kind that parents are thought to provide; and for many people meeting its demands, conforming to its ideal and winning its approval is a source of satisfaction. Their ego feels itself transported and strengthened, and this is of capital importance. 'When the ego has brought the super-ego the sacrifice of an instinctual renunciation, it expects to be rewarded by receiving more love from it. The consciousness of deserving this love is felt by it as pride' (Freud: XXIII, 117).

It means an increase in their self-esteem, in so far as it makes them feel superior to others who are still slaves to instincts and desires and have failed where they have succeeded. They feel they are special and have a keen sense of being a people chosen for an exclusive mission, like the early Christians, the French during the Revolution and, more recently, the socialists.

It is not surprising that totemic leaders adapt themselves to the masses as they are and do not ask of them anything that would disturb them or that they would refuse to understand. They do the opposite, in fact, and continually seek to reassure them that their instincts and needs are sound and promise to satisfy them in full. On the other hand, they are ready to limit that satisfaction by means of external repression, the army and police being the most effective ways of achieving this. Such reassurance entails two kinds of consequences. On the one hand, both individuals and the mass more or less expect miracles and rediscover their childish faith in an omnipotent person or magic formula. This justifies their infinite growth, as does publicity every day, enclosing the masses in a world of illusions, a Utopia of abundance or boundless justice, a magic world, in fact.

The authority of leaders of this kind could be said to be of an economic nature in so far as it comes from the ability to satisfy needs or to promise that they will be satisfied. Even ideas are seen in this way. For example, Christianity is a way of satisfying the need for immortality and happiness and socialism is a means of satisfying that for comfort and the enjoyment of earthly riches. The inevitable result of this is a fall in the self-esteem of both the individual and the masses, but for the opposite reasons to those we have just seen, namely that the expected rewards do not come from the super-ego. Indeed, the latter is severely critical of each person's deeds, and the ego is consequently weakened. People feel inferior to the leaders, on whom the partly-illusory satisfaction of desires now depends, and also to those who have accepted a renunciation that reconciles them with the ideals of the ego. In short, Mosaic leaders can only govern if they strengthen the ego, and totemic leaders only if they weaken it. At least that is logically what should happen, but reality is not often synonymous with a logical framework.

The fact is also that crowd psychology began by describing mainly totemic leaders, with Napoleon as the prototype, and later, in Freud's work, offered an analysis of Mosaic leaders, whose prototype is the prophet of Israel. The contrast between them lies in the prohibition against setting up idols imposed on the masses and that against charming the masses imposed on leaders. Movement from one to the other would be like that from a science smacking of magic to one based on reason or from a society which refuses to recognise the autonomy of private and public life to a divided society which does recognise it and enshrines it in the ethic it imposes on its leaders. As Freud wrote:

Going back to ethics, we may say in conclusion that a part of its precepts are justified rationally by the necessity for delimiting the rights of society as against the individual, the rights of the individual as against society and those of individuals as against one another. (Freud: XXIII, 122)

But in mass societies the opposite is most often the case. That means that there is still something we do not know, which is why the latter, which is progress from the historical point of view, goes hand in hand with psychic regression. The very fact that we cannot solve this problem shows that we are operating at the limits of the hypotheses we have proposed in the attempt to provide some degree of rational explanation of a reality which still needs a great deal more.

## III

I would not like to risk giving the impression that those hypotheses do not have any specific or even contemporary application. To get rid of the idea, I have chosen to use the history of the socialist movement as an illustration. From its earliest days it has had a succession of both Mosaic and totemic leaders and, indeed, much argument about the matter, which still shows no sign of abating. In the interests of brevity, I shall restrict myself to the comparison between Marx and Lassalle that has already been mentioned and then to that between Lenin and Stalin.

We know that Marx was simultaneously engaged in producing the theory of socialism and directing the international workers' association and was also involved in the basic developments connected with the birth of social-democratic parties in Europe. There is no need to tell the story of his life, which, as is well known, was characterised by privation and modesty. As a revolutionary, he made many enemies and engaged in bitter polemics to defend his own ideas and defeat those of his adversaries. His importance was quickly recognised, however, and supporters soon flocked to him. Both his writings and his letters show how resolutely opposed he was to any confusion between theory and myth. He firmly rejected any subordination of political organisation to the authority of an individual and, in his reflections on the Gotha programme, came out strongly against the overblown rhetoric and poverty-stricken generalities that deceive the intelligence because they are addressed to prejudice.

We also have overwhelming evidence that Marx was inflexibly opposed to any show of devotion to himself, rejecting fervent tributes to his genius and discouraging the chorus of praise it aroused. His sole concern was his work, the working-out and discussion of his doctrine, and he was convinced that the only means that should be used to propagate it were books, workers' education and the practice of revolution. As he confided to the German socialist Bloss, however, Lassalle subsequently did exactly the opposite.

The latter saw socialism as a form of religion and the workers' association as built on the model of a church, with himself as a leader raising the masses towards freedom. Since personal dictatorship had a *de facto* existence, he argued, it should be theoretically justified and declared essential in practice. He openly asked the association to follow its leader blindly, saying that it should be like a hammer in his hands. Acting in accordance with his views, he surrounded himself with a circle of admirers and allowed himself to be idolised by the wildly-enthusiastic masses. He was given a hero's welcome at meeting after meeting, demonstrating his undeniable gifts as an agitator and an organiser of grandiosely-produced rallies.

One historian describes him arriving at a station, where he was met by a deputation, and choirs gave a concert beneath the windows of his hotel. He arrived at the meeting-halls escorted by flower-bedecked cars, and there, too, he was often accompanied by a choir. In certain areas, the procession passed beneath triumphal arches set up across the streets. But the high point of each meeting was his speech, which could go on for over two hours, and on such occasions the orator or his message were of decisive importance, as the liturgical nature of the meeting turned the orator into a symbol (Mosse, 1975: 184). More accurately, he could be described as a hypnotist capable of fascinating the masses by the magic of his language. The struggle between the rival socialist factions, the supporters of Marx and those of Lassalle, left a deep mark on the German workers' movement between 1863 and 1875. The main focus of argument was the mode of authority and action on the masses.

Goethe said that if a man wanted to make his mark on the world, he needed two things, the first being to have a good head and the second a good inheritance, like Napoleon inheriting the legacy of the French Revolution, Frederick the Great that of the Silesian War, and so on. Lenin did so on the heritage of the Great War and the socialist revolution which had been heralded but never achieved.

His life as the exiled leader of the Bolshevik Party was like that led by Marx. Both had had a traditional education and lived in similar surroundings, thrashing out ideas and experiencing similar difficulties. For many years their practical energies were divided out between libraries and meetings, a clear warning to states that they should distrust solitary men buried in a book-lined study much more than extravert leaders wooing crowds and sacrificing themselves. The influence of the former is deeper, and there is no antidote to the contagious power of their example and ideas.

To come back to Lenin. It is true that for a short time, three or four years at most, he had to face the ordeal of initiation into violence and power. He did so with determination, even brutally eliminating his opponents. Nevertheless – and this is a fact of history, which has little regard for the rivers of blood in the memory of peoples or the betrayals carried out in their name – he seems to have remained faithful to his principle of transforming the idea of socialism into an effective force by means of the action of the party, propaganda and fierce argument. He would have no truck with the pomp and circumstance of power or the blatant symbol of authority. Victor Serge describes him thus:

In the Kremlin he still occupied a small apartment built for a palace servant. In the recent winter he, like everyone else, had had no heating. When he went to the barber's he took his turn, thinking it unseemly for anyone to give way to him. An old housekeeper looked after his rooms and did his mending. He knew that he was the Party's foremost brain and recently, in a grave situation, had used no threat worse than that of resigning from the Central Committee so as to appeal to the rank and file! (Serge, 1963: 101–2)

His gifts as a philosopher were certainly of a lower order than his political genius, but he used neither of them as a means of filling the empty place left by the tsar, the idol of the Russian people, who had been toppled after centuries of oppression. Indeed, he was well aware of the propensity of leaders to set themselves up on a pedestal and the tendency of the masses to worship them happily, and constantly tried to avoid it. Khrushchev reminds us that he bitterly criticised any manifestation of the cult of the individual and unremittingly fought against non-Marxist ideas about the 'hero' and the 'crowd', and any attempt to set the former off against the masses and the people (Lazitch, 1976: 55).

Ideas of that kind are certainly non-Marxist, but they are part of reality and crowd psychology. The very fact that it was necessary to fight them shows just how powerful they are, and the subsequent introduction of the cult of personality is a proof of their effectiveness. It was as a result of them that after Lenin's death, his heirs canonised him and laid his embalmed body in state opposite the Kremlin, like a holy relic or an immortal god. We know that his widow and certain members of the ruling stratum were against such things, which seemed more in keeping with the religions of the tsars of the pharaohs than with scientific Marxism.

His successors, however, knew what Gorky had recognised long ago. The image of a universally-venerated man short-circuits thought and emotions and commands loyalty. In short, they had agreed to treat the crowd as a crowd. As early as 1920, Gorky was writing that Lenin was becoming a legendary character and approving the fact, since he believed that most people needed faith before they could begin to act. There was no time for them to begin to think and understand, for meanwhile the evil genius of capitalism would stifle them faster and faster with wretchedness, exhaustion and drink.

It is politically useful to use a dead man against the living to subject respect for his mission to admiration for his person and to use that admiration ultimately for one's own benefit. With Lenin on his catafalque and shrouded in legend, the succession was open. Several of his former comrades were contenders, amongst them Trotsky, who was the most prestigious, and Bukharin, the most obvious choice. Only one, however, Stalin, had the courage and will to win at all costs. He subsequently eliminated them one by one and became the hero of a merciless struggle against the enemies he made a conquered people believe in. Lenin's mausoleum was thus put to its use as a stepping-stone and a pedestal. The crowd, which had made the pilgrimage to bow down before the dead god, threw itself at the feet of the living and terrible leader.

The rest is spread through the writings of the time. In my view, the most authentic is still Khrushchev's report, because it is a partial political document. Everything is in it – Stalin's determination, his sense of omnipotence, his unfaltering cruelty and his desire for vengeance. But these are secondary characteristics. The primary one is the orchestration of a whole range of ways of arousing devotion and love for himself, the father-figure constantly surrounded by children and enfolded by his loving and obedient people.

By grabbing all the civil and military titles a single man could hold, the Leader and Head shows how powers previously shared out amongst several 'brothers'-in-arms and party comrades were concentrated on a single individual. At the same time, calling streets, towns and institutes after him established a direct link between the leader and the masses, who celebrated him by singing a hymn in praise of him: 'Stalin has brought us up to be faithful to the people. He has brought us up to carry out our great tasks and shown us what our actions should be . . .' and so on.

He demanded that everyone should take part in maintaining his cult by means of continuous praise of his glory, reference to his genius and their own self-abnegation. This included those he was later to murder, like Kirov, or subject to slanderous trials, like Bukharin. Both were at the same seventeenth congress, the former referring to him as 'the greatest leader of all times and all peoples' and the latter as 'the glorious marshal of the proletarian forces, the best of the best revolutionaries'.

His own was merely the first of the countries in the world to be flooded with portraits of him that made his presence and the improved propaganda image of him ubiquitous. He held peoples from distant corners of the world in the gaze that he was careful to use to subjugate those near him. As a convinced hypnotist, Stalin thought himself able to impress and dominate them. This characteristic of his was striking enough for

Khrushchev to stress it, telling us that Stalin was capable of looking at someone and asking him why he was so shifty-eyed on that particular day, or why he kept turning away and could not look straight at him.

Questions of that nature were far from indications of a morbid suspicion. They were in fact orders, specifically intended to submit one gaze to the power of another and test its strength. Hugo knew what he was talking about when he said that forcing the crowd to examine one was an act of power. By the piecemeal removal of those displeasing or resisting him, the leader built up around himself a huge mirror that returned his thoughts and his will to him and reflected his omnipotence (Lazitch, 1976: 177).

Knowing as you do how the man was venerated, obeyed and adulated by multitudes of human beings of all sorts and conditions from every nation, this commentary will seem rather short. It will have achieved its aim, however, if it helps us to see our ideas about the nature of totemic leaders a little more clearly. We should never let ourselves be obsessed by the sheer scale of phenomena, for there is always a simple explanation for them. So much so, in fact, that we often wonder if that is really all there is to it. Yes, it is, and in the case of Stalin it probably was. No doubt we must also take into account the state of the Soviet economy and Soviet society if we really want to understand the circumstances in which he reached the high point of a power that few other men have achieved. But totemic leaders have not only flourished and undergone changes since he arrived on the scene. Nor was he anything new in either the socialist movement or the Soviet Union. He has had a great and equal number of heirs and imitators there, and despite everything that has been written on the subject in recent years, I do not think we have seen the last of the phenomenon.

The double nature of the two kinds of leaders remains to be illustrated in other historical milieux.[1] The important thing is not that it exists, for anything can be divided by two, or that the contrasts are those that I have described. What is fundamental is that it comes from the basic prohibition on making a man into a god who shapes both history outside us and the most personal ego in us.

# PART IX

# Secular religions

---

## 1. *The secret of a religion*

---

I

SO FAR, we have considered leaders as men possessed of charisma, defining them as a combination of two characters in a single person, the shadow of both the founding father and the heroic son. But the shadows are attached to a doctrine, an aim that they have set out to achieve. That much is clear, even if the explanation provided of it is surprising.

On the one hand, mass psychology has shown that leaders can only complete their mission if they recruit individuals who are temporarily detached from their usual group. They are the embryo of a crowd and are subject to the leader's ascendancy over them, which turns their encounter into a stable form of organisation. Tarde, and to an even greater extent Freud, boldly recognised that the Church and the army are the model for any crowd of that kind. In a society like our own, which is no longer governed by family, local and aristocratic tradition, political parties perform the function of both. In brief, parties are both the churches and the armies of the age of the crowd, and that is why in every party, church or army there is a crowd struggling to get out. The worst fear any political, military or religious leader can know is that his organisation might return to the crowd state as a result of some mistake on his part. This fear is greater than his fear of defeat or even of rebellion, since a crowd is the antithesis of an army or the Church, being a collection of people united not by discipline but by mood or tradition and a prey to powerful and contagious emotions that can cause it to disintegrate. Soldiers or party members are extremely scornful of those leaders, such as Gamelin, Kerensky, Cadorna and many others, whose army or party has fallen apart in their hands. The common characteristic of all such artificial crowds and the thing that shows they are in good health is always and everywhere a system of beliefs. It is the cement that holds them together and enables them to mobilise men even to the extent of asking them to lay down their lives. Without such a system, no leader could found and rule a party of the kind his mission necessitates. This is because the masses are only moved by a belief, and a belief does not exist without the masses. That is precisely why, in our times, the prophet has become the archetypal leader. The simple fact is that he has to be able to create a strong faith in those around him.

Religion is the prime example and the most complete form of a system of beliefs. Influenced by science, men turned away from transcendental religion at the precise moment when political demi-gods were presenting it in a new form to gather followers around them and mobilise the masses. Gramsci sums up this development when he says that the modern version of *The Prince* will have to contain an important section devoted to the question of moral and intellectual reform, that is, to the question of religion or world outlook (Gramsci, 1953: 8). It is clear that the masses cannot live beneath an empty heaven.

## II

I am talking, of course, of a secular religion, which proposes neither a god nor life eternal, one which atheists can subscribe to. Each nation has created one for itself. It is of course precisely as religions that the various socialist visions exalt and raise the oppressed masses. Their actions imply the 'madness of faith' that Zola spoke of in *Germinal*. They all have their dogmas, their sacred texts that command obedience and their heroes reminiscent of the saints.

Secular religions of this kind also meet certain psychic needs, such as the need for certainty and the regression of individuals in the crowd, but nothing else. They are never based on a so-called religious sense inherent in human nature, nor do they ever reckon on the intervention, even in a hidden form, of a divine being in the affairs of men. Indeed, the opposite is rather the case, for they claim to be based on various entities – nature, history, the fatherland, industry and so on – which are supposed to govern our destiny in an objective way. Basically, we see them as able to mobilise human beings by appealing to their attachment to either values (liberty, justice, the revolution and the like) or communities (the French, the workers and so on) for 'religion is an immense power which has the strongest emotions of human beings at its service' (Freud: XXII, 161).

They permeate mass society, becoming the substance of human life and the energy of an empty belief without which everything slowly dies. The idea of them was one of the discoveries of the French Revolution, and Robespierre was the first to see them as a powerful way of regenerating a nation and an instrument enabling him to make the Republic replace the monarchy completely. Secular celebrations of Reason and the Supreme Being crowned the discovery.

Let us look closely at such religions,[1] ignoring their more spectacular manifestations, which have already been described. What purposes do they serve? The first is that they create a total view of the world as a palliative to the fragmentary and divided nature of all science and technology and indeed of knowledge in general. There is a deep and basic human need to fit everything that we experience as incompatible and inexplicable into a meaningful whole. If we no longer have simple principles of a single kind that can explain what is happening in and around us, we feel threatened or – and this is perhaps the awful truth – powerless in the face of economic forces, psychic problems and the mass of uncontrolled events. This lack of coherence stops us taking part in any definable social action. There is no possible order or security for individuals in a society with more questions than answers.

It is true that the scientist or technologist can come to terms with this fragmentation and accept the constant oscillation between contradictory solutions and the uncertainty of ephemeral truths. In everyday life, however, we reject it. We need solid certainties and unchanging truths, for they alone enable us to control present forces and form plans for the future. We need an overall view with a single cause (social class, race etc.) a universal principle (the class struggle, natural selection and so on) and a definite picture of the human and non-human world. What secular religions essentially do is provide us with a total view of that kind. They offer us a concept of the world in which every problem has its solution. This is what liberal or nationalist political philosophies do, and even what Marxist theory does since it has, according to Freud, in Soviet Russia 'constructed a *Weltanschauung*, consistent and self-contained to an unparalleled degree, and alarmingly like the one it opposes' (Freud: XXII, 161).

It can be said that the constant progress of modern science has, by constantly making them more fragmented and by vastly increasing the number of unanswerable questions, driven God from the human mind. At the same time, it has made it more important, useful and necessary to have a view of the world that keeps only the vocabulary, arguments and images of science and combines them in new ways as the need arises. But there is a basic difference. All transcendental religions offer a concept of the physical world, explain the origin of the universe and predict its future. Secular religions, however, are centred around a view of the social world, explain the origin of society (nation, race, class and so on) and minutely describe the stages it will go through before a perfect and hopefully permanent state is reached. This change is probably explicable in terms of the development I have just mentioned, that is that we have driven the idea of divinity out of nature and it has taken refuge in society.

The second function of secular religions is to harmonise relationships between the individual and society and to reconcile the social and antisocial tendencies present in the former. It achieves this by substituting interior for exterior forces and replacing the constraints enforced by crude repression with those of the individual conscience. That demands patient effort and is the work of civilisation itself. It means that from the attachment to a human being and consent to his wishes, the same things can be obtained as were formerly procured by threats and violent domination. As we know, its only *modus operandi* is identification. As Freud tells us, the alternative is obvious.

We have seen that a community is held together by two things: the compelling force of violence and the emotional ties (identifications is the technical name) between its members. (Freud: XXII, 208)

Such attachments can no doubt be brought about in many ways, by the kinship system, for example, by belonging to a military corps or a profession and so on, but in mass society all these have lost their prestige and hence their effectiveness. Only religions (and their missionary groups) can still produce them, because they urge individuals to an inner acceptance of what society asks of them. In a more general way, they both take account of and deal with the fears that every individual has in connection with his physical self, sickness and death, and also his work and the injustice he is subject to in material life. Religions recognise the striving for happiness and the need of protection that everyone feels from his earliest years. They paint the darkest possible picture of the forces threatening human beings and then propose a solution. They show men how and why a limpidly clear and safe world, where there is no sickness, no conflicts or classes in society, no hatred, no masters and no gods, will one day come.

They are therefore religions of hope. They guarantee that men will emerge from torment victorious for ever if only they will identify with an ideal that goes beyond them and obey the rules they prescribe. This means that they can propose a scale of values making a clear distinction between two categories of actions, thoughts and emotions, the permitted and the forbidden. If they respect these rules, all individuals will avoid the conflicts that could set them at odds with society. They lose the burden of choice and avoid the risk of straying from the communal straight and narrow path, and this spares them a great deal of mental and moral suffering. Religion, Freud observes, 'restricts this play of choice and adaptation, since it imposes equally on everyone its own path to the acquisition of happiness and protection from suffering' (Freud: XXI, 84). And this means that it can reconcile things that are irreconcilable. It gives a social significance to individual existence, an aim to a life that can only acquire one if it renounces its desires and sees its own reality through the eyes of others, the eyes of the collective super-ego, which then becomes part of the individual, who obeys it.

Recognising these two functions of secular religions – proposing a concept of the social world and seeing individuals and the collective as one and the same thing – does not mean that we are advocating them or that we are learning something new about them. We had to clarify our ideas, however.

## III

They have a third and primordially important function, that of hiding a mystery. Every religion has its own. In its name it imposes rules and proclaims truths it does not explain. Indeed, it clouds the reasons for them and hides them so well that no-one can detect them. Everything is arranged so that there will be no chance contact and all things work together to make sure that the secret thus hidden from the mass of the faithful will not be revealed. The secret sometimes has a benevolent and sometimes a malevolent aspect. Only extraordinary circumstances call for it to be revealed, and the man who reveals it has to expiate his sin and sometimes even to pay for it with his life, as was the case with the Greek mathematician who divulged the secret of the right-angled triangle, which had been jealously guarded by the Pythagorean sect. In such circumstances, the whole body of believers seems a prey to violent emotions and overcome by a panic out of all proportion to what is at stake.

We can say that most artificial crowds (armies, churches, parties) are in touch with a mystery of that kind. They have a whole range of ceremonies, emblems and passwords (one need only think of the freemasons) that protect it and attack any attempt to reveal it. It serves to justify the hierarchy. The individual who rises in it comes closer to the sacred point that others remain distant from. What gives it its importance and prohibitory power? Why should the risk that it might be revealed set off such violent reactions?

We could suggest a social cause, self-defence in the face of a hostile environment, enemies and persecutors. Most social movements have experienced persecution of that kind, and their existence has been to some degree clandestine. The early Christians in the catacombs are an example of a struggle to survive in a hostile atmosphere, for they endured martyrdom as a testimony to their faith and refused to disclose their tie and whom it bound. This means that the secret concerns faith, for love of which human beings are ready to suffer the worst tortures. It is true that every movement from Christianity to socialism still has the traces of a fear of danger from the outside, that of discovery, and from the inside, that of betrayal. They continue to behave as if they all belonged to the same kind of society, a secret one. Such characteristics are still visible in our own times in many parties, in the Church and masonic-type societies. The features are those of a secret society slotted into an open one (Simmel, 1908).

There is an element of truth in that view, but it does not explain why this secret understanding still persists when the double danger has disappeared or why reactions are still excessive when what had been so carefully concealed has been divulged. In such cases, it is as if the ground on which history is built is about to open up and swallow the whole social or political edifice. Telling the secret seems such a disturbing possibility that even when it is partly known, it is still tacitly ignored. We have recently seen this in the way Communist parties have dealt with the revelation of the cult of Stalin. Even when Khrushchev had decided to break the enforced silence, he did no more than widen the circle of those knowing the secret. For the great mass of party members and the Soviet people, nothing had happened. He declared that the question of the cult of personality needed serious attention, that not a word of it must reach the outside world, and that the press in particular was not to be told of it. That was why the matter was to be examined in closed meetings of the Congress (Lazitch, 1976: 150).

Everything was arranged so that the recognition of errors and deadly lies should not break the wall of silence and that the existence of the report should itself remain a mystery. Hence the meetings behind closed doors, the silence in the press, with information limited to inner circles and members of the Congress forbidden to take notes or pass on reports of the meeting to outsiders. This was the case to such an extent that when a member of the Central Committee asked him whether the report was genuine or not, Maurice Thorez was able to reply that in his view it did not exist and would soon never have existed (Robrieux, 1975: 466).

## IV

The reader is perhaps by now inclined to think that I have some strange illusions about the ability of crowd psychology to explain these strange general phenomena. He will soon see that his fears are not groundless. Everything we have said flows largely from the available historical and sociological data, but that does mean that he should not follow us along a different path that other data might one day justify. Without such intellectual adventures there would be no astronomy, cosmology or chemistry. You will not be surprised to learn that the purpose of this warning is to prepare the way for a return to the hypothesis of the totemic cycle started by the murder of the original father. But every time we come back to it, we approach it from a different angle and a different starting-point.

If the enslaved victims of paternal repression rebelled, it must have been because they began to create, with the help of their experience, a vision of a better society. We can suppose that it was egalitarian in intention and allowed of a reasonably open morality. If it was to be set up, however, the brothers had to conspire. The means by which they would gain their freedom was the murder of the tyrant. It is not difficult to imagine the situation, for all regicides, parricides and even sometimes genocides are similar to each other.

What happened afterwards? According to Freud, the conspirators were torn by remorse and fear and decided to make their victim a god in the hope of removing all traces of their crime. But perhaps their remorse was an excuse for turning themselves into gods and a way of becoming successors rather than usurpers, of legitimising themselves, in short. They disguised a violent death as a natural one. We should remember that crying 'The king is dead, long live the king!' is often another and more diplomatic way of saying that he has been murdered, long live his murderers. On the basis of these and other factors, an observation can be suggested. By definition, all religions are created by conspiring sons and not by founding fathers. The former have psychic and political reasons for weaving a web of illusions about the origin of the new society and their own part in it.

What was the subsequent effect of the crime? It created a double social tie between the brothers. Let me explain. In the first place, they renounced sexual relationships with their mothers and sisters and com-mitted themselves to respecting the rights of all and setting up suitable institutions. Secondly, we must remember that they were partners in crime. Their conspiracy tied them all to a shared secret, which they would only refer to in guarded terms and in certain places, for fear of reviving painful memories and letting out the facts of what had happened. As Freud writes,

Society was now based on complicity in the common crime; religion was based on the sense of guilt and the remorse attaching to it; while morality was based partly on the exigencies of this society and partly on the penance demanded by the sense of guilt. (Freud: XIII, 146)

There is a blind spot in every society as there is in the human eye. In both cases, it is hard to locate it. We now know that in society it has the shape of a plot or conspiracy originally entered into to reverse the order of things and crowned by a frightful crime which its perpetrators themselves find unbearable. Without the fear and bloodshed, their crime would have been pointless and would never have marked both an end and a beginning. Once it had been committed, the conspirators were bound together by their complicity. That, rather than interests or laws governing association, is what holds the members of society together. A plot of that kind, which persists because it has to be hidden, is perhaps also the basis of all institutions.

Having made these two sets of observations, we can end this chapter quickly. Religions are created by 'sons', the successors of the founding father of a people or a given society. Their function is both to exculpate and legitimise the conspirators by disguising their crime to such an extent that no-one any longer sees them as its authors.

The main point, however, seems to me to be that by hiding the traces of crime and conspiracy, religions maintain, re-establish and celebrate the link between the conspirators and perpetuate the connivance latent in legal society. This is because nothing holds men closer together than complicity in a series of crimes of which no individual wants to be seen as guilty. Talking of what is known and revealing what is hidden would mean arousing the brothers' anger, risking exclusion and losing them for ever. Silence thus becomes a proof of group solidarity, and everyone refrains from telling the truth in order to remain in the community. A religion is needed to give it a meaning and to justify the sacrifice of reason. It makes silence the sign of perfect connivance between men who might be called blood brothers and who are united by the formula *Credimus quia absurdum*. The truth would bring anxiety and discord. Only a shared faith can stifle it.

## 2. *The prohibition of thought*

I

WE SHALL NOW TURN to an example from our own times to give these reflections a more concrete quality. It must not be supposed that they are only relevant to the religions of the past and have no connection with the present age. We can use the Russian Revolution as an illustration here. Once it had taken place, everyone thought that the new socialist society would have no hidden places and, unlike previous ones, would allow everyone to read the book of truth. Everyone would be able to consult it, examine the facts and give his opinion. This was probably to ignore historical experience and crowd psychology.[1]

Very soon, of course, a device for hiding events and the real relationships between the ruling echelons came into being. It also involved the masses of those supporting the party in actions which even in their eyes were sometimes criminal, such as arrests, torture and assassinations. If at the same time Marxism was already acquiring the characteristics of a secular religion still associated with science, it was because it was now becoming necessary to ensure that complicity was universal and the movement was, in its relationship with society, impermeable to scrutiny. Let us pass over the judgements that can be or have been made on this development and have the wisdom to remember that the greatest undertakings, those that have had the deepest effect on human beings, offer a wealth of unedifying details if we look at them closely, including injustice, cruelty, selfish passions and even cowardice.

In the events we are concerned with, the notorious Moscow trials of 1936–1938 were perhaps the major turning-point. They demonstrated a plot against the new society, and hence against the party, to divulge secrets that should have remained hidden. The way they were organised recreated a number of stock figures. On the one hand there were the traitors, who had to expiate their sins, and on the other the faithful guardians of the mystery, the heroes of the Revolution. The due legal forms and the language used were aimed at rousing popular fear and hatred of the enemy within. The arguments were not concerned with truth and falsehood, but with what hides those questions, good and evil and the perpetual conflict between them. The Chinese philosopher Lao-tse was well aware of this. 'If a man wishes to know the whole truth,' he wrote, 'he should not concern himself with good and evil. The conflict between them is the sickness of the mind.'

For a considerable period of time, the trials turned the political universe into a religious one, since the actors were called upon to confess a fault and call for its expiation by the innocent. In his own way, each participant was a martyr to a cause, whether he was accusing himself of a crime he did not commit or accusing someone else of imaginary ones to safeguard the shared values of a revolution that they had carried out together. Some would speak of a majestic sacrifice, others of dreadful repression. But why did the accused confess? What were they afraid of? Neither police brutality nor the death penalty, as has sometimes been claimed.

All of them – Bukharin, Kamenev, Zinoviev and others – had experienced prison and exile, and some of them torture. In the courts of tsarist Russia, they had become ferocious accusers and transformed a legal trial into a political one. Now, they knew that they had no hope of gaining clemency from their accusers by denouncing themselves. They knew that the accusations against them were lies and that they had been arrested for nothing. From the beginning to the end of the trial, neither they nor anyone else asked what these veterans of the Revolution were guilty of.

The nature and composition of the tribunal set up to judge these participants in history are still obscure. There was always an unspoken understanding that the accused were guilty, but more of being what they were than of doing what they had done. And the verdict, on their very existence rather than their so-called crimes, could only be radical, as if they had been judged by a god. It was of course a death-sentence. Necessity, rather than truth, lay behind it. If the accused were afraid of anything, it was of not playing their part properly, of divulging what ought to be kept hidden or of compromising a party they had created and to which they were attached by every fibre of their being.

In other words, they were all fettered by a group and doctrinal solidarity that was simply complicity. Everyone was held by each of his fellows; no-one was his own master any longer. Even when they had come through it and were in exile, the condemned men still thought that 'the Party that was excommunicating, imprisoning, and beginning to murder us, remained our Party, and we still owed everything to it: we must live only for it, since only through it could we serve the Revolution. We were defeated by Party patriotism: it both provoked us to rebel and turned us against ourselves' (Serge, 1963: 245).

If a Bukharin, a Radek, a Zinoviev and a thousand other

supernumeraries did conspire, it was not with Hitler, capitalism or some intelligence department, as the trial papers claimed, but with their jailers, their brothers and long-time acolytes, the Stalins, Molotovs and Vyshinskis. They participated in a scenario that was intended to hide a truth that they knew well, a hindered, reticent, remorseful truth, paralysed by scruples and the pangs of conscience. When these old revolutionaries were called police spies, cunning traitors, the dregs of humanity and lubricious vipers, they went further, assured others and themselves of their fidelity and unimpaired solidarity. One historian said that, at the Moscow trials, there had been a prolonged rift among the Communists which had arisen from their horror at the methods of Stalin's government and their fundamental solidarity with Stalin's regime (Deutscher, 1961). Opting for the latter choice gave them the strength to debase themselves and drag themselves through the mud of a history they had entered with clean hands and heads held high and from which they emerged degraded and permanently soiled.

The effect of their confessions, however, was to create a shared major secret, that of the Revolution and the origins of the new society. The very high degree of improbability in the statements of the judges and prosecuting counsel showed just how arbitrary and distorted their revelations concerning these origins were. Once this had been confirmed by those who had been the architects of the Revolution and accepted by a stunned party, they took on all the force of a truth confirmed by the connivance of those chiefly involved. All these trials (of a nature not exclusive to the Soviet Revolution) turned conspiracy, which had previously been directed against outside force, namely the hated imperial order, into something directed inwards, against the party and the society that had emerged from it.

At the same time, clandestinity and secrecy as a device for protection against enemies and traitors became a means of defence against oneself, one's friends and the faithful. Everyone was afraid of being betrayed by the truth rather than of betraying it. Before the Revolution, truth had been repressed and forbidden. After it, it was something to which any recourse was eschewed, just as before they rebelled, the father forbade his sons to have incestuous relationships with the women in the group and after it they maintained the situation by banning incest. The trials really marked a special area within which everything was to remain secret and unknown. All those who kept it inviolate became accomplices in the conspiracy. The party leaders guarding it and the intellectuals brought in to justify it were caught up in a spiralling complicity of which the first circle was that of the parricides, regicides and deicides that mark the beginning of any history.

Through the mass public trials they showed how eager they were to draw the whole people into it. Newspapers and loudspeakers broadcast the accusations across the length and breadth of the land, the streets, factories and barracks echoed to cries of 'Death to the traitors!' and 'Stamp out the snakes!' There had never been such an awareness and knowledge of just how unconvincing the charges were, and that awareness and knowledge had never gone so unheeded. The vehemence with which the people applauded, the depths of their veneration, the fact that socialist revolutionaries and party leaders could accept and ultimately idolise men, and more particularly the man Stalin who imposed on them as a truth the absence and neglect of truth, would be a miracle in individual psychology.

But to mass psychology it is quite to be expected, for all such events are part of the logic of re-establishing a mystery concerned with the part played by those who have fomented a revolt against the despotic power of the father they have identified with and the nature of the indissoluble tie they have created by their joint striving towards that end. The mystery is maintained by sacrificing designated victims, made to look like traitors, in atonement. In addition, the tie that unites them is periodically strengthened and extended by their part in the whole pretence.

The trials were perhaps one of the most intense moments of the Marxist passion, since they stamped a leaden seal over the origins of the Revolution and made that particular period into a black hole in the collective memory. This completed the break between doctrine and the scientific study of history, which was no longer to be a search for a now forbidden truth. It was to assume all the consistency of a system of beliefs with the past forgotten and its fictitious reconstitution in public places as its dogmas. All the images surfacing in the feverish atmosphere of the times and the value of unquestioning obedience were included in it. This acceptance of doctrine necessarily became an act of faith.

There was clearly nothing surprising in the fact that it was very like a religion in which parties played a missionary role, a twofold religion with two societies in it, those who shared the secret and those who did not. Nor is it surprising that the same parties seem to deny it and even to give an objective explanation of it. For such parties may make history, but they do not know the history they are making or all the forces shaping them. We, however, do not have the same excuse. Over the last ten years, the mass of facts at our disposal has increased and the scales have fallen from all eyes. The reasons for the conduct of those who led the blind are disappearing one by one. These striking scenes from world history are strangely consonant with the principles of crowd psychology, so much so, in fact, that the latter seem to have been produced to fit them, and it would be tempting to reject them as tailor-made if they had not been formulated much earlier.

## II

Those who gave the expected verdicts a standing ovation and those who accepted the confessions all knew that the former were inevitable and the latter untrue. They all gave their approval to things that had been fought against for years: torture, executions, corrupt judges and corrupt courts. In addition, however, they were united in celebrating the birth of a new mystery that became the crux of their history and the instrument of power. In connection with it, there grew up a prohibition which is to a Church or religion what the forbidding of incest is to the family and marriage, that is, its very basis. I mean the prohibition of thought. It did not betoken a censorship of truth or free rein for illusion and deceit. It was an interdict on the primacy of reason in the mental life of crowds. How, asks Freud in wonder, 'can we expect people who are under the dominance of prohibitions of thought to attain the psychological ideal, the primacy of the intelligence?' (Freud: XXI, 48).

Historically, the demands made by a prohibition on thought have always been almost intolerable. For thousands of years there has been constant documentary evidence of rebellions and spasmodic returns to former freedoms. Marx must have turned in his grave when men with his name constantly on their lips not only did not return to those liberties but also renewed the prohibition and made his ideas the opium of the people. It was not that they wanted to avoid errors in methods of explanation in the future. If there is no error and no-one ever goes astray or gets caught up in it, the truth will never be discovered. For those proscribing it, however, error becomes a crime because it means breaking the taboo. For that, millions of men have been condemned to death in the name of a truth that can only be illusory.

This does not mean that logic then becomes powerless, but it does mean that it is made to serve another end more powerful than itself: faith. It is as if the cycle starting with an affective, empirical utopian socialism moved through a phase of intellectual, theoretical socialism and then on to one of a religious and entirely political and social nature. The pattern, which seems to repeat others, has been described by Freud in these words:

Thus we are faced by the phenomenon that in the course of the development of humanity sensuality is gradually overpowered by intellectuality and that men feel proud and exalted by every such advance. But we are unable to say why this should be so. It further happens later on that intellectuality itself is overpowered by the very puzzling emotional phenomenon of faith. Here we have the celebrated *'credo quia absurdum'*, and, once more, anyone who has succeeded in this regards it as a supreme achievement. (Freud: XXIII, 118)

Let us try for a moment to imagine why, using our main hypothesis, which gives us a certain amount of elbow-room if we refer to the murder of the primitive father. In order to deal with the most urgent problem, the sons accepted both really and inwardly the incest taboo he imposed on them. They learned to renounce their instincts, and not only their sexual ones. The primacy of the senses gave way to that of the mind and intelligence needed to idealise or sublimate them. Subsequently, however, they had to hide the murder by making a god of the father and concealing their own crime. This was demanded by their real solidarity: they had been accomplices in crime and went on to be, so to speak, accessories after the fact. To do that, they forbade both themselves and the clan to think of their crime, asking the latter to accept the totemic fiction in its place.

This abandonment of truth thus seems to lie at the root of the movement from intellectuality to faith and from knowledge to belief. The fact that they had accepted such a sacrifice for the sake of the unity of the tribe (or that of the Church or the army or the party today) gave the individuals concerned a feeling of pride that made martyrdom preferable to adjuration. The victims of the Moscow trials were in some degree exemplary. Such a refusal to accept what is obvious to the intelligence is possible and even necessary.

It would seem that renouncing the instincts is the lynch-pin of transcendental religions and that renouncing truth and thought is specific to secular ones. If the conjecture is right, it is easy to see why the prohibition on thought is the negative aspect – because it rules out all questions, all reflection and all searching – of the phenomenon of which *credo quia absurdum* is the positive one. I see it as positive to the extent that by zealously adhering to a declaration formulated on behalf of absolutely everyone and taking as rational and proven what is certainly neither, we help preserve our collectivity and our place within it. If, as Heidegger said, the axiom on which science is based is that we should never believe anything, as everything needs proving, then religion is based on the opposite one that we must always believe everything, as nothing needs proving. Freud saw the danger of this, warning us that 'The prohibition against thought issued by religion to assist in its self-preservation is also far from being free from danger either for the individual or for human society'[2] (Freud: XXII, 171).

I am not venturing to suggest that the examples I have used in this chapter – which a great many competent scholars have investigated –

prove all these aspects of crowd psychology, or even less explain them. It would be wrong to see them as any more than illustrations of ideas, just as one might use slides, films or drawings to illustrate notions which would otherwise remain abstract and bloodless. But there are also ideas which are compelling because of their power of mere deduction. If it is true that every religion obeys a prohibition on thought, then each religion must follow the logical pattern of the 'as if', that is, the pattern of our illusions. From the moment men obey it, they are obliged to act as if the world of fictions and conventions were ultimate reality, as if they were responsible for their own actions or for those ascribed to them, as if the innocent were guilty when in fact each of them could say to his accuser what Tiresias replied to Oedipus: 'You who accuse me and believe yourself to be innocent, you – oh miracle! – are the guilty one. The man you are hounding is merely yourself.'

That kind of logic provides solutions to the questions that everyone is asking and presents unilateral interpretations of events, using a basis of carefully selected facts and ignoring the rest. Yet it has no hesitation in giving them a general application, as if they were based on carefully-scrutinised and impartial data. It uses vague and ambiguous words with both an exoteric and an esoteric meaning which conceal and reveal their sense at the same time. These are communicated to the masses by the appropriate experts, and those masses are induced to react in a stereotyped way. Of this kind of logic, Freud says:

This asserts that our thought-out activity includes a great number of hypotheses whose groundlessness and even absurdity we fully realize. They are called 'fictions', but for a variety of practical reasons we have to behave 'as if' we believed in these fictions. This is the case with religious doctrines because of their incomparable importance for the maintenance of human society. This line of argument is not far removed from the *'credo quia absurdum'*. (Freud: XXIII, 28–9)

# 3. *The cult of the father*

I

I
N ALL SECULAR – and political – religions the same implicit but major
idea is at work. Both the unity and the actions of the mass depend on a
universal complicity in a mystery that marks it out and cements its
identity. Truth lies outside and perhaps even above the jurisdiction of
reason. What gives a free rein to internal rivalries and dissensions in
parties or nations is not the existence of the complicity but a slackening of
it, for the latter encourages individuals to withdraw from society and
weakens their faith in collective beliefs.

In the last chapter, we saw that the *form* of such beliefs, their internal
logic, is determined by the need to hide the complicity from the lower
strata of society. I now go on to say that, in the light of the totemic
hypothesis, their *content* is dependent on two phenomena: the divinisa-
tion of the father and the resurrection of his *imago*. He is transformed into
a true god of the masses, becomes infallible and legendary and protects
them as they prostrate themselves before him. At the same time, he gives
new life to all the attachments and identifications current in the past and
remembered with poignancy and nostalgia. De Gaulle resurrected not
only Napoleon, but all the kings of France, and to such an extent that
there was a fear, mixed with a touch of hope in certain quarters, that he
was restoring the monarchy.

There is perhaps no need to repeat that during this process of turning
the father into a god, one of the fraternal conspirators separates himself
from the others, takes the father's place and assumes his charisma. To the
people, however, the two men are one, a living and a dead leader united
in one person. The result is strange. In a complex and technically and
economically advanced society, it is surprising to see that one man takes
on such stature, since what he is doing is bringing back to life the
elementary prototype of the leader surrounded by an admiring crowd
which thinks that it has his love. A blueprint for the cult of the individual,
in fact.

We have been mistaken in trying to account for the phenomenon in
terms of his monopoly of state power. In many Asian and Latin-American
countries there are absolute military dictatorships in which the masses do

not venerate the leader or share his beliefs. We were even more mistaken when we saw it as the work of political terror carried out by the party and the police in unison. That explanation ignores the fact that power was conceived in a relatively democratic way and takes no account of the spread of the cult of Stalin far beyond the borders of the Soviet Union, for example. Khrushchev's view of Stalin was correct:

I will give Stalin credit for one thing: he didn't simply come with a sword and conquer our minds and bodies. No, he demonstrated his superior skill in subordinating and manipulating people – an important quality necessary in a great leader.                                                        (Khrushchev, 1971: 6)

Seen in the light of mass psychology, the cult is a link in the process of changing a theory (Marxism, for example) into a view of the world with all the strength of a faith, that is, into a secular religion. It is only incidentally the cult of a particular man, such as Stalin or Mao. Wherever religion has spread and taken possession of a nation, this type of cult has reappeared at regular intervals. Most observers – and Khrushchev in particular – have seen the link between the two things:

A personality cult is a little like a religion. For centuries people have been droning, 'Lord, have mercy upon us; Lord, help and protect us.' And have all the prayers helped? Of course not. But people are set in their ways and continue to believe in God despite all the evidence to the contrary.                     (Khrushchev, 1971: 271)

God or the father. We should note at once that the cult, which can take many different forms, is first and foremost a cult of fatherhood, celebrating the fathers of the Church, the father of the nation, the father of the Party, and so on. Was not Stalin called the beloved father of the Soviet peoples? The splendour the leader surrounds himself with, the artificial brilliance of the ceremonies organised around his person and his inordinate right to every title and privilege serve to emphasise the fact that he is the deified father. There is no doubt that he influences the life of the masses. Tito's former companion Djilas writes that his luxuries illustrated how he subjugated the party and introduced the cult of universal adulation of his personality (Djilas, 1981: 96).

We must accept that the cult, which comes into being and persists against all reason, is in practical terms very similar to the famous *credo quia absurdum*. It may weaken and lose its appeal for a time, but the soil it is rooted in and will one day thrive again in is kept well watered and weeded.

## II

The cult of the individual grows as the distance between the mentality of the individual (i.e. the leader) and that of the masses increases. Let us take our hypothesis a little further. After a long period of uniformity and complete equality, the relationships between the brothers deteriorate. One of them sets himself up as a special individual with his own particular qualities such as self-esteem, the ability to endure conflict, a dominating gaze and so on. From the very earliest times, such men have served a myth or belief to that end, for myth, in Freud's words, is 'the step by which the individual emerges from group psychology' (Freud: XVIII, 136).

For the group, religion – or its precursor, myth – is a device to secure uniformity, but for the individual it is the means of achieving liberation. There have always been two dominant factors whenever it has been created. The first tends towards *deifying* the father in the strict sense of the word. This is achieved by raising his person above the ordinary human level and putting it beyond all judgement. No criticism of his teaching is permitted. He becomes a totally non-material figure, immortal, legendary, perfect and infallible. The instigators of this process are the sons who have conspired. They surround the father with pious sentiments and revere him as if he were still amongst them. Even before he becomes immortal, he has a place amongst those who have created peoples and beliefs, in the Pantheon in the minds of the masses, and is the object of a cult that was no concern of his while he was alive. 'The primal father of the horde was not yet immortal, as he later became by deification' (Freud: XVIII, 124).

When there is such a change of nature and an individual is transformed into a great man, it is hard to say, in the long run, whether he ever was a real historical figure. In the case of Marx, Lenin, Napoleon and Mao, we are sure – for a time, at least – that they actually were. Christ, Moses or Lao-tse are more problematic. In recent times we have had examples of such things occurring. Lenin is a useful one.

During his lifetime, he was recognised by those close to him, his companions and disciples, as one of the leaders of the party and the Russian Revolution, and that is also how he saw himself. We know that he was against any glorification of himself, which was incompatible with Marxism, against blind obedience to his ideas, which was incompatible with science, and against absolute obedience, which was incompatible with democracy. The Russian revolutionary Clara Zetkin describes him as acting like one of a peer group to which he was attached by every fibre of his being. We also know that he scorned the trappings of power and all excessive servility. The Soviet poet Tvardovsky called him the man who hated ovations.

And yet he was barely cold in his coffin before there was a move to deify him. His written and spoken words were seen as containing an imperishable message. Their authority was such that not a single letter of them could be changed, for they were the definitive truth. They were invoked with solemnity and treated with respect. As regards the man himself, the words used to describe him belong to the vocabulary of legends and the images to that of religion. Everything that had touched him or that he had touched became a holy relic, except his will, dealing with his 'sons' and his successors. That passed into the domain of the collective mystery ruled by silence.

All the 'sons', the Bolshevik 'Old Guard' including Trotsky, Zinoviev, Bukharin etc. as well as Stalin, took part in the deification, responding to the same tragic desire to raise him above humble mortals. The way they celebrated him would have revolted him. When they embalmed him like an Egyptian pharaoh and declared him an idol of the Revolution, they were changing the man who had fought for a world without gods or masters into a god. The ceremony, Isaac Deutscher writes,

was calculated to stir the mind of a primitive, semi-oriental people into a mood of exaltation for the new Leninist cult. So was the Mausoleum in the Red Square, in which Lenin's embalmed body was deposited, in spite of his widow's protest and the indignation of many Bolshevik intellectuals.        (Deutscher, 1961: 269)

That was only one possible aim amongst many, however. They were all probably under some internal compulsion to disinter some ancient ceremony, and probably used it to impress themselves. They wanted to give free expression to their admiration for the man with whom they had identified during his lifetime (when that admiration had been repressed) and whom they had certainly feared. Lenin also died at the hands of an assassin, as unnaturally as the tsar himself, and the murder demanded reparation of an exceptional character and the removal of any trace of guilt that might have fallen on themselves. A weight of deep emotions was needed to make those hardened atheists treat the dead man like a god in the view of all the world and to let the public gaze on him as if he were still alive, as if waiting for his resurrection. *Mummification* is one of the strongest propensities of the mentality of the crowd (and if there are no mummies, statues and monuments are ready substitutes) precisely because it is a denial of the death of the admired being. It also shields his successors from the charge of killing him (which is often exactly what they have done) or of not having opposed the conspiracy against him vigorously enough. It is also a way of trying to prevent the disappearance of his *imago* and of capturing it for ever. A way, in short, of making his resurrection in the minds of future masses that much easier.

The language used to address the deified leader becomes codified as ceremonies are repeated. You know the kinds of phrases Stalin used and the liturgical tone he adopted when taking what amounted to a religious oath before Lenin's catafalque: 'On leaving us, comrade Lenin ordered us to keep the great title of member of the party pure and lofty. We swear to you, comrade Lenin, that we shall carry out your behest to the full . . .' and more in that vein.

When a god is created, a name is created too, linking party, Church and doctrine to a person and making them part of his immortal nature. Lenin, once he had moved from the world of mortal to the world of immortal beings, gave rise to a whole new onomastics. His name became a designation for everything. The Bolshevik Party, socialist theory, Marx's ideas and many other things all took his name. From that point on, joining the party and accepting its teaching meant becoming the servant of a demi-god, becoming a Leninist. 'He sealeth up the hand of every man,' we read in Job, 'that all men may know his work.'

Names also confer an identity and impose an identification, indicating which of the voices of the super-ego will be the dominant one. The bearer is grateful to the person conferring it, feeling himself to be a son of the great man, a member of his family. When it is applied to more or less everything and is on everyone's lips, it means that the great man is everywhere. Everyone is obliged to submit to everything originating from him. It is as if everything that exists bears his name and everything that bears his name exists. Lenin's was even more ubiquitous than most. No other twentieth-century figure has had such a profound effect on the consciousness of a people or changed a culture more visibly, even more than he changed society. And the man who wanted the impersonal rule of science and democracy to take the place of religion and heroes did not live to see the huge crowds processing past his catafalque, mentally baring their heads when his name was mentioned and sacrificing themselves to his cult. The deification of Lenin, which was at first something exceptional, has since become a procedure to spread a secular religion (and there are many examples of this, from Mao to Tito) just as canonisation helps to spread a transcendental one. There is no way to prevent what starts as a spontaneous creation and expresses an uncontainable urge from becoming a system.

**III**

What makes up the second process determining the content of a secular religion? It provides a *historiated* account of the conspiracy of the 'sons' and the pattern of events up to the point where one of them emerges from the group and takes the father's place. There is a real power-struggle. What is chiefly of interest here is which of the many possible forms it takes. According to the Oxford English Dictionary, 'historiated' means 'decorated with figures of men or animals', and that is the sense in which it should be understood here, except that the scenes are real and recreate the images of the past with exceptional vividness. The result is that in terms of the effects they produce, truth appears in the guise of fiction. The events that have been treated in this way may be incredible, but they bring the enthusiasm of millions to fever-pitch.

To come back to the cult of Lenin. His successors worshipped both his person and his ideas, and this tendency soon spread to those who had been his companions and then in turn to each of the party leaders. The Soviet historian Roy Medvedev describes in his *Let History Judge* how streets, factories, collective farms (the Rykov factory, the Bukharin tramway depot, etc.) and towns were named after them. In 1925, with the consent of the politburo, not only Leningrad and Stalingrad appeared on the map, but also towns such as Trotsk and Zinovievsk. At the end of the twenties, virtually every *oblast* and republic had its cult of a local leader.

At times of crisis and shifting rivalries, the mass of leaders perpetuate a climate of permanent anxiety that adds its effect to those of economic worries. One man with authority is felt to be more efficient than assemblies and deliberative bodies in terms of making things work smoothly and rapidly, taking decisions promptly and co-ordinating the general working of society. That is why the crowd feels bereft of a leader when he dies and begins to pine for him as children sometimes pine for an absent parent. The result is that one of the 'brothers' decides to take his place and is tempted to break their tacit agreement and reintroduce everything they had conspired to abolish. Writing about the events which ensue after the death of the parent, Freud states that the sense of deprivation which is felt eventually has the power to make one individual or another detach himself from the crowd and take on the role of the father. According to this view of things, the children undo all the work of the revolution, for when one of them decides to act in this way, he takes on himself the merits of all and eliminates them in order to remain in sole command.

The ten years after Lenin's death and deification saw both a more consolidated regime and the perfect flowering of the cult devoted to him.

Everyone had some share of his person, his name and even of his body. A typical poster of the time announced that everyone had a drop of his blood running in his veins. In the meantime, the man who intended to take his place had made himself known. His name was Stalin. As early as 1926, he announced in a closed meeting that there was a need to restore the rights of paternal authority, maintaining that in Russia, the land of the tsars, the people preferred to have a single man at the head of the state.

It would perhaps be disappointing to learn that Stalin was a sophisticated and mentally subtle man, for he was after all a great leader, which surely more or less rules out sophistication and subtlety. He could, however, gauge exactly what weight to give to the feelings and ideas of the masses and knew that if power of any kind was to have a firm basis, commands and ceremonies had to be of a type in accordance with what they believed.

He was tenacious and filled with his own ideas and took full advantage of the universal disorientation prevalent in a period of major social unrest to pick off his former comrades one by one, for they were now his competitors. He began with the greatest, Trotsky, and finished with the closest, Bukharin. During that whole period, he devoted himself to the detailed, thankless and bloody task of eliminating those who had seen the Revolution with their own eyes, which were still full of the images of those glorious October days. Individuals were repressed chiefly by wiping out their memory and destroying their identification with the party of revolution. The American historian Malia states that it was at this point that the regime firmly took shape.

At the same time, Stalin laid the guilt for the fictitious parricide on their shoulders in order to be able to demand an expiation of it. Writing on his orders, the author of an article in a journal of the time had no hesitation in claiming that Bukharin had been the instigator of and accomplice in the attempt on the life of the greatest genius of the human race, Lenin. These machinations made Stalin the one great *hero*. Of this archetypal figure, Freud writes:

It must remain uncertain whether there was a ringleader and instigator to the murder among the band of brothers who rebelled against the primal father, or whether such a figure was created later by the imagination of creative artists in order to turn themselves into heroes, and was then introduced into the tradition.
(Freud: XXIII, 135–6)

This was all the great orchestrator of the masses needed to be able to call his brothers, who were now presumptively guilty, filth and vermin. As a result of his propaganda, they had been transformed into a swarm of loathsome beetles and insects, like the characters in Kafka's stories. It is not too hard to believe that Stalin wanted to show that archaic mental structures are effective and recurring. Be that as it may, his own speeches and those given under his direction were full of the figures of sacred and profane mythology, aimed at separating the individual psyche from that of the crowd.

One such construct attributed individual guilt to a deed which could only have been performed by the entire tribe:

> The hero claims to have acted alone in accomplishing the deed, which certainly only the horde as a whole would have ventured upon. But, as Rank has observed, fairy tales have preserved clear traces of the facts which were disavowed. For we often find in them that the hero who has to carry out some difficult task (usually the youngest son, and not infrequently one who has represented himself to the father-substitute as being stupid, that is to say, harmless) – we often find, then, that this hero can carry out his task, only with the help of a crowd of small animals, such as bees or ants. These would be the brothers in the primal horde, just as in the same way in dream symbolism insects or vermin signify brothers and sisters (contemptuously considered as babies). (Freud: XVIII, 136)

It is a charming analogy, showing how one of the band of conspiring brothers took his revenge on the others and, by reducing them to the status of small animals, made them into mere Lilliputians in comparison with himself. At the same time, he took the credit for what they had done, uniting in his own living self all the virtues of those who were now dead. The expropriation was so blatant that a veteran of the Revolution wrote to Stalin accusing him of having used those he had murdered by taking all the credit for what they had done and achieved.

It is just possible to understand why he took their lives and made use of the fact that most people tacitly ignored what he was doing, for although no-one actively advocates a reign of terror, very few people rebel against it. But what is impossible to understand is the sight of all those men and women stripping themselves of their past and begging the forgiveness of the man who had taken its place, as if they too felt themselves to be guilty of murdering their father, at least in terms of his achievement. As Isaac Deutscher writes, 'But all those unfortunates on whom the limelight was turned appeared in sackcloth and ashes, loudly confessing their sins, calling themselves sons of Belial and praising *de profundis* the Superman whose feet were crushing them into the dust' (Deutscher, 1961: 373).

As they fell away and Stalin took the credit for all that they had achieved, his name ousted those of Trotsky, Bukharin and Zinoviev, as prominent and eye-catching as a winking light on a headquarters map. His status increased. As the single great man of the Revolution, he was doubly a usurper, for he had triumphed over both his comrades, the 'brothers', and Lenin, who had wanted to remove him from the succession. He declared himself the model that all should follow and obey like a father. The great Stalin, in fact. Such usurpations brought him no discredit, and indeed enhanced the trust he enjoyed. In a sense he took by force not only the life-histories of his victims, but also the affection the masses felt for them, and when that affection was left without an object, they directed it towards the new father-figure, the man who had put things back on their proper course. In his own words, the state was a family, and he was their father.

## IV

Once he was the only one of Lenin's companions left alive, Stalin turned Marxist theory into a total and hence powerful view of the world that offered simple formulas and explanations for almost everything. The major devices it used were firstly a canon of writings establishing principles and speeches describing how they should be applied and putting them into a definitive form of language. According to Djilas, this met 'a need, not only in the Soviet Party, but throughout International Communism as well, where his dull scholastic but easily assimilated compendium became very influential' (Djilas, *Encounter*, December 1979: 27).

The second device was rewriting the history of the Revolution and describing the working of history as a succession of conspiracies hatched by the old revolutionaries. The latter were depicted as fundamentally evil beings over whose machinations Stalin had triumphed and whom he had defeated in much the same way as Saint George killed the dragon. He created something like a demonology of traitors and enemies of the kind that no religious faith can survive without, traitors and enemies that he, Stalin, the hero, had defeated with the help of the masses who followed him. In an anonymous history of the Russian Communist Party it is explained that this battle against sceptical and indifferent elements, against Trotskyists, Zinovievists, Bukharinists and Kamenevists, enabled the power base of the party to find a means of achieving absolute unity after Lenin's death. Under Stalin's banner, this power base with its rallying call was to pull the Soviet people out of oblivion and to lead them forward to national industrialisation and rural collectivism. These largely fictitious labels and classifications and the 'fraternal' faction in the party and their role in the historical drama became an integral part of the body of accepted beliefs. Even when one corner of the veil was lifted, the historical leaders of the Revolution were still wicked men. The dead could not ask for justice, and the living dared not question the basis of the system or reveal the mystery it hid. A compromise was reached. There could be a silent forgiveness of the dead for the wrong done to them, provided that the living were not obliged to speak of it and break a prohibition stronger than themselves. What happened, in fact, was that all the revamping of history meant that Stalin was in a position to separate himself from the many and become the one who assumed the role of the father.

With that aim in view, he made sure that he was always and everywhere seen as the only man who had been at Lenin's side during the years of exile and at the worst point in the Revolution and the only one to have continued with his work after his death. Their names were linked in books, newspapers and films, and all others were excluded. In short, it was a case of Stalin as Lenin *redivivus*, back from the dead. Molotov described him as the man who worked with Lenin to build up the party, and Jaroslavski as the universal father. At every street corner, every time a new theme was introduced in a speech, on every streamer, the image of the dead father and his living successor was manifest. The master/disciple couple was a reincarnation of another legendary couple, Marx and Engels. Even in the Academy of Sciences, it was declared, with an unblushing disregard for verisimilitude, that from the end of the (eighteen!) nineties, Lenin and Stalin were to the development of the revolutionary movement of the new age . . . what Marx and Engels had been to the preceding one.

In order to engrave the sequence of revived images more firmly in the minds of the masses, Stalin produced a historiated version of the development of the movement and of socialism as if it were building up to the climax of his appearance, changing collective history into his own biography, that of a divine demiurge. It should not be surprising, Freud remarks, that most frequently

The lie of the heroic myth culminates in the deification of the hero. Perhaps the deified hero may have been earlier than the Father God and may have been a precursor to the return of the primal Father as a deity. (Freud: XXIII, 137)

From that point – about 1930 – onwards, Stalin was treated and could behave like an omniscient, omnipotent and infallible demi-god. It would be disheartening to quote texts and names proclaiming him to be such. They make him a true heir not only of Lenin, but also of the tsars in everything except the non-hereditary nature of his power. He gradually dissolved all egalitarian relationships, condemning them by declaring that the introduction of equality in the field of necessity and individual life was a petty-bourgeois absurdity. Above all, he brought back the authority he and his comrades had rebelled against. He acted as God the Father, with a whole hierarchy arranged in due order beneath him. The top party members were a privileged class; ordinary citizens were another but rather less brilliant one.

The fact that such an about-turn was possible and that it was scientific Marxist theory and not the extravagant vision contained in some archaic poetry that provided a pedestal for a great man and fed the faith that grew up around him proves how difficult it is to leave crowds out of any account of the life of societies. In this context, we talk thoughtlessly of deviations and historical errors and go on to say that by and large they have helped progress and reason to gain a little ground. To talk in that way is to forget that although it is always possible to reinterpret history, it is never possible to remake it. There is no guarantee that where the masses are involved things would happen any differently.

What we really observe is that those so-called errors or deviations have a stubborn habit of repeating themselves. This seems to indicate that they are part of some regular pattern, since, as the formula has it, the same causes produce the same effects. It is difficult to know whether they have really helped the cause of progress. Of the merits of Stalin and his imitators one can, I believe, say what an English historian said of Napoleon: 'He destroyed only one thing: the Jacobin Revolution, the dream of equality, liberty and fraternity, and of the people rising in its majesty to shake off oppression' (Hobsbawm, 1974: 76). We need only substitute 'Bolshevik' for 'Jacobin'.

## V

The cult of the father is associated with the birth of a secular religion. We can see that happening all around us. The Soviet writer Ehrenburg notes the fact in his memoirs, pointing out that from 1938 it was more exact to use the word 'cult' in its original religious sense, for in the minds of millions of human beings Stalin had been transformed into a mythical demi-god.

As I said I would, I have used such observations and historical material to illustrate the totemic hypothesis and its significance for crowd psychology. That discipline would see Stalin (or anyone else in his place) as important specifically in that he made the birth and spread of that religion possible. The necessity has been a cause for protest and has been seen as a survival. Attempts to find a cause have been fruitless. Perhaps our hypothesis provides us with the hidden reason. The means could have been different and better controlled by civil law, but the end would inevitably have been achieved.

If we follow what is by now a familiar path, we can suppose that socialism arrives from the outside, by way of a party and a leader prepared outside the destined recipients, by an Egyptian Moses, so to speak. We are talking, of course, of Lenin and his lieutenants. They revealed the theory and imposed it after a series of extraordinary events, of which the revolution was the main one. Also, once the Revolution was over and Lenin dead, the Russian people rejected the doctrine and the men who represented it. Once can even speak of a dilution of the party itself. This surface rejection, however, can be seen (still in terms of our hypothesis) as hiding its descent to the depths, its long route through crowd psychology. During that incubation period, it came into contact with other traditions, enmeshing itself with them and becoming one of them. At the end of its journey, it came back to the surface. It now demanded to be recognised from within and spread by a leader from within, a product of the mass itself, a Jewish Moses this time.

His task was to bring the party and the people back to the true teachings and to impose on them something that after its sojourn in the unconscious was now no longer a science but a vision of the world. In other words, he now had to ensure the primacy of faith instead of the previous primacy of reason or even spirituality. By inducing people to give up the latter, he enhanced their stature and gave them pride in their success. The person demanding the sacrifice, Stalin, inevitably became '. . . the remote, inaccessible ruler, the Life-giving Sun, the Father of all the two hundred millions of Soviet citizens, if not the totem whom the tribe considers as its forebear and with whom all the members of the tribe must feel themselves in a close personal relationship' (Deutscher, 1953: 51).

In the hands of its leader, the Soviet Union became a one-man show. From start to finish, authority was his alone and absolute. He was worshipped like a god, and the party and Soviet society (but they were not alone in this) became a quasi-religious community welded together by a common allegiance and a shared cult. When death showed him that only illusion was immortal, no-one dared lay claim to his place. Such is the common lot of charismatic leaders.

These conjectures about religious illusions and the observations preceding them should not lead us into the more dangerous illusion that they are necessarily valid. I should like to quote word for word what Freud wrote to Einstein in this connection:

It may perhaps seem to you as though our theories are a kind of mythology and, in the present case, not even an agreeable one. But does not every science come in the end to a kind of mythology like this? (Freud: XXII, 211)

Mass psychology has been subject to the pressure of the circumstances it grew up in and the problems it has had to resolve. It seems to me that, after all it has taught us during the present century, it deserves the most serious attention. There is, of course, a whole area of reality that lies outside its scope, but there is another area that it has made its own, one which decides now, as it has done in the past, the success or failure of a party or an idea. That means that its methods and explanations are of the greatest concern both to men of action and men of science. As a general rule, when there is no contradiction between life and theory, it is better to reflect on theory, which is richer. Where there is a contradiction, it is better to reflect on life, which is more certain. As far as mass psychology is concerned, we must reflect now on the one and now on the other, for as Homer tells us, one thinks under the pressure of harsh necessity.

# Conclusion: The planetary age of the crowd

PSYCHOLOGY discovered the energy in crowds at the time when physics was discovering the energy in atoms. Their influence on historical events has been of a similar order of magnitude. I could go on giving an account of hypotheses that are of just as great an interest to the scientist as to the man of action, but it would be better to stop at this point for several reasons.

The first is that to follow the deductions of this discipline one has to stray much too far from the normal road science takes. Your immediate response to this statement will no doubt be a critical one. If there is such a gap between mass psychology and science, why bother to compose a system out of this hotch-potch of images, notions and speculation? I accept your criticism, for it is undeniably justified. The answer I will give you may seem simple, but I think it is the only valid one. The problems that the discipline has brought to light again are major and practical ones. By comparison, a number of those in which the human sciences abound are abstract and secondary. The very variety of causes that brought mass psychology into being invites us to reflect on the hypotheses it proposes, once they have been reformulated in a coherent and general way. This I have tried to do, as I am sure that they are just as important for us now as they were in the past.

But that is not all. From time to time there creeps into these extravagant hypotheses a truth that is so intolerable and unverifiable by any other scientific method that it would, I know, be almost madness for any scientist to defend it and to dare to suggest it. That cannot be helped. They are the truths that show us that it is possible to think rationally about mass phenomena and to have an idea of a meaningful system of causes, even if this were to take us into the labyrinthine byways of ideas that border on myths. That fact in itself is a major trump card for crowd psychology. We should not let ourselves be over-impressed by the popular and official images of science (which are often the same, in fact). Cosmological and biological myths, for example, have been and still are, if we are to believe certain scientists, a pre-condition for formulating theories about the universe or the origin of life. Psychological myths, to the extent that it is not only a question of myths, can produce theories about the universe of the masses.

There is also the reason that the hypotheses put forward have limits. I am well aware of these: they are obvious. I have not tried to hide the fact that crowd psychology pays too little attention to economic and social factors. It even goes to some trouble to prove that the class and culture of those making up the mass are of no consequence in an explanation of collective movements. That is something which runs counter to our whole view of society, especially as in practice there is no justification for ignoring these factors. If we are to advance our analysis of such movements, they have to be taken into account. A knowledge of social and economic circumstances is no less essential for the scientist than for the men of action. At the same time, and for similar reasons, mass psychology has tended to play down the intellectual and human value of the groups it studies. Neither truth nor necessity compels us to adopt that attitude. Such judgements add nothing to our knowledge of the masses, and since they are pointless and even harmful, I have taken no account of them.

The last reason is that crowd psychology does not see history in the same way as the other sciences. In its view, the despotic leaders and urban masses of ancient Rome, the princes of the Church and the peasant masses of the Middle Ages and even the urban masses of our own age are more or less identical. They belong to the same series of phenomena and are the effects of the same causes. That is a seriously wrong view, of course, but it is easy to correct it, and that is what certain historians engaged in studying them are doing. That does not mean that crowd psychology is not interested in history (and history is certainly very concerned with it). The opposite is the case. It sees it as an important factor in what crowds think and do, even if in its own way. Most theories in the field look towards the future and see the growth of human groups as the solution to the difficulties we all encounter in life. The past is an obstacle to overcome, an abyss to be avoided, the thing one turns away from. Crowd psychology, however, stresses the past and the recurrence of the solutions men have invented for their problems throughout history. It is a means of action and a living memory without which nothing is possible. It bases a practical rule on that principle, which is that whatever happens in the present, one must look just as much, if not more, to the resurgent past as to the inchoate future that is taking shape. These are some of its limitations, but they should not be used as an excuse for rejecting it. We can more profitably see them as the stones we can use to rebuild it in a different way.

Crowd psychology is misunderstood. Nothing shows this more clearly than the conclusions that have been drawn from its hypotheses now and

in the past. It is seen as being opposed to democracy and favouring
individual authority over the majority. We have seen unbridled power at
work, with men becoming passive brutes, killing because they were
ordered to, because they were afraid, or because they were loyal, and all
this while a people sank into silence, the law was perverted and all rights
to truth were abolished. The innocent have been found guilty, and free
men have been imprisoned because of their religion, race or class.
Countless millions have been sacrificed. For all these reasons, we are
bound to reject such an intolerable abuse with every ounce of our
strength.

It is true that crowd psychology asks one question that most other
sciences never raise. Why do we find the power of leaders over us so
profoundly unattractive? In normal conditions, can we not simply see it
as one of the many painful necessities that life inflicts on us? It seems to be
something habitual in the political field, to have a certain social justification and often to be unavoidable. When we ask that question, we are
coming up against the reality of power in a very precise, concrete and
specific form. When we talk of power (parties or organisations) we are
necessarily talking about leaders, and when we are talking about leaders
we are talking about power. Everything else is clever talk and juggling
with ideas.

It is no less true that crowd psychology foresaw the rise of increasingly
powerful leaders when we were all busy ruling out the possibility. But to
see it as responsible for that rise would be to shrug off our own
responsibility and that of civilisation and to criticise it for having
announced a truth instead of stifling it. Such criticism is all the more
unjustified since crowd psychology saw the danger to democracy and
tried to prevent its collapse.

The way it set about showing the danger was a very uncomfortable one.
Our confidence in mass law and our hope for a future we would all control
was sapped. This was because everything we saw as steps towards
progress and democracy – the growth of an urban population, of the
media and of production – involves in its eyes a renewal of authority and
its concentration in the hands of a single individual. Crowd psychology
tells us that we cannot save our threatened freedom by continually
repeating outworn formulas when we are faced with a changing reality,
or by stimulating the same old emotions in hearts that have been
anaesthetised by mass anonymity. We have to listen to what it has to say,
for events have proved it right in even its most doubtful predictions.

What it has to say does not have to be new to be true. The lesson it
teaches us is a simple one. What transforms power radically in the age of
the crowd? Totally unexpectedly, leaders appear as a remedy for the

psychic misery of the masses. Any attempt to hide the importance of this is to refuse to face up to the most overwhelming fact of society, to change it into a non-fact and to retreat into fantasy again. So the alternatives are clear: either the first response emerges triumphant, or there is another, that of democracy pure and simple. But we cannot go backwards through history to recapture it in its liberal form. There has to be another one that takes the leader into account and finds a remedy for the syndrome, one that must be able to reconstitute, using different means, the psychic equivalents of relationships, values and institutions, of, in short, collective life, which the masses have lost but which is still hauntingly present in their memory. Only this kind of equivalent will make it possible to mobilise them in order to act and govern. The ingredients of such a form of democracy are to some extent already known. They would include making the powers of the state subject to those of elected representatives, restoring the autonomy of individuals (and of minorities in general) separating private and public life and restricting the power of the media in order to make better use of the general area of dialogue and public conversation. All this, of course, without neglecting social justice in the true sense of the term. Education would be based on democratic traditions, which it would revitalise with the spontaneity of irresistible feelings and memories. Those various elements all tend to exclude any magical or idolatrous exercise of power of the kind that could make it seem omniscient and omnipotent to the masses. Never before has there been so much 'magical' sovereignty, never has it had such a range of techniques at its disposal, and it is for those reasons that choosing it or rejecting it is now as serious as choosing or rejecting atomic weapons.

The scientific nature of crowd psychology is of a very provisional kind, but its contemporary relevance is of prime importance. On a continent-wide scale throughout the world, mass phenomena are becoming increasingly apparent. There seems to be some tendency towards stability in Europe, but in Latin America, Africa and Asia, they are becoming much more marked. In those parts of the world, we are witnessing in the late twentieth century a repetition, with some variations, of what happened in Europe at the end of the nineteenth. There has been an explosion of urban populations, and four hundred million men, women and children eke out a precarious existence vegetating in makeshift homes around the cities. They have been driven from the countryside by poverty, hunger and war and have huddled together in hastily-thrown up slums or shanty-towns. The illusion of peace and well-being provided by the town has been a magnet to them, keeping them in places where no-one would have dreamed of living. Every year, there is at least a ten per cent increase in the size of these human galaxies. They have lost their traditional links, and those caught up in them no longer have any contact with their natural traditions or ties with the communities they came from. They have been cut off from the organic life of society and drawn into an orbit of casual and occasional work and the cycle of the mass media and communications according to what we might call the American model, which is foreign to them.

We know why these migrations take place, but the consequences of them are still not properly understood. The individuals involved, who have been uprooted from their own surroundings and thrown haphazardly into ghettoes on the edges of large towns, are the forerunners of new masses. New leaders will sprout upon this fertile compost and are indeed already beginning to appear. In short, such phenomena are the very first signs of a future world-wide age of the crowd. Since similar causes produce similar effects, there is every reason to believe that it will be based on the sort of principles we have already seen. It will make use of means of suggestion already tried out in Europe, but adapted to fit the huge scale involved. It will be a severe test of the explanations offered by crowd psychology and the ways it has been put into practice in other regions.

Like a cock crowing while it is still dark, science heralds the dawn and is of its time because it is a step ahead of it. That is why it is so valuable, both for the man of action who can steal a march on those of his rivals who are more ignorant or more respectful of tradition, and for the man of science looking for a new field to exercise his talents and his curiosity in.

If the prospect of a world-wide age of the crowd corresponds to what is really going to happen, then this book, which deals with a traditional branch of knowledge and our recent past, will help those who want to be aware of developments and to understand some of the features of the future. Of a future, in fact, that has already begun.

# Notes

## Part I

### 3 What do we do when faced with the masses?

**1.** The part played by mass psychologists, and in particular those with whom this work is concerned, in forming the notion of this new kind of politics is widely ignored. The exception is the very great intellectual historians with the necessary learning and openness of mind. Thus the English historian Berlin includes Le Bon, Tarde and Freud amongst those who transformed the simple model of human nature 'with which political theorists from Hobbes to J. S. Mill had operated, and shifted emphasis from political argument to the less or more deterministic descriptive disciplines that began with Tocqueville and Taine and Marx, and were carried on by Weber and Durkheim, Le Bon and Tarde, Pareto and Freud, and their disciples in our time' (Berlin, 1979: 323–4).

### 4 Eastern and western varieties of despotism

**1.** The rather dangerous parallels K. Wittfogel draws in the work referred to show how hazardous it is to ignore these limits and to change an analogy which is only useful in describing reality into an identity which is supposed to explain it, in brief, to try to find a model for the present in the past.

## Part II

### 2 The Machiavelli of mass societies

**1.** Regarding this book, Michels wrote to Le Bon on 23 November 1911, 'I have simply applied to political parties and their administrative and political structure the theories that you have so luminously established concerning the collective life of crowds.'

**2.** The history of ideas in France is full of gaps and we are nourished by many myths. If it is ever tackled seriously, it will become apparent that Durkheim's sociology exerted a massive influence in university circles, whereas Le Bon's crowd psychology permeated the military and political world and, through Sorel, made some impression on socialist thought. Not only did Sorel know Le Bon's work and review it in laudatory terms, he was also unstinting in his admiration for him. Comparing him to Ribot and Janet, Sorel had no hesitation in writing that he was undeniably the greatest living French psychologist (Sorel, 1911: 3).

**3.** M. Charles Morazé, one of General de Gaulle's advisers and confidants, has given me a first-hand piece of information of great value, for which I thank him most sincerely. He had, he told me, heard de Gaulle speak of Le Bon on several occasions, and also mentioned that the general was passionately interested in the practical questions of crowd psychology, which he saw as being decisive in the political field.

### 3 Four reasons for saying nothing

**1.** Along with many other peole such as Richet and Ribot, Le Bon helped establish psychology as a discipline in France. Although a marginal figure, he had consistent and even deep relationships with scholars and philosophers. Amongst these was Henri Poincaré, who in his time was considered to be the most eminent mathematician and physicist of the age. It could be said, and indeed it has been said, that there was a genuine collaboration between the two men. Bergson exchanged letters with Le Bon and wrote, on the occasion of the latter's last birthday, 'I take this opportunity to express my deep liking and great esteem for one of the most original minds of our time' (Bergson, 1931).

**2.** Le Bon was of less weight as a thinker than Max Weber, but their political positions were close. There was much common ground in their nationalism, their faith in the importance of the leader and their descriptions of the nature of leaders and masses. One sometimes has the impression that certain of Weber's views of charismatic authority and mass democracy reflect those in Le Bon's writings, which were well known in Germany at the time. And did not Michels achieve a synthesis between Weberian sociology and crowd psychology? With regard to his relationship with Nazism, many historians have noted that Weber unintentionally prepared the ground for it. (See Mommsen, 1974 and Beetham, 1974.) Several sociologists have explained and justified him from this point of view. To the best of my knowledge, no-one has pointed out his blameworthiness.

**3.** The real problem is not to discover why Le Bon influenced Fascism, as he is not the only writer to have done so, but why France did not become the first Fascist state in Europe. We have resolutely avoided raising and answering the question. In André Gide's *Journal* for 5 April 1933 there is the following sentence: 'What aborted it [Nazism] in France? Circumstances or men?'

### 5 Mass hypnosis

**1.** In *The Horla*, Maupassant describes a case of delayed suggestion and puts forward a theory similar to Le Bon's. Literature, of course, had seen the importance of such phenomena before science did.

**2.** The medical practitioners who introduced hypnosis called their therapy by suggestion 'medicine of the imagination' and the illnesses produced by an obsession were given the label 'illnesses of the imagination' (but not imaginary illnesses!) By analogy, we can say that the politics conceived of by the earliest crowd psychologists, with Le Bon in first place, was a 'politics of the imagination'.

### 6 The mental life of crowds

**1.** From its first beginnings to our own times, psychology has seen itself as a science of conscious phenomena. Le Bon saw crowd psychology as to some extent an autonomous discipline, since it was the study of unconscious phenomena. It is true that he did not interpret them in the same way as Freud, but they did have a similar role for him. Both men started from hypnosis. One discovered the unconscious in 'the crowd mind', the other saw it in that of the individual, and each based a science on his discovery.

## Part III

*1 Collective matter: the impulsive and conservative crowd*

**1.** Revolutionary leaders themselves have justified the revolutionary role of parties by the spontaneously reformist, even apolitical, nature of the masses. That at least was Lenin's argument, and Trotsky came close to Le Bon when he wrote in his *History of the Russian Revolution* that the rapid changes of mood and opinion amongst the masses at a time of revolution did not come from flexibility and mobility of the human mind, but rather from its conservative nature.

**2.** This idea is still heard even in our own times with regard to the socialist countries. The German philosopher R. Bahro sees the immediate needs of the secondary strata and classes as still being conservative in nature and never really looking forward to a new way of life (Bahro 1979: 137). See also Birnbaum, 1979 with regard to the policy of left-wing parties.

**3.** Lenin maintained that the strength of tradition in millions and tens of millions of human beings was the most redoubtable force.

*2 Collective form: the dogmatic and utopian crowd*

**1.** This point has been greatly developed and confirmed in the work of Pierre Bourdieu. See in particular his *Le Sens pratique*, 1980.

**2.** In *Le Médecin de campagne*, Balzac wrote: 'With the people, infallibility is always necessary. It made Napoleon, and would have made a god of him had the universe not heard his fall at Waterloo.'

**3.** The reader's attention is drawn to this point. Europe is obsessed with the search for a secular religion. Crowd psychology is interested in religion not as a residue from the past, which is how sociology sees it, nor as an aspect of primitive cultures, which is how anthropology presents it, but as a present and future factor in advanced cultures. It was in this way that Le Bon studied it and Freud was concerned with it for almost twenty years.

*4 Charisma*

**1.** The question of abolishing Mao's divine status is largely at the heart of the present Chinese political system, as was that of abolishing Stalin's in the Soviet system in the recent past.

**2.** I hasten to add that everything I have just said about political leaders also holds good for artistic, sporting, literary and cinematographic ones. Even science, which is forewarned and therefore ought to be forearmed, finds it difficult to escape the phenomenon.

*6 Conclusion*

**1.** The Marxist philosopher Lukács makes the same criticisms as Sorel, but links them with a total condemnation of crowd psychology, maintaining that such a society is incapable of development from the purely scientific point of view, since it is hopelessly caught up in the circle of false problems arising from a false problematics of that kind insofar as it does not prove itself able to understand the social class nature of its errors (Lukács, 1978: 122).

## Part IV

### 1 *The paradox of mass psychology*

**1.** For a modern version of this theory, see R. Debray, 1979.

### 3 *The leader principle*

**1.** In the development of crowd psychology, the idea of the *social ego* prepared the ground for the move from Le Bon's idea of the *crowd soul* to Freud's concept of the *ego ideal* or *super-ego*.

**2.** This is summed up in the famous German expression the *Führerprinzip*.

**3.** Crowd psychology sees the hierarchy principle and the organisation principle as simply two aspects of the leader principle. The former cannot therefore be developed without finally reaching the latter.

**4.** It is important to appreciate this distinction. Many psychologists attempt to define the submissive, dependent and conformist personality type. Others speak of a genetic propensity to obedience. In the view of crowd psychology the need to obey, like other manifestations of the psyche, is a product of the mass state and disappears once the individual is alone again. It is important to avoid moving without good reason from the collective to the individual when discussing submissive and suggestible individuals or from the individual to the collective when discussing the relationships between crowds and leaders in sado-masochistic terms. The latter type of confusion has recently been much used to 'poeticise' Nazi crimes.

## Part V

### 4 *The Republic in France*

**1.** Whiffs of a Bonapartist or Orleanist temperament might be found in varying proportions in either of the two, but that kind of antithesis is no longer of any interest.

## Part VI

### 1 *The black books of Doctor Freud*

**1.** Many books contain accounts of the relationships between Freud, Le Bon and Tarde. See in particular Giner, 1976, Adorno, 1972: VIII, 35; Sherif, 1956: 339 and Broch, 1979: 29.

*Mass Psychology and Analysis of the Ego* attracted so much attention that Lukács, the Hungarian Marxist philosopher, devoted a full review article to it (Lukács, 1978).

**2.** There was a more concrete link between Freud and Le Bon than a book and a common field of study: Princess Marie Bonaparte, who from 1925 was the former's patient and trusted friend, sharing many of his thoughts that remained a secret to others. She was also, however, from a very early date one of the friends and admirers of Le Bon and with another friend and admirer, Princess Marthe Bibesco, was present during his last moments (M. Bibesco, 'Le Docteur Faust de la rue Vignon', *Annales Politiques et Littéraires*, 15 March 1932, 259–60.) She also dedicated one of her last books (*Les Glanes des jours*, 1950) to him.

**3.** The task that Freud set himself in this connection was to transfer, by means of pertinent analogies, psychoanalytical images to crowd psychology. The method was that of the 'scientific metaphors' (or 'models' as we now call them) urged by the English physicist Maxwell. It was not, however, a question of 'mass psychoanalysis', as in that domain it is impossible to distinguish between the 'normal' and the 'pathological' and even less possible to have recourse to any therapy. A transfer of this kind was also in keeping with Freud's idea that 'psychoanalysis is nothing but psychology, one of the parts of psychology, and that one does not need to apologize for employing analytical methods in a psychological study which is concerned with the deeper psychic facts' (Freud and Bullitt, 1966: xiii–xiv).

**4.** Freud's pessimism in his mass psychology is a favourite butt of his biographers and critics and was seen as a symptom of his conservatism and even of his lack of understanding of social reality. It is of course a question of whether the role of the scientist is to face up to and express disagreeable truths or to look for soothing solutions to the sometimes insoluble problems that have so long beset the human race, a question in short of whether he should act as a real thinker or as a priest (Adorno, 1972: 36).

## 2 *From classical to revolutionary mass psychology*

**1.** It is thus an error to speak of Freud's sociology, or anthropology or history and, *a fortiori*, to define them in terms of psychology, or vice versa.

**2.** The case of Roheim is an interesting one. In his *Animism, Magic and Divine King* he has attempted to express in a concrete way the nature of political links as traced by Freud in *Group Psychology* and also to reconcile at the scientific level the various positions of psychoanalysis and social and political criticism.

**3.** Whether their initiators were aware of it or not, most of the attempts to combine Marxism and psychoanalysis took place within the context of mass psychology. To the end of his life, Freud resisted any such link. This was not, as has often been maintained, because he remained faithful to a view of man as an individual, whereas Marxism saw society as the ultimate reality. The real explanation lies rather in the difference between the two ways of conceiving and representing society. To the extent that Freud was a mass psychologist, his model of society was not compatible with Marx's model of the class society. Reich, Adorno, Marcuse and the like, however, merely tried to reconcile the two models, and all the differences between them arise from the respective importance they attached to each. Reich favoured the idea of mass society, Marcuse that of class society. Adorno used each as a critique of the other. Freud was also opposed to associating them for other reasons, particularly in connection with the autonomy of ideological phenomena, but the first reason given here was the major one.

**4.** The same was true in economics. Ricardo's classical labour theory of value remained the basis of Marx's theory, even when it assumed revolutionary significance in his hands.

## 5 *The origin of affective attachments in society*

**1.** The compulsion to repeat can be better explained as a compulsion to imitate and identify oneself, with the aim of maintaining oneself and remaining the same. In that situation, one is one's own model, which is seen as better than or preferable to any other. That is why there are people whose lives contain the same indefinitely-repeated and uncorrected features. Once we have identified with someone, we end up identifying with ourselves, because we are no longer simply like that person but *are* him to such an extent that we forget it. This gives rise to a destructive aspect, as we might want to get rid of that person, perhaps even for good. In the case of John Lennon's killer, mentioned above, one might say that the motive for the killing was to get rid of the original and replace it with the copy. In intellectual life, where plagiarism and the theft of ideas are frequent, a similar mechanism is set in motion. At any rate, many of the phenomena attributed to the death-wish, and particularly those involving aggression, come into this category.

**2.** We know that the idea of identification was first consistently put forward in Freud's 1921 essay, *Group Psychology and the Analysis of the Ego* and that of the ego in *The Ego and the Id*, the essay that followed it and developed the latter topic. We are indebted to the second essay since in western society each individual is made up of the id, the ego and the super-ego. It is unnecessary to add that the question of the latter was the result of the break dealt with in the first chapter of this section and is a major element in general psychoanalytical theory. We should also note that one of the reasons for Freud's rejection of compromise with Marxism was his view of the autonomy of the super-ego.

**3.** Many analytical studies of identification are incomplete for a number of reasons. They pass over the fact that in *Beyond the Pleasure Principle* it is clearly identification in general that is at issue. In addition, they also depict the child as a partner or stake in family relationships when in fact he is the mediator, the go-between between the mother and the father, with whom he establishes alternating coalitions based on love and hate. The dual aspect of identification, the decrease in drives on the one hand and the pursuit of their aims by alternative means on the other, has been missed. The voice of instinct is too strong ever to be silenced.

**4.** Psychoanalysts seem on the whole to have developed a psychology of the id first and then one of the ego. They were out of touch with crowd psychology and neglected the fact that it was central to the second topic and consequently developed virtually no theory of the super-ego worthy of the name. The latter, however, was the main concern and the unfinished part of Freud's later work.

## 6 *Eros and mimesis*

**1.** Just as in psychoanalysis there is a tendency to reduce the mimetic model to an erotic one, so there has recently been a trend in the opposite direction (i.e. from the erotic to the mimetic) aimed at accounting for the origins of religion (Girard, 1972).

## 7 *The end of hypnosis*

**1.** There has been little attention devoted to the part played by the gaze in politics. Goering was certainly neither the first person nor the last to order people at a rally to look at the steely eyes of the Führer. From this point of view, a history of the question would be of absorbing interest.

**2.** It would seem that the most exemplary leaders of our time (Stalin, Mao, Tito, de Gaulle, Khomeini and so on) all observed this prohibition. Of contemporary French politicians, a certain number have wished to charm and posses. Or at least this is the impression they give, and that attitude limits their hold over the masses.

**3.** 'The expression "mass hypnosis", usually used rather vaguely, was taken seriously by Freud and modes of mass behaviour similar to those in hypnosis were developed on the basis of the instinctual behaviour of individuals uniting to form a mass. By this means, Freud's theory gave expression to a social situation in which the formation of a mass is assumed to be based on the atomisation and alienation of human beings' (Adorno, 1972: 435).

**4.** Over the last few years there has been a rebirth of interest in crowds and collective behaviour. Some important studies have tended to deny any difference between masses and individuals, to ignore the importance of leaders and to take only rational factors into account. But it is a fact that, unlike crowd psychology, these studies are aimed at an exclusively academic and administrative readership. See for example Olson (1978), Oberschall (1973), Tilly (1978).

## Part VII

### 3 *The primal secret*

**1.** In his study, Freud started from the supposition of internecine warfare within the primitive band led by a male, as described by Darwin. I have extended this scientific myth a little to relate it to the sex war and the sexual division of labour. This has occasionally meant changing one or two ideas about the origin of laws and the meaning of the incest taboo. There had to be some degree of modification, since on the one hand the idea of the primitive band is no longer valid and on the other Freud never shows how the murder of the father led to matriarchy, for example. In addition, in his theory and others, the role of women is that of a crowd of dumb and absent shadows. I have dealt with some of these questions in my *Society against Nature* (Moscovici, 1976b).

## Part VIII

### 1 *'The Man Moses'*

**1.** The choice of Moses is not easy to explain, and there is no single reason for it. It is possible to imagine a number of hypotheses all equally true. One has its origins in the rise of the charismatic leader in mass society. A second is based on the fact that Moses fascinated contemporary politicians. We know that that was the case with Hitler, who was probably not the only one. Moses became the paradigm of the revolutionary leader who founds a nation, especially as there were so many Jews in the Communist and socialist revolutionary movements of the time. For a very illuminating work, see Ekart (1926).

The third hypothesis, which is the most transparent one, is this. Freud elaborates the 'poetic myth' of what the 'great man' necessarily is when carrying out such a huge task. By making Moses an Egyptian and removing his Jewishness, Freud gives him a universal value. By depriving, as he says, the Jewish race of one of its sons, he sees himself as giving the human race a father. We are of course justified in adding to these hypotheses a further one connected to Freud's personal life. In setting them out, I have tried once more to make the point that the choice of Moses as an archetype was based on wider reasons than could be expressed in a 'political myth'. The fact that crowd psychology has been obliged to formulate it is no less significant.

## 2 *The family romances of great men*

**1.** There are of course two types of family romance, an ascending and a descending one. In the former, the 'native' family is of humble origins. In the latter, the opposite is the case. One thinks of all those who have identified with poor, pure, persecuted and rebellious parents and followed their example. They are often said to have done so as a result of their awareness of social injustice, but we cannot rule out the possibility that the family romance they created for themselves in their childhood had prepared them for it. Even if they had forgotten it, it came back into conscious awareness under the pressure of external events. From a psychological point of view, the family romance corresponds to identical conditions, whether they be ascending or descending.

**2.** There is doubtless a whole pathology of family romances amongst people who are unsure of themselves either because they fear that they have not made a success of their own or because they imagine that they have sacrificed it to the family complex. Its symptoms are an obsessive concern with genealogies, arguments about its place in history and comparisons with outstanding characters (Napoleon, Freud, Einstein and so on). One has the impression that their 'native' family has been consumed by their 'noble' and imaginary parents. Those are probably the symptoms of what we might see as an obsession with the 'romance'.

## 3 *Creating a people*

**1.** By analogy, the cycle can be extended to artificial crowds such as churches, armies and parties. To the Catholic Church, for example. The first phase would be that of the secularised nineteenth century when the Pope, the infallible father chosen by Italian cardinals, was its single and tyrannical head. The second, that of the revolt of sons and brothers against him, would be the conciliar revolt, with the Church entering a period of relative democracy with a full quota of reforms and discussion, opening itself up to the problems of the outside world and using its methods, particularly in the field of communications. Gilson has pointed out that Vatican II marked the beginning of a new conciliar style, which historians will see as being influenced by mass societies and their methods. (Gilson, 1967: 111) Since the election of John Paul II (and this would be the third phase) we have seen the resurrection of the *imago* of the Pope, the one father of the Church, and a return to identifications and rules that we thought progress had swept away. It should also be pointed out that the present Pope is a Pole, and hence his election was a break with tradition. This explains why when he took the throne of Peter as a usurper he received the charisma it bestows. The masses are drawn to him and give him, as it were, all the love and veneration they had been keeping back until a father-figure arrived.

## 4 Mosaic and totemic leaders

**1.** Psychoanalysis itself is not without its own totemic leaders. See Georges, 1979.

## Part IX

### 1 The secret of a religion

**1.** It may be surprising to find no mention of the concept of ideology here. It has been expressly avoided for two reasons. In the first place, it is part of neither the field nor the vocabulary of classical crowd psychology and is not found in Le Bon, Tarde or Freud. Secondly, secular religion is different from ideology in that it presupposes the existence of a faith, and hence an influence of the past on the present which is partly independent of economic factors. In other words, unlike ideology, it is not a superstructure.

### 2 The prohibition of thought

**1.** One of those taking part stresses the areas which are ignored when a totally social and economic view is taken: 'The Russian Revolution, although led by men who were upright and intelligent, did not resolve this problem; the character of the masses had received, from the experience of despotism, a fatal stamp whose effects were imprinted in the leaders themselves. In making this judgement, I do not mean to disown the importance of economic–historical factors; they broadly condition action, but they do not determine its entire quality' (Serge, 1963: 375).

**2.** In institutional religion, the prohibition on thought is expressed in the axiom that religion has always been right and always will be. This is included in the propositions of Gregory VII known as the papal *Dictatus*: 'The Church has never erred and, as Scripture states, never will err.'

# References

Adorno, T. W. 1951, 'Freudian theory and the pattern of Fascist propaganda', in Roheim, G. (ed.), *Psychoanalysis and the Social Sciences*, Vol. III, New York.

Adorno, T. W. 1972, *Gesammelte Schriften*, Vol. VIII, Suhrkamp, Frankfurt.

Alberoni, F. 1968, *Status nascenti*, Il Mulino, Bologna.

Arendt, Hannah, 1967, *The Origins of Totalitarianism*, third edition, Allen and Unwin, London.

Ayçoberry, P. 1979, *La Question nazie*, Le Seuil, Paris.

Bahro, R. 1979, *L'Alternative*, Stock, Paris.

Bainville, J. 1959, *Napoléon*, Fayard, Paris.

Bartlett, F. 1932, *Remembering*, Cambridge University Press, Cambridge.

Barthou, Louis, *La Liberté*, 31 May 1931.

Baudelaire, 'Les Foules', *Le Spleen de Paris*.

Bechterev, W. 1905, *Die Bedeutung der Suggestion im sozialen Leben*, J. F. Bergman, Wiesbaden.

Bechterev, W. 1957, *La Réflexologie collective*, Delachaux et Niestlé, Neuchâtel.

Becker, H. and Barnes, H. E. 1961, *Social Thought from Lore to Science*, Dover, New York.

Beetham, D. 1974, *Max Weber and the Theory of Modern Politics*, Allen and Unwin, London.

Bell, D. 1960, *The End of Ideology*, The Free Press, Glencoe, Ill.

Bergson, Henri, *La Liberté*, 31 May 1931.

Berlin, I. 1979, *Against the Current*, Hogarth Press, London.

Bernheim, H. 1888, *De la suggestion*, O. Doin, Paris.

Bibesco, M. 1932, 'Le Docteur Faust de la rue Vignon', *Annales Politiques et Littéraires*, 15 March 1932.

Biddis, M. D. 1980, *L'Être des masses*, Le Seuil, Paris.

Binet, A. and Féré, C. 1887, *Le Magnétisme animal*, Paris.

Birnbaum, P. 1979, *Le Peuple et les gros*, Grasset, Paris.

Bloch, Ernst, *Maintenant*, 2, 19 March 1979.

Borges, Jorge Luis, 1962, *Ficciones*, Weidenfeld and Nicolson, London.

Bourdieu, P. 1980, *Le Sens pratique*, Ed. de Minuit, Paris.

Broch, H. 1979, *Massenwahntheorie*, Suhrkamp, Frankfurt.

Canetti, Elias, 1973, *Crowds and Power*, Penguin, London.

Cassirer, E. 1961, *The Myth of the State*, Yale Paperback, Yale University Press, New Haven.

Chanlaine, 1932, *Mussolini parle*, Tallandier, Paris.

Chertok, L. 1979, *Le Non-savoir des psy*, Payot, Paris.

Clemenceau, G. 1916, *La France devant l'Allemagne*, Payot, Paris.

Daniel, J. 1979, *L'Ere des ruptures*, Grasset, Paris.

Debray, R. 1979, *Le Pouvoir intellectuel en France*, Ramsay, Paris.

## References

De Felice, P. 1947, *Foules en délire, extases collectives*, Albin Michel, Paris.

De Gaulle, Charles, 1944, *Le Fil de l'épée*, Livre de Poche, Paris.

De Gaulle, Charles, 1955, *Mémoires de guerre*, Plon, Paris.

Deutscher, I. 1953, *Russia after Stalin*, Hamish Hamilton, London.

Deutscher, I. 1961, *Stalin, a Political Biography*, Oxford University Press, London (Oxford Paperbacks).

Djilas, M. Interview in *Encounter*, December 1979.

Djilas, M. 'Le sens du danger', *Le Monde*, 6 May 1980.

Djilas, M. 1981, *Tito, the Story from Inside*, Weidenfeld and Nicolson, London.

Duhamel, A. 1980, *La République giscardienne*, Grasset, Paris.

Durkheim, Emile, 1938, *L'Evolution pédagogique en France*, Alcan, Paris.

Einstein, Albert, 1954, *Ideas and Opinions*, Alvin Redman, London.

Ekart, D. 1926, *Der Bolschevismus von Moses bis Lenin. Zwiegespräche zwischen Adolf Hitler und mir.*

Ellenberger, H. F. 1970, *The Discovery of the Unconscious*, Basic Books, New York.

Emmanuel, Pierre, *Le Figaro*, 20 December 1979.

Fauconnet, P. 1920, *La Responsabilité*, Alcan, Paris.

Fischer, R. 1961, *Masse und Vermassung*, G. Vehlin, Schopfheim.

Flaubert, G. 1952, *L'Education sentimentale*, Ed. Pléiade, Paris.

Forel, A. 1906, *Hypnotism*, Ribman, London.

Freud, Sigmund, 1966–1974, *The Standard Edition of the Complete Psychological Works of Sigmund Freud*, 24 vols., Hogarth and the Institute of Psycho-Analysis, London.

Freud, S. and Bullitt, W. C. 1966, *Thomas Woodrow Wilson: a Psychological Study*, Weidenfeld and Nicolson, London.

Fromm, E. 1962, *The Dogma of Christ*, Anchor, New York.

Fromm, E. quoted in Sollner, A. 1979, *Geschichte und Herrschaft*, Suhrkamp, Frankfurt.

Furet, F. 1978, *Penser la Révolution française*, Gallimard, Paris.

Geiger, T. 1926, *Die Masse und ihre Aktion*, F. Enke, Stuttgart

Georges, F. 1979, *L'Effet'yau de poêle de Lacan et des lacaniens*, Hachette, Paris.

Gilson, E. 1967, *La Société de masse et la culture*, Vrin, Paris.

Giner, S. 1976, *Mass Society*, Martin Robinson, London.

Girard, P. 1972, *La Violence et le sacré*, Grasset, Paris.

Giscard d'Estaing, V. 1976, *Démocratie française*, Livre de Poche, Paris.

Glaser, H. 1979, *Sigmund Freud*, Fischer, Frankfurt.

Gramsci, A. 1952, *Il materialismo storico e la filosofia di Benedetto Croce*, Einaudi, Turin.

Gramsci, A. 1953, *Note su Macchiavelli*, Einaudi, Milan.

Gramsci, A. 1957, *The Modern Prince and other writings*, New World International, New York.

Gregor, A. J. 1969, *The Ideology of Fascism*, The Free Press, New York.

Habermas, J. 1978, *L'Espace public*, Payot, Paris.

Hanotaux, G. 1925, *Le Général Mangin*, Plon, Paris.

Hégédus, A. *Le Monde*, 3 August 1980.

Herzstein, R. E. 1979, *The War Hitler Won*, Abacus, London.

Hobsbawm, E. J. 1971, *Primitive Rebels*, Manchester University Press.

Hobsbawm, E. J. 1974, *The Age of Revolution*, Weidenfeld and Nicolson, London.

Horkheimer, M. and Adorno, T. 1973, *Aspects of Sociology*, Heinemann, London.

House, F. N. 1936, *The Development of Sociology*, McGraw Hill, New York.

Jacoby, R. 1975, *Social Amnesia*, The Harvester Press, Hassocks, Sussex.

Katz, E. and Lazarsfeld, P. 1965, *Personal Influence*, The Free Press, New York.

Kautsky, K. 1970, *Die Aktion der Masse*, in Grunnenberg, A. *Die Massenstreik-debatte*, Europäische Verlagsanstalt, Frankfurt.

Khrushchev, Nikita, 1971, *Khrushchev Remembers*, André Deutsch, London.

Korsh, K. 1970, *Marxism and Philosophy*, Johns Hopkins University Press, Baltimore.

Laplanche, J. and Pontalis, J. B. 1967, *Vocabulaire de la psychanalyse*, PUF, Paris.

Lazitch, B. 1976, *Le Rapport de Khrouchtchev et son histoire*, Le Seuil, Paris.

Le Bon, Gustave, 1895, *Les Lois psychologiques de l'évolution des peuples*, Alcan, Paris.

Le Bon, Gustave, 1910, *La Psychologie politique*, Flammarion, Paris.

Le Bon, Gustave, 1911, *L'Opinion et les croyances*, Flammarion, Paris.

Le Bon, Gustave, 1924, 'L'Evolution de l'Europe vers les formes diverses de dictature', *Annales Politiques et Littéraires*, March 1924.

Le Bon, Gustave, 1925, 'Les Difficultés de la politique moderne et les formes futures de gouvernement', *Annales Politiques et Littéraires*, February 1925.

Le Bon, Gustave, 1952, *The Crowd*, Ernest Benn, London.

Le Bon, Gustave, 1963, *La Psychologie des foules*, PUF, Paris.

Le Bon, Gustave, 1980, *The French Revolution and the Psychology of Revolution*, Social Science Classics, Transaction Books, New Brunswick.

Lederer, E. 1940, *State of the Masses; the Threat of the Classless Society*, Norton, New York.

Lefèbvre, G. 1954, *Etudes sur la Révolution française*, PUF, Paris.

Lenin, V. I. 1971, *Que faire?*, Ed. Sociales, Paris.

Lindzey, G. and Aronson, E. (eds.), 1969, *Handbook of Social Psychology*, IV, Addison-Wesley, Reading, Mass.

Lukács, G. 1978, *Littérature, philosophie, marxisme*, (1922–3), PUF, Paris.

McDougall, W. 1908, *Introduction to Social Psychology*, Methuen, London.

McDougall, W. 1920, 1939, *The Group Mind*, Cambridge University Press, Cambridge.

McDougall, W. 1936, *Psychoanalysis and Social Psychology*, Methuen, London.

Mackay, C. 1847, *Extraordinary Popular Delusions and the Madness of the Crowd*, L. C. Page, Wells, Vermont.

Malia, M. *Comprendre la Révolution russe*, Le Seuil, Paris.

Mann, T. 1975, *Considérations d'un apolitique*, Grasset, Paris.

Mannoni, M. 1952, *Conditions psychologiques d'une action sur les foules*, C. E. Nancy.

Maser, W. 1970, *Hitler's Mein Kampf*, Faber and Faber, London.

Masser, W. A. 1972, *Adolf Hitler, Legende, Mythos, Wirklichkeit*, Munich and Esslingen.

Maupassant, Guy de, 1924, *La Horla*, Flammarion, Paris.

Maupassant, Guy de, 1979, *Sur l'eau*, Ed. Encre, Paris.

Mauss, M. 1973, *Sociologie et anthropologie*, PUF, Paris.

Medvedev, R. 1976, *Let History Judge*, Spokesman Books, London.

Michelet, J. 1974, *Le Peuple*, Flammarion, Paris.

Michels, R. 1971, *Les Partis politiques*, Flammarion, Paris.

Moscovici, M. 1980, 'Résurgences et dérivés de la mystique', *Nouvelle Revue de Psychanalyse*, 1980, pp. 71–101.

Moscovici, S. 1968, *Essai sur l'histoire humaine de la nature*, Flammarion, Paris.

## References

Moscovici, S. 1976a, *Social influence and Social Change*, Academic Press, London.
Moscovici, S. 1976b, *Society Against Nature*, The Harvester Press, Hassocks, Sussex.
Moscovici, S. 1980, 'Toward a theory of conversion', *Advances in Experimental Social Psychology*, 1980, p. 13.
Moscovici, S. 1981, 'Bewusste und unbewusste Einflüsse in der Kommunikation', *Zeitschrift für Sozialpsychologie*, 12, 1981, 93–103.
Mommsen, W. J. 1974, *Max Weber und die deutsche Politik*, J. C. B. Mohr, Tübingen.
Mosse, G. L. 1975, *La nazionalizzazione delle masse*, Il Mulino, Bologna.
Newmann, S. 1965, *Permanent Revolution: Totalitarianism in the Age of International Civil War*, Praeger, New York.
Noir, M. 'L'utilisation des techniques de marketing dans une campagne présidentielle', *Pouvoirs*, 1980, p. 14.
Nye, R. A. 1975, *The Origin of Crowd Psychology*, Sage Publications Ltd, London.
Oberschall, A. 1973, *Social Conflicts and Social Movements*, Prentice Hall Inc., Englewood Cliffs.
Odajnyk, W. W. 1975, *C. J. Jung und die Politik*, Stuttgart.
Olson, M. 1978, *Logique de l'action collective*, PUF, Paris.
Park, R. E. 1975, *Society*, The Free Press, Glencoe, Ill.
Porchnev, B. 1970, *Social Psychology*, Progress Publishers, Moscow.
Porchnev, B. *La Science léniniste de la révolution et la psychologie sociale*, Ed. Novosoki.
Poulantzas, N. 1974, *Fascisme et dictature*, Maspéro, Paris.
Proust, M. 1978, *A la recherche du temps perdu*, Vol. III, Ed. Pléiade, Paris.
Reich, Wilhelm, 1972, *Reich parle de Freud*, Payot, Paris.
Reich, Wilhelm, 1975, *The Mass Psychology of Fascism*, Penguin, London.
Rieff, Philip, 1979, *Freud, the mind of a moralist*, University of Chicago Press, Chicago.
Reinwald, P. 1949, *De l'esprit des Masses*, Delachaux and Niestlé, Neuchâtel.
Robert, M. 1964, *La Révolution psychanalytique*, Payot, Paris.
Robert, M. 1974, *D'Œdipe à Moïse*, Calmann-Lévy, Paris.
Robinson, P. A. 1970, *La sinistra freudiana*, Astrolabio, Roma.
Robrieux, P. 1975, *Maurice Thorez, sa vie secrète et sa vie publique*, Fayard, Paris.
Robrieux, P. 'Un tyran et son mythe', *Le Monde*, 22 December 1979.
Roheim, G. 1972, *Animism, Magic and Divine King*, International Universities Press, New York.
Rouget, G. 1980, *La Musique et la transe*, Gallimard, Paris.
Sartre, J. P. 1971, *L'Idiot de la famille*, Gallimard, Paris.
Schumpeter, J. A. 1976, *Capitalism, Socialism and Democracy*, Allen and Unwin, London.
Serge, U. 1963, *Memoirs of a Revolutionary*, Oxford University Press, London.
Sevenster, J. N. 1975, *The Roots of Pagan Antisemitism in the Ancient World*, E. J. Brill, Leyden.
Sherif, M. and Sherif, C. 1956, *An Outline of Social Psychology*, Harper and Row, London.
Shorske, C. 1973, *Politics and Patricide in Freud's Interpretation of Dreams*, American Historical Review.
Sighele, S. 1898, *Psychologie des sectes*, V. Girard and E. Brière, Paris.
Silone, I. 1962, *La scuola di dittatori*, Mondadori, Milan.
Simmel, G. 1908, *Soziologie*, Dunker and Humbold, Leipzig.

Sorel, Georges, *Le Devenir social*, November 1895.

Sorel, Georges, *Le Bulletin de la semaine*, 11 January 1911.

Sorel, Georges, 1915, *Reflexions on Violence*, P. Smith, Gloucester, Mass.

Stein, A. 1955, 'Adolph Hitler and Gustave Le Bon', *Geschichte in Wissenschaft und Unterricht*.

Stendhal, 1952, *Le Rouge et le noir*, Vol. I, Ed. Pléiade, Paris.

Stendhal, 1955, *Vie de Henry Brulard*, Ed. Pléiade, Paris.

Sternhell, Z. 1972, *Maurice Barrès et le nationalisme français*, A. Colin, Paris.

Suares, G. 1939, *Briand*, Vol. I, Plon, Paris.

Tarde, G. 1890, *La Philosophie pénale*, A. Storck, Lyon.

Tarde, G. 1895a, *La Logique sociale*, Alcan, Paris.

Tarde, G. 1895b, *Les Transformations du pouvoir*, Alcan, Paris.

Tarde, G. 1899, *Social Laws* (translated by Howard C. Warren, preface by James Mark Baldwin), Macmillan, London.

Tarde, G. 1910, *L'Opinion et la foule*, Alcan, Paris.

Tarde, G. 1962, *The Laws of Imitation* (translated from the second French edition, Introduction by Franklin H. Giddings, reprint of 1903 edition by Holt and Co.), Peter Smith, Gloucester, Mass.

Tarde, G. 1968, *Penal Philosophy* (translated by Rapelje Howell, editorial preface by Edward Lindsey, Introduction by Robert H. Gault), publication N° 16 in Patterson Smith reprint series in Criminology, Law Enforcement and Social Problems, Patterson Smith, Montclair, New Jersey.

Tarde, G. 1969, *On Communication and Social Influence*, ed. Terry N. Clark, University of Chicago Press, Chicago.

Tchakhotine, S. 1939, *Le Viol des foules*, Gallimard, Paris.

Thorez, M. *Le Monde*, 23 January 1980.

Tilly, C. 1978, *From Mobilisation to Revolution*, Addison-Wesley, Reading, Mass.

Todd, E. 1979, *Le Fou et le prolétaire*, Laffont, Paris.

Tournier, M. 1977, *Le vent Paraclet*, Ed. Folio, Paris.

Trepper, L. 1975, *Le grand jeu*, Albin Michel, Paris.

Trotsky, L. 1950, *Histoire de la révolution russe*, Vol. I, Le Seuil, Paris.

Vierkandt, A. 1928, *Gesellschaftslehre*, F. Enke, Stuttgart.

Von Wiese, L. 1924, *Allgemeine Soziologie*, Dunker and Humbold, Munich and Leipzig.

Weber, M. 1958, *Gesammelte politische Schriften*, Tübingen.

Weber, M. 1965, *The Sociology of Religion*, Methuen, London.

Weber, M. 1968, *Economy and Society*, 3 vols., Bedminster Press, New York.

Weber, M. 1980, *Le Judaïsme antique*, Plon, Paris.

Weil, S. 1955, *Réflexions sur les causes de la liberté et de l'oppression sociale*, Gallimard, Paris.

Wilson, B. R. 1975, *The Noble Savages*, University of California Press, Berkley.

Wittfogel, K. A. 1964, *Le Despotisme oriental*, Ed. de Minuit, Paris.

Wurmser, A. 1949, *Nouvelle critique*.

Zinoviev, A. 1979, *The Yawning Heights*, Bodley Head, London.

Zinoviev, A. 'Victimes et complices', *Le Monde*, 22 December 1979.

Zola, E. 1965, *La Débâcle*, Livre de Poche, Paris.

# Index of Names

Adorno, T. W.  47, 56, 57, 64, 143, 234, 236, 389–90, 392, 395, 396
Ahad Haam  328
Akhenaten  331–3
Alberoni, F.  311, 395
Alessandri, A.  61
Alexander the Great  120, 293
Allport, G. W.  55
Amenophis IV  331
Aquinas, T.  95
Aragon, L.  177
Arendt, H.  148, 176, 395
Ariosto, L.  221
Aristotle  108, 112, 122, 219
Aronson, E.  55, 397

Bacon, F.  145
Bahro, R.  388, 395
Bainville, J.  276, 395
Baldwin, J. M.  399
Balzac, H. de  58, 96, 173, 198, 298, 325, 388
Barbusse, H.  177
Barnes, H. E.  56, 395
Barre, M.  175
Barrès, M.  103, 399
Barthou, L.  54, 62, 395
Bartlett, F.  13–14, 395
Baudelaire, C.  22, 58, 71, 301, 395
Bechterev, W.  244, 257, 395
Becker, H.  56, 395
Beetham, D.  387, 395
Bell, D.  24, 395
Bergson, H.  54, 58, 387, 395
Berlin, I.  386, 395
Bernard, St  168
Bernheim, H.  81–3, 85–7, 225, 395
Bibesco, M.  54, 390, 395
Biddis, M. D.  65, 395
Binet, A.  84–6, 395
Birnbaum, P.  102, 104, 388, 395
Bloch, E.  111, 395
Blum, L.  289
Bonaparte, M.  54, 389
Borges, J.-L.  243, 395
Bourdieu, P.  388, 395

Bradley, F. H.  10
Brandt, W.  126
Breton, A.  87
Briand, A.  54, 62, 399
Broch, H.  28, 39, 47, 69, 234, 389, 395
Broglie, L. de  219
Bruno, G.  333
Brutus  140, 304, 308
Buddha  115, 241
Bukharin, N.  127, 351, 362, 371, 374–6
Bullitt, W. C.  263, 267, 320, 321, 390, 396
Burckhardt, J.  46

Cæsar  98, 120, 139, 145, 203, 293–5, 301, 304, 308, 317
Caligula  177
Canetti, E.  25, 42, 174, 175, 272, 273, 395
Carter, J.  175
Cassirer, E.  29, 121, 395
Castro, F.  1, 2, 137
Chagall, M.  325
Charcot, L.  81, 83, 395
Chateaubriand, F. R.  38, 41, 130, 170
Chekhov, A. P.  338
Chirac, J.  216, 217
Christ  96, 115, 135, 160, 166, 171, 174, 219, 241, 252, 278, 279, 286, 297, 298, 301, 303, 308, 325, 330, 370, 396
Churchill, W. S.  104, 290
Cicero  267
Clark, T. N.  399
Claudel, P.  72
Clemenceau, G.  62, 395
Comte, A.  21, 120
Corradini, E.  63
Croce, B.  396
Cromwell, O.  293
Cyrus  326

Daniel, J.  125, 209, 395
Danton, G. J.  124
Darwin, C.  171, 219, 297, 392
de Gaulle, C.  38, 45, 62–3, 96, 99, 125, 130–3, 135–7, 139, 145, 166, 172, 175, 203, 208–14, 252, 289–90, 293, 301, 317, 336, 340, 368, 386, 392, 396

Debray, R.   212, 389, 395
Descartes, R.   315, 330
Desmoulins, C.   204
Deutscher, I.   363, 371, 375, 379, 396
Djilas, M.   39, 133, 251, 369, 376, 396
Dostoyevsky, F. M.   58
Dreyfus, A.   189
Duhamel, A.   211, 214, 396
Durkheim, E.   10, 57, 67, 102, 172, 208,
   219, 386, 396

Ehrenburg, I.   378
Einstein, A.   14, 166, 175, 219, 224, 227,
   300, 316, 325, 379, 393, 396
Ekart, D.   392, 396
Eliot, T. S.   31
Ellenberger, H. F.   222, 396
Eluard, P.   177
Emmanuel, P.   212–13, 396
Engels, F.   35, 61, 343, 377

Fauconnet, P.   73, 396
Federn, P.   233, 234
Felice, P. de   72, 282, 396
Féré, C.   84–6, 395
Fischer, R.   256, 396
Flaubert, G.   22–3, 50, 69, 75, 258–9, 324,
   396
Floriban, G. de   109
Forel, A.   84, 396
Franco, F.   177
Franklin, B.   330, 340
Frederick II (The Great)   14, 349
Freud, S.   8–9, 11, 17–18, 26, 28, 36, 57–8,
   69, 79, 81–2, 87, 93, 102, 135, 151, 157,
   171, 181, 218–43, 245–50, 252–3, 256–9,
   261, 263–70, 273–5, 277, 279, 281–2, 284–
   9, 297–300, 303–9, 311, 314–18, 320–4,
   326–8, 330–5, 337–40, 343, 346–7, 353–7,
   359, 365–7, 370, 373–5, 377, 379, 386–94,
   396, 398
Fromm, E.   47, 89, 227, 233–4, 396
Furet, F.   51, 124–5, 396

Galileo   298, 315, 333
Gamelin, M.   353
Gandhi, M.   2, 129, 144, 289, 342
Gault, R. H.   399
Geiger, T.   56, 396
Genghis Khan   115
Georges, F.   394, 396
Giddings, F. H.   399
Gide, A.   323, 387
Gilson, E.   393, 396
Giner, S.   53, 158, 389, 396
Girard, P.   391, 396

Giscard d'Estaing, V.   208, 211–16, 289,
   396
Glaser, H.   233, 396
Gobineau, A. de   52, 58
Goebbels, P. J.   64, 146
Goering, H.   267, 391
Goethe, J. W.   126, 130, 145, 256, 349
Gorgias   139
Gorky, M.   350
Gramsci, A.   14–15, 22, 34, 59, 166, 295,
   313, 354, 396
Gregor, A. J.   63, 396
Gregory VII, Pope   394
Grillparzer, F.   14

Habermas, J.   196, 396
Hanotaux, G.   61, 396
Hegedus, A.   119, 396
Hegel, G. W. F.   46, 293
Heidegger, M.   366
Heine, H.   130
Hercules   326
Hermotines   301
Herzstein, R. E.   65, 396
Hitler, A.   2, 7, 36, 56, 63–4, 69, 76, 99,
   104, 110–11, 120, 125, 127, 144, 147, 152,
   176, 180, 234–6, 293, 316, 363, 392, 396–7,
   399
Hobbes, T.   313, 386
Hobsbawm, E.   21, 378, 396
Hofmannsthal, H. von   122
Homer   380
Horkheimer, M.   56, 64, 236, 396
Hugo, V.   170, 352

Jacoby, R.   235, 397
Jancourt, Chevalier de   344
Janet, P.   386
Jaroslavski, General   377
Jaurès, J.   326
Joan of Arc   102–3
John Paul II, Pope   37, 120, 290, 293, 301,
   393
Jung, C. J.   58, 240, 257, 398

Kafka, F.   304, 322, 324, 374
Kamenev, L. B.   362, 376
Kant, I.   173, 221
Katz, E.   191, 397
Kautsky, K.   60, 114, 397
Kennedy, J. F.   126, 211
Kepler, J.   221
Kerensky, A.   353
Khomeini, Ayatollah   37, 120, 146, 392
Khrushchev, N.   127, 345, 351–2, 358, 369,
   397
Kirov, S.   351

Korsh, K.  233, 397
Kropotkin, P.  205

Lao-tse  362, 370
Lanoux, A.  50
Laplanche, J.  298, 397
Lazarsfeld, P.  191, 397
Lazitch, B.  346, 350, 352, 358, 397
Le Bon, G.  7–9, 11, 18, 23–4, 28, 30, 40–1,
    47, 49–70, 74–82, 87–90, 93–105, 108–13,
    115, 117–20, 122–4, 126–30, 134–6, 138–
    40, 142–5, 147–8, 150, 153, 155–6, 163,
    165, 167, 172–3, 179, 206–8, 210, 217–19,
    221–2, 230, 232–3, 235–42, 253, 282, 285,
    287, 289, 294–5, 297, 314, 320–1, 386–90,
    394, 397, 399
Lederer, E.  224, 397
Lefèbvre, G.  57, 76, 397
Leibniz, G. W.  287
Lenin, V. I.  35, 78, 127, 129, 165, 252,
    280, 293, 301, 308, 325, 330, 333, 336,
    340, 345, 348–51, 370–9, 388, 396–7
Lennon, J.  260, 391
Leonardo da Vinci  219
Lindsey, E.  399
Lindzey, G.  55, 397
Lloyd George, D.  63
Lombroso, C.  73
Louis XIV  203, 260, 301
Louis XVI  298
Louis, St  167
Lukács, G.  388–9, 397
Ludwig, E.  111
Luther, M.  123, 279
Luxemburg, R.  109

McDougall, W.  55, 64, 87, 221, 397
MacLuhan, M.  158
Machiavelli, N.  58, 63, 125, 313, 396
Mackay, C.  72, 397
Mahomet  115, 129, 241, 317, 330, 342
Maimonides  256
Mallarmé, S.  93
Malia, M.  374, 397
Malraux, A.  210
Mann, T.  40, 128, 397
Mannoni, M.  63, 397
Mao Tse-tung  1–3, 89, 97, 104, 120, 151,
    157, 177, 233, 287, 289–90, 308, 317, 330,
    339, 344, 369–70, 372, 388, 392
Marat, J.  204
Marchais, G.  102, 116, 217, 289
Marcuse, H.  235–6, 390
Mark Antony  98, 308
Marx, K.  10, 24, 35, 61, 121, 174, 205,
    219–20, 224, 325, 342–3, 348–9, 365, 370,
    372, 377, 386, 390

Maser, W.  64, 397
Masser, W. A.  65, 397
Maupassant, G. de  15–16, 184, 223, 283,
    387, 397
Mauroy, M.  175
Mauss, M.  26, 319–20, 397
Maxwell, J. C.  390
Medvedev, R.  373, 397
Mendès-France, P.  140
Mesmer, F. A.  49, 246
Michelangelo  314
Michelet, J.  6, 172, 207–8, 397
Michels, R.  57, 60, 63, 175, 180, 295, 386–
    7, 397
Milgram, S.  55
Mill, J. S.  386
Mirabeau, G. H. R.  124
Mirabeau, V. de R.  49
Mitterrand, F.  216, 289
Molotov, V. M.  363, 377
Mommsen, W. J.  387, 397
Morazé, C.  386
Morin, E.  213
Mosca, G.  63
Moscovici, M.  258, 397
Moscovici, S.  55, 108, 171, 331–3, 335,
    338, 392, 397–8
Moses  115, 135, 219, 228, 241, 284, 308,
    314–16, 318, 325–43, 345, 370, 379, 392–3,
    396, 398
Mosse, G. L.  65, 349, 398
Mozart, W. A.  179
Mussolini, B.  1–2, 63, 69, 89, 111, 114,
    137, 316, 395

Napoleon Bonaparte  6–7, 38–9, 42, 45–6,
    59, 69, 85, 96, 103–4, 110, 113, 115, 126,
    129–31, 133, 135–6, 139–41, 147, 165,
    174–5, 181, 198, 203, 233, 275, 277, 279,
    291, 293–4, 298, 300, 301, 308, 314, 317,
    325, 347, 349, 368, 370, 378, 388, 393, 395
Napoleon III  50, 276
Nehru, J.  1
Newmann, S.  224, 398
Newton, I.  157, 221, 245
Nietzsche, F.  28, 58, 113, 124, 221, 231,
    311
Noir, M.  217, 398
Nye, R. A.  54, 62, 65, 68, 398

Oberschall, A.  31, 56, 392, 398
Octavius Romulus  301
Odajnyk, W. W.  58, 398
Oedipus  326–9, 367, 398
Offenbach, J.  50
Olson, M.  392, 398
Ortega y Gasset, J.  27, 29

Orwell, G.   274

Pareto, V.   63, 386
Park, R. E.   56, 398
Parsons, T.   67
Pascal, B.   93, 289
Pericles   203
Peter the Hermit   123, 168
Picasso, P.   325
Pinochet, General   2
Plutarch   98
Poincaré, H.   54, 387
Poincaré, R.   54, 62–3
Pol Pot   3, 36, 137
Pompey   294
Pompidou, G.   126, 134
Pontalis, J. B.   298, 397
Porchnev, B.   78, 280, 398
Proust, M.   33, 118, 189, 226, 257, 260–1,
   324, 398
Pythagoras   301, 303

Radek, K.   362
Radiguet, R.   250
Rank, O.   375
Reagan, R.   175
Reich, W.   28, 35, 47, 234–6, 390, 398
Reinwald, P.   66, 222, 398
Renan, E.   51
Ribot, T.   54, 386, 387
Ricardo   390
Rieff, P.   231, 398
Rimbaud, A.   108
Rivière, J.   226
Robert, M.   220, 222, 224, 398
Robespierre, M.   59, 109, 123–4, 129–30,
   136, 147, 203, 251, 289, 293, 305, 314,
   336, 340, 354
Robinson, P.   235, 398
Robrieux, P.   127, 358, 398
Roheim, G.   143, 390, 395, 398
Romulus   326, 336
Roosevelt, T.   54, 61, 137, 203, 289, 317
Rouget, G.   143, 398
Rousseau, J.-J.   123, 170
Rumi   345

Saada   301
Saint-Simon, C. H. de   31, 49
Salazar, A.   137
Sand, G.   50
Sartre, J.-P.   259, 398
Schachter, S.   108
Schiller, J.   14, 307
Schönberg, A.   332
Schumpeter, J. A.   68, 69, 398
Serge, V.   350, 394, 398

Shakespeare, W.   36, 98, 291, 310
Sherif, C.   55, 389, 398
Sherif, M.   55, 389, 398
Shorske, C.   227, 398
Sighele, S.   73, 172, 242, 398
Silone, I.   61, 398
Simmel, G.   55, 358, 398
Skinner, B. F.   67
Socrates   203
Sollner, A.   89, 396
Solon   14
Sorel, G.   49, 59–60, 63, 113, 153, 386, 388,
   398–9
Stalin, J.   1–3, 6–7, 43, 89, 103, 120, 126–7,
   133, 147, 157, 160, 171, 174, 176, 180,
   233–4, 236, 279, 290, 293, 301, 308, 316,
   340, 345, 348, 351–2, 358, 363–4, 369,
   371–2, 374–9, 388, 392, 396
Stein, A.   64, 399
Stendhal   143, 266, 322, 399
Sternhell, Z.   58, 399
Suares, G.   61, 399

Taine, H.   24, 51–2, 386
Talleyrand, C.-M. de   140
Tarde, G.   8–9, 11, 24, 37–8, 41, 54–6, 67,
   77, 87, 102, 155–8, 161–70, 172–6, 178–9,
   181, 183–208, 212–13, 215–19, 221–2, 230,
   232–3, 235, 242, 245, 256–7, 282, 286–9,
   297, 303, 307, 321, 353, 386, 389, 394, 399
Tasso, T.   221
Tchakhotine, S.   66, 111, 399
Thorez, M.   102–3, 358, 398–9
Tiberius   115
Tilly, C.   392, 399
Tiresias   367
Tito, J. B.   1–2, 39, 133, 135, 174, 177, 251,
   290, 293, 369, 372, 392, 396
Toch, H.   55
Tocqueville, A. de   24, 49, 386
Todd, E.   215, 399
Toller, E.   107
Tönnies, F.   20
Tournier, M.   110, 399
Trepper, L.   277, 399
Trotsky, L.   127, 135, 152, 345, 351, 371,
   374–6, 388, 399
Tvardovsky, A.   371

Valéry, P.   46, 54, 297
Vasarely, V.   325
Vico, G.   311
Vierkandt, A.   55, 75, 399
Virgil   261
Von Wiese, L.   55, 399

Wagner, R.   170

Washington, G.   340
Weber, M.   24, 57, 67, 69, 174, 219, 290–4,
  296, 301, 314, 340, 344, 386–7, 395, 398–9
Weil, S.   16, 399
Wilson, B. R.   294, 399
Wittfogel, K. A.   41, 386, 399
Woodrow Wilson, T.   134, 263, 396

Wurmser, A.   177, 399

Zetkin, C.   370
Zinoviev, A.   7, 16, 127, 177, 362, 371,
  375–6, 399
Zola, E.   51, 204, 276, 354, 399
Zweig, S.   225, 232

# Subject Index

action 2, 14, 17–18, 21–2, 29–30, 32, 34–5, 38, 42, 47, 60, 66, 78, 101, 104, 112, 120, 123, 126–7, 150, 152, 169, 237, 313
admiration 179–81, 295
advertising 66–7, 181, 216–17, 294
affirmation 145–8
altruism 75–6
anarchy 6–7, 73, 75, 178, 205, 274
antisemitism 60, 96, 224, 227
apathy 115, 117
authoritarianism 44, 47, 63–5, 89, 117, 233, 235
authority 1–2, 6–7, 18, 36–7, 40–4, 77, 89, 135–6, 142, 176, 179, 208, 212, 238, 241, 266, 290–5, 308–9, 313–14, 323, 328, 343, 345–7, 350, 377, 383, 387

belief 30–1, 34–5, 38–9, 41, 45, 54, 90, 92, 97, 115–24, 140–1, 145, 147–8, 150, 155, 158, 164, 175, 196, 203, 209, 232, 301, 303, 313–14, 368

ceremonial 141–3, 149, 210–11, 225, 232, 235, 238, 301, 303, 369, 371
charisma 1–3, 4, 43, 45–6, 120, 129–39, 168, 175, 179, 181, 194, 208–11, 214, 216, 235, 285, 290–8, 301, 303, 307, 310–11, 314, 353, 368, 379, 387; vs prestige 131–6, 174
class 24–6, 29, 51, 54, 59–60, 66, 71, 74, 78–9, 113, 129, 153, 155, 176, 199, 206–7, 214–15, 235, 247, 255, 263, 281, 314, 356, 378, 388
*coincidentia oppositorum* 299, 337, 364
collective hypnosis 82–3, 143–4
madness 15, 18, 72–6
unconsciousness 58–9, 92–4, 102–3, 109, 114, 116, 147, 171, 205, 240
communications, means of 158, 183–200, 210–13, 216, 385
community vs society 20–3, 186, 275, 285
conflict 20–2, 50–3, 272, 333, 370
conformity 22, 31, 74, 180, 235, 162, 273, 280, 284, 299
consciousness 171–2, 238, 254, 284; levels of 24, 31, 36, 78, 81–8, 90, 92–3, 139

conservatism, of crowd 60, 90, 113, 209, 233
conversation and power 183–8, 190–2, 197, 384
conversion 338–41
criminal behaviour 1, 4, 72–9
crowd, the 4–11, 14–16, 20–8, 31, 33, 39, 42, 52, 54, 56–7, 60, 69, 71–81, 84, 86, 88, 90–1, 107–31, 133–4, 136, 139–46, 149–53, 155–7, 162–71, 173–5, 178–80, 189–95, 197–200, 205–6, 209, 214, 222, 230, 232–3, 237, 240–55, 269, 271–83, 285–7, 291, 295–6, 298, 306, 314–17, 335, 342, 346, 350, 352–4, 368, 375, 378, 381, 385
hypnotic 83, 88–90, 94, 109
soul of 54, 116, 119, 172, 218, 246, 388–9
thinking vs individual 94–7
crowd psychology 1, 4, 6–11, 18–20, 24, 27–34, 37, 40, 42, 46–9, 54–62, 66–70, 73, 77–82, 86–92, 105, 107–11, 114–15, 120–1, 124, 127–31, 140, 144, 148–53, 155–60, 167, 171–2, 178–81, 190–3, 199, 201–2, 206–8, 213, 217–18, 220–3, 225–8, 230–6, 239–42, 244–6, 252, 256, 270, 277, 279, 282, 287–9, 294–8, 300, 303–4, 317–21, 326, 341–2, 347, 353, 358, 361, 364, 369, 378–84, 386–94
crowds, artificial 160–9, 242–3, 249, 252, 275, 303–4, 307, 310, 353, 357, 393
mental life of 90, 92–105, 150, 297–8, 365, 371, 386
natural 160–9, 242, 282, 310

demagogy 110, 170, 224
democracy 10, 33–4, 39–40, 42–44, 46–7, 52–3, 62, 68–9, 97, 101, 153, 167, 178, 181, 192, 201, 205, 207, 218, 224, 273–4, 294, 372, 383–4, 387
despot, personality of 47, 76–7
despotism 32, 39–48, 61, 115, 304
dictatorship 3, 40, 46, 64, 69, 127, 132, 137, 153, 176, 187
disorders 246, 275–6, 281, 293

405

domination   57, 64–5, 133, 173, 192, 253, 304–5

economics   28, 33–5, 47, 153, 215, 234–6, 271
ego   222, 240, 247–8, 250–1, 253, 257, 264, 266–9, 280–1, 284, 311, 320, 326, 346–7, 352, 389
egotism   251, 253–4
emotion   4–6, 16, 26, 31–2, 34, 37, 92, 104, 108–9, 140, 142–4, 148, 163, 175–6, 194, 205, 212, 233, 237, 244, 246, 251, 253
equality, principle of   1, 21, 41–4, 46, 51, 78, 101, 133, 186–7, 192, 201, 251–2, 271–5, 283, 308–9
Eros   255, 270, 278, 282, 287, 320–1, 323
erotic tendencies   246–8, 250, 253, 255, 267, 271, 278, 280, 285, 286, 296, 300, 320–1
exchange, means of   24–5
extremism of crowds   112

familiarity and distance   132–4, 175, 209, 250–1
family   37, 47, 181, 228, 241–3, 252, 264, 267–8
   romances   321–30, 393
Fascism   61, 63–5, 68–9, 113, 141, 235
father   37, 43, 228, 241, 252, 264–8, 304–11, 318, 322–3, 325, 333, 359, 366, 368–80
fear   16, 73–5, 77, 81, 133, 144, 162, 179, 222, 224, 275–7, 280
femininity   110–12, 114, 130, 139, 163, 280
France   49–51, 53, 62–3, 65, 68–9, 82, 102, 110, 117, 119, 125, 167, 187, 196, 200–1, 207–18, 386–7
Frankfurt School   56, 69, 235–6
freedom   1, 10, 26, 42–3, 46–8, 216
French Revolution   4, 6, 21, 25, 39, 41, 44, 51, 75–7, 89, 109–10, 112–13, 116–17, 124–6, 136, 153, 186, 204, 207, 242, 301, 308, 346, 354

Germany   51, 53–4, 60, 63–5, 82, 125, 207, 223–4, 234–5
government   1, 62–3, 66, 80, 213–15
great men   316–19, 324–5, 327
group mind   241

hero, myth of   1–2, 46, 150–1, 210, 285, 308, 316–17, 322, 326–7, 333–4, 374–5, 377
history   1–2, 4, 7, 9, 11, 24–5, 27–8, 36–7, 39–41, 46–7, 57, 60–1, 65, 72, 76–7, 79, 91, 95, 105, 107–8, 116–17, 119–20, 125, 127, 135, 141–2, 150, 155, 157, 170–1, 205, 207–8, 212, 223–5, 229, 231, 236, 249, 257, 267, 271, 295–9, 302, 308, 311, 316–17, 328, 330, 331–2, 338–41, 358, 361–3, 377–8, 381–2
hope   118–19, 173, 275
hypnosis   81–95, 112, 125, 130, 136, 139–40, 142–3, 145, 149–52, 161, 174, 185, 189, 194, 200, 205, 213, 225, 227–8, 232–3, 238, 244, 246, 263, 283–8, 296, 342, 351, 387, 392
hysteria   18, 20, 76–7, 79, 86, 163

identification   222, 228, 255–70, 272–8, 280–1, 283, 286, 288, 296, 299, 300–2, 321, 323, 325, 333, 368
ideology   24, 37, 41, 67–8, 78, 119, 124, 171, 173, 224, 235, 394
illusion   38–9, 47, 54, 62, 72, 84–5, 95, 109, 118, 138–9, 150, 162, 178, 232, 238, 252–3, 276, 297, 342, 367, 379
images vs ideas   91–105, 116
   repeated   101–2, 144–5, 217
imagination   39, 87, 89, 90, 99, 104, 140, 150, 175, 300
*imago*   298–307, 310–11, 368
imitative behaviour   1, 157–8, 160–1, 164–6, 168–9, 174–5, 181, 185, 205, 218, 222, 256–7, 259, 260–1, 263–8, 270–2, 274, 277, 279, 391
incubation   334–5, 341, 379
individuals   4–5, 13–20, 22–31, 33–4, 37–9, 42, 48, 66, 74, 76–7, 81–2, 86, 88, 90, 92, 94, 97, 101, 103–4, 107–8, 112, 117–18, 134, 141, 144, 150, 157–8, 163, 170, 174, 184, 195–6, 198, 209, 211, 228, 231, 237, 239–41, 244–53, 255, 258, 262–3, 268–9, 271, 274–7, 280–1, 283, 286–8, 291, 295, 297, 314, 319–20, 330, 347, 354, 357, 368, 370, 375, 383–5, 387
influence   17–20, 22, 25, 27, 45, 64, 66, 115, 213, 217, 245, 249, 285
intuition   95–101
irrationality   35–7
Italy   61, 63–5, 82, 207

jealousy   260–1, 272, 275
journalists   197–8, 202, 204, 213, 294
justice   26, 35, 251, 273–4

law   1–2, 72–4, 77–8, 305–7, 309–10, 383
leaders   1–7, 9, 11, 26, 36–48, 54, 61–8, 76–7, 80, 84, 88, 90, 101, 107–8, 119–20, 122–51, 157–8, 165, 168–83, 185, 194–5, 200, 202–4, 208–15, 217, 222, 232–6, 240–2, 244, 250–3, 265, 267, 269, 275–6, 278, 283–96, 301, 303, 306–10, 313–15,

317, 320, 325, 330, 332–53, 369–83, 385,
387–9
death of   177–8, 228, 371–2
liberation   4, 235, 370
liberty, paradox of   32, 38–9, 41, 186–7
libido   228, 244–56, 262–4, 269–70, 286,
320–1, 325
love   245–55, 260–1, 270–6, 278–9, 281,
283, 285–7, 320–1, 326, 346, 368
lowest common denominators   14, 165,
199
*lumpenproletariat*   71–4

madness   15, 18, 86; collective vs
individual   18, 72–3, 75–6, 123–5, 127–
8, 162
marketing, political   216
mass communication   11, 22, 66, 95, 152,
158, 183–98, 201
mass media   37, 40, 68, 111, 194, 198, 294,
385
mass production   22, 90, 100, 121, 213
mass psychology   *see* crowd psychology
masses, the   4–9, 11, 13–23, 25–30, 32–40,
45–8, 51, 53–4, 56–61, 63–8, 71, 75, 77–
8, 89–91, 94, 101–4, 108, 113–15, 123,
125, 128, 132, 136, 138–40, 142–3, 148,
150–1, 153, 155–6, 160, 163, 166–7, 170,
174, 176–7, 179–81, 195–6, 199–200,
207–18, 222, 231, 233, 235–40, 242, 244,
250, 256, 265, 268, 271, 274–5, 277,
285–8, 290, 292, 296, 300–1, 303, 308,
310, 313, 316–19, 330, 334, 343, 346–7,
354–5, 357, 367–70, 372, 374, 377, 379,
381, 384, 387–8
mediocrity, law of   14
*Mein Kampf*   64, 127, 144
memory   112, 296–300, 308, 335–6, 384
mental illness   20, 76, 127–8
mimesis   256, 259, 263, 270–2, 274, 277,
280, 282, 286–7, 300, 320–1, 391
mob   20–1, 60, 71–3, 164, 176
moral prohibitions   4, 10, 73, 77, 252, 281,
316, 332, 349
Moses   228–9, 314–16, 318, 326–52, 379,
392–3
mystery   132–5, 149, 175, 315

narcissism   247–56, 259, 277–8, 286, 320–1,
324
Nazism   35, 47, 64–5, 111, 114, 125, 127,
146, 224, 234–5, 277, 387, 389
neurosis   18–19, 223, 228–9, 231–2, 320,
322
newspapers   183, 188–90, 192–5, 197–9,
204, 206, 208
nostalgia   298–9, 336, 368

Oedipus complex   228, 322, 325, 327–9
opinion poll   7, 68, 193, 206, 216–17
vs public opinion   195–8, 204, 206, 212,
216, 237, 244
orderedness   71–4, 236, 278
organisation, systems of   166, 193–4, 209,
222, 242

panic   275–8, 280, 283
passion   34, 39, 61, 98, 130, 189, 203, 247,
260
personality, cult of   7, 44–6, 120, 127, 176–
7, 217, 219, 358, 369–79
persuasion   141, 144, 147, 149, 181, 183,
206, 213
plebiscites   42, 44, 216
pogroms   60, 96, 224, 278
political systems   40–2, 47, 52–3, 207–8,
386
politics   2, 6, 8, 30–7, 41, 66, 68, 80, 126,
144, 200, 206
power   1–4, 6, 9, 21–2, 29–30, 35–7, 45, 65,
141–2, 157, 179, 183, 188, 190–1, 201,
205, 207, 251, 253, 288, 304–6, 309–10;
of crowd   15, 22–3, 32, 71–80, 142,
175, 384; of leader   1–5, 7, 11, 32, 36,
41–4, 46, 54, 75–7, 84, 88, 90, 107, 122–
49, 151, 174, 208, 210–12, 288, 313–14,
342, 345, 369, 371, 383
prejudice   15, 67, 111–12, 189, 196, 207,
247
prestige   131–6, 174, 201, 203, 208–11
progress   4, 36, 53, 60, 115, 155, 242, 326,
348, 378
propaganda   11, 37, 60–1, 64–7, 89–90, 95,
111, 119, 138–49, 151, 181, 350
prophets   293–5, 314–15, 325, 327, 330–41
psychoanalysis   57, 220–2, 225–6, 228–30,
234–5, 240, 242, 244–6, 273, 287, 322,
390–1, 394
publicists   183, 199–200, 204, 213, 217
publics vs crowds   193–5, 197–200, 202,
205–18

racialism   52, 247, 263
radio   183, 189–93, 195, 199–201, 204, 210,
213
reason   6, 9, 13–16, 19, 30–2, 35, 38, 48,
59, 68, 88, 93–7, 100–4, 115, 126, 138,
140, 147, 150, 163, 194, 198, 237–9, 269,
296, 355, 360, 368, 378–9
regression   235, 237–8, 240, 242, 244, 253,
286, 348
religion   5–6, 24, 35, 119–21, 124, 144, 148,
224–5, 228–32, 238, 241, 255, 279, 303,
306–7, 324, 328, 331–43, 353–61, 364,
366–70, 372–3, 378–9, 391, 394

repetition, functions of   101–2, 144–8,
    160–1, 174, 213, 217, 232, 255, 257–8,
    261, 270, 272
repression   179–80, 234–5, 237, 240, 255,
    266, 276, 300, 347, 356, 359, 361–367
resurrection   300, 301, 302, 309, 311, 368,
    377
revelation   332
revolt of the masses   27–8, 235–6
revolution   1, 10, 20–1, 24, 44–5, 67–8,
    113–14, 124, 148, 152, 167, 207, 223,
    233–4, 236, 301, 311
revolutionary thought   60, 64, 127, 168
riot   20–1, 72–4, 77, 167, 210–11, 238, 281
Russian Revolution   112, 127, 141, 223,
    301, 308, 361–3, 376–7, 379, 388

satisfaction of desire   247–8, 255
sexuality   233, 245–9, 252–5, 257, 264, 272,
    274, 278, 284–6
socialism   21, 49, 51, 59–61, 63, 67, 73,
    101–2, 109, 114, 121, 129, 148, 168, 205,
    209, 234, 348–52, 358, 365, 370–2,
    378–9
sociology   4, 28, 55, 71, 115, 208, 230, 231,
    236, 386, 388
society   1–4, 8, 10–11, 20–4, 36, 69, 91,
    102, 118, 129, 156, 161, 233, 249, 255–
    69, 279, 281, 286, 288, 301, 356, 359,
    360, 368, 373, 378, 384
    mass vs class   24–29, 40, 42, 44, 48, 56,
    66, 77, 79, 80, 105, 107, 111, 132, 190,
    235, 294, 348, 354, 390
spontaneity   78, 103, 140, 242, 248, 282
submission   38, 47–8, 83–4, 176–7, 180–1,
    252, 292, 307–8

suggestibility   87, 90, 92, 111, 122, 226,
    244
suggestion   17–20, 45, 66, 83–94, 102–3,
    108, 130–2, 138–49, 150–2, 155, 157–8,
    161, 169, 179, 181, 185, 194, 206, 225–8,
    237, 244–6, 249, 283, 286, 288, 385
super-ego   228, 266–7, 269, 280–1, 284,
    287, 317–18, 320–1, 326, 346–7, 357,
    372, 389, 391

television   183, 189–94, 199–201, 204, 210,
    213
terror   52, 73, 176–8, 275, 279–80, 283,
    361–7, 369, 375
thought   14–18, 22, 35, 47, 78, 84–5, 94–7,
    101, 105, 113, 120, 158, 179, 234–7, 287,
    361–7
totalitarianism   44, 47, 61, 63–5, 69, 143,
    148, 176, 224, 227
totemic cycle   304–5, 311–12, 330, 342–52,
    359, 368
truth   361–6, 368, 371, 383
tyrants   2, 32, 40, 115, 173, 176–7, 235,
    306–7, 310, 359

unconscious   222, 228, 231, 239–40, 261,
    273, 300, 379, 387
usurpation   45–6, 135–6, 208–9, 293

violence   7, 13, 72–6, 144, 178, 180–1, 201,
    238, 274–81

working class   21–2, 59–61, 67, 71–4, 77–8,
    114, 124, 128, 168
wretchedness of the masses   5, 20–1, 39,
    232, 236, 277, 280, 384